Design in Reading

Design in Reading

An Introduction to Critical Reading

Second Edition

RICHMOND GARRIGUS
Reedley College

New York   San Francisco   Boston
London   Toronto   Sydney   Tokyo   Singapore   Madrid
Mexico City   Munich   Paris   Cape Town   Hong Kong   Montreal

Vice President/Editor-in-Chief: Joseph Terry
Senior Acquisitions Editor: Steve Rigolosi
Senior Marketing Manager: Melanie Craig
Supplements Editor: Donna Campion
Media Supplements Editor: Nancy Garcia
Senior Production Manager: Eric Jorgensen
Project Coordination, Text Design, and Electronic Page Makeup:
    Electronic Publishing Services Inc., N.Y.C.
Cover Design Manager: Nancy Danahy
Cover Design: Keithley and Associates, Inc.
Cover Image: Nancy Danahy
Manufacturing Buyer: Lucy Hebard
Printer and Binder: Hamilton Printing Co.
Cover Printer: Phoenix Color Corporation

For permission to use copyrighted material, grateful acknowledgment is made to the copyright holders on p. 544, which are hereby made part of this copyright page.

Library of Congress Cataloging-in-Publication Data

Garrigus, Richmond, 1941-
    Design in reading: an introduction to critical reading/Richmond Garrigus.--2nd ed.
        p. cm.
    Includes index.
    ISBN 0-321-09630-4
    1. Reading (Higher eduction) 2. Study skills. I. Title.

    LB2395.3 .G37 2003
    428.4'071'1--dc21

                                            2002066058

Please visit our website at http://www.ablongman.com

ISBN 0-321-09630-4

2 3 4 5 6 7 8 9 10-HT-05 04 03

Brief Contents

v

Detailed Contents

Part III Persuasion to Action   439

12 DETERMINING WHAT NEEDS TO BE DONE: PROBLEMS AND SOLUTIONS   441

Preface

If, at the end of a reading course, a student is able to approach a text strategically, explain in his or her own voice the author's main points, as well as summarize those points concisely and respond thoughtfully to them in writing—a teacher of reading would be entitled to feel that his or her efforts had been well rewarded. The goal of *Design in Reading* is to help students reach such a level of proficiency and thus find a way to participate effectively in the academic discourse that is the foundation of the collegiate experience.

Design in Reading provides students with a structured approach to building fundamental critical thinking and reading skills to enable them to participate effectively in academic discourse. It incorporates an analytical reading system that promotes interactive reading in order to address two key problems:

- Developmental readers are often unaware that writers can have very different purposes and that the readers' relationship with the writer thus varies according to the writer's intentions and interests. They might read an op-ed article or advertising copy in the same way as they would a computer manual. They find it difficult to tell fact from opinion and evaluate evidence.

- Students have great trouble in getting the "big picture"—the main idea. They are unsure of what an idea is, often responding in fragments to questions regarding a thesis or topic sentence, and they are unable to distinguish important ideas from minor details. As a result, they can easily get lost and very frustrated.

ORGANIZATION OF THE TEXT

The three-part organization of *Design in Reading* allows for the simultaneous and progressive development of skills addressing these two problems throughout the text.

RECOGNIZING PURPOSE AND TONE

The three parts of the text present three purposes in writing: mastering information, using evidence to support an opinion, and persuading to action. In each of these, the relationship of writer to reader shifts significantly and grows more complex. This framework allows the instructor to initiate a discussion of purpose and tone at the beginning of the course and to integrate them throughout.

FINDING MAIN IDEAS

The text brings together the concepts of idea and patterns of organization by defining a core of main idea types and organizational patterns. The student discovers that there are different kinds of main ideas, and that the kind of idea being developed determines the pattern of development. Throughout the text, students practice recognizing and mapping eight idea patterns. Part I introduces the student to working with these patterns in sentences, paragraphs, and short passages. In Parts II and III, these eight main ideas provide the controlling organizational patterns for selections from college textbooks and for full-length articles.

■ FEATURES

RELEVANT READING SELECTIONS

A number of criteria have governed the choice of the readings in the book. The foremost consideration has been that the selections provide clear examples of the types of structures or concepts being presented. A substantial number of articles come from authors reflecting diverse cultural vantage points and experiences. Reading selections also reflect issues of concern and interest to the student; several selections used in the text were found and submitted by students for Reading Portfolio assignments.

AUTHENTIC PARAGRAPH EXERCISES

All paragraph and short passage exercises in Part I are taken from current text sources rather than paraphrased or manufactured to support a model. These sources represent the kind of textbooks college students will be using (psychology, history, biology, etc.). These materials also introduce students to issues and topics that they will need to incorporate as part of their essential background information.

EXERCISES FOR ANALYTICAL THINKING

The text contains over 80 exercises for improving thinking and reading skills.

Basic Critical Thinking Skills.   Readings are followed by questions aimed at critical thinking skills rather than rote recall. Students practice

- ■ Distinguishing topical organization from organization by ideas
- ■ Finding the main idea of paragraphs, multiparagraph units, and articles
- ■ Identifying idea patterns of organization
- ■ Recognizing transitions that signal relationships among pattern elements and supporting details

HIGH-LEVEL THINKING SKILLS

Where appropriate to the chapter content and the type of reading, questions involving high-level critical thinking skills require students to

- Draw inferences and state implied main ideas
- Synthesize two or more sentences to formulate divided main ideas
- Distinguish fact and opinion
- Evaluate evidence
- Explain figurative language (including analogy)
- Identify basic logical fallacies and emotional appeals

MAPPING PRACTICE

"Mind maps" are not simply discussed as a study skills option and then dropped, but are incorporated throughout the text. Students discover that idea patterns can have their own distinctive maps. Paragraph exercises and those following many articles give practice in pattern mapping as a way to achieve mastery of structure and idea, and as an invaluable preliminary to writing balanced and acceptably paraphrased summaries.

VOCABULARY BUILDING

Students work with vocabulary in two areas.

Vocabulary in Context.   The use of context in determining meaning is introduced in Chapter 3 and remains a focus throughout the text. Context questions follow many of the readings, and frequent exercises direct the students to create context sentences of their own for new words that they meet.

Word Parts.   Four of the chapters in Part II introduce the student to the importance of word parts in vocabulary building by providing a core of high-frequency prefixes and roots. A brief exercise follows each and occasional exercises after readings encourage the use of word parts along with context to help unlock the meaning of words.

STUDY SKILLS

Study skills guides frequently tell students to find and mark "the most important information," but how do readers decide on what is important? Part I thoroughly grounds students in the fundamentals of topic, main idea, and major and minor detail, and thus provides the students with the machinery for deciding what is most important. In Chapter 5, summarizing and paraphrasing are integrated with recognizing and mapping organizational patterns as students learn that only through in-depth analysis can they determine what information a summary must capture. Chapter 1 covers the basic purposes of graphics in textbooks and gives students practice in learning how to utilize graphic information.

METACOGNITIVE FEATURES

Chapter Previews and Reviews.   An outline Chapter Preview of each chapter advises students of new terms and of the skills they will practice. Chapter Reviews provide a quick ten-question check of content mastery.

Interactive Text.   Beginning in Chapter 5, extended textbook selections and full-length articles are preceded by two features designed to aid the student in developing metacognitive abilities.

- *Setting Your Reading Goals* includes framing information to help students focus on both the author's purpose and their own. It provides previewing strategies for forming a main idea hypothesis. This section is followed by a selected list of *preview vocabulary* words.
- *Annotating as You Read* provides the student with a structure for interacting with the text. Suggestions are given for finding and marking important information and for being on the lookout for transitional words and phrases that help to indicate organizational relationships.

An additional interactive feature is designed to keep students aware of the need for constant feedback and reevaluation of hypotheses. Questions or directions may appear in midtext to remind the student of the task at hand or to allow a self-check of progress.

FRAMES OF REFERENCE

Throughout the text, the student is reminded of the importance of activating and increasing schema. Students are encouraged to begin building general reference frameworks (timelines, classifications, etc.) that will help them see connections in information. In Parts II and III, the Academic Connection relates idea patterns to large reference frameworks in major fields of study, such as time in history or causation in medical studies and criminology.

READING PORTFOLIO

A feature unique to this text are the Reading Portfolio assignments. These provide an opportunity for ongoing reading and writing activity throughout the course.

- *Applying knowledge.* All chapters end with suggested assignments (many with options) that invite students to apply what they have learned to outside reading materials by finding articles for analysis on their own.

- *Writing and responding.* Through assignments requiring students to carefully summarize and thoughtfully respond, the instructor is able to integrate written work smoothly and relevantly into a reading course.

- *Summarizing and evaluating.* As students reinforce their identification of idea types, they also practice summary and paraphrase techniques under close supervision, and are encouraged to evaluate as they respond to what they read.

- *Lifelong reading.* By finding and responding to articles that arouse their interests, students become more familiar with print resources. Through this exposure their chances of developing positive lifelong reading habits greatly improve.

COLLABORATIVE LEARNING

Opportunities for large- and small-group activities are provided and encouraged in every chapter. Pattern map exercises, especially in Part I, are especially appropriate for small-group formats and overhead projector work.

ADDITIONAL WRITING ASSIGNMENTS

The Reading Portfolio assignments provide for regular written assignments throughout the text. In addition, many group and individual writing assignments can be generated from the Questions for Writing/Discussion sections following many readings.

NEW TO THE SECOND EDITION

Comments and suggestions from colleagues and reviewers have led to many changes and additions for this edition.

INTRODUCTION: JOINING THE ACADEMIC DIALOGUE

This new section clarifies for students exactly what it is that instructors expect from them. It introduces students to the importance of developing the critical thinking and reading skills that are essential to academic discourse. Here, and in several sections added to the chapters in Part I, the student learns how reading involves dialogues on many levels: with the author, with oneself, with peers, and with the world outside.

EXPANDED DISCUSSION ON TONE

A new approach to tone for the student is provided through a graphic that lists tone descriptors in several general categories that may or may not apply to a reading. The student is encouraged to realize that because a writer's attitude can be complex, more than one word is often required to describe tone.

ADDITIONAL CHAPTER IN PART I

A more in-depth coverage of fundamentals has required expanding the chapters in Part I from four to five. Additional explanations and exercises for key topics—topic, idea, and main idea—have resulted in splitting the former initial chapter into two in this edition.

CHANGE IN PRESENTATION OF MAPPING STRATEGIES

New "mind map" approaches appear in Chapter 4. Organization patterns are grouped under three types of maps: umbrella maps, enumeration maps, and relationship maps.

NEW SECTION ON METHODS OF DEVELOPMENT

Discussion has been added for several techniques that authors frequently employ: restatement, clarification, order of importance, and the use of subpatterns. Exercises have been added for these topics, and questions regarding methods of development are integrated into the reading throughout the text.

ADDITIONAL READINGS FROM TEXTBOOKS

In response to reviewers comments, new selections from textbooks in a variety of fields—astronomy, business, computer science, biology, sociology, health, fitness, and history—have been added to many chapters in the text.

FOCUS ON ISSUES OF MEDIA AND TECHNOLOGY

Several of the articles new to this edition focus on the issues relevant to students both in the present and the future. Articles deal with the effect of media and advertising on students and the benefits and threats of the rapidly changing world of technology.

THE LONGMAN READING SKILLS PACKAGE

A complete **Instructor's Manual/Test Bank** is available to accompany *Design in Reading*. This print supplement includes a complete answer key for the text, as well as teaching strategies, a book report guide, and preformatted tests/practices for each chapter. Ask your Longman sales representative for ISBN 0-321-09632-0.

In addition, a series of other valuable ancillaries is available.

ELECTRONIC AND ONLINE OFFERINGS
[NEW WEB VERSION] Longman Reading Road Trip Multimedia Software, CD Version and Web Version.   This innovative and exciting multimedia reading software is available either in CD-ROM format or on the Web. The package takes students on a tour of 15 cities and landmarks throughout the United States.

Each of the 15 modules corresponds to a reading or study skill (for example, finding the main idea, understanding patterns of organization, and thinking critically). All modules contain a tour of the location, instruction and tutorial, exercises, interactive feedback, and mastery tests. To shrinkwrap the CD or the access code to the Website with this textbook, please consult your Longman sales representative.

[NEW] Longman Vocabulary Website.   For additional vocabulary-related resources, visit our free vocabulary Website at http://www.ablongman.com/vocabulary.

The Longman English Pages Web Site.   Both students and instructors can visit our free content-rich Web site for additional reading selections and writing exercises. From the Longman English pages, visitors can conduct a simulated Web search, learn how to write a resume and cover letter, or try their hand at poetry writing. Stop by and visit us at **http://www.ablongman.com/englishpages**.

The Longman Electronic Newsletter.   Twice a month during the spring and fall, instructors who have subscribed receive a free copy of the Longman Developmental English Newsletter in their e-mailbox. Written by experienced classroom instructors, the newsletter offers teaching tips, classroom activities, book reviews, and more. To subscribe, visit the Longman Basic Skills Web site at **http://www.ablongman. com/basicskills**, or send an e-mail to **BasicSkills@ablongman.com**.

FOR ADDITIONAL READING AND REFERENCE

The Dictionary Deal.   Two dictionaries can be shrinkwrapped with *Design in Reading* at a nominal fee. *The New American Webster Handy College Dictionary* is a paperback reference text with more than 100,000 entries. *Merriam Webster's Collegiate Dictionary,* Tenth Edition, is a hardback reference with a citation file of more than 14.5 million examples of English words drawn from actual use. For more information on how to shrinkwrap a dictionary with your text, please contact your Longman sales representative.

Penguin Quality Paperback Titles.   A series of Penguin paperbacks is available at a significant discount when shrinkwrapped with any Longman Reading Skills title. Some titles available are Toni Morrison's *Beloved,* Julia Alvarez's *How the Garcia Girls Lost Their Accents,* Mark Twain's *Huckleberry Finn, Narrative of the Life of Frederick Douglass,* Harriet Beecher Stowe's *Uncle Tom's Cabin,* Dr. Martin Luther King, Jr.'s *Why We Can't Wait,* and plays by Shakespeare, Miller, and Albee. For a complete list of titles or more information, please contact your Longman sales consultant.

***The Pocket Reader* and *The Brief Pocket Reader,* First Edition.**   These inexpensive volumes contains 80 brief readings and 50 readings, respectively. Each reading is brief (1–3 pages each). The readers are theme-based: writers on writing, nature, women and men, customs and habits, politics, rights and obligations, and coming of age. Also included is an alternate rhetorical table of contents. 0-321-07668-0

The Longman Textbook Reader.   This supplement, for use in developmental reading courses, offers five complete chapters from Addison-Wesley/Longman textbooks: computer science, biology, psychology, communications, and business. Each chapter includes additional comprehension quizzes, critical thinking questions, and group activities. Available FREE with the adoption of this Longman text. For information on how to bundle *The Longman Textbook Reader* with your text, please contact your Longman sales representative. Available in two formats: with answers and without answers.

Newsweek **Alliance.**   Instructors may choose to shrinkwrap a 12-week subscription to *Newsweek* with any Longman text. The price of the subscription is 57 cents per issue (a total of $6.84 for the subscription). Available with the subscription is a free "Interactive Guide to *Newsweek*"—a workbook for students who are using the text. In addition, *Newsweek* provides a wide variety of instructor supplements free to teachers, including maps, Skills Builders, and weekly quizzes. For more information on the *Newsweek* program, please contact your Longman sales representative.

FOR INSTRUCTORS

[NEW] Electronic Test Bank for Reading.   This electronic test bank offers more than 3,000 questions in all areas of reading, including vocabulary, main idea, supporting details, patterns of organization, language, critical thinking, analytical reasoning, inference, point of view, visual aids, and textbook reading. With this easy-to-use CD-ROM, instructors simply choose questions from the electronic test bank, then print out the completed test for distribution. CD-ROM: 0-321-08179-X Print version: 0-321-08596-5

CLAST Test Package, Fourth Edition.   These two 40-item objective tests evaluate students' readiness for the CLAST exams. Strategies for teaching CLAST preparedness are included. Free with any Longman English title. Reproducible sheets: 0-321-01950-4 Computerized IBM version: 0-321-01982-2 Computerized Mac version: 0-321-01983-0

TASP Test Package, Third Edition.   These 12 practice pre-tests and post-tests assess the same reading and writing skills covered in the TASP examination. Free with any Longman English title. Reproducible sheets:0-321-01959-8 Computerized IBM version: 0-321-01985-7 Computerized Mac version: 0-321-01984-9

Teaching Online: Internet Research, Conversation, and Composition, **Second Edition.** Ideal for instructors who have never surfed the Net, this easy-to-follow guide offers basic definitions, numerous examples, and step-by-step information about finding and using Internet sources. Free to adopters. 0-321-01957-1

[NEW] **The Longman Guide to Classroom Management.** is the first in a series of monographs for developmental educators. Written by Joannis Flatley of St. Philip's College, it focuses on issues of classroom etiquette, providing guidance on dealing with unruly, unengaged, disruptive, or uncooperative students. 0-321-09246-5

[NEW] **The Longman Instructor Planner.** is an all-in-one resource for instructors. It includes monthly and weekly planning sheets, to-do lists, student contact forms, attendance rosters, a gradebook, an address/phone book, and a mini-almanac. It is free upon request. 0-321-09247-3

FOR STUDENTS

[NEW] **The Longman Reader's Journal, by Kathleen T. McWhorter.** This reader's journal offers students a space to record their questions about, reactions to, and summaries of materials they've read. Also included is a personal vocabulary log, as well as ample space for free writing. For an examination copy, contact your Longman sales consultant. 0-321-08843-3

[NEW] **The Longman Reader's Portfolio.** This unique supplement provides students with a space to plan, think about, and present their work. The portfolio includes a diagnostic area (including a learning style questionnaire), a working area (including calendars, vocabulary logs, reading response sheets, book club tips, and other valuable materials), and a display area (including a progress chart, a final table of contents, and a final assessment). Free when packed with this text. 0-321-10766-7

Researching Online, **Sixth Edition.** A perfect companion for a new age, this indispensable new supplement helps students navigate the Internet. Adapted from *Teaching Online,* the instructor's Internet guide, *Researching Online* speaks directly to students, giving them detailed, step-by-step instructions for performing electronic searches. Available free when shrinkwrapped with this text. 0-321-11733-6

Ten Practices of Highly Successful Students. This popular supplement helps students learn crucial study skills, offering concise tips for a successful career in college. Topics include time management, test-taking, reading critically, stress, and motivation. 0-205-30769-8

[FOR FLORIDA ADOPTERS] *Thinking Through the Test,* by D.J. Henry. This special workbook, prepared specially for students in Florida, offers ample skill and practice exercises to help students prep for the Florida State Exit Exam. To shrinkwrap this workbook free with your textbook, please contact your Longman sales representative. Available in two versions: with answers and without answers. Also available: two laminated grids (one for reading, one for writing) that can serve as handy references for students preparing for the Florida State Exit Exam.

The Longman Planner.   This free planner helps students organize a business life. Ask your Longman sales representative for an examination copy. 0-321-04573-4

◼ ACKNOWLEDGMENTS

"It takes a village to raise a child." Likewise, it takes a village to create a book. I am extremely grateful for the people in my village whose contributions have been invaluable in shaping both the first and second editions of this textbook. I thank colleagues and friends whose feedback, advice, and support I continue to rely on: Yvonne and Gordon Taylor, Steve Usher, Rose Kahn, Kris Lewis, and Ceroasetta Simba of Fresno City College, and Norma Kaser, Jan Reyes, and Sheryl Young-Manning of Reedley College.

Appreciative thanks go also to the following reviewers whose thoughtful comments and constructive advice have led to substantive improvements in many aspects of this text.

For the first edition I am grateful to Pamela Cervi, Henry Ford Community College; Miriam Kinard, Trident Technical College; Leslie King, S.U.N.Y. at Oswego; Audrey J. Roth, Miami Dade Community College; Patricia Rottmund, Harrisburg Area Community College; Nancy Smith, Florida Community College at Jacksonville; and Suzanne Weisar, San Jacinto College South.

For the second edition, I would like to thank Brenda G. Armbrecht, Georgia Perimeter College; Mary Gilbert, Tompkins Cortland Community College; Robert S. Mann, Des Moines Area Community College; Natalie Miller, Joliet Junior College; and Sheila Novins, Nassau Community College.

Working with the experienced editorial staff of Longman Publishers has been a pleasure. I am particularly indebted to Senior Editor Steven Rigolosi for his encouragement and for the focus and direction he has provided to make this revision a reality.

Richmond Garrigus

To the Student

Think for a moment about the following situations that you will face often in college:

- Taking notes in a class where you know you will be tested on lecture material
- Reading a textbook chapter in preparation for an exam
- Being asked to complete a one-page summary of a lengthy article

For many students, these are moments of panic. In all of these situations, the advice may be to identify "the most important ideas." But the problem is, how do you decide what is and isn't important? For that matter, what *is* an idea really?

This textbook will help you develop the ability to recognize ideas and thus make useful decisions, in situations like those above, about what is important. You will learn that simply running your eyes over words and sentences is not enough to gain true comprehension: reading requires analysis. To *analyze* means to break things and ideas into parts, to see connections, and to make a carefully planned examination. By reading this book and working through the exercises, you will come to know the main types of ideas and how they work in patterns to help you make better sense of the world.

This textbook will also help you to see how senders of communications have a variety of intentions, not all of which are obvious at first glance. Think, for example, of what an average week's delivery of mail brings to your home: personal letters, bills and advertisements, perhaps an announcement of a public hearing or upcoming event, one or more magazines full of news and commentary, and almost certainly a large amount of annoying bulk-rate mail, ranging from pleas for money for various causes to official-looking announcements that you have "won" millions of dollars. All of these differ not just in content, but in their purpose as well. Wise readers learn to recognize that the announcement of the public hearing gives important information, that the articles in a newsmagazine may present an interpretation of some current event, that a pamphlet might contain arguments intended to persuade a voter to support a cause or candidate, while that official-looking envelope is less likely to contain a check than clever gimmicks to get your dollars.

Take some time to preview the table of contents of this textbook. Note that the three parts of the text cover various aims of communication:

Part I: To inform

Part II: To prove

Part III: To persuade or manipulate to action

These purposes involve you with writers in very different ways. To be an effective reader, you must understand these differences and act accordingly. This text will encourage you to pay close attention to not only *what* is being said but also the *motive* behind it.

Think of reading as an activity like playing a sport or mastering a musical instrument. You can only get out of it what you put into it and, at least at the start, winning (or getting the right answer) is really not as important as committing yourself to mastering the fundamentals. What you will be asked to do in this textbook is not easy. Nothing worthwhile ever is. Critical thinking/reading is hard work, but it can be enjoyable while at the same time giving you a payoff in personal satisfaction and greater success in your college work and in your career.

Introduction: Joining the Academic Dialogue

dialogue (dīˊə lôg) n. 1. talking together, conversation 2. interchange and discussion of ideas, esp. when open and frank, as in seeking mutual understanding or harmony (*Webster's New World Dictionary,* 3rd College Ed.)

During your early college experience, you may, like many students, be bothered by a nagging but usually unspoken question: "What is it exactly that these teachers want from me?" You may study diligently and turn in all assignments, and yet the tests always seem to ask questions that you never anticipated and written assignments don't come back with the grades you want. Courses do present a core of factual information that students are expected to remember. But just being able to recall facts and data for a course isn't enough. All fields of inquiry share a common set of underlying skills and attitudes that take the learner from merely accumulating or memorizing information to unifying and understanding it. This ability to think at higher levels underlies success in all classes and melds teachers and students into a community of learners engaged in **academic dialogue.**

In the course of your life you will be engaged in many dialogues: private ones with family and loved ones, social ones with friends and associates, civic dialogues through participation in public life, professional ones in the world of work. Academic dialogue is another, unique form of communication. Below is a short list of some of its key features. Academic dialogue

- Consists of careful analysis and thoughtful discussion
- Requires playing by rules of reasonable discourse—giving sound, relevant evidence for judgments and conclusions
- Goes beyond gathering data and information to connecting and understanding it
- Helps us to become aware of our strengths and our weakness as learners
- Holds up the principles of honesty and integrity to direct our search for knowledge
- Develops in us the tools to overcome biases or prejudices that cloud our judgment

The teacher-student relationship has always been a special one. Over time, the role of teacher has evolved from acting as a strict master to being more of a partner, advisor, mentor, and guide. The instructional community offers the student this standing invitation: "Join us. Learn to use your mind and speak in your voice to the best of your capacity." In short, what your teachers want is for you to join, and eventually become full partners in, the academic dialogue that is the foundation of education and civic life. Critical thinking and reading skills are essential for engaging in academic dialogue across the curriculum, for vocational and technical courses as well as those in general education. Mastering these skills is therefore vital for your success and growth as a college student.

■ A COMMITMENT TO GROWTH AND CHANGE

Learning involves not just a change in the knowledge we have; it involves changes in the way we process information and experiences. A college education is more than something you get; it is something you become. Participating in academic dialogue will change forever the way you see the world.

But change can be threatening. It is sometimes difficult to give up old habits, even when they don't work. Many students have had very negative experiences in the past. "Math anxiety" is a condition familiar to many teachers; students are so convinced that mathematics is beyond them that they tune out and give up. A similar situation can happen in reading. A student may be able to read and understand most of the words and sentences in a text but simply can't connect it to a world of ideas. The information remains a disconnected hodgepodge of pieces and chunks, and any kind of a dialogue through discussion and sharing of ideas is impossible. In *Speaking of Reading,* Nadine Rosenthal has recorded oral conversations with readers from various walks of life and levels of ability. The book includes the observations of many readers who were able to overcome negative experiences with reading and to change, not just the way they read, but the way they connect to their world. Below is the story of a student who underwent a transformation as a result of experiences in education. As you read, note the profound differences in the student before and after—changes in his outlook on life, his readiness to accept new challenges, his confidence, and his self-esteem.

John Moran from *Speaking of Reading*

1   On the first night of my master's degree class, I knew I was in trouble. I was totally unprepared. I did not have the tools to do what they were requesting. I knew it the minute I stepped foot in the classes. It was a real eye-opener for me. The teachers said, "We expect this, this, and this. Read these many chapters. And we need this paperwork. Turn it in next week." I said to myself, "I've never seen this before." It really frightened me. At this point, I realized I had a major stumbling block regarding the process of reading.

2   Going to the library the next day was an adventure for me. I walked in and saw all these people that were in class the night before, all studying. I said to myself, "I don't think I've been in the library more than five times in my life." I felt the handicap at that point, knowing I didn't have the tools.

3   In the beginning, the driving, motivating force was more a fear of failure than a desire to enhance my learning. I was so afraid to fall. I even fought a few teachers during the beginning of my master's program. I was constantly nail-biting them and bickering over the smallest of things because I knew I didn't have it. So I said, "Well, why can't I do this?" And they would say, "These are the requirements here. This is the way we do things." One teacher was really outstanding. He'll never realize how much he helped me. It was his openness and his relentlessness in not allowing me a crack to slip through, because I'd have taken it. He said, "No, John, no. Understand, this is psychology which can be applicable to anything. I'm just giving you the process on how to do it." It was the word, process, that helped me.

4   As time went on, I found that I was very capable of understanding what was required, and I also found a joy that had never appeared to me before. It was like flowers blooming in the library, realizing that I was OK being there. My thesis required almost eight months of fourteen, fifteen hours a day in a medical library, and that's where I learned to feel comfortable. I hibernated

Nadine Rosenthal, *Speaking of Reading,* (Nadine Rosenthal, 1995), 199–202. Reprinted by permission of the author.

there, and I came to be able to read for three, four hours at a time, and put off taking a break because I didn't think I had done enough. I was able to deliver, too. I was able to go back to class and sit and participate with all these people and know that I had remembered what I read.

5   Confirmations come in a variety of ways. Sometimes we don't need to have people pat us on the back and say how great we are. For me the confirmations came when somebody would talk about something in class and I would think, "I read that last night." That's right. And I can remember even raising my hand and saying, "And this is also related to that." It got me feeling real comfortable at being able to talk about what I read, how I remembered it, how I comprehended it.

6   All of a sudden there was a real gleam in reading. As the discomfort of reading ended, and feeling good about it started, I branched out with it. Prior to graduate school, I was narrow-minded as to reading. I would say, "I don't want to read this. I don't want to read that." But it's not so much that I didn't want to, but that I didn't know how. I was scared. The more I read, the less scared I became, and as a result, what happened? I wasn't as narrow minded.

7   Reading was never reinforced in my family. Everybody was a blue-collar worker, and due to the streets and the activities in the neighborhood, reading and education took a back burner. Even though we were put in a Catholic school, there was no reinforcement, so I just hit the streets; that's what everybody in my family did. Nobody went to college. The joy of being in the streets with friends far outweighed going into a classroom. How could you match the two? The street had such an allure. Peer identity and peer acceptance were so important. I mean, if you hang out with people who don't do book work, who don't go into a library, it's not an option. It doesn't exist. You're not going to go to a library in front of your friends. It's not going to happen.

8   The kids today are a lot like I used to be. They want to go into the streets and hang out. They'd rather be in a doorway than come and sit in a library. They don't realize the safeness and the comfortableness of the place. They could actually drop their guard in the library and not have to look over their shoulders. You can't tell me there's not something in a library that can attract every kid out there. There has to be. It's a matter of getting them there to find it, and showing them the tools for finding the books.

9   That's what the graduate degree did for me. It gave me the confidence and self-esteem to be able to be comfortable in a library. I'm an incredibly different person now. Reading has allowed me to enter into a new arena and feel comfortable. I find myself going on journeys and picking out books that I never would have years earlier. Reading has given me the freedom to grow from inside out and be wiser. There's things in reading you don't have to go out and shout about, but they're discoveries you make inside.

10   I'm reading a book now that's a thousand pages on Japan. It's three inches thick. You have to be kidding! And we're talking fourteenth century. It's about the history of the Japanese samurai and how their spiritualness and their emotional development resulted in being a samurai without violence. I go to bed reading it at night. I told my friend who gave me the book that it's so powerful, I'll have to read it again. And he said, "Well, that's right. I read it twice."

11   I think there are a lot of young people like me out there. Education could open up their world, but how do you bring them over to the other side? That is the fascinating part of this whole experience of education—finding a vehicle to get them to the other end so they can discover they're capable of learning. So many kids are knocking on the door out there, and we have to pay attention to hear them. We have to figure out how to help them discover reading the way I did. If we teach them how to read, then they read for life and everything opens up for them.

12   I thought I was going to graduate school to get a degree, but I found out that the degree is miscellaneous. The end result was the incredible discovery of what reading is all about, which is the last thing I expected. There are a few times in life when we have special experiences that stay with us forever and warm our insides. I truly believe that learning to read in graduate school was one of them for me. I can read now. I can read a thousand-page book and learn about so many things. It makes me smile.

Exercise

Work in groups of three or four to answer the questions below. Numbers in parentheses refer to paragraph numbers.

1. Moran admits in paragraphs 1–2 that he "was in trouble." What problems was he facing? _____

   _____

   _____

   _____

2. What factor (1–3) motivated Moran at the beginning of his studies? Explain in what ways this factor is negative or positive. _____

   _____

   _____

   _____

3. What does Moran mean by "process" (3) and how did the word help him?

_____

_____

_____

4. "It was like flowers blooming in the library, realizing that I was OK being there." (4) What change in his outlook has occurred?_____

_____

_____

_____

5. Moran speaks of "confirmation"—that is, evidence that gives value to what we do. What gave Moran confirmation in his academic pursuits?_____

_____

_____

_____

6. How did reading affect Moran's mental outlook on life (6)? _____

_____

_____

_____

7. Moran speculates in paragraphs 7–8 on factors that might have affected his performance and that of others. What conclusions does he draw about the following?

a. Home life: _____

_____

_____

b. Peer group pressure:_____

_____

_____

c. Attitudes toward the library: _____

_____

_____

8. In paragraphs 9–10, Moran talks about how he has changed to the point where he is able fully to join the academic dialogue.

     a. What did the graduate degree do for him? _____

     _____

     _____

     b. "Reading has given me the freedom to grow from inside out and be wiser." What example of this does he give? _____

     _____

     _____

9. "I thought I was going to graduate school to get a degree, but I found out that the degree is miscellaneous." (12) In Moran's view, what was the most important function of his educational experience? _____

     _____

     _____

     _____

10. "I think there are a lot of young people like me out there. Education could open up their world, but how do you bring them over to the other side?" (11) What suggestions would you give to solve this problem? _____

     _____

     _____

     _____

Instructors, students, authors, texts, data, ideas—all of these elements interconnect in various ways to create the academic dialogue of the college classroom. Several sections in the early portions of your text will help you understand that academic dialogue can take a variety of forms—not just with the author, but a dialogue with yourself, your peers, and the world around you.

Reading for Information

"You must learn to walk before you hope to run." Whether playing a sport like golf or an instrument like the piano, if you intend to master a skill, you must have a solid grounding in the fundamentals—and you must practice. The same is true for the skill of reading. To become an effective reader, you must learn the terms and concepts that are necessary for analysis and discussion to occur. In Part I you will build a firm foundation for academic dialogue by mastering fundamental skills involved in processing information from texts.

Responding to Factual Information: Topics, Ideas, and Graphics

CHAPTER 1

In the original TV series *Dragnet,* Detective Joe Friday was famous for asking for "the facts, Ma'am, nothing but the facts." All college majors require students to master certain basics in the field. Much of the reading you will do in college and on the job—textbooks, manuals, statistical studies, and reports—involves reading to find and retain factual information. This chapter will introduce you to the most basic elements involved in understanding factual information.

CHAPTER PREVIEW

In this chapter you will

- Become aware of how reading is a dialogue with an author
- Learn to recognize topics and subtopics
- Discover how the terms general and specific relate to topics
- Observe how questions lead us from topics to ideas
- Use outlines and spider maps to show topics and subtopics
- Work with a variety of graphic aids
- Be introduced to an ongoing term activity, the Reading Portfolio

Communication requires at least two participants; at any one point, someone is sending information and someone is receiving it. Reading, as a form of communication, involves first of all a dialogue with the writer. Obviously, the dialogue is not "out loud"—no audible conversation is involved. Yet there is an exchange of ideas. Authors have certain points in mind that they hope eventually will, by means of the text, end up in the their readers' minds.

SHARING INFORMATION: A DIALOGUE WITH THE AUTHOR

Depending on the kind of reading material, the dialogue between reader and writer can range from generally impersonal writing (an instruction manual) to the highly personal (an opinion essay on an editorial page). Indeed, a reader can become worked up to the point of shouting at the page or pursuing further dialogue by telephone, e-mail, or a letter to the editor. As you read the passage below, pay attention to the ways in which the act of reading invites a dialogue between reader and writer.

The Etiquette of Talking Back

by Mortimer Adler

1   Reading a book is a kind of conversation. Now you may think it is not conversation at all, because the author does all the talking and you have nothing to say. If you think that, you do not realize your opportunities and obligations as a reader.

2   As a matter of fact, the reader has the last word. The author has had his say, and then it is the reader's turn. The reader has an obligation as well as an opportunity to talk back. The opportunity is clear. Nothing can stop a reader from pronouncing judgment. The roots of the obligation, however, lie a little deeper in the nature of the relation between books and readers. If a book is of the sort which conveys knowledge, the author's aim was to instruct. He has tried to teach. He has tried to convince or persuade his reader about something. His effort is crowned with success only if the reader finally says, "I am taught. You have convinced me that such and such is true, or persuaded me that it is probable." But even if the reader is not convinced or persuaded, the author's intention and effort should be respected. The reader owes him a considered judgment. If he cannot say, "I agree," he

---

Mortimer Adler, *How to Read a Book* (Simon and Schuster, © 1967 by Mortimer Adler).

should at least have grounds for disagreeing or even for suspending judgment on the question.

3   I am saying no more than that a good book deserves an active reading. The activity of reading does not stop with the work of understanding what a book says. It must be completed by the work of criticism, the work of judging. The passive reader sins against this requirement, probably even more than against the rules of analysis and interpretation. He not only makes no effort to understand; he dismisses a book simply by putting it down or forgetting it. Worse than faint praise, he damns it by no critical consideration whatsoever.

4   What I mean by talking back, you now can see, is not something apart from reading.... There is a tendency to think that a good book is above the criticism of the average reader [and that] the reader and the author are not peers.... It is true that a book which can enlighten its readers, and is in this sense their better, should not be criticized by them until they understand it. When they do, they have elevated themselves almost to peerage with the author. Now they are fit to exercise the rights and privileges of their new position. Unless they exercise their critical faculties now, they are doing the author an injustice. He has done what he could to make them his equal. He deserves that they act like his peers, that they engage in conversation with him, that they talk back.

Exercise 1.1

Work in groups of three or four to answer the questions below. Numbers in parentheses refer to paragraph numbers.

1. In what way (1–2) is reading a book actually a conversation?

   _____

   _____

2. Explain the difference (2) between the "opportunity" and the "obligation" to talk back to the author. _____

   _____

   _____

3. "The reader owes him a considered judgment." (2) How does the phrase "considered judgment" relate to the ideals of academic dialogue? _____

   _____

   _____

4. What are the "sins" (3) of a passive reader? Have you ever been "guilty" of any of them? _____

_____

_____

5. "There is a tendency to think that a good book is above the criticism of the average reader." (4) Under what conditions, according to the author, is it acceptable to criticize—i.e., "talk back to"—a book? _____

_____

_____

The "conversation" in informational writing is not very personal. Feelings or attitudes are usually not emphasized. In scientific reports and studies, for example, you will rarely see the first person pronoun "I." If opinions appear, they are usually reported rather than proposed by the authors. The goal of informational writing is to share objective data and concepts. Writers try to anticipate the expectations of their readers. When we read for information, our dialogue with the writer reflects our expectations through the following types of questions:

- Are the writer's directions and explanations clear? Nothing can be more frustrating, for example, than trying to learn to use a tool or put together an object from an instruction manual that misleads or confuses.
- Is the information presented by the writer accurate? This is especially crucial if we use it to support our own research or opinions.
- Is the information current? This does not mean that older sources are automatically outdated, but in many technical areas, information does change rapidly and yesterday's facts may be changed by new studies or advances.

Many of your college texts will be largely informational, though some will include sections to get you to examine controversies and engage in debate. You will find, however, that informational does not necessarily mean easy. The content, format, and vocabulary of college texts present a big challenge. To carry on a successful conversation with textbooks, you need to master fundamental reading and study strategies.

■ IDENTIFYING TOPICS AND SUBTOPICS IN READING

The starting point for effective reading and note taking is identifying the topics and subtopics on which textbooks provide information. The word "topic" means about the same as "subject." Everything in the world that can be named—for example, baseball, politics, music, voting—provides us with topics for investigation. To find the topic of a passage, look for the answer to this question: "What is this about?"

For example, what is the topic of the previous paragraph?

a. note taking

b. textbooks

c. topics

d. baseball

All of these terms appear in the paragraph, but clearly the answer is "topics." It is the subject that everything else connects to. One good technique for identifying the topic is to look for repeated words or phrases. In the paragraph above, for example, the words *topic* and *topics* are mentioned four times.

Topics that are **general** (broad) cover large areas of material. Topics can themselves be further subdivided into smaller categories (subtopics)—which are more **specific** (less broad). It is vital in reading and writing to understand this distinction between general and specific. For example, look at the list below:

The category at the top—"mammals"—is the most general; the detail at the bottom the most specific. Trying to picture a broad category like "mammal" is difficult; each of us would have something quite different in mind. In picturing a specific chimpanzee, "Bozo," our "mind pictures" would probably be much more alike. Don't be confused by the fact that general and specific can be relative terms. Here, although the first three are general classes, we would say that chimpanzees are "more specific" than primates, and primates are "more specific" than mammals. However, as one single thing, only Bozo can be a "specific" chimpanzee.

Because topical material is packed full of information, you will need to use special strategies in reading and studying textbook passages. You have probably been told to concentrate on what is "most important," but the first big problem is how to decide what is important. What should be highlighted/underlined, annotated, and remembered? Fortunately, most textbooks contain headings and subheadings that will help you recognize broad major topics and subtopics. For example, examine the short passage below from a nutrition textbook.

Muscle Structure and Contraction

Muscle Structure   Skeletal muscle is a collection of long thin cells called *fibers*. These fibers are surrounded by a dense layer of connective tissue called *fascia* that holds the individual fibers together and separates muscle from surrounding tissues. Muscles are attached to bone by connective tissues known as *tendons.*

Muscle Contraction   Muscle contraction is regulated by signals coming from motor nerves. Motor nerves originate in the spinal cord and send nerve fibers to individual muscles throughout the body. The motor nerve and individual muscle fiber make contact at the neuromuscular junction (where nerve and muscle fiber meet). Each motor nerve branches and then connects with numerous individual muscle. The motor nerve and all of the muscle fibers it controls is called a motor unit.

(Powers and Dodd, *Total Fitness: Exercise, Nutrition, and Wellness,* 2nd ed., 105)

The order and size of the boldface headings clue us that "Muscle Structure" and "Muscle Contraction" are subtopics of a larger category that contains them both.

Major Topic: **Muscle Structure and Contraction**

Subtopic 1:   *Muscle Structure*

Subtopic 2:   *Muscle Contraction*

Exercise 1.2

Part A

Identify the topic of each paragraph below by asking yourself "What is this about?" Then circle the letter of the word or phrase that best states the topic. Look for repeated words or phrases.

(Ferl and Wallace, *Biology: The Realm of Life,* 3rd ed.)

1. The human thumb is a refinement of a specialization that is possessed, to some degree, by other primates. Originally, the opposable thumb evolved as an adaptation that allowed for grasping branches. But for most primates it is relatively short, poorly muscled, and much less capable of precise movement. The human thumb has evolved special musculature and can be rotated readily. Apes can be trained to use simple tools and to open beer cans, but they are comically clumsy all the same. With our much greater dexterity, we can make precise tools, and many of us have been known to open beer cans with great dexterity. (p. 337)

   a. the human thumb

   b. the opposable thumb

   c. human adaptations

   d. opening beer cans

2. *Imperfect* is not a derogatory term in botany. Instead, it refers to the presumed absence of sexual reproduction. There are thousands of poorly under-

stood species of *Fungi Imperfecti,* which apparently will occupy the energies of taxonomists for decades to come. Undoubtedly, many of these species will eventually be placed among either the sac or club fungi. The *Fungi Imperfecti* include a number of human parasites such as *Trichophyton mentaprophytes,* which causes athlete's foot. Another causes ringworm. (p. 389)

   a. absence of sexual reproduction

   b. human parasites

   c. taxonomists

   d. *Fungi Imperfecti*

3. A new, drastically modified reproductive device—the land egg—first introduced by the early reptiles, was a vital adaptation to complete terrestrial life. The land egg was surrounded by a tough leathery shell (later replaced by a calcium shell in birds). Included within the egg was a supply of water and food, everything necessary for the embryo's development. (p. 463)

   a. reproductive devices

   b. early reptile adaptation

   c. the land egg

   d. embryo development

4. In some cases an individual may have a dominant genotype without showing it, a condition known as incomplete penetrance. For instance, the gene that gives one the ability to roll his or her tongue is dominant, yet not all persons with the dominant allele will be able to roll their tongues. But for any one person, it is all or nothing. There are no people who can roll their tongue only part way. (p. 205)

   a. genotypes

   b. incomplete penetrance

   c. dominant alleles

   d. tongue rolling

5. You are probably aware of the persistent controversy over the connection between saturated fats and cholesterol. You may have even switched to foods with high levels of unsaturated fats—the ones so heavily touted in advertisements for margarine and cooking oils. Indeed people generally assume that it is good to avoid fats in the diet. Although this is generally a good practice for Americans, who consume too much fat, fats are not all bad. In fact, some amount of fat is essential in the diets of many animals. (p. 667)

   a. saturated fats

   b. cholesterol

   c. margarine and cooking oils

   d. fats

Part B

In the textbook selection below, the main topic heading and three major subtopic headings have been removed. Fill in those headings from the list on the left. The items in the list on the right are the topics of the seven paragraphs. Fill in the blank at the end of each paragraph with the appropriate topic.
(Capron, *Computers: Tools for an Information Age*, 6th ed., 261–262)

<u>Headings</u>

Setting up an Internet

Intranets

The Internet Too

Intranets at Work

<u>Paragraph Topics</u>

Linking intranet and internet

Components of an intranet

Extranets

Intranet web pages

Distinguishing intranets from internets

Employee use of internet at work

Typical applications at work

Main Topic Heading: _____

1. Although many businesses use the internet to promote their products and services to the public, they are finding that an even more useful application is for their internal—company only—purposes, hence the intranet. Vendors promoting their intranet software products in magazine advertisements often make a play on the word, perhaps inTRAnet or even In<u>tra</u>net. They do not want you to think that they are simply misspelling internet. In fact, an intranet is a private Internet-like network internal to a certain company. The number of intranets has been growing rapidly. Every Fortune 500 company either has an intranet or is planning one. Part of the phenomenal growth is the relative ease of setting up an intranet.

Paragraph topic: _____

Major Subtopic Heading: _____

2. It's fast, it's easy, it's inexpensive. Relatively speaking, of course. The components of an intranet are are familiar ones: the same ones used for the Internet. Hardware requirements include a server and computers used for access. These probably exist because most companies already have local area networks; this is why the intranet setup is fast, easy, and inexpensive. The Internet TCP/IP protocols must be in place. The server, which will act as a clearinghouse for all data regardless of source, needs its own software. The server will process

requests and also perhaps pull data from traditional sources such as a mainframe computer. As on the Internet, each access computer needs a browser.

Paragraph topic: _____

3. The intranet developers will doubtless devote the most time and attention to writing the web pages that employees will see and use. The pages must be well designed and easy to follow, opting for function over glitz. A typical opening page, for example, would probably have an attractive company logo and several clickable generic icons to represent functions. One click leads to a more detailed page and so on. By presenting information the same way to every computer, the developers can pull all the computers, software and files that dot the corporate landscape into a single system that helps employees find information wherever it resides.

Paragraph topic: _____

Major Subtopic Heading: _____

4. A well-designed intranet can be used by most employees from day one. They can point and click and link to sites that contain information previously locked away behind functionaries and forms. Suppose, for example, that an employee needs to check up on the status of her benefits. Traditionally, she would probably have to find the right form, fill it out correctly, submit it, and wait a few days for a response. Now, it is point and click, give some identifying information such as Social Security number, and the information shows up on the screen and can be printed.

Paragraph topic: _____

5. Employee information is just the beginning. Typical applications are internal job openings, marketing, vacation requests, corporate policy information, and perhaps company training courses. Some even include the local weather report and the daily cafeteria menu. Intranets even cut down on the flow of e-mail. A manager can, instead of sending out mass e-mail to employees, post notices on his or her own web site and leave it to employees to check it regularly.

Paragraph topic: _____

Major Subtopic Heading: _____

6. An intranet can remain private and isolated, but most companies choose to link their intranets to the Internet. This gives employees access to Internet

resources and to other employees with their own intranets in geographically dispersed areas. The employer access to the public Internet would not be confused with public access to the company intranet: the intranet is private.

Paragraph topic: _____

7. However, companies may choose to link some parts of their intranet together. Such a hookup, intranet-to-intranet, is called an **extranet**. Some companies are finding that their longstanding relationships with customers and suppliers can often be handled more easily and more inexpensively with an intranet than with more traditional electronic data interchange— EDI—systems.

Paragraph topic: _____

■ FROM TOPICS TO IDEAS

Asking "What is this about?" helps us to identify a topic, but a topic alone doesn't communicate much. If an instructor walks into class and says "cats," students would have various images in their minds but they would likely all be quite different. We do not really initiate a dialogue until we ask a slightly different question: "What about cats?" To communicate we need to generate ideas **about** a topic. For example, the open-ended question "What about cats" or "What are cats?" leads to many more pointed questions and answers about a topic: **who, what, which kind of, when, where, why,** or **how:**

What are the personality traits of cats?

Why do cats make better pets than dogs?

What are the responsibilities of owning a cat?

How can cats best be trained?

When are cats a potential danger to small children?

These questions generate ideas about a topic that can be discussed, agreed with, or disputed:

Cats have both positive and negative personality traits.

Cats can be even more loving and loyal pets than dogs.

Owning a cat brings many responsibilities.

Training a cat requires knowledge of training techniques and patience.

An untrained cat can pose a real hazard when unsupervised around small children.

From the above examples you should now be able to draw one very important rule:

A *topic* is stated as a **fragment.** It is a subject only.

Ideas are stated in **complete sentences.** An idea must have a subject and a complete predicate.

Length is not always a good guide. A long string of phrases may still be only a fragment; an idea sentence, on the other hand, may be very short.

Exercise 1.3

Part A

Answer the questions that follow each of the numbered items below. Study the two examples below before proceeding.

Example 1   Due to clever advertising, cigarette smoking is increasing among teenagers.

What is the topic? ___advertising and teen smoking___

Is there a complete idea? _____yes_____

If *yes,* what question about the topic is answered? Has cigarette ___

advertising directed at teens been successful?___

If *no,* make up a question about the topic that will lead to an idea.

Question: _____

Idea: _____

Example 2   The challenges of the future for today's workforce.

What is the topic? workers in the future___

Is there a complete idea? _____no_____

If *yes,* what question about the topic is answered? _____

_____

(continued)

> If *no,* make up a question about the topic that will lead to an idea.
>
> Question: _How can workers meet tomorrow's challenges?_
>
> Idea: _Workers must be trained in new technologies to meet the_ _challenges of work in the future._

1. Too many Americans today fail to follow a sensible fitness plan.

   What is the topic? _____

   Is there a complete idea? _____

   If *yes,* what question about the topic is answered? _____

   _____

   If *no,* make up a question about the topic that will lead to an idea.

   Question: _____

   Idea: _____

2. Overemphasis on competitive sports in colleges and high schools.

   What is the topic? _____

   Is there a complete idea? _____

   If *yes,* what question about the topic is answered? _____

   _____

   If *no,* make up a question about the topic that will lead to an idea.

   Question: _____

   Idea: _____

3. Political parties work against true democracy.

   What is the topic? _____

   Is there a complete idea? _____

   If *yes,* what question about the topic is answered? _____

   _____

   If *no,* make up a question about the topic that will lead to an idea.

   Question: _____

   Idea: _____

4. The rapidly increasing problem of families without fathers.

What is the topic? _____

Is there a complete idea? _____

If *yes*, what question about the topic is answered? _____

_____

If *no*, make up a question about the topic that will lead to an idea.

Question: _____

Idea: _____

5. Pressure to raise the speed limit on America's highways.

What is the topic? _____

Is there a complete idea? _____

If *yes*, what question about the topic is answered? _____

_____

If *no*, make up a question about the topic that will lead to an idea.

Question: _____

Idea: _____

6. The spiraling costs of medical insurance in the United States must be brought under control.

What is the topic? _____

Is there a complete idea? _____

If *yes*, what question about the topic is answered? _____

_____

If *no*, make up a question about the topic that will lead to an idea.

Question: _____

Idea: _____

7. American cars are now comparable in quality to Japanese cars, and often lower in price.

What is the topic? _____

Is there a complete idea? _____

If *yes*, what question about the topic is answered? _____

_____

If *no,* make up a question about the topic that will lead to an idea.

Question: _____

Idea: _____

8. Motivation and organization are more important for success in college than "brains."

What is the topic? _____

Is there a complete idea? _____

If *yes,* what question about the topic is answered? _____

_____

If *no,* make up a question about the topic that will lead to an idea.

Question: _____

Idea: _____

9. The deadly epidemic of violence by teenagers against teenagers sweeping our streets today.

What is the topic? _____

Is there a complete idea? _____

If *yes,* what question about the topic is answered? _____

_____

If *no,* make up a question about the topic that will lead to an idea.

Question: _____

Idea: _____

10. News reporting today is shallow and inaccurate.

What is the topic? _____

Is there a complete idea? _____

If *yes,* what question about the topic is answered? _____

_____

If *no,* make up a question about the topic that will lead to an idea.

Question: _____

Idea: _____

Part B

Below are two paragraphs for which you earlier identified topics. Answer the questions that follow in order to express the key ideas that the paragraph contains. **Be sure your answers are in complete sentences.**

1. Although many businesses use the internet to promote their products and services to the public, they are finding that an even more useful application is for their internal—company only—purposes, hence the intranet. Vendors promoting their intranet software products in magazine advertisements often make a play on the word, perhaps InTRAnet or even Intranet. They do not want you to think that they are simply misspelling Internet. In fact, an intranet is a private Internet-like network internal to a certain company. The number of intranets has been growing rapidly. Every Fortune 500 company either has an intranet or is planning one. Part of the phenomenal growth is the relative ease of setting up an intranet.

   a. For **what** do many businesses use the Internet?

   _____

   b. **What** new application have they discovered?

   _____

   c. **What** play on words do vendors make?

   _____

   d. **Why** do they make this play on words?

   _____

   e. **What** is an intranet?

   _____

   f. **Why** are they growing rapidly?

   _____

2. The intranet developers will doubtless devote the most time and attention to writing the web pages that employees will see and use. The pages must be well designed and easy to follow, opting for function over glitz. A typical opening page, for example, would probably have an attractive company logo and several clickable generic icons to represent functions. One click leads to a more detailed page and so on. By presenting information the same way to every computer, the developers can pull all the computers, software and files that dot the corporate landscape into a single system that helps employees find information wherever it resides.

a. **How** will intranet developers use most of their time?

_____

b. **What** characteristics do the pages need to have?

_____

c. **What** would a typical opening page have?

_____

d. To **what** will one click lead?

_____

e. **What** effects will result from presenting information the same way on every computer?

_____

TOPICAL ORGANIZATION

Materials organized around a topic give a variety of information that defines it and identifies its various aspects. Much information we encounter every day uses an organizational pattern of a main topic and any subtopics that fall under it. A dictionary entry for a word is an example of a very basic topical unit. For example, one dictionary provides this definition for the entry word _chair:_ "A piece of furniture for one person to sit on, having a back and, usually, four legs." As you can see, this entry answers a number of questions about the topic:

To **what** general group does a chair belong?	furniture
For **whose** use is it designed?	one person
What is its function?	to sit on
What are its parts?	a back and legs
How many legs does it have?	usually four

Other reference books are also topical. An entry on "automobiles" in an encyclopedia would respond to the question "What about automobiles?" or "What are automobiles?" by answering many more specific questions about them: their history, their types, their components, their effect on society, and so on. Owner manuals, from lawn mowers to computers, provide the user with information on different aspects of the product—components, how to use, warranties, troubleshooting, etc. Articles in magazines and popular newspapers are sometimes topical, giving a general survey of one or more aspects of a subject.

By far your most important contact with topical material will be your college courses and their required textbooks. Most courses use texts that cover a wide range of topics in a field of study. Chapters generally deal with various subtopics, and frequently—especially in science textbooks—individual paragraphs will have topical organization. A number of strategies have been suggested over the years in making notes from lectures or from text readings. The traditional Roman numeral outline can be effective in showing the relationships of topics to subtopics and specific detail. More recently students have been encouraged to use various mapping strategies to help visualize relationships. Maps that use lines and boxes or circles can accomplish the same purpose as the outline. For example, we could represent the main topic and subtopics of a previous selection by either a traditional outline or by a "spider map":

Traditional Outline
I. Muscle Structure and Contraction
    A. Muscle Structure
        1. fibers—skeletal muscle
        2. fascia—connective tissue
        3. tendon
    B. Muscle Contraction
        1. regulated by motor nerves
        2. nerve/muscle meet at junction
        3. motor unit: motor nerves plus fibers

Spider Map

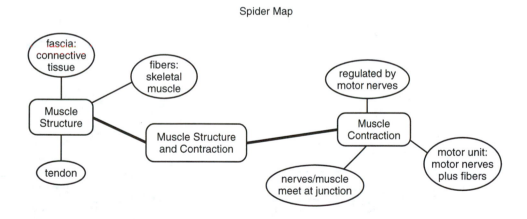

Exercise 1.4

On the following page are the topic and subtopic headings and paragraph topics that you worked with on the article about intranets. Use your results to fill in both the blank outline and spider map below

<u>Headings</u>

Setting up an Internet

Intranets

The Internet Too

Intranets at Work

<u>Paragraph Topics</u>

Linking intranet and internet

Components of an intranet

Extranets

Intranet web pages

Distinguishing intranets from internets

Employee use of internet at work

Typical applications at work

Outline

Topic: _____

Introduction:

I.

    A. _____

    B. _____

II. _____

    A. _____

    B. _____

III. _____

    A. _____

    B. _____

Spider Map

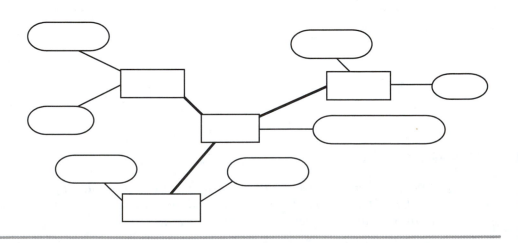

Making outlines and maps like these will put you in a much better position to decide what is most important to study or memorize for a test. If you were asked on a test to write a short essay on this topic, recalling the information on the map or outline would be sufficient for a satisfactory response. In general, however, tests covering topically organized materials tend to use objective questions: multiple choice, true/false, matching, or fill in the blanks. These require familiarity and recognition, but not the same degree of memorization and recall as a detailed essay response. The degree to which you map and memorize will also depend greatly on an instructor's teaching and testing methods.

You have been introduced to basic reading and study techniques in working with textbooks: looking for main headings and subheadings and devices such as bold-faced type, underlined text, or italicized words. However, in addition to the main text itself, there are other modes of conveying information that require special instruction and practice.

REPRESENTING FACTUAL INFORMATION THROUGH GRAPHICS

A selection titled "Bias of the Media" in a text on American government contains the following:

> The emphasis upon human interest stories also means a focus on which candidate in an election is going to win, rather than on the issues and which candidate should win. The media cover elections as horse races, with "front-runners" and "dark horses" [see Table 1.1 on page 30].
>
> (Welch et al., *American Government*, 4th ed., 235)

Table 1.1 is one example of visual aids called **graphics**: representations of factual information in the form of tables, graphs, charts, maps, drawings, photographs, and so forth. You have already created simple graphics in mapping various idea patterns from paragraphs and passages. In many college textbooks, authors present information through graphics, which are often more visually effective and economical than written text alone. Following are some general features of graphic materials.

1. Graphics do more than simply present a series of facts. They present information in idea patterns, especially classification, comparison/contrast, time sequence, and part/whole relationships. In Table 1.1 from "Bias of the Media," for example, note how the column "Subject of Coverage" is divided into two main types of subjects, "Horse race" and "Substance." The columns with percentages represent three different types of media—the newspaper, newsmagazines, and television—and the reader is directed to contrast the three.

2. Graphics also contain text of their own, as labels and sometimes as commentary. Note in the table caption the sentences beginning with "According to a study...."

Table 1.1

Presidential Election News Emphasizes the Horse Race

According to a study of the 1976 presidential campaign, the media devoted considerably more attention to the horse-race aspects than the substance. But note the differences among the media.

Subject of Coverage	Los Angeles Times	Time, Newsweek	ABC, CBS, NBC Evening News
Horse race	51%	54%	58%
Winning and losing	20	23	24
Strategy and logistics	19	22	17
Appearance and hoopla	12	9	17
Substance	35	32	29
Issues	21	17	18
Candidates' characteristics and records	8	11	7
Endorsements	6	4	4
Other	14	14	13

Source: Thomas E. Praeger, *The Mass Media Election* (New York, 1980), p.24

3. Graphics interact with the text in varying degrees:
- Some graphics are added mainly for interest and emphasis. Photographs and illustrations often have this function.
- Graphics can present information that is relatively independent of the text. For Table 1.1, the text simply mentions that the media covers elections as horse races and then lets the table speak for itself.
- Graphics sometimes interact with the text very closely. This is especially common when the text is describing in detail the various components of a subject and/or the process by which it functions.

To get the most benefit from your study time when working with graphic materials, follow these guidelines.

1. Always respond to references to tables and figures or other graphics in the text. They often convey detail or explanations of major importance.

2. Determine the purpose of the graphic. This is usually indicated by the label next to the table or figure. For example, Table 1.1 is clearly labeled "Presidential Election News Emphasizes the Horse Race." However, sometimes the graphic may not be clear without reference to the main text.

3. Make sure you understand fully the relationships of the labeled elements of the graphics—horizontal and vertical columns with data, figures showing parts, and processes. In Table 1.1 the vertical column specifies types of coverage, the horizontal column lists types of media, and the areas of intersection show percentages of coverage.

4. Pay attention to any footnotes to the graphic. These may provide key information on identifying elements in the graphic or help to explain data. Note also the source of the data.

5. Evaluate any conclusions regarding the graphic made in the text and draw conclusions of your own based on the facts presented. Occasionally the text will direct you to some possible connections, as in Table 1.1: "But note the differences among the media."

6. When studying graphic materials for a test, don't waste time trying to memorize specific facts and figures. As a general rule in highly detailed material, if it's not practical to memorize everything, don't memorize anything. What is important is that you remember what the graphic shows and what conclusions you can draw from it.

TABLES

Tables provide a way to include a large number of facts, statistics, or other details, and to organize these in a clear and economical manner. The layout in columns and rows makes it easy for the reader to compare and contrast the data and draw inferences from it.

Exercise 1.5

Study Table 1.2 and the text below. Answer the following questions by circling the correct letter choice and filling in the blanks where indicated.

Current Reverses In spite of these gains, African Americans continue to lag behind in politics, economics, and education. Only one U.S. Senator is African American, when by ratio in the population we would expect 12. As Table 1.2 (page 32) shows, African Americans average only 55 percent of white income, have much more unemployment and poverty, and are unlikely to own their own home.

(Henslin, *Sociology*, 3rd ed., 330–31)

1. Table 1.2 provides data on the relationship between _____ and _____.

2. Racial and ethnic groups are listed in the column

    a. alphabetically.

    b. from largest to smallest.

    c. from smallest to largest.

    d. most recent to longest here.

Table 1.2

Race and Ethnicity and Comparative Well-Being

	Median Family Income	Percentage of White Income	Percentage Unemployed	Percentage of White Unemployment	Percentage Below Poverty Line	Percentage of White Poverty	Percentage Owning Their Homes	Percentage of White Home Ownership
White Americans[a]	$39,308	—	5.3	—	12.1	—	68	—
Afican Americans	21,548	55	11.5	217	32.9	272	42	62
Latinos	23,912	61	10.6	200	29.3	242	40	59
Country of origin								
Mexico	23,714	60	10.7	202	30.1	249	44	65
Puerto Rico	20,301	52	12.8	242	36.5	317	23	34
Cuba	31,015	79	7.8	147	18.1	150	53	78
Central and South America	23,649	60	NA[c]	NA	26.7	221	26	38
Asian Americans[b]	44,456	113	4.1	77	15.2	126	52	76
Native Americans	21,619	55	NA	NA	31.2	258	NA	NA

Note: The racial and ethnic groups are listed from largest to smallest.
[a]Non-Latino.
[b]Includes Pacific Islanders.
[c]Not available.
Source: Statistical Abstract 1995: Tables 49, 50, 52, 53, 997.

How did you arrive at your answer to this question? _____
_____

3. From the text and table you can infer that the data concern people currently living in

    a. the United States.

    b. North America.

    c. North and South America.

    d. North, Central, and South America.

4. The text that accompanies the table is mainly concerned with statistics regarding which ethnic group? _____

5. The only ethnic group to be subdivided by countries is _____.

6. Latinos from which country are worse off than African Americans in all three categories of Percentage Unemployed, Percentage Below Poverty Line, and Percentage Owning Their Homes? _____

7. The only ethnic group better off in income and employment than white Americans is _____.

8. Which subgroup of Latinos appears to be the best off? _____

9. What percentage of Native Americans are unemployed? _____

   What did you have to do to get your answer? _____

   _____

10. If you were studying for a test, which *one* of the statements below would be most important to remember?

    a. 18.1 percent of people from Cuba living in the United States are below the poverty line in income.

    b. Asian Americans rank above white Americans in family income and employment, whereas African Americans lag significantly behind.

    c. 44 percent of Latinos from Mexico own their homes, compared to 53 percent of Latinos from Cuba.

    d. The percentage of Asian Americans owning homes is less than that of white Americans owning homes.

GRAPHS

The term **figure** is used by many texts to include a number of types of **graphs,** such as bar, line, pie, and symbol. Graphs function primarily to provide comparisons of quantity among items or relative changes over time.

Bar graphs and **line graphs** are alternative ways of presenting much the same data. Line graphs are often the graph of choice for showing trends over time. In the following example, the author uses both types to give special emphasis to the data.

Postponing Marriage

Figure 1.1 (page 34) illustrates one of the most significant trends in U.S. marriages. The average age of first-time brides and grooms declined for about eighty years. In 1890 the typical first-time bride was 22, but by 1950 she had just left her teens. After plateauing in the 1950s and 1960s, age at first marriage turned sharply upward about 1970. *Today the average first-time bride is older than at any time in U.S. history.* The average first-time groom is considerably older than he was in 1970, but still somewhat younger than he was in 1890.

Figure 1.2 (page 35) is another way to portray this remarkable change. Note how the proportion of never-married younger Americans has climbed, with the percentage of unmarried women now almost *double* what it was in 1970.

Why did this change occur? As sociologist Larry Bumpass points out, if we were to count cohabitation, we would find that this average age has changed little (Bumpass et al., 1991). Although Americans have postponed the age at which they first marry, they have *not* postponed the age at which they first set up housekeeping with someone of the opposite sex.

(Henslin, *Sociology*, 3rd ed., 448–9)

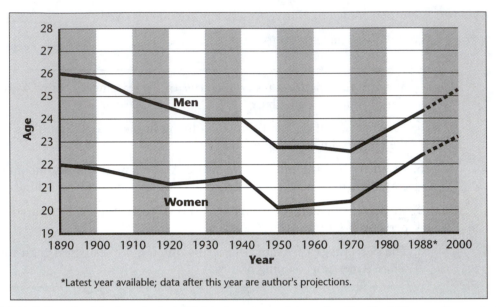

FIGURE 1.1   **The Median Age at Which Americans Marry for the First Time**   (*Source*: Statistical Abstract 1995: Table 145, and earlier years)

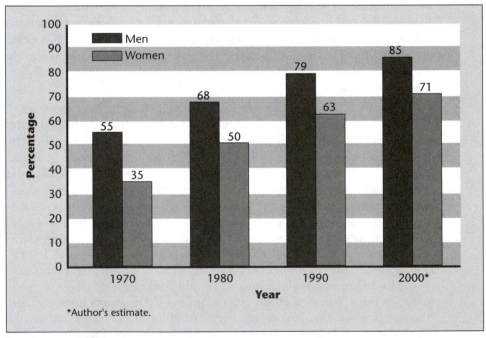

FIGURE 1.2   **Americans Aged 20–24 Who Have Never Married**   (*Source*: Statistical Abstract 1993: Table 60; 1995: Table 59)

Exercise 1.6

Circle the correct letter choice for each of the following questions.

1. According to Figure 1.1, since approximately what year has the median age of marriage been rising at a parallel rate for men and women?

   a. 1890

   b. 1900

   c. 1950

   d. 1970

2. According to Figure 1.1, in what decade did the median age of marriage drop most rapidly for both men and women?

   a. the 1920s

   b. the 1940s

   c. the 1960s

   d. the 1970s

3. In approximately what year (Figure 1.1) is the median age for women equal to the lowest median age for marriage ever recorded for men?

   a. 1920

   b. 1949

   c. 1988

   d. 2000

4. From Figure 1.2 we can see that every ten years the difference in percentages between unmarried men and women has declined

   a. 20 percentage points.

   b. 2 percentage points.

   c. 17 percentage points.

   d. not at all.

5. For Americans aged 20–24, Figure 1.2 shows

   a. a steady rise in ages for men and women who are unmarried.

   b. a rise in age for unmarried women but a decline for men.

   c. a decline in age for unmarried men and women.

   d. an erratic up and down movement in the ages of unmarried men and women.

6. We could estimate from Figure 1.2 that the percentage of unmarried women equaled the figure for men in 1970 in approximately what year?

    a. 1976

    b. 1984

    c. 1990

    d. 1995

7. The graphs in Figures 1.1 and 1.2 are similar in all of the following except

    a. they give data on men and women.

    b. they allow comparisons to be made for men and women.

    c. they give data over a number of years.

    d. they both list data by ages.

8. Figure 1.2 gives data for the same period as that shown in approximately what portion of Figure 1.1?

    a. the first quarter

    b. the second half

    c. the middle third

    d. the last quarter

Pie graphs provide another means of presenting distribution and percentages. They have the advantage of giving a very clear visual image of relative proportions.

Exercise 1.7

Study Figure 1.3 and circle the correct letter choice.

1. Which of the regions below has the largest percentage of Latinos?

    a. Southwest

    b. Northwest

    c. East Coast

    d. Midwest

    e. insufficient data to determine

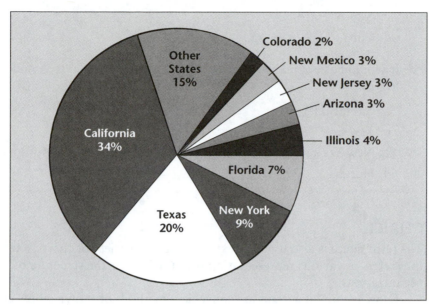

FIGURE 1.3 **Where U.S. Latinos Live** (*Source:* Statistical Abstract 1995: Table 38; from Henslin, *Sociology,* 3rd ed., 334)

2. Which is the only region from which no states are specifically named?

    a. Southwest

    b. Northwest

    c. Midwest

    d. East Coast

3. Which region has the smallest percentage of Latinos?

    a. Southwest

    b. Northwest

    c. East Coast

    d. Midwest

    e. insufficient data to determine

4. The two states with the most Latinos have a common border with

    a. Arizona.

    b. Mexico.

    c. New Mexico.

    d. Cuba.

5. It would be reasonable to expect that Latinos from Cuba would most likely live in

    a. California.

    b. Texas.

    c. New York.

    d. Florida.

CHARTS

The term **figure** is also used by texts to include a variety of charts, a catchall term that refers to various representations of processes or the structure of objects and organizations.

Drawings and **diagrams** are convenient methods of showing how components interact in the steps in a process, as in Figure 1.4.

Exercise 1.8

Study Figure 1.4. Circle the correct letter choice and fill in the blank where indicated.

1. The main purpose of Figure 1.4 is to

    a. show the structure of a neuron.

    b. demonstrate the function of synaptic vesicles.

    c. explain the process of neuronal transmission.

    d. illustrate electrical changes.

2. The synapse is

    a. a solid.

    b. a liquid.

    c. a space.

    d. an electrical charge.

3. The neurotransmitters in the diagram are shown

    a. to move somewhat in a circle.

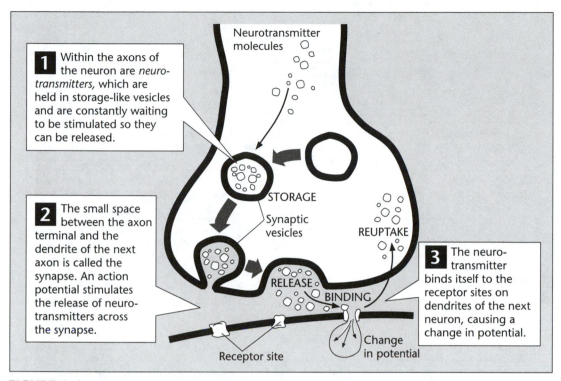

1 Within the axons of the neuron are *neurotransmitters,* which are held in storage-like vesicles and are constantly waiting to be stimulated so they can be released.

2 The small space between the axon terminal and the dendrite of the next axon is called the synapse. An action potential stimulates the release of neurotransmitters across the synapse.

3 The neurotransmitter binds itself to the receptor sites on dendrites of the next neuron, causing a change in potential.

Neurotransmitter molecules

STORAGE

Synaptic vesicles

REUPTAKE

RELEASE

BINDING

Change in potential

Receptor site

FIGURE 1.4   Major Steps in Neuronal Transmission   (*Source:* Lefton, *Psychology,* 5th ed., 48)

    b. to move in a straight line.

    c. to move only from left to right.

    d. to be stationary.

4. The large, hoof-like structure that contains the smaller circles represents

    a. a complete neuron.

    b. the axon of the neuron.

    c. an expanded view of a synapse.

    d. a cross section of the dendrite.

5. In which of the three steps are neurotransmitters released across the synapse?

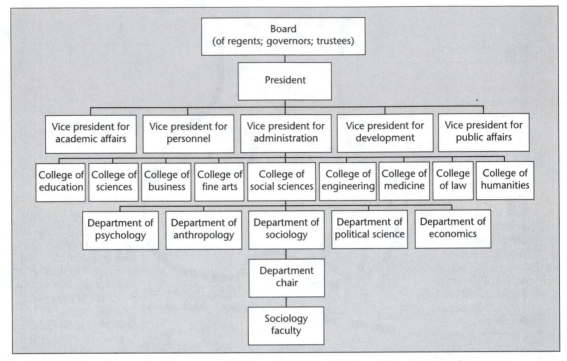

FIGURE 1.5   The Typical Bureaucratic Structure of a Medium-Sized University   This is a scaled-down version of a university's bureaucratic structure. The actual lines of authority of a university are likely to be much more complicated than those depicted here. A university may have a chancellor and several presidents under the chancellor, with each president responsible for a particular campus. Although extensions of authority are given in this figure only for the vice president for administration and the College of Social Sciences, each of the other vice presidents and colleges has similar postions. If the figure were to be extended, departmental secretaries would be shown, and eventually, somewhere, even students. (*Source:* Henslin, *Sociology,* 3rd ed., 172)

Flowcharts, like the one in Figure 1.5, are useful for diagraming very formalized processes and directions. These often include arrows showing the flow of movement. They are also effective in giving a comprehensive picture of the structure and line of authority in an organization.

Exercise 1.9

Study Figure 1.5 and answer the following questions by circling the correct letter choice and filling in the blanks where indicated.

1. Direct access to the board is given only to

   a. vice presidents.

    b. department chairs.

    c. the president.

    d. faculty.

2. From this flowchart, we can conclude

    a. the college of social sciences is traditionally the largest on all campuses.

    b. departments of sociology have more faculty members than other departments.

    c. every campus has its college of social sciences under a vice president for administration.

    d. none of the above

3. The only complete representation of structure in this chart is under which vice president? _____

4. The explanatory text accompanying the flowchart tells us that

    a. the chart is a simplified example.

    b. department secretaries are unnecessary.

    c. a university usually has a number of chancellors.

    d. all of the above

5. What criticism is implied by the last sentence in the caption, "If the figure …"?

_____

MAPS

We typically think of **maps** as a means of reducing in scale the physical features of large areas. You are familiar with road maps and have also probably seen topographical maps, which show features like lakes and mountains. Maps can also show weather and climate, distributions such as population, or political divisions and boundaries. Maps can also be used to feature other kinds of information, as in the example shown in Figure 1.6 (page 42).

Exercise 1.10

Study Figure 1.6 and answer the following questions by circling the correct letter choice and filling in the blanks where indicated.

1. The map represents data for what years? _____

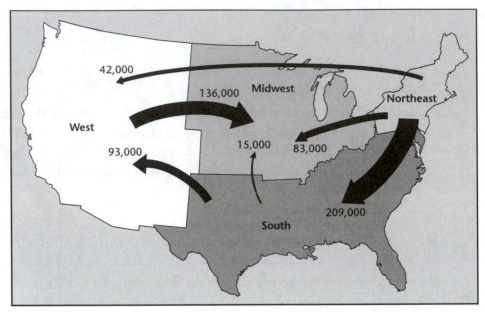

FIGURE 1.6   **Net Migration Flows Between Regions, 1992–1993**   (*Source:* Statistical Abstract 1995: Table 32; from Henslin, *Sciology,* 3rd ed., 569)

2. Which region is closest to having a balance between net gain and net loss?

   a. West

   b. Midwest

   c. Northeast

   d. South

3. Which region had the greatest net loss?

   a. West

   b. Midwest

   c. Northeast

   d. South

4. The total net gain for the South would be

   a. 317,000.

   b. 101,000.

   c. 108,000.

   d. 194,000.

5. The arrow and the number 15,000 mean

    a. a total of 15,000 people left the South for the Midwest.

    b. a total of 15,000 people left the Midwest for the South.

    c. 15,000 more people went from the Midwest to the South than went from the South to the Midwest.

    d. 15,000 more people went from the South to the Midwest than went from the Midwest to the South.

CHAPTER REVIEW

Circle the correct letter choice.

1. Which of the following is the most *general* term?

    a. television

    b. game shows

    c. media entertainment

2. Which of the following is the most *specific* term?

    a. television

    b. game shows

    c. media entertainment

Identify each of the following sentences or phrases as TOPIC *or* IDEA.

3. _____ Today's schools face a great number of difficult challenges.

4. _____ America's never-ending appetite for sporting events.

5. _____ The numerous challenges that are facing today's wage earner.

6. _____ Children should be protected from seeing violence in movies.

Fill in the blank.

7. One effective way to turn a topic into an idea is to ask a _____.

8. Topical organization may be shown by using a traditional _____.

9. Topical organization can also be shown by using a _____ map.

10. A graph can show data by means of (a) _____.

    a. bar.

    b. pie.

    c. line.

    d. all of the above.

If you are truly serious about improving your reading comprehension, vocabulary, and background knowledge, then commit yourself to keeping a **portfolio of articles** and completing portfolio assignments during the semester or year.

1. *Collect articles of interest, keep them in a file, and write a short summary and reaction for each article as soon as you read it.* You'll be surprised at how many connections in your information you will begin to make. A good start would be to find some articles on at least one current area of local, state, national, or world interest.

2. *Become familiar with sources you can use for finding articles.* The Internet is an invaluable source of information. Websites can lead you to great variety of reading materials. Check out the services of your college resource center. Try to browse through one or more newspapers every day. Most libraries have reading rooms with local newspapers and also with nationally distributed newspapers like *The New York Times*. Read more than the front page or the sports section. Look for feature sections and the editorial-opinion section. Many key current issues are debated there. Also, there are hundreds of magazines available in all sorts of interest areas, from computers to home decoration to sports. You should, however, be sure to include informative weekly news magazines in your reading diet. *Time, Newsweek,* or *U.S. News and World Report,* for example, are good sources for keeping up with current events.

3. *Keep a notebook handy when you read.* Write down and identify any people and places you aren't familiar with and look these up in reference sources. Your reading will also provide you with an excellent opportunity to increase your vocabulary. Practice your skill at using the context, and make note of any new vocabulary words whose meaning you can't determine so that you can look them up later in your dictionary.

Recognizing Important Information: Main Ideas and Supporting Details

On virtually all reading tests—school achievement, college placement, job testing—the first question you will be asked about a paragraph or a selection is "What is the main idea?" A common saying, "He can't see the forest for the trees," applies to the difficulty we often have of finding main points and seeing their relationship to the specific details that develop them. Without the main idea, we find ourselves lost on the forest floor, our vision blocked by the details of the trees. Finding the main idea takes us high above where we see the whole, with the various parts forming an understandable unit.

■ CHAPTER PREVIEW

In this chapter you will

- Learn the difference between ideas and main ideas
- Identify and map topical and main idea paragraphs
- Apply the terms **general** and **specific** to main ideas and supporting details
- Discover the function of definitions in paragraphs
- Identify and use signals that point to main ideas
- Practice identifying eight kinds of main ideas and their key signal words
- Recognize the importance of listening in your dialogue with your peers

In Chapter 1 you were given an example of the range of ideas we could generate from questions about a topic ("cats"), such as:

Cats have both positive and negative personality traits.

Cats can be even more loving and loyal pets than dogs.

Owning a cat brings many responsibilities.

Training a cat requires knowledge of training techniques and patience.

An untrained cat can pose a real hazard when left unsupervised around small children.

Suppose for a composition course you decide to write an assigned essay of 600 words on this topic. You might be tempted to include most or all of the ideas you have listed from your questions, since all of these ideas relate to the topic "cats." However, the odds are that your grade will not be high, because reading and writing assignments in college often involve creating a different kind of unity of material. Although you might cover the topic by stating several ideas about it, your instructor will likely comment that the paper is "too broad" or "lacks a focus," which means that it needs to give the reader more than a survey of one or more aspects of a topic.

■ MAIN IDEAS AND SUPPORTING DETAILS

Your instructor will be asking you to make a critical shift from "topical" to "main idea" writing. This kind of writing focuses on answering *one dominant question* that everything in the text helps to develop. The answer to that question, the **main idea,** is expressed in a complete sentence that limits, controls, and unifies what can appear in the essay. Using our example above, we could develop an essay with a main idea by limiting our inquiry to a single area:

Cats have both positive and negative personality traits.

However, for a short essay, this idea would still prove too broad. We would be wise to limit our paper even further by asking and answering an even more specific dominant question:

Question: What personality trait is most characteristic of cats?

Main idea: Most cats are egotistical loners.

Our paper would now include only details about personality traits that directly relate to the egotism and antisocial leanings of cats. Of course someone else could write an essay on the same topic but with an entirely different dominant idea requiring a different selection of details for support:

Cats may appear to be egotistical loners but are really just shy and insecure.

Examining the two paragraphs below will give you a clearer idea of the difference between topical and main idea organization:

<u>Topical Organization</u>

Disneyland is a famous amusement park in Southern California. The genius behind the operation was Walt Disney, who began as a cartoonist in the 1920s and later founded his own movie studio. The park features scientific and historical attractions, along with exciting and creative rides. Part of its success must be attributed to its careful attention to detail. Millions of visitors from all over the globe visit it each year.

<u>Idea Organization</u>

Part of Disneyland's success must be attributed to its careful attention to detail. From intricately designed rides like Pirates of the Caribbean to precise historical accuracy in shops and stores on Main Street, the Disney creators have done their homework. Maintenance workers repaint and refurbish continually. Groundskeepers trim shrubs and lawns neatly. Not a scrap of trash is to be seen anywhere on the grounds.

Note first that the general topic of both paragraphs is "Disneyland." If we try to frame a dominant question for the first one, we soon find that the paragraph answers a number of questions of equal importance.

- What and where is Disneyland?
  Disneyland is a famous amusement park in Southern California.
- Who originated it and when did he begin his career?
  The genius behind the operation was Walt Disney, who began....
- What attractions and features does the park offer?
  The park features scientific and historical attractions....
- Why has it been so successful?
  Part of its success must be attributed to its careful attention to detail.
- How many people visit it and where do they come from?
  Millions of visitors from all over the globe visit it each year.

This paragraph has a unity in that all the details support a topic—Disneyland—but their connection ends there. There is no single dominant observation about Disneyland that holds all the details together. The various details are coordinate—that is, they are relatively equal in value. Just about any piece of information could be included in the paragraph as long as it relates to the topic of Disneyland.

The idea paragraph, in contrast, focuses on the fourth sentence of the topical paragraph, which answers the question "*What about that success?*" or "*Why has it been successful?*" We could take the answer to that question as a main idea hypothesis:

Part of Disneyland's success can be attributed to its attention to detail.

If our our hypothesis is correct, no matter what questions the other sentences might answer, they must all relate to the answer to the dominant question: "Why has it been successful?" Do the following all give us evidence of "success through attention to detail?"

- Intricately designed rides
- Precise historical accuracy in shops and stores
- Groundskeepers trim lawns and shrubs

Relating these details back to our main idea confirms our hypothesis. The details of the paragraph have a unity beyond just the topic. They are **subordinate** (supporting) in their relation to the more general main idea. Thus the main idea controls the paragraph by limiting it to only those details that relate to "success through attention to detail."

A number of terms are used to designate the elements that make up main idea units. These relate to the concepts of general (broad) and specific (narrow, concrete) that you were introduced to earlier. For the main idea of an entire article, chapter, or book, the terms **controlling idea** or **thesis** are frequently used. The main idea of a paragraph is often termed the **topic sentence.** The rest of a paragraph or essay consists of **supporting material,** including specific details: concrete examples, statistics, data, physical descriptions, and precise accounts of actions. Note the following pair of statements:

1. Uncle Elmo is the biggest cheapskate I know.
2. Uncle Elmo is 6 foot tall and has brown eyes.

The first statement is a generalization that can be developed as a main idea by a number of specific details:

- The stale fruitcakes Uncle Elmo recycles as Christmas gifts
- The way he disappears into the restaurant bathroom when the check appears
- The times he has "forgotten" his wallet and borrows money he never repays

Statement 2 is already specific. We could make it a little more precise—"6 foot, one-quarter inch tall, and has dark brown eyes"—but we can't really *develop* a statement that already represents a specific observation.

Exercise 2.1

For each group of four items, put T *for the topic (not a complete sentence),* MI *for the item that is the main idea (a complete sentence), and* S *for the two supporting details.*

> **SAMPLE**
>
> ___S___   Children's reading skills may not develop at the proper rate.
>
> ___MI___   Excessive T.V. viewing may have harmful effects on children.
>
> ___T___   Television's effects on children.
>
> ___S___   Lack of exercise and obesity may result from excessive T.V. viewing

1. _____   Joe received the Most Valuable Player award in football.

   _____   Joe's accomplishments in football.

   _____   Joe excels in football.

   _____   Joe was voted All-Conference quarterback.

2. _____   Pleasanton Community College needs a new library.

   _____   The community colleges are in dire financial straits.

   _____   Community colleges in California are awaiting budget cuts.

   _____   Finances in community colleges.

3. _____   Fruit is an essential source of nutrition for humans.

   _____   Bananas provide needed potassium.

   _____   An orange is an excellent source of vitamin C.

   _____   The importance of fruit for humans.

4. _____   Students at American high schools.

   _____   Madison High School students prefer partying to studying.

   _____   Fred, a junior at Edison High, refuses to study history or algebra.

   _____   American high school students are lazy.

5. _____   Many young people hate vegetables.

   _____   Food preferences of young people.

   _____   A lot of teenagers simply refuse to eat carrots.

   _____   Broccoli is not a favorite of children.

▓ MAPPING TOPICAL AND MAIN IDEA PARAGRAPHS

Textbooks in some academic fields—for example history, philosophy, or political science—rely primarily on main idea organization of paragraphs and passages. Texts in other fields—particularly in the science areas—mix in a significant number of topical paragraphs. To distinguish more important from less important information in textbooks, and mark and annotate accordingly, it is important to recognize when material is organized around a topic and when it has a main idea focus.

In the previous chapter, you were introduced to two methods of highlighting important information in topical materials—the outline and the spider map. Pattern maps can help in visualizing the difference between topical and main idea units. To show connections in topical organization, a variation of a spider map— a pinwheel map—may be used. To show relationships in main idea organization, we can use a cartwheel map. Compare the maps of the topical and main idea paragraphs on Disneyland in Figure 2.1.

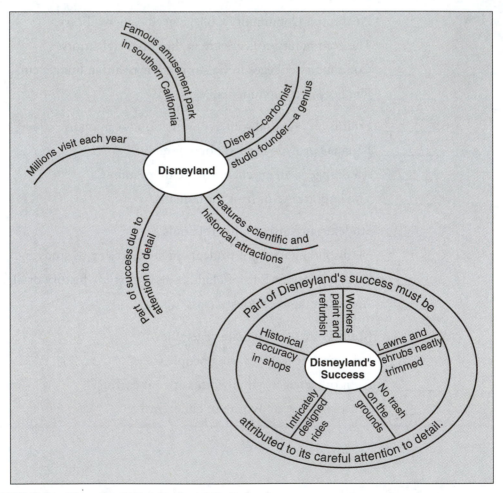

FIGURE 2.1   Disneyland Pinwheel and Cartwheel

The pinwheel (topical) map shows that all the details support a topic—Disneyland is the common hub—but their connection ends there. There is no single dominant observation about Disneyland that relates or holds all the details together. In the main idea (cartwheel) map, the details of the paragraph (the spokes) have unity beyond just the topic (the hub). The main idea controls the paragraph by limiting it to only those details that relate to "success through attention to detail."

Exercise 2.2

Part A

In the following pairs, one paragraph is topical and one is controlled by a main idea. Use questions and hypothesis testing to see if a paragraph is controlled by a main idea or by a topic only. For each paragraph in the pair, write its letter next to the correct organizational pattern wheel. Then complete the pattern map for each, adding or deleting "spokes" where necessary.

1. a. Of all the aquatic plants, green algae bears the greatest resemblance to land plants. They, too, accumulate starch in chloroplasts. They, too, have an abundance of chlorophylls and most have cell walls with cellulose. These and other similarities support the theory that land plants evolved from ancestral green algae.

1. b. Most brown algae live just offshore or in intertidal zones. Giant kelps often are 50 meters tall, forming underwater forests that are among the most productive ecosystems. They have hollow, gas-filled bladders that keep blades near the sunlit surface waters. The brown alga *Sargassum* floats as extensive masses through the vast Sargasso Sea, which lies between the Azores and the Bahamas.

(Starr, *Biology*, 2nd ed., 276–277)

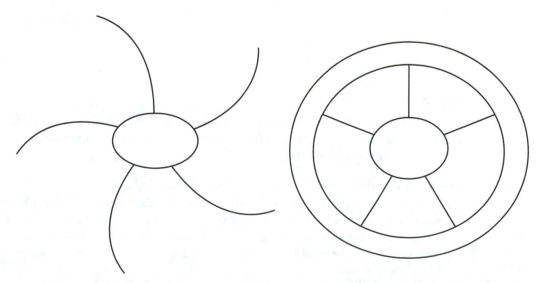

2. a. Anorexia nervosa, a starvation disease that affects as many as 40 out of every 10,000 young women in the United States, is an eating disorder characterized by an obstinate and willful refusal to eat. Individuals with the disorder, usually adolescent girls from middle-class families, have a distorted body image. They perceive themselves as fat if they lack muscle tone or deviate from their idealized body image. Victims may sustain permanent damage to their heart muscle tissue, sometimes dying as a result.

2. b. Anorexia nervosa victims require a structured setting and are often hospitalized to help them regain weight. To ensure that the setting is reinforcing, hospital and staff members are always present at meals, and individual and family therapy is provided. Clients are encouraged to eat and are rewarded for consuming specified quantities of food. Generally, psychotherapy is also necessary to help these people maintain a healthy self-image. Even with treatment however, as many as 50 percent suffer relapses.

(Lefton, *Psychology,* 5th ed., 354–355)

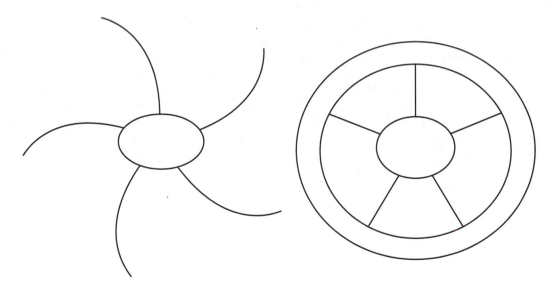

Part B

Below are sets of paragraphs on a common topic. In each pair, one paragraph has topical organization and one has a main idea. For each paragraph, circle the letter of the correct choice.

Set I   (Ferl and Wallace, *Biology: The Realm of Life,* 3rd ed., 600)

  1. Thermoreceptors occur in a wide variety of animals. For example, thermoreception may be important to many invertebrates. Heat detection is especially important to the ectoparasites of birds and mammals—leeches, fleas, mosquitoes, ticks, and lice—parasites that must find a warm-blooded host.

(Their thermoreceptors are generally located on the antennas, legs, or mouth parts.) Thermoreception among invertebrates is not well understood.

   a. Thermoreceptors occur in a wide variety of animals.

   b. Thermoreception may be important to many invertebrates.

   c. Ectoparasites must have a warm-blooded host.

   d. Thermoreceptors are generally located on the antennas, legs, or mouth parts.

   e. None of the above. The paragraph has a topical organization.

2. Most human thermoreceptors are located in the skin. These receptors respond not only to temperature, but particularly to changes in temperature (so that a change from cold to cool might be registered as warmth). Their precise mechanism of reception remains a mystery, although some physiologists ascribe thermoreception to the free nerve endings and to specialized skin receptors called Ruffini corpuscles and Krause end bulbs. The latter are far more numerous and are stimulated by a greater temperature range than are the former.

   a. Most human thermoreceptors are located in the skin.

   b. Thermoreceptors respond to temperature and also to changes in temperature.

   c. Their precise mechanism of reception remains a mystery.

   d. Krause end bulbs are far more numerous than are Ruffini corpuscles.

   e. None of the above. The paragraph has a topical organization.

Set II   (Powers and Dodd, *Total Fitness: Exercise, Nutrition, and Wellness,* 2nd ed., 152)

1. Nutrition can be broadly defined as the study of food and the way the body uses it to produce energy and build or repair body tissues. Good nutrition means that an individual's diet supplies all of the essential foodstuffs required to maintain a healthy body. Although dietary deficiencies were a problem of the past in many industrialized countries, a primary danger associated with nutrition today is overeating.

   a. Nutrition is the study of food and the way the body uses it.

   b. For good nutrition, one's diet must supply foodstuffs to maintain a healthy body.

   c. Dietary deficiencies were a problem of the past in many industrialized countries.

   d. A primary danger associated with nutrition today is overeating.

   e. None of the above. The paragraph has a topical organization.

2. Many diets are high in calories, sugar, fats, and sodium, and diseases linked to these dietary excesses, such as cardiovascular disease, cancer, obesity, and diabetes, are the leading killers in the United States today. According to the U.S. Department of Health and Human Services, over one-half of all deaths

in the United States are associated with health problems linked to poor nutrition. Nevertheless, through diet analysis and modification, it is possible to prevent many of these nutrition-related diseases.

   a. Many diets are high in calories, sugar, fats, and sodium.

   b. Diseases linked to dietary excesses are the leading killers in the United States today.

   c. Over one-half of all deaths in the United States are linked to poor nutrition.

   d. Many diseases related to poor nutrition can be prevented by diet analysis and change.

   e. None of the above. The paragraph has a topical organization.

Set III   (Donatelle, *Access to Health*, 7th ed., 363)

1. Emphysema is a chronic disease in which the alveoli (the tiny air sacs in the lungs) are destroyed, impairing the lungs' ability to obtain oxygen and remove carbon dioxide. As a result, breathing becomes difficult. Whereas healthy people expend only about 5 percent of their energy in breathing, people with advanced emphysema expend nearly 80 percent of their energy in breathing. A simple movement such as rising from a seated position may be painful and difficult for the emphysema patient. Since the heart has to work harder to do even the simplest tasks, it may become enlarged and the person may die from heart damage.

   a. Emphysema is a disease in which the alveoli are destroyed, thus impairing the lungs.

   b. Emphysema impairs the lungs, which makes breathing difficult and enlarges the heart.

   c. People with advanced emphysema expend 80 percent of their energy in breathing.

   d. A simple movement may be painful and difficult for the emphysema patient.

   e. None of the above. The paragraph has a topical organization.

2. Chronic bronchitis is the presence of a productive cough that persists or reoccurs frequently. It may develop in smokers because their inflamed lungs produce more mucus and constantly try to rid themselves of this mucus and foreign particles. The effort to do so results in the "smoker's hack," the persistent cough experienced by most smokers. Smokers are more prone than nonsmokers to respiratory ailments such as influenza, pneumonia, and colds.

   a. Chronic bronchitis is the presence of a cough that persists or reoccurs frequently.

   b. Bronchitis develops in smokers because their inflamed lungs produce more mucus.

c. The effort to get rid of mucus and foreign particles results in "smoker's hack."

d. Smokers are more prone than nonsmokers to various respiratory ailments.

e. None of the above. The paragraph has a topical organization.

USING SIGNALS TO LOCATE MAIN IDEAS

It would be easier to find main idea sentences if they were always placed in the same position, first or last. However, although those are its most frequent positions, the main idea sentence can appear anywhere in a paragraph—first, last, or somewhere in the middle. This makes finding the topic sentence more challenging, but there are some common signals that can help you locate main ideas.

QUESTIONS

The presence of a question, especially at the start of paragraph, is a good hint that the sentence that answers it is the main idea. Note in the example below how the question leads directly into the main idea of the passage (main idea underlined):

> Why does negative advertising work when most people say they do not like it? <u>People may say they like to hear about issues, but their actions belie their words.</u> Politics is just not that important to most people, and indeed many are woefully ignorant about specific issues. If one out of seven Americans cannot find the United States on a world map, how interested are they going to be in a discussion of foreign policy?
>
> (Welch et al., *American Government,* 4th ed., 204)

There are of course situations in which questions do not lead to main ideas. Note, for example, that the last sentence of the paragraph poses a question that really is a statement. A question that answers itself is called a *rhetorical question* and is used for emphasis or effect.

DIRECTIONAL SHIFTS

Shifts to new topics and main ideas are often signaled by contrast words like *but, however, nevertheless,* or by a phrases like *in fact* or *in truth*. When these occur in the first sentence of a paragraph, they may relate back to the previous paragraph, in order to add a qualification to a previously developed idea or to give the other side of a situation (main idea underlined):

> … until then. The movement of women into highly skilled blue-collar work such as construction and automaking was sharply limited by the very slow growth in those jobs. In 1991, only 3.7 percent of mechanics, 1.3 percent of carpenters, and 0.8 percent of auto mechanics were women.

> *However*, <u>some women made inroads into traditionally male jobs in the highly paid primary sector.</u> The years 1970 to 1990 found more women in the fields of law, medicine …

Signal words can also designate a shift within the paragraph itself. These paragraphs seem to be going in one direction but quickly take a turn elsewhere, requiring us to modify a main idea guess (main idea underlined):

> *Although* the fundamental unit of speech—logically and descriptively—is the phoneme, <u>research suggests that psychologically the fundamental unit is larger.</u> For example …

Internal shifts also occur often in the second or even third sentences (main idea underlined):

> We seem to view solar power as a new concept, an untouched source of energy for human endeavors. *In fact,* <u>sunlight has long provided us with our most fundamental source of energy.</u> Such fossil fuels as …

LISTING PHRASES

When a main idea has multiple or compound elements, it may be phrased to suggest that a list of items will be enumerated. Listing phrases usually appear in the first sentence of a paragraph. They usually (but not always) combine a word or phrase of number (*three, several, a few, a number of,* etc.) with one designating a plural category (*steps, types, kinds, similarities, traits,* etc.). Below are some examples of common listing phrases; note how they help you to anticipate the structure of the passage that will follow:

- There were *several key stages* in the development of American industry.
- There are at least *two good reasons* why eligible Americans should register to vote.
- President Jones has demonstrated important leadership *qualities*.

FIRST ITEM IN A LIST

Certain signal words and phrases—e.g., *then, third, next, finally*—work with listing phrases to indicate specific items. Those that go with the first item in such a list—e.g., *first, to begin with, one reason, the initial step,* (and, occasionally, *for example*)—almost always occur in the sentence directly following a listing phrase/main idea.

EXAMPLES

Examples can occur throughout a paragraph. However, if an example is placed near the beginning of a paragraph and follows a general statement, the sentence that goes before it is very likely to be main idea. The connection is even clearer when authors use signal words such as *for instance, for example, to illustrate,* or *including* to indicate the transition from main idea to supporting detail:

> <u>Farmers have used violence on occasion to fight economic exploitation.</u> Between the Revolutionary War and 1800, *for example,* Shay's rebellion....

SUMMARY/CONCLUSION SIGNALS

Signal words such as *therefore, thus, in summary, in conclusion, indeed,* and *clearly* alert us to a general statement of summary or conclusion that may be the main idea sentence. In such cases, the main idea is most likely to be the last sentence of the paragraph. Some authors restate main ideas for emphasis or to ensure comprehension. The main idea may be introduced early in the paragraph and then repeated, often using one of the summary signal words or phrases, at or near the end of the paragraph:

> <u>The use of the eating-right pyramid in forming a diet accomplishes two important goals.</u> First, the relative proportions of foods known to promote disease are minimized. Second, "nutrient dense" foods, that is, foods high in micronutrients per calorie, are maximized. *Thus,* <u>by following the pyramid approach, you are assured of getting the proper balance of macro- and micronutrients.</u>

> (Powers and Dodd, *Total Fitness: Exercise, Nutrition, and Wellness,* 2nd ed., 165)

DRAWING A GENERAL CONCLUSION

When a paragraph has no clear main idea signals, use a 5 step process to find a sentence broad enough to provide a main idea:

1. Identify the *topic.* Look for a frequently repeated term.
2. Focus on a main *question* that all the ideas in a passage help to develop.
3. Answer the question in the form of a *main idea hypothesis* (an educated guess).
4. *Test* your hypothesis as you read to see if new information continues to support your main idea guess.
5. If you can't confirm your hypothesis, you have either
   a. missed or misread key signals and need to reread for a new hypothesis
      or
   b. the passage has a *topical* rather than an *idea* organization.

When in doubt, give preference to the sentence in the first or last position, since these are statistically the most likely places where main ideas occur.

Exercise 2.3

In the following paragraphs, <u>underline</u> the main idea sentence of the paragraph and check <u>all</u> signals that gave you a clue on the list that follows the paragraph.

1. It takes a great deal of evolutionary change for a reptile to fly, and birds have certainly changed from their reptilian stock. However, beneath their obvious fight modifications lie many ancient reptilian traits. Their legs, for example, are still covered with reptile-like scales. And feathers, complex as they are in today's birds, can be traced back to reptilian scales. Today, the feathers provide not only an aerodynamic flight surface but also insulation for a body that must carefully regulate its temperature.

    (Ferl and Wallace, *Biology: The Realm of Life,* 3rd ed., 463)

    This is the main idea because it:

    _____ answers a question stated in the paragraph.

    _____ has a listing phrase: _____.

    _____ is followed by a first item in a list signal word or

    phrase: _____.

    _____ is followed by an example (signal word or phrase,

    if used: _____).

    _____ has a change of direction signal: _____.

    _____ has a summary/conclusion signal: _____.

    _____ has no signal but states a general conclusion that all details lead to.

2. Individuals are, by their nature, social beings. There are two fundamental reasons for this assumption. First, human babies enter the world totally dependent on other people for their survival. This initial period of dependence means, in effect, that each of us has been immersed in social groups from birth. A second basis for the social nature of human beings is that throughout history people have found it to their advantage to cooperate with other people (for defense, for material comforts, to overcome the perils of nature, and to improve technology).

    (Eitzen and Zinn, *In Conflict and Order,* 7th ed., 5)

    This is the main idea because it:

    _____ answers a question stated in the paragraph.

    _____ has a listing phrase: _____.

_____ is followed by a first item in a list signal word or

phrase: _____.

_____ is followed by an example (signal word or phrase,

if used: _____).

_____ has a change of direction signal: _____.

_____ has a summary/conclusion signal: _____.

_____ has no signal but states a general conclusion that all details lead to.

3. Another relatively powerless group resorting to violence to achieve its aims has been organized labor. In the 1870s workers attempted to organize for collective action against unfair policies of the industrialists. Unions, such as the Knights of Labor, American Federation of Labor, and the Industrial Workers of the World, formed. Their primary tactic was the strike, which in itself is nonviolent. But strikers often used force to keep persons from crossing the picket lines.

(Eitzen and Zinn, *In Conflict and Order,* 7th ed., 66)

This is the main idea because it:

_____ answers a question stated in the paragraph.

_____ has a listing phrase: _____.

_____ is followed by a first item in a list signal word or

phrase: _____.

_____ is followed by an example (signal word or phrase,

if used: _____).

_____ has a change of direction signal: _____.

_____ has a summary/conclusion signal: _____.

_____ has no signal but states a general conclusion that all details lead to.

4. When we speak to someone, we produce a series of sounds in a continuous stream, punctuated by pauses and modulated by stress and changes in pitch. We write sentences as sets of words, with spaces between them. But we say sentences as a string of sounds, emphasizing (stressing) some, quickly sliding over others, raising the pitch of our voice on some, lowering it on others. We maintain a regular rhythmic pattern of stress. We pause at appropriate times—for example, between phrases—but we do not pause after pronouncing each word.

Thus, speech does not come to us as a series of individual words; we must extract the words from a stream of speech.

(Carlson and Buskist, *Psychology: The Science of Behavior,* 5th ed., 303)

This is the main idea because it:

_____ answers a question stated in the paragraph.

_____ has a listing phrase: _____.

_____ is followed by a first item in a list signal word or

phrase: _____.

_____ is followed by an example (signal word or phrase,

if used: _____).

_____ has a change of direction signal: _____.

_____ has a summary/conclusion signal: _____.

_____ has no signal but states a general conclusion that all details lead to.

5. The automatic nature of syntactical analysis is nicely illustrated by experiments performed with artificial grammars. For example, Reber and Allen devised a set of rules for combining the letters M, V, R, T, and X. For example, MVRXR and VXTTV were "grammatical," but MXVTR and VMRTX were "ungrammatical." (The rules were rather complex.) They asked subjects to look at twenty "grammatical" strings of letters, printed on index cards. The subjects were told to "pay the utmost attention to the letter strings" but were not instructed to do anything else. Later, the subjects were presented with fifty different strings of letters, half of which were "grammatical" and half of which were not. Some of the "grammatical" strings were ones they had already seen, and some were new to them. The subjects were asked to indicate whether the strings were "grammatical." The subjects did quite well; they correctly identified 81 percent of the strings of letters. Obviously, they had learned the rules.

(Carlson and Buskist, *Psychology: The Science of Behavior,* 5th ed., 305)

This is the main idea because it:

_____ answers a question stated in the paragraph.

_____ has a listing phrase: _____.

_____ is followed by a first item in a list signal word or

phrase: _____.

_____ is followed by an example (signal word or phrase,

if used: _____).

_____ has a change of direction signal: _____.

_____ has a summary/conclusion signal: _____.

_____ has no signal but states a general conclusion that all details lead to.

6. Some memories (implicit memories) cannot be described verbally, whereas others (explicit memories) can. Apparently, the syntactic rules are learned implicitly. Later, we can be taught to talk about these rules and recognize their application (and, for example, construct diagrams of sentences), but this ability is not needed to speak and understand the speech of others. In fact, researchers found that patients with anterograde amnesia were able to learn an artificial grammar even though they had lost the ability to form explicit memories. In contrast, as other researchers observed, such patients are unable to learn the meanings of new words. Thus, learning syntax and word meaning appears to involve different types of memory—and consequently, different brain mechanisms.

(Carlson and Buskist, _Psychology: The Science of Behavior,_ 5th ed., 305)

This is the main idea because it:

_____ answers a question stated in the paragraph.

_____ has a listing phrase: _____.

_____ is followed by a first item in a list signal word or

phrase: _____.

_____ is followed by an example (signal word or phrase,

if used: _____).

_____ has a change of direction signal: _____.

_____ has a summary/conclusion signal: _____.

_____ has no signal but states a general conclusion that all details lead to.

7. _Word class_ refers to the grammatical categories (such as noun, pronoun, verb, adjective) that we learn about in school. But a person need not learn to categorize these words deliberately in order to recognize them and use them appropriately. For example, when we hear a sentence containing the word _pretty,_ we recognize that it refers to a person or a thing. Consider these two sentences: _The pretty girl picked the strawberries_ and _The tablecloth was pretty._

Although the word *pretty* is used in two different ways, at the beginning or end of the sentence, we have no trouble identifying what the word refers to.

(Carlson and Buskist, *Psychology: The Science of Behavior*, 5th ed., 305–306)

This is the main idea because it:

_____ answers a question stated in the paragraph.

_____ has a listing phrase: _____.

_____ is followed by a first item in a list signal word or

phrase: _____.

_____ is followed by an example (signal word or phrase,

if used: _____).

_____ has a change of direction signal: _____.

_____ has a summary/conclusion signal: _____.

_____ has no signal but states a general conclusion that all details lead to.

8. It is clear that eating a balanced diet is the key to good nutrition. Now the critical question is "How how do I know if I'm eating a well-balanced diet?" The answer is to perform a dietary analysis by keeping a daily record of everything you eat. It is a good idea to include both weekdays and weekends in your record (two weekdays and one weekend day is generally recommended). The process of analyzing your diet by hand is often time consuming and can be simplified by using computerized dietary analysis software.

(Powers and Dodd, *Total Fitness: Exercise, Nutrition, and Wellness*, 2nd ed., 168)

This is the main idea because it:

_____ answers a question stated in the paragraph.

_____ has a listing phrase: _____.

_____ is followed by a first item in a list signal word or

phrase: _____.

_____ is followed by an example (signal word or phrase,

if used: _____).

_____ has a change of direction signal: _____.

_____ has a summary/conclusion signal: _____.

_____ has no signal but states a general conclusion that all details lead to.

9. In village societies, so-called cunning folk played a positive role in helping people cope with calamity. People turned to them for help when such natural disasters as plague and famine struck or when such physical disabilities as lameness or inability to conceive offspring befell either humans or animals. The cunning folk provided consolation and gave people hope that such natural calamities might be averted or reversed by magical means. In this way they provided an important service and kept village line moving forward.

(Kagan, Ozment, and Turner,
Western Heritage, Vol. 1, 5th ed., 522)

This is the main idea because it:

_____ answers a question stated in the paragraph.

_____ has a listing phrase: _____.

_____ is followed by a first item in a list signal word or

phrase: _____.

_____ is followed by an example (signal word or phrase,

if used: _____).

_____ has a change of direction signal: _____.

_____ has a summary/conclusion signal: _____.

_____ has no signal but states a general conclusion that all details lead to.

10. There is also a relationship between income and voting. A considerably higher percentage of citizens with annual incomes over $40,000 vote than do citizens with incomes under $10,000. Income level is, to some degree, connected to education level, as wealthier people tend to have more opportunities for higher education and more education also may lead to higher income. Wealthy citizens are also more likely than poor ones to think that the "system" works for them and that their votes make a difference.

(O'Connor and Sabato, American Government:
Continuity and Change, 1997 ed., 524–525)

This is the main idea because it:

_____ answers a question stated in the paragraph.

_____ has a listing phrase: _____.

_____ is followed by a first item in a list signal word or

phrase: _____.

_____ is followed by an example (signal word or phrase,

if used: _____).

_____ has a change of direction signal: _____.

_____ has a summary/conclusion signal: _____.

_____ has no signal but states a general conclusion that all details lead to.

■ DEFINITIONS AND INTRODUCTORY INFORMATION IN PARAGRAPHS

Topical sentences are at times inserted into idea paragraphs, and topical paragraphs may turn up in longer passages. In these cases, their function is usually to provide introductory or important factual background information. For example, the idea paragraph on Disneyland could have begun with

> Disneyland, located in Anaheim, California, was the brainchild of animator Walt Disney. Part of Disneyland's success can be attributed to....

The first sentence obviously does not relate to "attention to detail" but the presence of a background information sentence would not be enough to affect the main idea focus of the paragraph.

The presence of a definition—particularly if it occurs in a complete sentence at the beginning of a paragraph—has a tendency to misdirect our attention from what may be the main idea of a paragraph or passage. A definition may be a main idea of a paragraph:

> <u>Probably the most important factor unifying society is the phenomenon of _functional integration_ (the unity among divergent elements of society resulting from a specialized division of labor).</u> In a highly differentiated society such as the United States, with its specialized division of labor, interaction among different segments occurs with some regularity. Interdependence often results because no group is entirely self-sufficient. The farmer needs the miller, the processor, and retail agents, as well as the fertilizer manufacturer and the agricultural experimenters. Manufacturers need raw materials, on the one hand, and customers, on the other. Management needs workers, the workers need management.
>
> (Eitzen and Zinn, _In Conflict and Order,_ 7th ed., 68)

Often, however, the author includes a definition only to clarify a central term or the topic itself. Here it functions as important background information. If it were removed, however, the paragraph would still stand as a complete unit with a main idea:

> A business is a profit-seeking activity that provides goods and services that satisfy consumers' needs. Businesses play a number of key roles in society and the economy. They provide society with necessities such as housing,

clothing, food, transportation, communication, and health care; they provide people with jobs and a means to prosper; they pay taxes that are used to build highways, fund education, and provide grants for scientific research; and they reinvest their profits in the economy, thereby creating a higher standard of living and quality of life for society as a whole.

(Bovee and Thill, *Business in Action,* 3)

It is the second sentence that tells us "what about" the topic. It answers the question ("What roles does business play?") that the rest of the details relate to:

Main idea: Businesses play a number of key roles in society and the economy.

The first sentence provides a helpful definition of the topic. It tells us what a business is, but its omission would not alter the main point of the paragraph.

Exercise 2.4

Underline the definition given in each paragraph below and decide whether the definition is the main idea. If not, write the sentence that is the main idea. Then list any signals that gave you a clue to the main idea.

1. Substances contained in food that are necessary for good health are called nutrients. They can be divided into two categories: macronutrients and micronutrients. Macronutrients, which consist of carbohydrates, fats, and proteins, are necessary for building and maintaining body tissues and providing energy for daily activities. Micronutrients include all other substances in food such as vitamins and minerals that regulate the functions of the cells.

   (Powers and Dodd, *Total Fitness: Exercise, Nutrition, and Wellness,* 2nd ed., 152)

   Is the definition the main idea sentence? _____ Yes _____ No

   If *no,* write the main idea sentence: _____

   _____

   _____

   Signals (if any): _____

2. Photosynthesis is the conversion of light energy into chemical energy. The energy of sunlight is first used to sharply increase the energy level of certain chlorophyll electrons. Such energy-rich electrons then flow through highly ordered carriers in electron transport systems, powering proton pumps as they go, and finally reducing NADP+ to NADPH. Proton pumps generate the great energy of the chemiosmotic systems responsible for forming the

energy-rich bonds of ATP. Both ATP and NADPH provide energy that is used to form food (such as glucose) from carbon dioxide and water.

(Ferl and Wallace, *Biology: The Realm of Life,* 3rd ed., 103)

Is the definition the main idea sentence? _____ Yes _____ No

If *no,* write the main idea sentence: _____

_____

_____

Signals (if any): _____

3. Affixes are sounds that we add to the beginning (*prefixes*) or end (*suffixes*) of words to alter their grammatical function: -*ed* to the end of a regular verb to indicate the past tense (*drop/dropped*); -*ing* to a verb to indicate its use as a noun (*sing/singing*); and -*ly* to an adjective to indicate its use as an adverb (*bright/brightly*). We are very quick to recognize the syntactical function of words with affixes like these. For example, Epstein (1961) presented people with word strings such as the following:

a vap koob desak the citar molent um glox nerf

A vapy koob desaked the citar molently um glox nerfs.

The people could more easily remember the second string than the first, even though letters had been added to some of the words. Apparently, the addition of the affixes -*y, -ed,* and -*ly* made the words seem more like a sentence and they thus became easier to categorize and recall.

(Carlson and Buskist, *Psychology: The Science of Behavior,* 5th ed., 306)

Is the definition the main idea sentence? _____ Yes _____ No

If *no,* write the main idea sentence: _____

_____

_____

Signals (if any): _____

4. Coelomates have a mesoderm-lined body cavity called a coelum. The coelomates have a complex, complete gut lined with digestive and absorptive tissue, with specialized regions along its length. For instance, there are regions whose primary functions are grinding, swallowing, digesting, and absorbing food; there are others for the temporary storage of food; and yet others for the concentration and elimination of wastes. Such linear specialization permits food to be continuously processed, since, during a

given time, food in different regions will be undergoing significant stages of digestion.

(Ferl and Wallace, Biology: The Realm of Life, 3rd ed., 430)

Is the definition the main idea sentence?   _____ Yes _____ No

If *no,* write the main idea sentence: _____

_____

_____

Signals (if any): _____

5. Prosody refers to the use of stress, rhythm, and changes in pitch that accompany speech. Prosody can emphasize the syntax of a word or group of words or even serve as the primary source of syntactic information. For example, in several languages (including English), a declarative sentence can be turned into a question by means of prosody. Read the following sentences aloud to see how you would indicate to a listener which is a statement and which is a question.

> You said that.
> You said that?

(Carlson and Buskist, Psychology: The Science of Behavior, 5th ed., 306)

Is the definition the main idea sentence?   _____ Yes _____ No

If not, write the main idea sentence: _____

_____

_____

Signals (if any): _____

RECOGNIZING EIGHT KINDS OF IDEAS

Compare the statements below. They are all generalizations, they are all complete sentences, and they all could serve as the main idea of a paragraph or of an article:

Last year the Super Bowl was incredibly boring.

Many young people today are taking up smoking.

The team concept in football is very different from that involved in basketball.

Only five years after World War II, the United States was at war again in Korea.

These sentences share another feature: they could all be answers to questions. Yet the questions would be quite different, because they involve a variety of different mental activities that we use to understand and report about the world around us.

For example, questions using *where* show our concern with location, how things fit together in space, or how parts go together to make wholes. *When* points to time relationships, *how* to understanding steps in a process or tracking causes. Answering *why* leads us to determine causes and effects and into giving reasons for the way things are. It helps us see connections, assign responsibility, and suggest changes or solutions. Related questions like *who,* *which,* and *what* help us to identify and describe the characteristics of objects in our world.

We must keep in mind a very important truth about the ideas we create by giving answers to these kinds of questions: *Not all ideas are the same. Their forms vary with the kinds of thinking in which we are engaged.* The academic dialogue in various fields differs greatly depending on the concerns in those fields and the kinds of thinking they require. The following passage from Richard Samson's *Thinking Skills* (22–23) is a good starting point for keeping clear the difference among various kinds of ideas:

> There are many types of thoughts we can think about things. Not all of them are structural thoughts. How do we tell the difference? Let us consider eggs. When the most famous of all eggs, Humpty Dumpty, fell from the wall, the unhappy result was of a structural nature: pieces, parts—spatial elements of a static whole.
>
> If, instead of "breaking" an egg into parts, you take a basket containing many different kinds of eggs and "break them down" into types (chicken eggs, duck eggs, pigeon eggs), you are classifying, not analyzing the physical parts of a structure. If you take an egg and "break it down" into the things which happen to it (a hen lays it, a baby chick grows inside it, the chick picks through its shell and is born from it), you are analyzing an operation, not a static structure; you are "breaking" something into its "time-parts" rather than physical parts in a purely spatial sense. If you take an egg and "break it down" into its attributes (white, ovular, edible, fragile), you are [describing] it, not analyzing its structure—the spatial arrangement of its parts.

Below are listed eight common kinds of ideas. To illustrate the different kinds of thinking that can be applied to a single topic, we could extend the discussion about the topic of eggs in many different ways, depending on our interests.

Description: Eggs are usually ovular and most are very fragile.

Whole/part: An egg consists of a shell, a yolk, and albumen (egg white).

Classification: There are many kinds of eggs: e.g., chicken eggs, duck eggs, pigeon eggs.

Time sequence: A hen lays the egg; the chick grows, picks through its shell, and is born.

Comparison/contrast: Ostrich eggs are much larger than pigeon eggs.

Cause/effect: Eating eggs may result in higher cholesterol.

Opinion/reasons: You should eat eggs, for a number of reasons.

Problem/solution: Limit your consumption of eggs to avoid health problems resulting from dangerous levels of cholesterol.

Important transitions (signal words) reveal common relationships that can help a reader identify ideas. For example, imagine a situation in which your boss calls you into his office for a conference. Which of the following would you prefer to hear?

We have been very pleased with your work so far. Therefore,...

We have been very pleased with your work so far. However,...

Even before you get the news directly, you have been signaled what is to come. The first would cause a glow of anticipation: perhaps a raise or promotion. The second would send a shiver down your spine and thoughts of job hunting would float through your head.

Below is an expanded discussion on the eight types of ideas identified above. To help you recognize and understand the function of transitions and other signal words, a list of those most common to each pattern is included.

DESCRIPTION

This is the most common of all ideas. **Descriptive statements** tell us about the qualities and characteristics of persons, places, objects, or events. Adjectives carry the key meaning.

- Many of our health care programs are *wasteful.*
- President Washington was *wise* and *prudent* in foreign affairs.
- Mardi Gras is an *exciting, unpredictable* time of year.

A subject can also be described by statements regarding behaviors, significant actions, or characteristic functions. In these, action verbs provide the point.

- During World War II, many Japanese-Americans *fought heroically for the Allies.*
- The Savings and Loan scandal *will cost taxpayers over $500 billion.*
- The Small Business Administration *provides loans for family business ventures.*

Common Pattern Words

qualities	for example	moreover	also
traits	to illustrate	furthermore	next
characteristics	for instance	in addition	first of all
attributes	including	another	finally

WHOLE/PART

When we analyze the various parts that make up an entire structure—whether physical (the human body), geographical (a map of the United States), political (the U.S. Government), or mental (the human mind)—we are engaged in the thinking process of **structure (whole/part) analysis.**

- The average home *consists* of three bedrooms, a family room, a kitchen, a laundry room, and a bath and a half.
- Decision-making consists of an emotional *component* and a rational *component.*
- The Great Plains lie *east* of the Rockies and *west* of the Mississippi.
- The highest court *in the U.S. judicial system* is the Supreme Court.

Sometimes whole/part and classification are confused. In the latter, for example, you might sort a basket of apples into groups based on size (small, medium, large) or color (red, green, yellow). In contrast, whole/part ideas involve just *one* thing—the apple—and then separate it into parts: stem, skin, seeds, core.

Common Pattern Words

part	east, west, etc.	in front of	beyond
component	up, down	behind	around
aspect	right, left	next to	upon
divisions	in, out	adjacent to	far, near
branches	above, below	bordering	toward

CLASSIFICATION

Ideas regarding **placing** or **sorting** things into groups or categories involve us in the mental activity of classifying. The end result depends on our interests. Sorting your clothes into piles to wash, for instance, would result in groups very different from those you create when you sort the clean clothes into your dresser drawers. Often classification involves breaking large groups of items into subtypes, based on characteristics like age, vocation, and gender.

- Most workers find themselves at the mercy of one of *three kinds* of bosses.
- There are *two kinds* of roofers: those who have fallen, and those who are going to fall.
- Executives are *either Type* A or *Type* B personalities.

Common Pattern Words

types (of)	fall into	kinds (of)	divide into
categories	belong to	groups	separate into

TIME SEQUENCE

Since all our lives are "time-driven"—watches, calendars—ideas related to time are familiar to us from an early age. When we want to tell a story, recount events in our lives, create a "history" of a topic, or tell how to do something, we naturally find ourselves using **ideas of time.**

- Down the street came the parade, with *first* the circus performers and *then* the trained animals.
- The stock market crash of 1929 was *soon followed* by the Great Depression of the thirties.
- To change a tire, you must *first* loosen the lug nuts, jack up the car, and *then* remove the nuts and the old tire.

Common Pattern Words

stage	first, etc.	before	since
phase	next	after	until
era	then	during	at last
step	now	earlier	finally
while	later	at the beginning	

COMPARISON/CONTRAST

Many ideas involve observing **similarities** (comparison) and **differences** (contrast) among objects, processes, groups, or structures (although the word *comparison* is often intended to include both meanings). Contrast has some special uses. It can show contradiction, hypocritical actions, or note results contrary to our expectations.

- Renting a house and owning a condo are *radically different.*
- Schools preach creative thinking *but* reward conformity.
- *Although* Pete studied hard, he failed his history test.

Common Pattern Words

same	better than	although	but
like	worse than	however	yet
similarly	different from	conversely	still
likewise	opposite	in spite of	while
parallels	in contrast	nevertheless	despite
resembles	on the contrary	rather than	

CAUSE/EFFECT

When our ideas involve the question **why** or when we determine responsibility, we deal in **cause and effect relationships.** There is an aspect of time involved—the cause happens first, the effect follows—but there is also a relationship between the two: the effect would *not* have occurred without the cause, by itself or combined with others.

- Lack of exercise can *contribute* significantly to weight gain.
- A number of environmental factors can *influence* your success in college.
- One *effect* of the recession has been a decrease in tax revenues from businesses.

Also certain "how to" ideas—those that give advice on achieving a goal—don't occur in a series of steps as in a process; instead they show that, if the advice is followed (the cause), then desirable results will follow (the effect).

- To study effectively, you need a quiet place, good lighting, and a set schedule.

Common Pattern Words

influence	because	so
contribute to	for	thus
create	so that	therefore
determine	since	if ... then
result in	consequently	in order for

OPINION/REASON

Sometimes we have very strong ideas on current issues about what our fellow citizen should **believe, do,** or **value.** If we expect our ideas to be accepted, we must back up our **opinion** with **reasons** for our views.

- Many doctors believe that pregnant women *should* give up alcohol during pregnancy *due to* possible damage to the fetus and/or themselves.
- Youth football leagues *should be* abolished *because* they stereotype young athletes, overemphasize winning, and create the potential for dangerous injuries.
- *Because of* low tuition, good student–teacher ratios, and savings on transportation and housing, students *should* consider attending a community college for the first two years of their college education.

Common Pattern Words   Synonyms for *should* are commonly combined with causation words that lead to the reasons.

must	because
ought to	since
need to	for

The reasons are often listed with sequence words and signal words of addition.

first	moreover
second	furthermore
next	also
finally	in addition

PROBLEM/SOLUTION

Problem-solving ideas involve cause and effect relationships; the difference is that cause/effect simply explains why. Problem/solution goes beyond that to argue that **something is wrong and needs to be fixed.**

- Overcrowding of parking facilities, a result of a sudden increase of enrollment, requires that we plan immediately for expanded campus parking.
- The deadly increase in smoking among the young points dramatically to the need for drastic restrictions on tobacco advertising.
- Only parental involvement at all levels can prevent a further decline in the performance of our schools.

Common Pattern Words
synonyms for *problem*
synonyms for *solution*
signal words for cause/effect

Part A

Identify the kind of idea in each sentence by selecting from the list below and writing your answer in the space following each sentence. Then list key words that signaled the idea type.

description/support   classification
comparison/contrast   whole/part
time sequence   problem/solution
cause/effect   opinion/reason

1. After the jury deliberated for five hours, they returned with a verdict of guilty.

    Kind of idea: _____

    Signal words or phrases: _____

2. Ralph's winning basket at the buzzer is just another example of his excellent play all year.

    Kind of idea: _____

    Signal words or phrases: _____

3. Many citizens pay four types of taxes: income, Social Security, sales, and property.

    Kind of idea: _____

    Signal words or phrases: _____

4. Some students of above-average ability study many hours for a test but still fail.

    Kind of idea: _____

    Signal words or phrases: _____

5. The epidemic of violence on our streets, claiming young and old alike, will not be solved until all members of the community cooperate.

    Kind of idea: _____

    Signal words or phrases: _____

6. Many congressmen are reelected due to money from powerful political action committees.

    Kind of idea: _____

    Signal words or phrases: _____

7. Most written reports consist of an introduction, a body, and a conclusion.

   Kind of idea: _____

   Signal words or phrases: _____

8. You should limit the amount of red meat in your diet for two reasons: health and weight control.

   Kind of idea: _____

   Signal words or phrases: _____

9. To sink a putt, first visualize the ball going into the cup, and then stroke with confidence.

   Kind of idea: _____

   Signal words or phrases: _____

10. The banana split has a banana on the bottom, a layer of ice cream and chocolate sauce in the middle, and whipped cream, chopped nuts, and a maraschino cherry on top.

    Kind of idea: _____

    Signal words or phrases: _____

Part B

The paragraphs below will give you practice in finding and identifying main idea types. First, underline the main idea sentence for each paragraph. (For the one paragraph in which the main idea has been restated, underline both the main idea and the restatement.) Then, identify the kind of idea, using the list below. Each idea type is used once in paragraphs 1–8.

description/support	classification
comparison/contrast	whole/part
time sequence	problem/solution
cause/effect	opinion/reason

Next, circle the letter of the correct response regarding signals used to locate the main idea.

1. Several types of tactile receptors are located in the human skin. Touch receptors include Merkel's disks, Meissner's corpuscles, and free nerve endings, all of which are located near the skin surface. (Free nerve endings also register pain.) Pressure is detected by bulbous Pacinian corpuscles that are located deeper in the skin and in some of the deep organs of the body, such as the

pancreas. Human touch receptors are more concentrated in the fingertips, lips, nipples, face, and genitals. Body hairs can also transmit signals since at their base they are generally wrapped by free nerve endings. (Try moving one hair without feeling it.)

(Ferl and Wallace, *Biology: The Realm of Life,* 3rd ed., 603)

Kind of idea: _____

This is the main idea sentence because it

    a. answers a question stated in the paragraph.

    b. has a listing phrase.

    c. has a first item in a list signal word.

    d. all of the above

2. A new, drastically modified reproductive device—the land egg—first introduced by the early reptiles, was a vital adaptation to complete terrestrial life. The land egg was surrounded by a tough leathery shell (later replaced by a calcium shell in birds), which, while admitting air, protected the embryo against desiccation and mechanical injury. Included within the egg was a supply of water and food, everything necessary for the embryo's development.

(Ferl and Wallace, *Biology: The Realm of Life,* 3rd ed., 463)

Kind of idea: _____

This is the main idea sentence because it

    a. answers a question stated in the paragraph.

    b. has a change of direction signal.

    c. has a conclusion signal.

    d. states a general conclusion that all details relate to (no specific signals).

3. Because speech is full of hesitations, muffled sounds, and sloppy pronunciations, many individual words are hard to recognize out of context. For example, when Pollack and Pickett (1964) isolated individual words from a recording of normal conversations and played them back to other people, those people correctly identified the words only 47 percent of the time. When they presented the same words in the context of the original conversation, the subjects identified and understood almost 100 percent of them. Miller, Heise, and Lichten (1951) found that subjects understood strings of words

such as "who brought some wet socks" in a noisy environment but failed to understand strings such as "wet brought who socks some." These findings confirm that the context of speech provides important cues to aid our recognition of words.

(Carlson and Buskist, Psychology: The Science of Behavior, 5th ed., 304)

Kind of idea: _____

This is the main idea sentence because it

    a. answers a question stated in the paragraph.

    b. has a change of direction signal.

    c. is followed by an example signal word.

    d. states a general conclusion that all details relate to (no specific signals).

4. The order model (sometimes referred to as functionalism) attributes to society the characteristics of cohesion, consensus, cooperation, reciprocity, stability, and persistence. A high degree of cooperation (and societal integration) is accomplished because there is a high degree of consensus on the societal goal and on cultural values. Moreover, the different parts of the system are assumed to need each other because of complementary interests. Because the primary social process is cooperation and the system is highly integrated, all social change is gradual, adjustive, and reforming. Societies are therefore basically stable units.

(Eitzen and Zinn, In Conflict and Order, 7th ed., 48)

Kind of idea: _____

This is the main idea sentence because it

    a. has a listing phrase.

    b. has a conclusion signal.

    c. is followed by an example signal word.

    d. states a general conclusion that all details relate to (no specific signals).

5. Proteins are the largest and most complex of food molecules. Essentially, protein digestion occurs in three steps, beginning in the stomach. Here, pepsin attacks the molecule, splitting it into peptide fragments of various lengths. The fragments are then subjected to a more specific disruption in the small intestine, where the pancreatic enzymes trypsin and clymotypsin break into

specific amino linkages. This leaves the protein in the form of peptide fragments only two to ten amino acids long. These are finally cleaved by enzymes of the small intestine into single amino acids.

(Ferl and Wallace, *Biology: The Realm of Life*, 3rd ed., 665)

Kind of idea: _____

This is the main idea sentence because it

    a. has a listing phrase.

    b. has a first item in a list signal word.

    c. has a change of direction signal.

    d. both *a* and *b*

6. Humans are homeotherms, which means same temperature. That is, body temperature is regulated around a set point; humans regulate their body temperature around the set point of 98.6°F. Variations in body temperature can result in serious bodily injury. Indeed, heat illness can occur when body temperature rises above 105°F. Cramps, dizziness, nausea, lack of sweat production, and dry, hot skin are all indications of impending heat illness. Therefore, the body must maintain precise control over temperature to avoid a life-threatening situation.

(Powers and Dodd, *Total Fitness: Exercise, Nutrition, and Wellness*, 2nd ed., 220)

Kind of idea: _____

This is the main idea sentence because it

    a. has a listing phrase.

    b. has a first item in a list signal word.

    c. has a conclusion signal.

    d. both *a* and *b*

7. There are many differences, including socioeconomic and attitudinal, between voters and nonvoters. First, people who vote are usually more highly educated than nonvoters. Other things being equal, college graduates are much more likely to vote than those with less education. People with more education tend to learn more about politics, are less hindered by registration requirements, and are more self-confident about their ability to affect public life. Therefore one might argue that institutions of higher edu-

cation provide citizens with opportunities to learn about and become interested in politics.

(O'Connor and Sabato, *American Government:*
Continuity and Change, 1997 ed., 524)

Kind of idea: _____

This is the main idea sentence because it

    a. answers a question stated in the paragraph.

    b. has a listing phrase.

    c. has a first item in a list signal word.

    d. both *b* and *c*

8. A variety of reasons are given to support employee drug testing; most focus on safety and productivity. The Department of Transportation, one of the strongest advocates of employee drug testing, rationalizes its decision to routinely test 4 million private-industry employees, out of concern for the public. Corporate legal liability and moral responsibility for the actions of its employees has been given as another compelling reason to allow corporations the right to test its employees for drug use. Lost productivity is another oft-cited reason for drug testing. Besides its positive effects on the workplace, drug testing is also considered to be an additional weapon in the war on drugs.

(Eshleman, Cashion, Basirico, *Sociology: An Introduction,* 4th ed., 134)

Kind of idea: _____

This is the main idea sentence because it

    a. has a listing phrase.

    b. has a first item in a list signal word.

    c. has a conclusion signal.

    d. both *a* and *c*

COLLABORATIVE LEARNING:
A DIALOGUE WITH PEERS

Reading and studying are often done in isolation from others, but at other times classes provide the student with opportunities for interaction. Instructors welcome questions from students and encourage classroom dialogue that develops from lectures or media presentations. Another opportunity for dialogue can occur in collaborative groups that analyze and discuss reading material. A peer discussion group can be very effective for learning but brings with it some special obligations. Obviously we cannot all speak at the same time. One of the most important aspects of dialogue, then, is knowing when to speak and when to be silent and listen. But does listening necessarily occur when we are being silent? In the passage below, the author clarifies for us what true listening really is.

Seek First to Understand, Then to Be Understood

by Stephen Covey

1   Communication is the most important skill in life. We spend most of our waking hours communicating. But consider this: You've spent years learning how to read and write, years learning how to speak. But what about listening? What training or education have you had that enables you to listen so that you really, deeply understand another human being from that individual's own frame of reference? Comparatively few people have had any training in listening at all.

2   We typically seek first to be understood. Most people do not listen with the intent to understand; they listen with the intent to reply. They're either speaking or preparing to speak. That's the case with so many of us. We're filled with our own rightness, our own autobiography. We want to be understood. Our conversations become collective monologues, and we never really understand what's going on inside another human being.

3   When another person speaks, we're usually "listening" at one of four levels. We may be ignoring another person, not really listening at all. We may practice pretending. "Yeah. Uh-huh. Right." We may practice selective listening, hearing only certain parts of the conversation. We often do this when we're listening to the constant chatter of a preschool child. Or we may even practice attentive listening, paying attention and focusing energy on the words that are being said. But very few of us ever practice the fifth level, the highest form of listening, empathic listening.

4   When I say empathic listening, I mean listening with intent to understand. I mean seeking first to understand, to really understand. It's entirely different. Empathic (from empathy) listening gets inside another person's frame of reference. You look out through it, you see the world the way they see the world. Empathic listening is so powerful because it gives you accurate data

to work with. You're dealing with the reality inside another person's head and heart. You're listening to understand.

Many of the exercises in this textbook, like the one below, are designed for group work. Before you engage in the exercise, think about these guidelines for group work:

<u>Roles and Functions of Group Members</u>	<u>Functions of the Group</u>
Listen as well as speak.	Sets its goal and uses time-management skills to reach it.
Do not wander off-track into personal issues.	Reaches agreement if possible and summarizes findings.
Respect the right of others to express contrary views.	
Are not afraid to disagree with the ideas of the majority.	
Remain open minded—views can be changed.	
Avoid personal attacks.	

<u>Group Leader</u>	<u>Note Taker</u>
Keeps the group to its purpose	Writes down brainstorming ideas
Sets a time line for completion	Assembles a final summary
Ensures an equal voice for all	May write findings on chalkboard or overhead
Presents findings to other groups	

Exercise 2.6

Form groups according to your instructor's directions. Assign the roles of group leader and note taker and follow the guidelines for effective participation. Numbers in parentheses refer to paragraph numbers.

1. "Communication is the most important skill in life" (1). Do you agree? What are some other important skills in life? _____

_____

_____

_____

2. "We're filled with our own rightness, our own autobiography" (2). Can you give an example from your experience that would help to explain what Covey means here? _____

_____

_____

_____

3. "Our conversations become collective monologues" (2). You've learned what is involved in a dialogue. What is a monologue? Is a conversation that is a monologue really a "conversation"? _____

_____

_____

_____

4. Which of the five levels of listening that Covey identifies (3) aren't really listening at all? Can you recall personal experiences in observing or engaging in these? _____

_____

_____

_____

5. What does the word "empathy" mean? What is the difference (3–4) between attentive listening and empathic listening? _____

_____

_____

_____

6. "You see the world the way they see the world" (4). What are some factors that cause people to see things differently from one another? _____

_____

_____

_____

7. "Comparatively few people have had any training in listening at all" (1). Describe any such training that you have had. Was it effective? _____

_____

_____

_____

CHAPTER REVIEW

Circle the correct letter choice.

1. Signal words like *because* and *therefore* would most likely be found in cause/effect and which of the following patterns?

    a. comparison/contrast and description/support

    b. classification and comparison/contrast

    c. problem/solution and opinion/reason

    d. whole/part and classification

2. A sequence of signal words including *first, next, then,* and *before* could be found in the pattern of

    a. description/support.

    b. time sequence.

    c. opinion/reason.

    d. classification.

3. Which of the following would function as a change of direction signal?

    a. but

    b. nevertheless

    c. on the other hand

    d. all of the above

Identify each of the following as T *for true and* F *for false.*

4. _____ Every paragraph has a main idea.

5. _____ Supporting details include statistics, examples, and specific descriptions.

6. _____ If a paragraph includes a definition, the sentence containing it is always the main idea.

7. _____ A sentence that begins with "for example" is very likely to be the main idea sentence.

Circle the correct letter choice and fill in the blank where indicated.

8. *Therefore* and *clearly* may signal a main idea statement of summary

   or _____.

9. A main idea can be

   a. the first sentence in the paragraph.

   b. the last sentence in the paragraph.

   c. a sentence in the middle of the paragraph.

   d. all of the above

10. The highest level of listening is

    a. attentive listening

    b. empathic listening

    c. pretend listening

    d. selective listening

READING PORTFOLIO   Developing a Filing System

You will need some type of organizer to keep your articles filed in order and easily accessible. This might be a three-ring binder with dividers and tabs or a compartmentalized accordion style filer. Whatever you use, you will need at least eight sections to file your articles according to the ideas that control them. Begin looking for and collecting articles built around the eight kinds of main ideas that have been identified and illustrated in Chapters 1 and 2. You may find them appropriate for later assignments.

1. *Description.* Magazines and newspapers feature **profiles** of people, places, or things: sports stars, entertainers, vacation spots, inventions. Many profiles will have a central focus on the special characteristics or behaviors of the subject, the good and/or the bad.

2. *Whole/Part.* Articles on geographic areas or changes in political boundaries involve whole/part analysis. These articles may also be on mechanical subjects—breaking down the parts of a new machine or a new weapon. Frequently an article will contain diagrams and illustrations with parts labeled.

3. *Classification.* These articles are fairly rare in popular, nonscientific publications, but you will find articles, for example, on political groupings or on racial and ethnic categories. Classification can often be humorous—"kinds of shoppers" or "types of bosses."

4. *Time Sequence.* Articles that give you a step by step sequence of "how to do" something are staples of magazines and feature sections of the newspapers. Time sequence articles may also deal with the history and development of institutions, movements, and traditions—how things started, how they grew.

5. *Comparison/Contrast.* These occur more frequently in magazines than in newspapers. Comparisons and contrasts are common in sports magazines (teams or individuals) and in car magazines and others dealing with product comparisons.

6. *Cause/Effect.* Look here mainly for articles that limit themselves to explaining why things have happened or will happen. Explanations may be physical or psychological—many articles that focus on *motives* fall into this category. Certain types of "advice" articles belong here—those that list a number of suggestions (not in a time sequence) that can lead to success or to achieving specific goals.

7. *Problem/Solution.* These articles share similarities with cause/effect, but go beyond to assert that things are "wrong" and need to be fixed. These articles can be very argumentative, and are usually found in feature sections of the newspaper and in the editorial section. Many magazine articles are devoted to problems in home life among spouses and family members and how to solve them.

8. *Opinion/Reason.* Opinions most often are found in the editorial section of the newspaper or in specially identified "columns" written by columnists. Newsmagazines often contain short essays written by nationally known journalists, who may also often appear on television. These articles cover a wide range of interest areas dealing with political and social issues of the time. However, sports, fashion, and entertainment also have issues that can be heatedly argued about.

Making Inferences: Context Vocabulary and Implied Main Ideas

When you take your car into an auto shop, the mechanic listens to your description of the car's behavior and may run some quick tests to come up with an initial guess about what's wrong. When you have a medical problem, your doctor asks questions carefully before making a tentative diagnosis, which is later confirmed or rejected depending on further tests. Detectives working a crime scene must try to reconstruct what happened on the basis of the available physical evidence. As different as these jobs may be, they all demand great skill in making inferences—a mental process that you will find is equally vital to reading, especially as you move into more difficult reading material.

■ CHAPTER PREVIEW

In this chapter you will

- Learn to distinguish the terms *imply* and *infer*
- Discover how to use four context clues for vocabulary
- Apply your inference skills to stories
- Use inference to determine implied main ideas
- Find and write about an article for your Reading Portfolio

INFERRING AND IMPLYING

There are many occasions in everyday life, as well as in reading, when we must attempt to draw conclusions based on a limited amount of evidence. When we make such reasonable guesses we are involved in the mental activity of **inference.** The verb *to infer* is often confused with the verb *to imply*—though related, they denote quite different mental activities. When we infer, we make a reasonable guess based on the partial evidence we have received. To imply, however, means "to suggest" and comes from the sender of a communication. For example, if a boss begins a conference with an employee by noting some performance problems of workers that the employee supervises, the boss may be suggesting indirectly that the employee is at fault. The boss is implying a criticism; the employee at this point should be inferring that his or her job may be in trouble.

In the story that follows, pay very careful attention to the details about Ildefonso, the "man without words." You will be able to draw some conclusions regarding his age, his past, his current situation, and the nature of his handicap—though none of this information is *directly* stated in the selection.

Ildefonso

by Susan Schaller

1   I read once that the human brain is unique in the primate family not because it is so much bigger or has developed such specialized parts, but because it has such a vast connection system—countless circuits and interchanges. My hope was that Ildefonso's unconscious connections between the sign "cat," the word *cat,* the cat picture, and a real cat might begin associations that would eventually surface.

2   Believing that at some level we had one sign in common, I began a new mime lesson. I pretended to see a cat. I signed "cat" and coaxed the invisible creature to approach, picked it up, stroked it, and held it in one arm as I signed "cat" again with the other.

3   Ildefonso imitated whatever he could and never stopped to watch me. Suddenly my back and neck ached with frustration as I placed Ildefonso's hands once again on the table. They rose immediately when I started my imaginary cat routine. We were an interlocked duo. My attempts at com-

---

Susan Schaller, "Idelfonso," from *A Man without Words,* (University of California Press, 1991), 43–45. Reprinted by permission of University of California Press and Susan Schaller.

munication turned the crank, and his hands jumped, popping up on cue like the head of a jack-in-the-box who forever hears the same nonsensical tune and springs up, smiling and oblivious.

4   The scraping of chairs on linoleum and rising bodies signaled the start of the morning break. I smelled the coffee from three buildings away and quickly took leave of Ildefonso. We were both exhausted from trying to figure out the other. The break was all too brief. Obsessed, I couldn't restrain myself from trying again. And again. I called my imaginary cat to my lap and petted it before signing "cat." Ildefonso called the cat to his lap and signed "cat." I hid the invisible cat behind my back and asked where it was with mime. Ildefonso did the same.

5   For four days, face to face, we failed to connect. My dependency on names blocked my view into his mind of no names. His survival strategy of mimicry kept him from listening—that is, paying attention to a conversation. Was it too late for him to learn language? Was I simply adding more confusion and frustration to his life?

6   The weekend provided a rest from these doubts, and I returned on Monday, determined to try again. It was the fifth working day since our meeting. He looked interested in everything I did, and I believed he was trying to communicate. So I kept trying too.

7   Cat sign, *cat,* cat picture, and imaginary cat danced together in various partnerships. I stayed with the same lesson, variation after variation. Still he insisted on copying everything I did. He didn't know how to receive. He could act and react, but he couldn't get the idea of conversing without doing. I wanted to scream at him: "I don't want you to *do* anything!"

8   I decided to ignore him. It was his searching eyes that had first attracted my attention; I must trust them to watch and study me. So I began the cat lesson again, but this time I had no eye contact with him. I looked instead at an imaginary student and taught him the cat connections. I stood at the blackboard facing an empty chair, signed "cat," and wrote *cat.* I petted an imaginary cat and read the word *cat* on the board. Sitting down in the chair, I became the imaginary Ildefonso. I studied the word and frowned. Then I tilted my head back, opened my mouth slightly, and nodded as if to say, "Oh, I get it. That's a cat." As Ildefonso, I went to the board and started petting the word *cat.* Of course, the chalk streaked. I looked bewildered. What happened? Wasn't that a cat? I turned back to the teacher position and explained via mime that *cat* is not a real cat but puts the idea of cat in my head. After pointing to *cat,* I mimed taking something out of my head and putting it in the invisible Ildefonso's head. Becoming Ildefonso again, I looked thoughtful while I pointed to the word, pointed to my head, held and stroked an imaginary cat, then pointed to my head again.

9   I carefully avoided meeting Ildefonso's eyes, but I knew he was watching. My peripheral vision showed me that his arms were folded and not echoing my movements. I repeated the teacher-student act over and over, varying it as much as possible without losing the main idea of *cat* or "cat" triggering a picture in the brain. The *cat* on the board was written, rubbed out, and rewritten until my fingers were white.

10   When it was time to go, Ildefonso stared at me. I stared back and sat down. While everyone else shuffled out the door, we sat looking at each other. I rose and nodded a farewell. He sat and stared at the space I had just occupied. For the first time, I had the feeling that he wouldn't show up the next day.

11   On Tuesday, I was truly surprised to find him sitting in his usual corner seat. I nodded hello and opened his book to the cat picture. I pointed and posed with a "what?" on my face. Ildefonso imitated the question and pointed to the picture. Already tired, I returned to what seemed to be our only hope—the imaginary Ildefonso skit. I set up the empty chair, headed for the blackboard, and repeated the days previous lesson. Time passed. I looked at Ildefonso. He straightened up in his chair and looked back. I went to the board, wondering if any new variations were possible. I tried a slow-motion version. At the next attempt, I looked the same, but in my head I had a Texas accent. I began to worry about my sanity. Fortunately, it was time for our fifteen-minute break.

12   As soon as it was over, Ildefonso returned to his seat and I to my stage. "One more time," I told myself. While I was correcting the imaginary Ildefonso, the real Ildefonso shifted in his chair. I stopped.

13   Suddenly he sat up, straight and rigid, his head back and his chin pointing forward. The whites of his eyes expanded as if in terror. He looked like a wild horse pulling back, testing every muscle before making a powerful lunge over a canyon's edge. My body and arms froze in the mime-and-sign dance that I had played over and over for an eternity. I stood motionless in front of the streaked *cat*, petted beyond recognition for the fiftieth time, and I witnessed Ildefonso's emancipation.

14   He broke through. He understood. He had forded the same river Helen Keller did at the water pump when she suddenly connected the water rushing over her hand with the word spelled into it. Yes, w-a-t-e-r and c-a-t *mean* something. And the cat-meaning in one head can join the cat-meaning in another's head just by tossing out a *cat*.

15   Ildefonso's face opened in excitement as he slowly pondered this revelation. His head turned to his left and very gradually back to his right. Slowly at first, then hungrily, he took in everything as though he had never seen anything before: the door, the bulletin board, the chairs, tables, students, the clock, the green blackboard, and me.

16   He slapped both hands flat on the table and looked up at me, demanding a response. "Table," I signed. He slapped his book. "Book," I replied. My face was wet with tears, but I obediently followed his pointing fingers and hands, signing: "door," "clock," "chair." But as suddenly as he had asked for names, he turned pale, collapsed, and wept. Folding his arms like a cradle on the table he lay down his head. My fingers were white as I clutched the metal rim of the table, which squeaked under his grief more loudly than his sobbing.

17   He had entered the universe of humanity, discovered the communion of minds. He now knew that he and a cat and the table all had names, and the fruit of his knowledge had opened his eyes to evil. He could see the prison where he had existed alone, shut out of the human race for twenty-seven years.

18   Welcome to my world, Ildefonso, I thought to myself. Let me show you all the miracles accomplished with symbols, all the bonds and ties between human beings, young and old, and even with those dead for centuries.

Exercise 3.1

Questions for Writing/Small-Group Discussion

1. How old is Ildefonso? What led you to your answer? _____

   _____

   _____

   _____

2. What is his problem/handicap? How do you know? _____

   _____

   _____

   _____

3. What evidence indicates a physical handicap that he is *not* suffering from?

   _____

   _____

   _____

   _____

4. What has his life been like to this point? _____

_____

_____

_____

5. What type of strategy has the teacher been using to teach him language? __

_____

_____

_____

6. How much success has the teacher had with him previously? _____

_____

_____

_____

7. What is the nature of the breakthrough he has just experienced? _____

_____

_____

_____

8. Find out who Helen Keller was, and why the reference to her is appropriate. Then look again at the passage describing Ildefonso's important break-through: "Yes, w-a-t-e-r and c-a-t *mean* something. And the cat-meaning in one head can join the cat-meaning in another's head just by tossing out a *cat*." How was Helen Keller's breakthrough similar to that of Ildefonso? How did it differ? _____

_____

_____

_____

_____

■ INFERENCE IN LITERATURE

One reason that students have difficulty understanding poetry, short stories, and novels is that creative literature makes real demands on our skill in drawing inferences. Modern authors especially do not often make direct statements about characters or themes. It is left to the reader to draw any conclusions or judgments based on the evidence in the text. In making inferences, we must pay close attention to how the characters are shown. We judge characters by what they do and say, how they react to other characters, by the choices they make, and by how the unfolding of the plot helps to reveal their values and the direction of their lives.

Gary Soto's *Living up the Street* is a remembrance of the author's growing up in the barrio of a California city. The following story, "Fear," details an encounter of the narrator with a fellow student. As you read, pay careful attention to details and descriptions that suggest meanings that are not directly stated.

Fear

by Gary Soto

1   A cold day after school. Frankie T., who would drown his brother by accident that coming spring and would use a length of pipe to beat a woman in a burglary years later, had me pinned on the ground behind a backstop, his breath sour as meat left out in the sun. *"Cabron,"* he called me and I didn't say anything. I stared at his face, shaped like the sole of a shoe, and just went along with the insults, although now and then I tried to raise a shoulder in a half-hearted struggle because that was part of the game.

2   He let his drool yo-yo from his lips, missing my feet by only inches, after which he giggled and called me names. Finally he let me up. I slapped grass from my jacket and pants, and pulled my shirt tail from my pants to shake out the fistful of dirt he had stuffed in my collar. I stood by him, nervous and red-faced from struggling, and when he suggested that we climb the monkey bars together, I followed him quietly to the kid's section of Jefferson Elementary. He climbed first, with small grunts, and for a second I thought of running but knew he would probably catch me—if not then, the next day. There was no way out of being a fifth grader—the daily event of running to teachers to show them your bloody nose. It was just a fact, like having lunch.

3   So I climbed the bars and tried to make conversation, first about the girls in our classroom and then about kickball. He looked at me smiling as if I had a camera in my hand, his teeth green like the underside of a rock, before he

---

Gary Soto, "Fear," from *Living up the Street* (Dell, 1985).

relaxed his grin into a simple gray line across his face. He told me to shut up. He gave me a hard stare and I looked away to a woman teacher walking to her car and wanted very badly to yell for help. She unlocked her door, got in, played with her face in the visor mirror while the engine warmed, and then drove off with blue smoke trailing. Frankie was watching me all along and when I turned to him, he laughed, "*Chale!* She can't help you, *ese.*" He moved closer to me on the bars and I thought he was going to hit me; instead he put his arm around my shoulder, squeezing firmly in friendship. "C'mon, chicken, let's be cool."

4   I opened my mouth and tried to feel happy as he told me what he was going to have for Thanksgiving. "My Mamma's got a turkey and ham, lots of potatoes, yams and stuff like that. I saw it in the refrigerator. And she says we gonna get some pies. Really, *ese.*"

5   Poor liar, I thought, smiling as we clunked our heads softly like good friends. He had seen the same afternoon program on TV as I had, one in which a woman in an apron demonstrated how to prepare a Thanksgiving dinner. I knew he would have tortillas and beans, a round steak maybe, and oranges from his backyard. He went on describing his Thanksgiving, then changed over to Christmas—the new bicycle, the clothes, the G.I. Joes. I told him that it sounded swell, even though I knew he was making it all up. His mother would in fact stand in line at the Salvation Army to come away hugging armfuls of toys that had been tapped back into shape by reformed alcoholics with veined noses. I pretended to be excited and asked if I could come over to his place to play after Christmas. "Oh, yeah, anytime," he said, squeezing my shoulder and clunking his head against mine.

6   When he asked what I was having for Thanksgiving, I told him that we would probably have a ham with pineapple on the top. My family was slightly better off than Frankie's, though I sometimes walked around with cardboard in my shoes and socks with holes big enough to be ski masks, so holidays were extravagant happenings. I told him about the scalloped potatoes, the candied yams, the frozen green beans, and the pumpkin pie.

7   His eyes moved across my face as if he were deciding where to hit me—nose, temple, chin, talking mouth—and then he lifted his arm from my shoulder and jumped from the monkey bars, grunting as he landed. He wiped sand from his knees while looking up and warned me not to mess around with him any more. He stared with such a great meanness that I had to look away. He warned me again and then he walked away. Incredibly relieved, I jumped from the bars and ran looking over my shoulder until I turned into my street.

8   Frankie scared most of the school out of its wits and even had the girls scampering out of view when he showed himself on the playground. If he caught us without notice, we grew quiet and stared down at our shoes until he passed after a threat or two. If he pushed us down, we stayed on the ground with our eyes closed and pretended that we were badly hurt. If he

riffled through our lunch bags, we didn't say anything. He took what he wanted, after which we sighed and watched him walk away peeling an orange or chewing big chunks of an apple.

9   Still, that afternoon when he called Mr. Koligian, our teacher, a foul name—we grew scared for him. Mr. Koligian pulled and tugged at his body until it was in his arms and then out of his arms as he hurled Frankie against the building. Some of us looked away because it was unfair. We knew the house he lived in: The empty refrigerator, the father gone, the mother in a sad bathrobe, the beatings, the yearnings for something to love. When the teacher manhandled him, we all wanted to run away. But instead we stared and felt shamed. Robert, Adele, Yolanda shamed; Danny, Alfonso, Brenda shamed; Nash, Margie, Rocha shamed. We all watched him flop about as Mr. Koligian shook and grew red from anger. We knew his house and, for some, it was the same one to walk home to: The broken mother, the indifferent walls, the refrigerator's glare which fed the people no one wanted.

Exercise 3.2

Write INF *for inference for any of the statements below that can be reasonably supported by evidence from the text. Then indicate the evidence or reasoning that led to your conclusion. Include paragraph numbers if applicable.*

1. _____   Despite occasional blowups, Frankie and the narrator are good friends.

   Evidence/reasoning: _____

   _____

2. _____   Frankie is a bully.

   Evidence/reasoning: _____

   _____

3. _____   The narrator really isn't afraid of Frankie.

   Evidence/reasoning: _____

   _____

4. _____   Frankie gets some of his ideas of the good things in life from T.V.

   Evidence/reasoning: _____

   _____

5. _____ Frankie is dangerous and unpredictable.

   Evidence/reasoning: _____

   _____

6. _____ The narrator and his friends try to survive their tormentor by being passive.

   Evidence/reasoning: _____

   _____

7. _____ Down deep Frankie is desperate to have a real friend.

   Evidence/reasoning: _____

   _____

8. _____ Frankie's mother cares nothing whatsoever about him.

   Evidence/reasoning: _____

   _____

9. _____ Frankie doesn't believe the narrator is telling the truth about his family's Thanksgiving dinner of ham with all the trimmings.

   Evidence/reasoning: _____

   _____

10. _____ Despite his fear of Frankie, the narrator has sympathy for him because he can relate to his home situation.

   Evidence/reasoning: _____

   _____

In "Fear," the narrator speaks directly to the reader, telling the sequence of events and describing the characters. At other times the techniques of authors are less direct. We might learn what a young or inexperienced character is thinking or we get self-justifications of characters who are either not aware of or who are dishonest about their own motives. In these kinds of stories, themes must be inferred, and readers may respond with different interpretations.

The story that follows demonstrates these latter techniques and thus requires very careful reading. The author, Dorothy West, is one of the foremost African-American writers. Her works span nearly seven decades; her most acclaimed novel, *The Wedding*, was published in 1995.

The Penny

Dorothy West

1   The little boy ran happily down the village street. His bunchy sweater and gaping shoes were inadequate to keep out the cold, but he felt nothing but joy. For the first time in weeks he had a penny to spend. His father had given it to him just five minutes before.

2   His father had brought home his piddling pay for his part-time job and dropped it into his mother's lap. His mother had counted it carefully with her customary sigh. As usual, there was never enough to last the week. Midway through the week there would not be food enough or fuel enough to carry them until next payday.

3   The little boy's stomach would growl in school. His face and faded shirt would show the scarcity of hot water and soap. His mother would leave her unheated flat and her empty kerosene heater and sit by the glowing heaters of her neighbors, gratefully gulping the coffee they gave her, and slyly pocketing the big, buttered slices of homemade bread. His father would beg a beer from some familiar at the bar to steel himself against the heartbreak of his wife and the hunger of his son. There was no joy in any hour of their day.

4   He was their husband and father. They had shared his good times. They loved him no less when his luck was bad. But his boy was so little, only six, and six was so young for sacrifices. Other boys had baseball bats and boxing gloves, and milk and butter in their bellies, and stout shoes and clean shirts, and pennies mixed with the marbles in their pockets.

5   The man could not remember the last time he had given the boy a penny to spend. It was surely in another and better world. To this pale creature with the pinched face and hollow eyes he had never given anything. The man had snatched a penny from the aproned lap of his wife and folded the boy's fingers over it. Instantly there had been a miraculous transformation. The gnome who clutched the penny had turned into a child.

6   And so the child raced toward the candy store, and his heart almost burst with happiness. There were beautiful things in the candy store. All the wonderful things the other kids pulled out of their pockets at recess. The things that could make a boy's mouth water with wanting. He could have his choice of any of these. He could show his penny to the shopkeeper and take as long as he liked to choose. He could stand outside and press his nose against the glass and not feel bad, for after a while he could go inside and put his penny on the counter. He could turn the knob of an ordinary door and walk straight into heaven.

7   The little boy's head was in the clouds. He did not know he had reached the curb. His feet slid into space. When he picked himself up, his hands were empty. His frantic eye saw the penny rolling toward the gutter. It vanished as he lunged. He limped back to the curb and sat down. A bruise was swelling on his cheek. His body was wrenched and sore. But just as he had not felt the cold, now he did not feel the pain. The penny, the round, shining penny, was gone. The end of the world has come at its bright beginning. The boy dropped his head on his knees and whimpered like a whipped puppy.

8   Miss Hester Halsey came down the street, walking in her prim way, with her nose, as always, a little disdainful. She had worked in the same office for twenty years and saved her money. She had no patience with people who were poor. They were simply shiftless. Miss Halsey saw the huddled figure of the boy. His back was to her, but she recognized his rags. He was the son of that worthless drunk and that lazy slattern. Miss Halsey's mouth grew grim. Her small, neat feet quickened their pace. Presently she stood over the boy. Delicately she touched him with her foot.

9   "Little boy?" His head jerked up. He scowled and snuffled. His grief was too immense for speech with this strange woman. He turned his face away and went on whimpering quietly. Miss Halsey saw the ugly bruise. She touched the boy with her foot again.

10   "Who hit you?" she asked in a soft, strained voice. The boy did not answer. "Your mother?" she urged. "Your father?"

11   The little boy was frightened. He could not have answered if he had wanted to. He moved crabwise along the curb. Miss Halsey moved along the curb with him. She did not move crabwise. She made a fluid movement after him. Her gloved hand touched his cheek. He winced and drew a sobbing breath.

12   "Does it hurt bad?" asked Miss Halsey eagerly. "Anyone who could beat a child …" her voice grew hoarse with righteousness, "ought to be reported to the proper authorities." She stooped, and her mouth was level with his ear. "Tell me, who did it, little boy?"

13   The boy took a quick, terrified look at her. Her burning eyes pulled him to his feet. He tried to escape, but his stiffening leg buckled. "Your leg, your leg, too," the relentless voice insisted. "Did they take a stick to you? Did they take a … a poker?"

14   The little boy felt as if he were drowning. This strange woman was pushing him down, down, and he was too tired to struggle. Once when he was three he had leaned too far over the rain barrel. He had fought his way to the surface, and his father had heard his cries. How he wanted the water to close over him to shut this woman out of sight and sound.

15   Feverishly Miss Halsey dug in her purse. She selected a coin, a shining penny, and held it out to him. "Look, little boy, a nice, new penny. Wouldn't you like a nice, new penny?" Once more he looked at her. His eyes were black with pleading. He did not want the penny. He only wanted to drown.

16   "You can have the penny," said Miss Halsey warmly, seeing the pleading look. "You can have it as soon as you tell me what happened. Poor little neglected boy, you'd be better off in a Home." Home, thought the little boy. If he drowned, he could never go back home. Tonight there would be fire and food. There would be hot water and a bath. He didn't want to drown. Oh, why didn't this lady let him go?

17   Miss Halsey was purring softly. "You can go and buy candy if I give you the penny. If you tell me what happened, you can go and buy candy." He could feel the water receding. She was going to let him go. She was going to give him a penny for candy. Everything would be as it was before. He stood up and smiled shyly at Miss Halsey. He was not afraid of her now. He felt happy and excited. Heaven was half a block away. In another minute he would enter it.

18   Miss Halsey let the penny lie in her open palm. The boy looked at it with an open mouth that began to moisten with wanting. Miss Halsey was as happy and excited as the boy. In a moment the long day would have some meaning. The dreary day of dull endeavor would end on a high note of moral victory.

19   "It was your father, wasn't it?" said Miss Halsey in a rich, full voice. "He came home drunk as usual and struck you with a poker. Your mother wasn't there to stop him. She was off gallivanting at some neighbors. You crawled as far as this corner, and I found you."

20   The thought of candy was driving him crazy. He was a timid little boy, but he could not restrain his hand any longer. The penny snuggled inside it, but Miss Halsey's fingers did not quite release it. He looked at her brightly, expectantly, ready to die for the penny.

21   "That's how it was, little boy, wasn't it?"

22   "Yes'm," he said joyously.

23   Miss Halsey released the penny. The little boy turned and scooted away. His leg was not sore anymore. He was not walking on earth anyway. He was walking on air. Miss Halsey continued down the street. She, too, was afloat in the clouds. She was thinking about the letter she would write to the minister.

24   In the whole town there were no two people happier than Miss Halsey and the little boy.

Exercise 3.3

Below are statements about "The Penny," followed by evidence that supposedly supports the inference. Decide if the inference is valid by asking these questions: Does the evidence really relate to the inference or does it actually support a different conclusion? Is there any other evidence that might point to a different con-

clusion? Check either Agree or Disgree for each and explain your decision. Include any additional evidence that supports your interpretation. Use paragraph numbers when possible. Study the example before completing the exercise.

Example

1. The little boy comes from an impoverished environment.

   Evidence: "The little boy's stomach would growl in school. His face and faded shirt would show the scarcity of hot water and soap."

   ___X___ Agree   _____ Disagree

   Explanation: Clearly the family is struggling to make ends meet. Other evidence (1, 2): "His bunchy sweater and gaping shoes were inadequate to keep out the cold....As usual, there was never enough to last the week."

---

1. The family is poor because the boy's mother mismanages the family's finances.

   Evidence: "Midway through the week there would not be food enough or fuel enough to carry them until next payday."

   _____ Agree   _____ Disagree

   Explanation: _____

   _____

   _____

2. The boy's mother is a lazy freeloader, not above stealing from others.

   Evidence: She would "sit by the glowing heaters of her neighbors, gratefully gulping the coffee they gave her, and slyly pocketing the big, buttered slices of homemade bread."

   _____ Agree   _____ Disagree

   Explanation: _____

   _____

   _____

3. The members of the family intensely hate each other.

   Evidence: "There was no joy in any hour of their day."

   _____ Agree   _____ Disagree

   Explanation: _____

   _____

   _____

4. The boy is greatly pleased by the father's gift of a penny.

   Evidence: "There had been a miraculous transformation. The gnome who clutched the penny had turned into a child."

   _____ Agree   _____ Disagree

   Explanation: _____

   _____

   _____

5. The boy had previously wanted things from the candy store, but couldn't buy them.

   Evidence: "He could stand outside and press his nose against the glass and not feel bad."

   _____ Agree   _____ Disagree

   Explanation: _____

   _____

   _____

6. The boy's parents had once worked in the same office as Miss Halsey but had been fired.

   Evidence: "She had worked in the same office for twenty years.... He was the son of that worthless drunk and that lazy slattern."

   _____ Agree   _____ Disagree

   Explanation: _____

   _____

   _____

7. Miss Halsey feels that the poor are totally responsible for their condition and lot in life.

   Evidence: "She had no patience with people who were poor. They were simply shiftless."

   _____ Agree   _____ Disagree

   Explanation: _____

   _____

   _____

8. The boy knows who Miss Halsey is, but doesn't want to talk to her.

   Evidence: "His grief was too immense for speech."

   _____ Agree   _____ Disagree

   Explanation: _____

   _____

   _____

9. Miss Halsey is trying to manipulate the boy by putting words into his mouth.

   Evidence: "'Who hit you?' she asked in a soft, strained voice. The boy did not answer. 'Your mother?' she urged. 'Your father?'"

   _____ Agree   _____ Disagree

   Explanation: _____

   _____

   _____

10. Miss Halsey is a righteous, moral, caring person.

    Evidence: "'Does it hurt bad?' asked Miss Halsey eagerly. 'Anyone who could beat a child ...' her voice grew hoarse with righteousness, 'ought to be reported to the proper authorities.'"

    _____ Agree   _____ Disagree

    Explanation: _____

    _____

    _____

11. Miss Halsey tries to kill the little boy by drowning him in the gutter.

Evidence: "The little boy felt as if he were drowning. This strange woman was pushing him down, down, and he was too tired to struggle."

_____ Agree   _____ Disagree

Explanation: _____

_____

_____

12. Miss Halsey's only motive in questioning the boy is to ensure his welfare.

Evidence: "'You can have the penny,' said Miss Halsey warmly.... 'Poor little neglected boy, you'd be better off in a Home.'"

_____ Agree   _____ Disagree

Explanation: _____

_____

_____

13. The boy would prefer to be in his own home, no matter how poor it was.

Evidence: "Home, thought the little boy.... Tonight there would be fire and food. There would be hot water and a bath."

_____ Agree   _____ Disagree

Explanation: _____

_____

_____

14. The little boy becomes convinced that Miss Halsey is a true friend.

Evidence: "He stood up and smiled shyly at Miss Halsey. He was not afraid of her now."

_____ Agree   _____ Disagree

Explanation: _____

_____

_____

15. Miss Halsey is a vicious busybody whose life gains meaning only in the pain of others.

    Evidence: "…the long day would have some meaning. The dreary day of dull endeavor would end on a high note of moral victory."

    _____ Agree   _____ Disagree

    Explanation: _____

    _____

    _____

16. The boy's bruises are the result of a vicious beating by his father.

    Evidence: "It was your father, wasn't it?" said Miss Halsey in a rich, full voice. "He came home drunk as usual and struck you with a poker."

    _____ Agree   _____ Disagree

    Explanation: _____

    _____

    _____

17. Miss Halsey is a brilliant detective who can figure out the truth.

    Evidence: "'That's how it was, little boy, wasn't it?' 'Yes'm,' he said joyously."

    _____ Agree   _____ Disagree

    Explanation: _____

    _____

    _____

18. The little boy doesn't realize the effect his words will have on his parents.

    Evidence: "Everything would be as it was before…. He was walking on air."

    _____ Agree   _____ Disagree

    Explanation: _____

    _____

    _____

19. Miss Halsey will try to have the little boy removed from his parents' custody.

    Evidence: "She, too, was afloat in the clouds. She was thinking about the letter she would write to the minister."

    _____ Agree   _____ Disagree

    Explanation: _____

    _____

    _____

20. Miss Halsey and the boy share the same kind of happiness because something has happened that will benefit everyone.

    Evidence: "In the whole town there were no two people happier than Miss Halsey and the little boy."

    _____ Agree   _____ Disagree

    Explanation: _____

    _____

    _____

■ CONTEXT VOCABULARY

There are better ways to improve vocabulary than to memorize lists of words. If you ever had a class that required this strategy, you may have done well when tested immediately after studying, but after three or four weeks you probably remembered very little. The truth is that we don't learn most of our words that way. As an infant first learning to talk, you didn't have a dictionary in your crib. Maybe you learned to point at that round thing that tasted good. When the thing wasn't in sight, you learned to say the magic word *cookie,* and a big person would bring it to you. You learned that a word is a **tool** that you come to value when you discover a need for it and are willing to practice with it. You cannot hope to learn new, often difficult, words without making them a part of yourself by (1) becoming aware of how you will be able to use the word, and (2) finding a way to put it to use.

This text will introduce you to two important ways of learning and remembering new and unfamiliar words. One of these techniques, which you will work with in Part II, is recognizing **word parts**—the smaller units of meaning (roots, prefixes, suffixes) that can combine to make complete words. This chapter will introduce another important use of inference in using **context clues** to figure out the meanings of words. Following the readings throughout this text, you will practice this skill and not only increase your vocabulary with these words but also develop a technique that you can apply to all your readings.

Using context clues will help you learn and remember vocabulary because you must think about the word, not just memorize a dictionary definition. You will also have to deal with some special problems many words present. For example, suppose you read this sentence: "We had not arranged to meet at a set hour."

To be sure of the exact meaning of *set*, you look the word up in your dictionary, only to find that the word takes up an entire page, can be used as a verb, adjective, or noun, and has many meanings under each. To answer your original question, "What does *set* mean?" you would first have to decide on its **part of speech** in this sentence. At this point you are already using the context— the situation, the environment in which something occurs—to decide that because of its placement between *a* and the noun *hour, set* was being used as an adjective. However your dictionary gives you nine different meanings for *set* as an adjective.

> **adj. 1** fixed or appointed in advance **2** established; prescribed as by author- ity **3** deliberate; intentional; purposeful **4** conventional; stereotyped; not spontaneous **5** fixed; motionless; rigid **6** a) resolute; determined b) obstinate **7** firm or hard in consistency **8** ready to begin some action **9** formed; built

Which one is it: intentional? motionless? built? Knowing the part of speech just isn't enough. You must look more closely at the context, not just the sentence with the word but at what goes before or after. Suppose the passage reads as follows:

> "We were planning to get together later in the evening, but we forgot one important thing. We had not arranged to meet at a set hour. Therefore, I ended up waiting two hours for the others."

With these clues—lack of planning, having to wait—we can now make a rational guess about the meaning of the word in its context: "fixed or appointed in advance."

You can often avoid having to stop to look up words by using the context clues to make an educated guess. When we first begin to read stories, we don't stop for every unfamiliar word. We let the story carry us along and we try to make intelligent guesses. After meeting a word on a few occasions, we build up a meaning for it, and at this point the word is in our recognition vocabulary. Later, the word becomes part of our writing and speaking vocabulary (our expres- sive vocabulary). Finally there will come a time when you will wonder how you ever got along without it.

Of course, no one is telling you to throw away your dictionary. There are many times when we must look up words.

- Sometimes there are no clear clues in the context—for example, with technical words or proper names.
- Sometimes words involve such difficult concepts that you cannot determine the meaning without using a dictionary.
- Even when good readers can make a reasonably confident guess, they often make note of the word so they can check for an exact meaning later.

Here are four useful types of clues to help you determine meaning from context.

SIMILARITY CLUES

Writers often use repetition for emphasis or clarity. As a result, two words or phrases that have much the same meaning sometimes appear in the same sentence. These clues are often in the form of **synonyms,** one-word equations in meaning. If you know one of the words, but not the other, you will still be able to determine the meaning of the unfamiliar term.

He proved to be very friendly; in fact, I have seldom met such a **congenial** host. (*congenial* = "friendly")

When I meet someone with that much knowledge in a field, I find that their **erudition** frightens me. (*erudition* = "great knowledge")

To say that he was talkative, even **garrulous,** would be no exaggeration. (*garrulous* = "very talkative")

Note, in the last example, how punctuation marks can work as a signal for a synonym or an equation phrase—commas, parentheses, and dashes can all be used for this purpose.

CONTRAST CLUES

Clues can also be negative equations. In situations involving contrast you often find an **antonym**—a word with a meaning opposite of another. If words are marked clearly as opposites by signal words like *but, however, in contrast,* and we know one of the words, we should be able to exchange a familiar word for the opposite.

John was very hard-working, but his brother was quite **indolent.** (*indolent* = opposite of "hard-working" = "lazy")

I expected truthfulness from a doctor; I was shocked by his **mendacity.** (*mendacity* = opposite of "truthfulness" = "deceit")

I felt only **antipathy**—no pity whatever—for the creature in the doorway. (*antipathy* = opposite of "pity" = "dislike")

One word of caution: contrast clues with negatives can be confusing, as shown in the following:

Some people feel he showed a lack of interest in life, but I myself never detected a hint of **apathy** in his attitude.

The contrast word *but* is canceled out by the word *never;* therefore, "lack of interest" means the same as "apathy." A substantial number of words and phrases function as useful signals of synonyms and antonyms. You were given a list of these in the section on comparison/contrast in Chapter 2.

EXAMPLE OR INSTANCE CLUES

Often the meaning of a noun that represents a group of things can be determined by one or more examples. Signal words such as *for example, for instance, to illustrate,* or *including* often help indicate the presence of a clue.

As part of his agreement with his parents, the boy was forced to make some **concessions.** He agreed to quit smoking and find a job. (The examples of things he was forced to do show that *concession* means "something given up or yielded.")

He finally got his **priorities** right; first came his wife and children, next his health, and finally his job. (*Priorities* are "things ranked in order of importance.")

He was definitely in favor of a **prohibition** against smoking and drinking. (Being **against** these examples indicates that *prohibition* must mean "a forbidding of an action; a ban.")

Many words in the language, both adjectives and nouns, are used to attribute qualities or characteristics to people, places, or things. For instance, "He is introverted" and "He is an introvert" say about the same thing. We use these words to represent conclusions or value judgments we have arrived at from our observations. Instances of behaviors or actions thus give us a clue to the meaning of an unknown descriptive word.

He was a real **introvert.** He refused to socialize with other students, preferring to bury his nose in a book by himself. (These behaviors would lead us to guess that an *introvert* is "one who directs his interests mainly toward himself, not others.")

Loreen defies her teachers and her parents. She is certainly a very **intractable** little girl. (Her actions lead us to decide that Loreen is "bratty" or "hard to control.")

Robert was arrested for robbing a gas station and a mini-market. I never suspected he had a tendency toward **larceny.** (Given his actions, we conclude that larceny means "theft.")

SITUATION CLUES

Sometimes we get clues to the meaning of a word from our own thinking processes. Using common sense or the overall logic of a situation allows us to narrow down the possible meanings of a word.

During her first semester Marisella's grades were excellent; **subsequently,** they dropped drastically.

The time sequence requires that subsequently must mean "following in time" because no grades could be given before the first semester.

Because hostilities had been started again by the enemy, our government had no choice but to **abrogate** the treaty.

By means of the logic of cause and effect and your knowledge of what the purpose of a treaty is, you would be able to figure out that *abrogate* must mean "to break" or "to cancel."

At times you need a certain amount of background information before you can make a good guess as to the meaning of a word.

Since we all know how much Conrad loves surfing, I find his desire to move to Minnesota **inexplicable.**

Someone uninformed on this country's geography would have no clue here. You would have to know the geography and climate (Minnesota is not near an ocean and its climate is much colder than California's) in order to guess that *inexplicable* means "puzzling" or "unexplainable."

Exercise 3.4

Use the context clues in the following sentences to determine the meaning of the word in italics. Circle the correct letter choice. Be prepared to explain how you figured out the definition.

1. Robert actually thinks that when Daylight Savings Time begins, the sun shines an hour longer. What an *ignoramus!*

   a. liar

   b. uninformed person

   c. bully

   d. comedian

2. Rudolpho studies hard, attends school regularly, and holds down a part-time job. I wish his brother was as *conscientious*.

   a. neurotic

   b. dependent

   c. governed by a sense of duty

   d. secure

3. All of the *media* sensationalize the news, but television is the worst offender.

   a. means of communication

   b. writers

   c. advertising agencies

   d. sponsors

4. The body builder kept staring contentedly at himself in the mirror in a *narcissistic* way.

   a. hypercritical

   b. self-loving

   c. analytical

   d. questioning

5. Several new stamps will be issued to *commemorate* the fiftieth anniversary of the end of World War II.

   a. criticize

   b. raise money for

   c. bring an end to

   d. honor the memory of

6. We thought that the mother would be very *distraught* at hearing of her husband's accident; however, she took the news quite calmly.

   a. extremely upset

   b. very angry

   c. disbelieving

   d. distrustful

7. After spending a night lost in the Rocky Mountains without a jacket, the child was found alive but suffering from *hypothermia*.

   a. heat stroke

  b. injuries from a fall

  c. snake bite

  d. low body temperature

8. John was in a real *quandary*. Although he needed time to finish his research paper, his boss expected him at work within the hour.

  a. muddy bog

  b. a place where stone is cut

  c. a perplexing situation

  d. a place for work and study

9. In this electronic age, a student who would prefer to go to a museum rather than watch television is a true *anomaly*.

  a. everyday occurrence

  b. unusual occurrence

  c. undocumented occurrence

  d. disappointing occurrence

10. It was refreshing to see students so excited, so *zealous* in doing their homework.

  a. enthusiastic

  b. careful

  c. sloppy

  d. upset

Exercise 3.5

One way to make a word part of your vocabulary is by writing a context sentence of your own. Take a look at each word in italics and at the definition that follows it. Before trying to write your sentence, visualize a situation in which the word could be used. "Situation clues" that might help you picture a way to use the word are given for you. The first one is done for you as a sample. These clues are general—you will need to think of specific examples. Make sure each sentence has specific details; it should clearly answer such questions as who, what, when, where, why, how. To test whether your sentence is a good context sen-

tence, ask yourself this: Would someone who doesn't know the word be able to guess the meaning from the clues in the sentence?

Example:

  strenuously: with great effort
  Situation clue: doing a difficult activity

Sentence: <u>The chain gang crew worked **strenuously** all afternoon to remove</u>

<u>the rocks from the road after the landslide.</u>

---

1. *elusive:* hard to get hold of; able to get away easily

   Situation clue: trying to grab something

   Sentence: _____

   _____

   _____

2. *dwindling:* slowly getting smaller

   Situation clue: a supply of something is getting used up

   Sentence: _____

   _____

   _____

3. *incarcerated:* put in jail

   Situation clue: somebody did something wrong; got caught

   Sentence: _____

   _____

   _____

4. *obligations:* duties

   Situation clue: can't do an activity you like because of things you must do

   Sentence: _____

   _____

   _____

5. *incredible:* unbelievable, hard to believe

Situation clue: somebody gives an excuse for not doing something

Sentence: _____

_____

_____

■ IMPLIED MAIN IDEAS

Earlier you were given some advice on identifying main ideas when they have no obvious signal clues: identify the topic, ask a specific question, form a hypothesis about which sentence is the topic sentence, and test it as you read by relating new information back to what has gone before. You were told that, if you could not confirm your hypothesis, you have either misread key signals and need to reread for a new hypothesis *or* the passage has a topical rather than an idea structure. However, another possibility exists: a passage can be given its unity by an **implied main idea** which is suggested rather than directly stated.

In a paragraph with an implied topic sentence, the details of the paragraph are all connected through a main idea, but the idea is not directly stated in one sentence. It is up to the reader to arrive at the main idea by seeing the unstated connection between the parts. As you read the paragraph below, note how the details reveal a connection:

> Alfredo is polite and attentive to his teachers. He cooperates with other children and works well in group situations. At home he helps his parents by watching his little sister and often reads to her. Last month he began an early morning paper route, which provides him with expense money.

The paragraph's general topic is obviously Alfredo and, as you read further, the topic narrows to report different examples of his behavior. To arrive at the main idea, ask yourself, Which of the following could I conclude about Alfredo from these details?

1. Alfredo's behavior is the result of excellent home discipline.
2. Alfredo is a conscientious, well-mannered boy.
3. Alfredo's sister is as well-behaved as he is.
4. Alfredo is a careless and thoughtless young man.

Obviously we would have to reject numbers 1 and 3. Though both might be true, the passage does not give us any solid information about ideas of either causation or comparison. What we do have are examples from school and home life that would lead us to attribute character traits to Alfredo, as expressed by choices 2 and 4. Our experiences in life have given us enough of a common background that we would agree that the supporting examples show positive behaviors. We would thus infer from the information received that number 2—"Alfredo is a conscientious, well-mannered boy"—is the best choice. One good test of a workable implied main idea is to put the sentence into the paragraph, usually at the beginning. It should clearly control all the supporting details.

> **Alfredo is a conscientious, well-mannered boy.** Alfredo is *polite and attentive to his teachers.* He *cooperates with other children* and *works well in group situations.* At home he *helps his parents* by watching his little sister and often reads to her. Last month he *began an early morning paper route,* which provides him with expense money.

Since all the details do clearly support the idea, your inference has been correct.

Implied main ideas are thus often a matter of **pattern completion**—inferring an unstated cause of an effect, for example, or determining an implied opinion from a number of stated reasons. In the example above, the nature of the details led us to complete the pattern of description/support. Implied main ideas can also frequently be in the form of listing phrases such as "several types of" or "a number of factors." This occurs when, as in the following example, we have compound main idea elements.

> Why is franchising so popular? For one thing, when you invest in a franchise, you know you are getting a viable business, one that has "worked" many times before. If the franchise is well established, you get the added benefit of instant name recognition. Besides, when it comes to marketing and advertising, the things that most businesses don't have time for, the franchise company does that for you. An independent hamburger stand can't afford a national television advertising campaign, but McDonald's, Burger King, and Wendy's can.
> (Bovee and Thill, *Business in Action: Step into the World of Opportunity in the 21st Century,* Pearson Education, Inc., p. 93)

The question posed in the first sentence indicates a pattern of cause/effect; we can infer that the paragraph will explain why franchises have become popular. However, the question is not fully answered in the second sentence, which begins a list of details (note the signal phrase "For one thing"). Further details are indicated by the signal words "added" and "Besides." Our implied main idea, therefore, must contain a listing phrase that will include all of these:

Franchising has become popular for several reasons.

To test our hypothesis, we can place the sentence back in the paragraph, in this case after the question:

> Why is franchising so popular? *Franchising has become popular for several reasons.* For one thing, when you invest in a franchise....

The sentence answers the initial question and provides the paragraph with a logical framework; we could conclude therefore that our implied main idea is correct.

In some paragraphs the main idea is directly stated, but the major parts of the idea statement will be stretched out over two or even more sentences, often separated by minor detail. These **divided main ideas** are very common in idea patterns with many elements, like opinion/reason, problem/solution, comparison/contrast, or cause/effect, but they can occur in any pattern. When you wish to state the main idea of reading material with a divided main idea, you must combine essential information into a single main idea statement. This may require minor changes in signal words or sentence structure.

> For presidential elections, candidates usually establish the agenda of policy issues. By emphasizing issues they think will resonate with the public and reflect favorably upon themselves, candidates pressure the media to cover these rather than the issues that do not rebound to their credit. **On the other hand,** the media usually establish the agenda of nonpolicy issues, involving candidates' personality and behavior. The media are able to set the agenda for nonpolicy issues because these are more likely to catch the public's fantasy.
>
> (Welch et al., *American Government,* 4th ed., 237)

The phrase "on the other hand" clearly indicates that we have a main idea of contrast; the first and the next to last sentences are general statements of what that main idea is. To state the main idea, we merge the two sentences into one (note the change of "on the other hand" to "but"):

> For presidential elections, candidates usually establish the agenda of policy issues, **but** the media set the agenda for nonpolicy issues.

Exercise 3.6

As you read the paragraphs—all unified by implied main ideas—try to see the connections between the details. Circle the letter of the sentence that is the best statement of the implied main idea of the paragraph. Identifying which kind of idea is controlling the paragraph can often help you in selecting the correct answer. To test your choice, reread the paragraph with your choice included to see if the sentence gives the paragraph a clearer unity.

1. Some parents are aware that they are mistreating a child but are unable to stop. Other abusive parents literally hate their children or are disgusted by them. The child's sloppiness, diapers, crying, or needs are unbearable to the parent. Often these parents expect the child to love them and make them happy. When the child (who is usually under 3 years old) cannot meet such unrealistic demands, the parent reacts with lethal anger. In addition, abusive mothers are more likely to believe that their children are acting *intentionally* to annoy them.

   (Coon, *Introduction to Psychology,* 7th ed., 422)

a. Few children are severely abused by their parents.

b. Parents of abused children were probably victims of abuse themselves.

c. Abusive parents show a variety of negative behaviors and attitudes.

d. Children under three are the most at-risk group.

Kind of idea: _____

2. Our current health care system is a crazy quilt of government and private funding. In itself that is not bad. However, in our current system only the elderly and some of the very poor have access to government aid. Many non-elderly poor have no access to health care at all because they can't afford it. Rapidly increasing costs are also making it difficult for businesses and middle-income people to cope. And even those covered by government programs find they must pay for a large amount of their care themselves, or in the case of Medicaid, find that they cannot get convenient, high quality care at all (many private physicians will not take Medicaid patients at all).

(Welch et al., *American Government,* 4th ed., 500)

a. Government programs have solved most of the problems of the health care system.

b. Our health care system is bad because government gets in the way of private funding.

c. Not all segments of our society are equally served by our health care system.

d. Private physicians should not be allowed to turn patients away.

Kind of idea: _____

3. Our society associates excellence with being Number 1. However, the data shows that competition—some students succeeding and other failing—actually impedes learning. David Johnson, a social psychologist and education professor at the University of Minnesota, noted the effectiveness of team learning by asserting that there is almost nothing that American education has seen that compares with its level of empirical support. Achievement and attitude of students are improved through cooperative learning.

(Lefton, *Psychology,* 5th ed., 366)

a. Being Number 1 has positive and negative sides.

b. In cooperative learning, no student is ever allowed to fail.

c. No students at the University of Minnesota prefer cooperative learning.

d. In education, cooperative learning is more effective than competition.

Kind of idea: _____

4. Immigration critics charge that newcomers take jobs away from people who are already here. They also charge that immigrant labor lowers wages because immigrants will work for less. In contrast, others argue that newcomers have little effect because immigrants take jobs that others do not want. Still others point out that immigrants might actually increase employment by making it possible for some industries to hire low-wage workers rather than move their operations to Third World nations to stay competitive.

(Welch et al., *American Government*, 4th ed., 9)

   a. There are a number of negative effects that immigration has on employment.

   b. Immigration has had a positive effect in keeping employers competitive.

   c. The truth is that immigration has actually little if any effect on employment.

   d. People have positive and negative views on the effects of immigration on jobs.

   Kind of idea: _____

5. In elementary school, developmentally advanced girls tend to have less prestige among peers. Presumably, this is because they are larger and heavier than their classmates. By junior high, however, early development includes secondary sexual characteristics. This leads to a more positive body image, greater peer prestige, and adult approval. In contrast, later-maturing girls have the possible advantage of usually growing taller and thinner than early-maturing girls. Other relevant findings are that early-maturing girls date sooner and are more independent and more active in school; they are also more often in trouble at school.

(Coon, *Introduction to Psychology*, 7th ed., 425)

   a. For girls, there are advantages and disadvantages to late and early maturing.

   b. Early-maturing girls experience more problems than late-maturing girls.

   c. Late-maturing girls are generally more successful in later life.

   d. Most elementary school girls are overweight.

   Kind of idea: _____

6. Bulimia nervosa is an eating disorder characterized by binge eating followed by purging. The ratio of female to male bulimics is 10 to 1. Researchers theorize that women more readily than men believe that fat is bad and thin is beautiful. Women of higher socioeconomic classes are at greater risk of

becoming bulimic, as are professionals whose weight is directly related to achievement, such as dancers, athletes, and models. Disharmonious family life and maladjusted parents appear to increase the likelihood of bulimia. Bulimics also have lower self-esteem than people who eat normally, and they may have experienced some kind of clinical depression in the past.

(Lefton, *Psychology,* 5th ed., 355)

   a. Almost all bulimics are involved in the entertainment business.

   b. Men run little risk of bulimia.

   c. A number of factors increase the risk of bulimia.

   d. Bulimics come from dysfunctional families.

   Kind of idea: _____

7. People with an internal locus of control feel a need to control their environment. They are more likely to engage in preventive health measures and dieting than are external people. College students characterized as internal are more likely than others to profit from psychotherapy and to show high academic achievement. In contrast, people with an external locus of control believe they have little control over their lives. A college student characterized as external may attribute a poor grade to a lousy teacher, feeling there was nothing he or she could have done to get a good grade.

(Lefton, *Psychology,* 5th ed., 449)

   a. People with a need to control their environment are more health and diet conscious.

   b. People with an internal locus of control differ from those with an external one.

   c. College students characterized as internal have little control of their lives.

   d. Both internal and external college students may be discriminated against on grades.

   Kind of idea: _____

8. Changing attitudes, and ultimately behavior, can be difficult if people have well-established habits (which often come with advancing age) or are highly motivated in the opposite direction. Consider attitudes toward seat belts. Although people believe in the effectiveness of seat belts and hold positive attitudes about using them, few people use them all the time. Mittal (1988) showed that getting people to use seat belts takes more than developing positive attitudes; it also takes instilling a new habit. Mittal argues that the more

often people use seat belts, the more likely they will be to use them in the future. Thus, education and devices to promote remembering (such as warning buzzers) can be helpful.

(Lefton, *Psychology,* 5th ed., 579)

    a. Changing attitudes can be difficult but education and memory devices can be helpful.

    b. Attitudes toward seat belts have been changed in several ways.

    c. Changing attitudes is difficult for the elderly and those with established habits.

    d. People do not always follow their beliefs in protecting their safety.

    Kind of idea: _____

9. Gum disease is three times more common among smokers than among nonsmokers. Smokers also lose significantly more teeth than do nonsmokers, despite efforts to practice good oral hygiene. Smokers are also likely to use more medications than are nonsmokers. Nicotine and the other ingredients in cigarettes interfere with the metabolism of drugs: nicotine speeds up the process by which the body uses and eliminates drugs, so that medications become less effective. The smoker may therefore have to take a higher dosage of a drug or take it more frequently.

(Donatelle, *Access to Health,* 7th ed., 363–364)

    a. Smokers are more likely to have tooth and gum problems than nonsmokers.

    b. Smokers use more medications and the medications are less effective.

    c. Nicotine speeds up the elimination of drugs, so that a smoker may take higher dosages.

    d. Smoking has several harmful effects upon people.

    Kind of idea: _____

10. Some groups in society are advantaged and others are disadvantaged. The former work to perpetuate their advantages while the latter sometimes organize to protest and change the system they consider unfair. But how can these persons work to change the system if they are self-defined as powerless? A first step is legitimate, polite protest which usually takes the form of voting, petitions, or writing to public officials. A second option is to use impolite, yet legitimate forms of protest (for example, peaceful demonstrations, picket lines, boycotts, and marches). The third alternative, used when others fail, is to use illegitimate forms of protest (for example, civil disobedience, riots, bombings, and guerrilla warfare).

(Eitzen and Zinn, *In Conflict and Order,* 7th ed., 61)

a. There are several reasons why advantaged groups perpetuate their advantages.

b. There are several solutions to the problem of being disadvantaged.

c. Disadvantaged groups organize to protest and change an unfair system.

d. Impolite and illegitimate protest has proved to be the most effective form of protest.

Kind of idea: _____

Part B

Below are five paragraphs on the topic of the great witch hunts of the second half of the sixteenth and early seventeenth centuries. Follow the same directions as for Part A above.

(Kagan, Ozment, and Turner, *Western Heritage,* Vol. 1, 5th ed., 522–524)

1. Possession of magical powers, for good or ill, made one an important person within village society. Not surprisingly, claims to such powers most often were made by the people most in need of security and influence, namely, the old and the impoverished, especially single or widowed women. Witch beliefs in village society may also have been a way of defying urban Christian society's attempts to impose its laws and institutions on the countryside. From this perspective, village Satanism became a fanciful substitute for an impossible social revolt, a way of spurning the values of one's new masters. It is also possible, although unlikely, that witch beliefs in rural society had a foundation in local fertility cults, whose semipagan practices, designed to ensure good harvests, may have acquired the features of diabolical witchcraft under Church persecution.

   a. Widowed and single women gained importance by possessing magical powers.

   b. There are several explanations for the formation of witch beliefs in villages.

   c. Witch beliefs played several roles in defying Church authority.

   d. Satanism was a way of revolting socially, while promoting fertility cults.

   Kind of idea: _____

2. Popular belief in magic was the essential foundation of the great witch hunts of the sixteenth and seventeenth centuries. Had ordinary people not believed that certain gifted individuals could aid or harm others by magical means, and had they not been willing to make accusations, the hunts could never have occurred. Yet the contribution of learned society was equally great. The Christian clergy also practiced magic, that of the holy sacraments, and the

exorcism of demons had been one of their traditional functions within society. Fear of demons and the Devil, which the clergy actively encouraged, allowed the clergy to assert their moral authority over people and to enforce religious discipline and conformity.

   a. Belief in magic by both the ordinary people and the clergy underlay the witch hunts.

   b. There were several reasons why the clergy practiced magic.

   c. A popular belief in magic or willingness to make accusations created the witch hunts.

   d. The Christian clergy practiced forms of magic but made no accusations.

   Kind of idea: _____

3. A good 80 percent of the victims of witch hunts were women, the vast majority between forty-five and sixty years of age and single. This fact has suggested to some that misogyny fueled the witch hunts. Based in male hatred and sexual fear of women, and occurring at a time when women threatened to break out from under male control, witch hunts, it is argued, were simply woman hunts. Older single women may, however, have been vulnerable for more basic social reasons. They were a largely dependent social group in need of public assistance and natural targets for the peculiar "social engineering" of the witch hunts. Some accused witches were women who sought to protect and empower themselves within their communities by claiming supernatural powers.

   a. Misogyny, based in male hatred and sexual fear of women, fueled the witch hunts.

   b. Most victims of the witch hunts were dependent women needing social assistance.

   c. The reasons for the witch hunts were purely social.

   d. Older, single women were the most likely targets of witch hunts for several reasons.

   Kind of idea: _____

4. It may be, however, that gender played a largely circumstantial role. Because of their economic straits, more women than men laid claim to the supernatural powers that made them influential in village society. For this reason, they found themselves on the front lines in disproportionate numbers when the Church declared war against all who practiced magic without its blessing. Also, the involvement of many of these women in midwifery associated them with the

deaths of beloved wives and infants and thus made them targets of local resentment and accusations. Both the Church and their neighbors were prepared to think and say the worst about these women. It was a deadly combination.

    a. The Church declared war against all who practiced magic or midwifery.

    b. Gender played a circumstantial role because of the economic straits of women.

    c. Along with gender, other reasons made women a target of the witch hunts.

    d. Because midwives were responsible for the death of children, the Church and their neighbors hated them.

    Kind of idea: _____

5. Why did the great witch panics occur in the second half of the sixteenth and early seventeenth centuries? The misfortune created by religious division and warfare were major factors. The new levels of violence exacerbated fears and hatreds and encouraged scapegoating. But political self-aggrandizement also played a role. As governments expanded and attempted to control their realms, they, like the Church, wanted to eliminate all competition for the loyalty of their subjects. Secular rulers as well as the pope could pronounce their competitors "devilish." Some argue that the Reformation was responsible for the witch panics. Having weakened the traditional religious protections against demons and the Devil, while at the same time portraying them as still powerful, the Reformation is said to have forced people to protect themselves by executing perceived witches.

    a. A combination of factors led to the occurrence of the great witch panics.

    b. The great witch panics occurred due to religious division, warfare, and scapegoating.

    c. The Reformation caused the witch panics by forcing people to protect themselves by executing perceived witches.

    d. Expanding governments, like the Church, wanted to eliminate all competition for the loyalty of their subjects.

    Kind of idea: _____

The following article portrays the situation of an at-risk single-parent family in a major U.S. city. As you read, try to make some inferences regarding what attitude towards the participants the author wants the reader to share, and what sort of action—if any—is recommended for their situation.

Tasha's Story

by Linda Ellerbee

1   Tasha loves her children. This is not in question. Tasha holds Patik and Felicia, ages 2 and 4, close to her, pulling their heads to hers smiling, singing the Barney song, "I love you ... you love me ..."

2   Her two older children, Robert and Honree ("I was 13 when I had him," says Tasha. "What did I know about spelling a French name?") are helping women lay out doughnuts, sandwiches and loaves of bread on a table set up on a sidewalk in inner city Baltimore.

3   The food is for giving away to hungry people. It has been donated to an organization which does that, and more. For four days, Tasha and her children have stayed in a shelter operated by this organization. While food is being laid out, a taxi pulls up, carrying a woman and a little boy. Both have been beaten by the boy's father. They, too, are looking for shelter.

4   Honree, at 8, the oldest of Tasha's children, watches the women giving away food, then asks if he, too, may have a pair of thin, white rubber gloves the women wear to handle food. The next time someone approaches the table, Honree is right there.

5   "May I help you?" he says. "You can have one sandwich, a doughnut and three loaves of bread, if you want to. May I get it for you? Here, will you sign this?" A man takes a second sandwich. "Please," says Honree, "there isn't enough. You can have only one sandwich." The man faces down this dignified boy and after a couple of beats, returns the second sandwich.

6   For several hours, Honree runs the free food table. He is polite and firm. When no one is wanting food he plays with his brothers and sisters and with the little boy who arrived by taxi, whose mother is inside the shelter, sleeping. But when someone approaches the table, Honree rushes to put on his food-handler gloves. He means to do it right.

7   Tasha has laid Patik down for his nap. Patik sleeps curled on a blanket on the sidewalk. His sweet baby face carries in it all the possibilities in the world. He does not yet know how limited his are.

8   Meanwhile, Tasha answers questions from the white, middle-class women who have come to help distribute food, only to find an 8-year-old boy doing it better.

9   "My own mother was a junkie," says Tasha. "She's been clean for six years now. She made me go to a parenting program for a year. My children's

Linda Ellerbee, "Tasha's Story," written by award-winning TV producer and best-selling author Linda Ellerbee, appeared in the July 1995 issue of the *Liberal Opinion*.

fathers? Two are dead from drugs. The other two, they don't do anything for the kids. Nothing at all. Yeah, I did drugs. I'm in the program now. AA, you know?"

10   Tasha looks at Felicia, who, at 4, is already beautiful. "I got to do what I can to make sure her life is different. I don't want her to be 13 and make the choices I made. Or only have the choices I had. But it's hard. I can't get a good job because I can't get my GED because I can't get child care. Actually, I can't get any kind of job until I can work out the child-care thing. I'm getting a place to live next Monday. The social worker called and said we'd go look at it. I told her I don't have to look at it. If it's got a roof and walls and locks on the door and windows and a toilet that flushes, I'll take it."

11   Tasha's children play with one another, and with others. Robert and Felicia sing a song about a rabbit and smile at everybody. Their smiles can light a whole day. They hug people, too, probably because they have been hugged. Honree works the food table. It seems clear he's been helping his mother take care of the smaller kids. This is an intelligent boy, alert, interested, quick, kind. One wants to do something. Something that will give Honree his chance. Something that will give Tasha an opportunity to give Honree—and Robert and Felicia and Patik—a chance.

12   Something.

13   One thinks of politics. But politics is theory and politicians take too long to do anything. Tasha, Patik, Felicia, Robert, and Honree are not theory—they are people—and they don't have too long.

14   Two men, old and wasted, approach the free food table. The sandwiches are all gone, Honree tells them. Tasha looks up and seeing the old men, takes two sandwiches which had been given to her children and says, "Here. Take these. My kids got fed last night. They're not as hungry as you."

Exercise 3.7

Write **INF** *for inference for any of the statements below that can be reasonably supported by evidence from the text.*

1. _____   Tasha's family is homeless.

2. _____   The children's fathers work at the shelter.

3. _____   Robert and Honree have been beaten by their fathers.

4. _____   Tasha's children have received some love and affection at home.

5. _____   Tasha is not very choosy about the kind of house they might move into.

6. _____   Honree is employed by the shelter to dispense food.

7. _____   Honree is determined to conduct things by the rules.

8. _____   The food giveaway is being conducted by a government agency.

9. _____   Tasha has been "clean" of drugs for six years.

10. _____   The author is not very optimistic about the future of Tasha and her children.

Comprehension Questions

Circle the best letter choice for the multiple choice questions below.

1. Which statement is the implied main idea of "Tasha's Story"?

   a. The welfare system has made too many people in America irresponsible.

   b. We must find some solution, other than a political one, to help families at risk.

   c. The problem of homelessness, single parent families, and what to do about it.

   d. Nothing can really be done to help Tasha and her family.

2. Tasha says she can't get a good job because she

   a. has no car.

   b. doesn't have the necessary education.

   c. needs child care.

   d. all of the above

   e. both *a* and *b*

   f. both *b* and *c*

3. How many dependent children does Tasha have?

   a. 2

   b. 3

   c. 4

   d. 5

4. Honree is described as

   a. dignified.

   b. intelligent.

    c. kind.

    d. all of the above

5. Tasha's children have

    a. one father.

    b. two fathers.

    c. three fathers.

    d. four fathers.

6. Honree gives out the food

    a. because he wants some for himself.

    b. politely, according to the rules.

    c. rudely and grudgingly.

    d. because his mother ordered him to.

7. The author makes a direct plea for help from

    a. local government.

    b. state government.

    c. the federal government.

    d. none of the above

8. Tasha's age is

    a. under 20.

    b. between 20 and 23.

    c. between 24 and 27.

    d. over 28.

9. Through her descriptions, we can infer that the author wants us to

    a. feel sympathy for the children, but not Tasha.

    b. feel sympathy for Tasha and her children.

    c. feel sympathy for Tasha's family and for the fathers of her children.

    d. recognize that the entire family has gotten what it deserves.

10. We can infer from the incident in the last paragraph that

    a. Tasha is indifferent to the needs of her children.

    b. Tasha's children really have more than most children.

c. the old men are more deserving than Tasha's children.

d. people need to look out for and share with one another.

Main Idea Pattern

Ellerbee's article consists mainly of descriptions and quotations, but it also contains the elements of the problem/solution pattern. Fill out the information in the pattern by referencing direct evidence from the article and by drawing inferences.

Problem: _____

_____

_____

Causes: _____

_____

_____

Effects: _____

_____

_____

Solution: _____

_____

_____

CHAPTER REVIEW

In the blanks below write either the word implied *or* inferred.

1. The teacher's frown at the start of class _____
   that the students had not done very well on the test that was about to be handed back.

2. When we saw the team get off the bus, silent and downcast, we _____
   _____ that they had lost the game.

3. When the moving van pulled up to our neighbor's house, we _____
   _____ that they had decided to move.

4. The smirk on the face of the child as it licked the ice cream cone _____
   _____ that the child felt it had got the better of its parents.

Circle the correct letter choice for questions 5–10.

5. "Jana is proficient in math; she gets an *A* every term." *Proficient* means:

    a. unmotivated.

    b. skilled.

    c. discouraged.

    d. graded too easily.

6. The kind of clue given above is one of

    a. example.

    b. contrast.

    c. similarity.

    d. definition.

7. "Charity contributions have been very sluggish this year. In contrast, last year at this time contributors were highly active." *Sluggish* most likely means

    a. profitable.

    b. unpredictable.

    c. slow moving.

    d. confident.

8. The kind of clue above is one of

    a. example.

    b. situation.

    c. equation.

    d. contrast.

9. "The screaming child's parents remained adamant. Throughout the child's tantrum they were unyielding in their refusal to let him have the candy." *Adamant* means

    a. unreasonable.

    b. firm.

    c. cruel.

    d. unhappy.

10. The kind of clue above is one of

    a. example.

    b. situation.

    c. similarity.

    d. contrast.

1. *Look for an in-depth article in a current newspaper or magazine on a topic which catches your interest and creates an emotional response* by making you angry or sad, or by making you laugh, or by causing you to experience some combination of these feelings.

2. *Ask who, what, when, where, why, and how questions about the content of the article.* Then, write an accurate summary of the main points in your own words (you will be given more information on summarizing in a later chapter). Your summary should be about 175 words in length.

3. *Respond to the subject matter by explaining your feelings about the topic, or by relating it to some personal experience of your own.* Make this part about the same length as the summary section.

4. *Be sure you include the article—or a copy of it—when you submit your paper.*

5. *See if you can find in the article at least five vocabulary words whose meanings you are unsure of.* Circle, underline, or highlight the five words in the article. For each word, determine its part of speech as it is used in the sentence. Make a guess as to its meaning in the context. Then look the words up in the dictionary. For each entry do the following:

   a. Define the word as it is used in the article.

   b. Write a context sentence of your own using the word. Visualize a situation that might provide a context for the word. Try to use a clear clue.

A good test for your sentence is to see whether someone unfamiliar with the word could likely guess its meaning from the way you used it.

Reading for Structure: The Organization of Ideas

Recognizing patterns enables readers to understand the organization of reading material, from a paragraph to a book, and to realize that writing is often built of smaller structures within larger ones. An effective reader is one who quickly and accurately recognizes main ideas and the patterns through which they are conveyed. This enables the reader to tell major from minor details, to map or outline structures, and to recall important material at test time—skills that are essential to joining fully in academic dialogue.

CHAPTER PREVIEW

In this chapter you will

- Learn how to recognize and predict organizational structure
- Illustrate the structure of paragraphs using a variety of organizational maps
- Identify common methods of development used by authors
- Understand how subpatterns are used to development a main pattern
- Work with subdivided and multiparagraph units

Y ou have learned that main ideas are developed by more specific material, the supporting details. These can be major details (very important) or minor details (of lesser importance). It becomes easier to identify major details and to understand their relationships when we recognize that major details are often typical elements of specific idea types. Some idea patterns have relatively fixed components: problem/solution, opinion/reason, and time sequence. Others are more flexible and can take a variety of shapes: e.g., cause/effect, description/support, and comparison/contrast.

RECOGNIZING AND MAPPING ORGANIZATIONAL PATTERNS

Recognizing the idea type is extremely important because it lets us make a reasonable **prediction** about the kind of detail to follow and the likely manner in which it will be organized. This recognition, in turn, focuses our attention on which details in the text (the "important" ideas) need to be highlighted and annotated.

As an example, take a main idea like the following:

To change a baby's diaper, follow these simple steps.

Recognizing this sentence as a time sequence (process) idea, along with noting a listing phrase ("these simple steps"), would lead us to predict with some certainty that the passage will be organized by enumerating the sequence detail (the steps) involved in the overall process. A good reading strategy would be to look for signal words for each step and annotate the text margins—for example, with numbers corresponding to stages or steps.

Traditional outlines are effective, especially for topical material, but an alternative analytic tool known variously as **idea maps** or **mind maps** can often give you a better mental picture of the organizational pattern of paragraphs, a passage, or even a chapter. You have already been introduced briefly to some types of idea maps—spider and pinwheel maps for topical materials and cartwheel maps for main idea paragraphs.

Such maps help you to visualize how the various parts connect. By analyzing paragraphs and passages, and completing pattern maps that reveal their organization, you will sharpen your strategies in note taking and studying and will strengthen your effort to become a contributing partner in academic dialogue. Following are some samples of common kinds of mind maps. Although there is usually a typical idea map associated with a particular idea, some idea types adapt to more than one kind of map.

UMBRELLA MAPS

Umbrella maps work well to support a broad main idea developed by specific details that can be presented in more or less random order. Support may include one or more examples/illustrations and/or specific detail such as historical facts, statistics, expert opinions, or scientific studies.

DESCRIPTION/SUPPORT

A descriptive pattern contains a main idea generalization about traits ("Marco is very bright"), behaviors ("My sister studies very hard for tests"), or significant actions ("Paula has contributed time and money to a number of local charities"), with appropriate support.

> One of the most striking characteristics of schizophrenics is the display of inappropriate affect—emotional responses. A patient with schizophrenia may become depressed and cry when her favorite food falls on the floor, yet laugh hysterically at the death of a close friend or relative. Some patients display no emotion (either appropriate or inappropriate) and seem incapable of experiencing a normal range of feeling. Their emotional range is constricted or *flat*. They show blank, expressionless faces, even when presented with a deliberately provocative remark or situation. Other patients exhibit *ambivalent* affect. They go through a wide range of emotional behaviors in a brief period, seeming happy one moment and dejected the next.
>
> (Lefton, Psychology, 5th ed., 524)

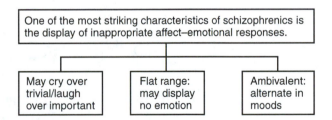

CAUSE/EFFECT

When the main idea is a direct statement of cause and effect, followed by examples, an umbrella map is effective. The map may include directional arrows to indicate cause-effect relationships.

The ability to engage in verbal behavior confers decided advantages on our species. Through listening and reading, we can profit from the experiences of others, even from those of people who died long ago. Through talking and writing, we can share the results of our own experiences. We can request from other people specific behaviors and information that are helpful to us. We can give information to other people so that their behavior will change in a way that benefits them (or us).

(Carlson and Buskist, Psychology, 5th ed., 303)

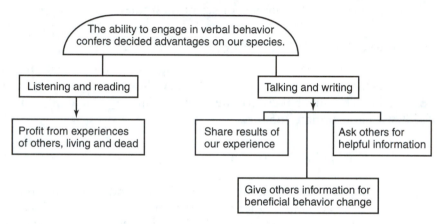

◼️ ENUMERATION MAPS

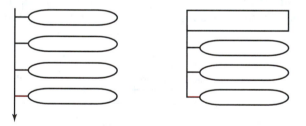

Maps like these are highly effective for graphically representing materials organized by listing phrases ("there are several reason why") along with other signal words showing items in a list (first, next, 1,2,3). Sequence arrows up or down are useful for showing the directions of time. Often dates or a period of years will be used to label units of time.

TIME SEQUENCE

The main elements here are the divisions we create in the flow of time. We divide narrative action into beginnings, middles and ends, using signals words and phrases ("*First* he calmed the dog, *then* finally freed him"). We create divisions occupying chunks of time to show steps in a process, phases or stages in growth, or eras and ages in history.

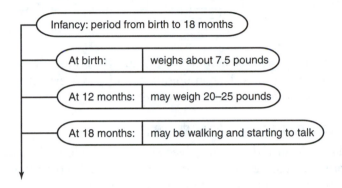

OPINION/REASON

The elements of this pattern include a position on an issue—the opinion that something should be believed, valued, or done—and a list of reasons given in support.

> The Founders opposed a "direct democracy" in which the will of the people becomes law. Some city-states of ancient Greece and medieval Europe had direct democracies but could not sustain them. The Founders thought that a large country would have even less ability to do so because people could not be brought together in one place in order to act. The Founders also believed that human nature was such that people could not withstand the passions of the moment and would be swayed by a demagogue to take unwise action. Eventually, democracy would collapse into tyranny.
>
> (Welch et al., *American Government,* 4th ed., 31)

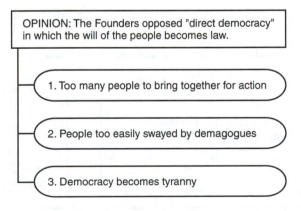

■ RELATIONSHIP MAPS

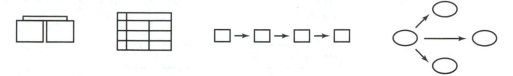

Relationship maps help us to visualize the connections in idea patterns with several components. Depending on the idea pattern, these maps may incorporate blocks, grids, diagrams, or even drawings.

COMPARISON/CONTRAST

This pattern always involves at least two elements—i.e., objects, ideas, viewpoints, qualities, or processes that are being compared or contrasted. Division into blocks aids in summarizing and organizing points of similarity or difference.

> After the end of the 1982 recession, employment grew steadily; by 1990, there were nearly nineteen million more Americans working than in 1980. There were losers as well as winners, however. Blue-collar jobs declined as American industry, notably steel and autos, streamlined operations by closing obsolete plants, switching to automated production, and farming out manufacturing to foreign producers with far lower labor costs. Companies that specialized in labor intensive consumer products, like Eastman Kodak and General Electric, virtually stopped all manufacturing in the United States, concentrating instead on marketing and distributing goods made abroad to their specifications. At the same time, however, the service sector expanded rapidly, especially the financial, transportation, and health-care industries. Accountants, lawyers, and technicians flourished, with women especially benefiting from the change from blue- to white-collar jobs.
>
> (Divine et al., *America, Past and Present,* 5th ed., 1059)

There were losers as well as winners after the 1982 recession.

Losers	Winners
Blue-collar jobs declined—American industry streamlined operations.	Service sector expanded rapidly—e.g., finance/transportation/health.
Labor-intensive product companies stopped manufacturing in U.S.	Accountants/lawyers/technicians flourished.
	Women benefited from change from blue- to white-collar jobs.

CLASSIFICATION

When we classify, we usually break a large category into subgroups. A grid is useful for showing both the subgroups and their distinguishing characteristics.

> There are several schools of thought on the essence of Humanism. Those who follow the nineteenth-century historian Jacob Burckhardt, who saw the Italian Renaissance as the birth of modernity, view it as an un-Christian philosophy that stressed the dignity of humankind and championed individualism and secular values. Others argue that Humanists were the very champions of authentic Catholic Christianity, who opposed the pagan teaching of Aristotle and the ineloquent Scholasticism that his writings nurtured. Still others see Humanism as a form of scholarship consciously designed to promote a sense of civic responsibility and political liberty.
>
> (Kagan, Ozment, and Turner, *Western Heritage,* Vol. I, 5th ed., 360)

Schools of Thought on the Essence of Humanism	
Followers of Burckhardt saw Italian Renaissance as birth of modernity	Viewed Humanism as un-Christian philosophy stressing dignity of humankind; championed individualism, secular values.
Humanists as champions of authentic Catholic Christianity	Opposed the pagan teaching of Aristotle and ineloquent Scholasticism that followed.
Humanism as a form of scholarship	Consciously designed to promote sense of civic responsibility and political liberty.

WHOLE/PART

The elements include the whole—whether the human body, the mind, the court system, or units in space, such as a continent—and whatever parts comprise it. For physical structures, textbooks and articles may provide illustrations or drawings to accompany text. In textbook passages without these aids, you might create a drawing for a physical structure—e.g., a plant, or, with a geographical structure, a proportional map. For abstract structures (e.g., the parts and connections of a judicial system), large and small boxes might be used to show relationships.

> The judicial system in the United States can best be described as a dual system consisting of the federal court system and the judicial systems of the fifty states. Both systems are basically three-tiered. At the bottom of the system are trial courts, where litigation begins. In the middle are the appellate courts in the state system and the courts of appeal in the federal system. At

the top of each pyramid sits a high court. (Some states call these Supreme Courts; New York calls it the Court of Appeals; Oklahoma and Texas call the highest state court for criminal cases the Court of Criminal Appeals.) The federal courts of appeals and Supreme Court as well as states courts of appeals and supreme courts are appellate courts that, with few exceptions, review on appeal only cases that have been decided in lower courts. These courts generally hear matters of both civil and criminal law.

(O'Connor and Sabato, *American Government:*
Continuity and Change, 1997 ed., 369)

U.S. Judicial System

3 Tiers	Federal Court System	State Court System
High courts	U.S. Supreme Court	State Supreme Courts
Appellate courts	U.S. Courts of Appeals (both civil and criminal)	State Courts of Appeals (both civil and criminal)
Trial courts	U.S. Trial Courts (litigation begins)	State Trial Courts (litigation begins)

PROBLEM/SOLUTION

Most often in this pattern you will not find a single main idea sentence that sums up all the pattern elements of problem-cause-effect-solution. To state the main idea, try to find a sentence that mentions at least both the problem and solution. Often you will need to treat the passage as having a divided main idea.

An adolescent's personality is affected both by the timing of puberty (a biological factor) and by how people react to that timing (an environmental factor). Parents and teachers can help both early- and late-maturing adolescents with feelings about body image. For example, research shows that involvement with athletics can be a buffer against the negative feelings that arise during this period. Increased time spent in sports is associated with increased satisfaction and higher self-ratings of strength and attractiveness for both boys and girls. Physical activity is associated with achievement, weight reduction, muscle tone, and stress reduction, all of which foster a positive self-image.

(Lefton, *Psychology,* 5th ed., 318)

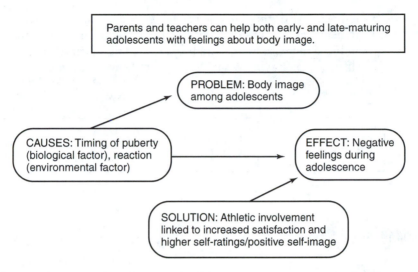

The emphasis on the elements in this pattern can vary greatly. For example, the solution sometimes aims at the effect (as shown by the arrow in the map above), sometimes at the causes, and sometimes directly at the problem itself. Mapping strategies thus need to be adjusted to fit the passage.

CAUSE/EFFECT

Relationship maps are best for showing multiple causes and effects. Horizontal boxes with directional arrows can help us to visualize various cause/effect connections. Relationships can be illustrated by drawing more than one arrow from a cause to its effects, or more than one arrow linking multiple causes to an effect:

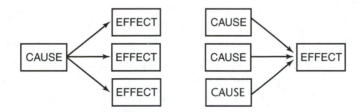

A chain of cause/effect reactions can be represented by a series of horizontal boxes with directional arrows from causes to effects.

The best way to determine if the environmental conditions are imposing a heat load on your body is to monitor your heart rate. An increase in body temperature during exercise in a hot environment will result in large increases in heart rate compared with exercise in a cool environment. A temperature-induced increase in exercise heart rate is significant because it increases the difficulty of staying within your target heart rate zone.

(Powers and Dodd, *Total Fitness: Exercise, Nutrition, and Wellness*, 2nd ed., 220)

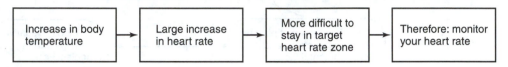

Exercise 4.1

Part A

For each paragraph, <u>underline</u> the sentence that contains the main idea. In the space provided, identify the main idea pattern as one of the following:

description/support   classification

comparison/contrast   whole/part

time sequence   problem/solution

cause/effect   opinion/reason

Complete the missing portions of each map for the main idea and supporting detail. Then answer the two multiple-choice detail questions that follow. It will be helpful in this exercise if you circle key transitions that may signal the pattern. Look back at the samples and the lists of signal words if you are unsure. Each pattern is used once.

1. Women and men perform tasks differently. Women tend to use both sides of the brain in cognitive tasks such as spelling, whereas men use primarily the left side. Women also listen with both ears equally, whereas men favor the right ear. Not all of the gender differences appear at all ages and at all phases of learning. Gender differences in problem solving, for example, tend to favor women in elementary school and men after puberty.

(Lefton, *Psychology*, 5th ed., 68)

Pattern: _____

Women and men _____ .

Women	**vs.**	**Men**

Women	Men
Use both sides of brain in cognitive tasks (spelling)	
	Favor right ear
Better at problem solving	Better at problem solving
_____	_____

1A. According to this passage,

    a. women are better listeners than men.

    b. most men have lost all hearing in the left ear.

    c. among fourth graders, a girl would likely be better at problem solving than a boy.

    d. gender differences appear at all ages and phases of learning.

1B. Women differ from men

    a. in the process by which they spell.

    b. in being better spellers.

    c. in choosing to whom they will listen.

    d. in the way they learn all elementary school subjects.

    2. We tend to judge people by the eye contact they make with us. Generally people prefer modest amounts of eye contact rather than constant or no eye contact. Job applicants, for example, are rated more favorably when they make moderate amounts of eye contact, and speakers who make more rather than less eye contact are preferred. Therapists report that a lack of eye contact in therapy suggests a lack of involvement. However, this is true only in Western cultures; some non-Western cultures consider direct eye contact a sign of disrespect. Witnesses in a court trial are perceived as more credible when they make eye contact with the attorney.

(Lefton, Psychology, 5th ed., 587)

Pattern: _____

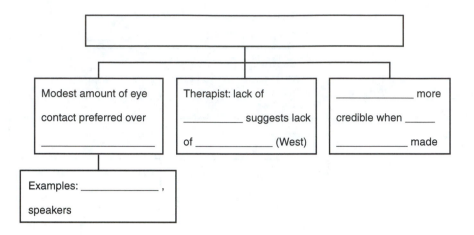

2A. According to the passage,

    a. judges try to make eye contact with us.

    b. either constant or no eye contact is preferred by most people.

    c. speakers who make eye contact are better received by their audience.

    d. few therapists are really involved in treating their patients.

2B. Lack of eye contact

    a. is practiced by therapists in treating patients.

    b. can make a witness less believable.

    c. is not a factor in being successful in a job application.

    d. is everywhere a sign of disrespect.

   3. Many behavioral, psychological, and physical disorders stem from biological factors. A child who acts out in class may have a neurological problem. A person with severe depression may have a chemical imbalance. Men and women may view and operate in the world differently because they have differing brain organization.

(Lefton, *Psychology*, 5th ed., 40)

Pattern: _____

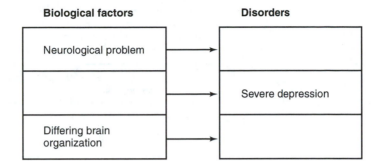

3A. A biological factor could be

    a. behavioral.

    b. psychological.

    c. neurological.

    d. all of the above

3B. Biological factors can cause disorders that are

    a. behavioral.

    b. psychological.

    c. physical.

    d. all of the above

    4. Not everyone experiences the infamous midlife crisis, but most people pass through a midlife transition, and some pass through two, three, or even more transitions. Often, a transition occurs at the beginning of adulthood, when people must give up adolescent freedom and accept adult responsibilities. At around age 30, another transition may occur; during this transition, careers and relationships begun in a person's 20s are reevaluated and sometimes rejected. In the transition of early and middle adulthood, people reorient their career and family choices—the midlife "crisis" at about age 40. Sometimes, parents experience another transition, called the empty nest syndrome, when their children leave home.

(Lefton, Psychology, 5th ed., 329)

Pattern: _____

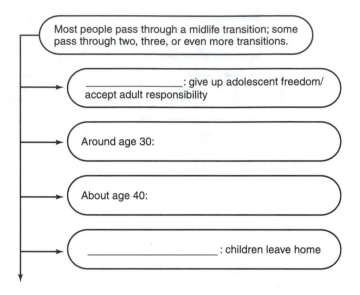

Most people pass through a midlife transition; some pass through two, three, or even more transitions.

_____: give up adolescent freedom/accept adult responsibility

Around age 30:

About age 40:

_____: children leave home

4A. According to the passage,

    a. all persons pass through at least two midlife transitions.

    b. adulthood begins at around age 30.

    c. careers and relationships are revaluated by persons in their 20s.

    d. none of the above

4B. Which of the following is NOT true of the "midlife crisis"?

    a. It can involve changes in careers.

    b. It includes the empty nest syndrome.

    c. It occurs at about age 40.

    d. It may result in changes in family choices.

5. The first root to poke through the coat of a germinating seed is the "primary" root. In most dicot seedlings, it increases in diameter and grows downward. Later, lateral roots start forming in internal tissues and erupt through the epidermis. The youngest of these lateral roots are closest to the root tip. A primary root and its lateral branchings are a taproot system. Carrot and dandelion plants have a taproot system. So does the oak tree.

(Starr, *Biology,* 2nd ed., 335)

Pattern: _____

```
┌─────────────────────────────────────────────────────────┐
│                                                         │
└─────────────────────────────────────────────────────────┘
┌─────────────────────────────────────────────────────────┐
│              WHOLE: _____                │
│                                                         │
│          Examples: carrot, _____,             │
│                      oak tree                           │
│                                                         │
│      PARTS:                                             │
│   ┌──────────────────────┐  ┌────────────────────────┐ │
│   │ _____ Root:   │  │ Lateral roots:         │ │
│   │                      │  │                        │ │
│   │ First to emerge      │  │ Form in _____ │ │
│   │                      │  │                        │ │
│   │ Increases in diameter│  │ Erupt through _____ │ │
│   │                      │  │                        │ │
│   │ Grows downward       │  │ Youngest closest _____ │ │
│   └──────────────────────┘  └────────────────────────┘ │
└─────────────────────────────────────────────────────────┘
```

5A. A primary root

   a. is the coat of a germinating seed.

   b. grows laterally, then downward

   c. is part of a taproot system.

   d. is not a feature of dandelions.

5B. Lateral roots

   a. begin growing inside the seed

   b. increase in size and grow downward.

   c. do not grow near the root tip.

   d. are not a feature of oak trees.

6. There are three types of neurons: sensory neurons, motor neurons, and interneurons. Sensory neurons convey information inward from the sensory organs to the brain and spinal cord. Motor neurons carry information from the brain and spinal cord to the muscles and glands. Interneurons connect neurons together and combine activities of sensory and motor neurons; there are many more interneurons than sensory or motor neurons, and they form the network that allows the neurons to interact with one another.

(Lefton, *Psychology,* 5th ed., 45)

Pattern: _____

Neurons

Types	Functions
Sensory	
	Connect neurons together

6A. According to the passage,

    a. interneurons are the most important of the neurons.

    b. sensory and motor neurons do not interact together.

    c. sensory and motor neurons carry information to the brain and spinal cord.

    d. none of the above

6B. Which of the following is NOT true of interneurons?

    a. They are one of three types of neurons.

    b. They bring together the activities of other types of neurons.

    c. They are less numerous than other types of neurons.

    d. They form an interactive network with other neurons.

7. Teenagers are still largely uninformed or ill informed about reproductive physiology and contraception. Too many underestimate the likelihood of pregnancy and have negative attitudes toward contraception, although they have trouble explaining why. Low levels of self-esteem, and feelings of powerlessness and alienation, are also associated with the personalities of those who fail to use contraceptives. School-based, comprehensive health-care programs that emphasize the complete picture of sexuality (attitudes, contraception, motivation, behavior) reduce the risks of pregnancy in teenagers.

(Lefton, *Psychology,* 5th ed., 326)

Pattern: _____

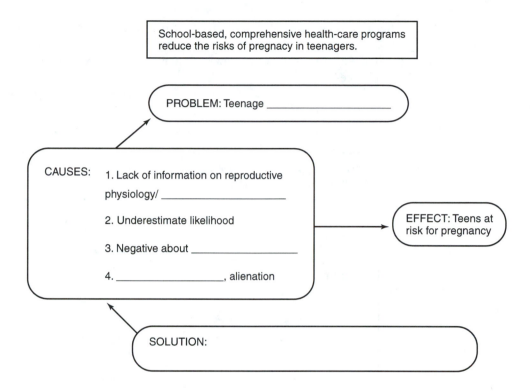

7A. Teenage pregnancy is the result of all of the following EXCEPT:

    a. a lack of information by teenagers on reproduction and conception.

    b. health care programs in the schools.

    c. low self-esteem.

    d. negative attitudes toward contraceptives.

7B. According to the passage, teenagers

    a. sometimes feel powerless and alone.

    b. generally have clear reasons why they oppose using contraception.

    c. fully understand the risks of pregnancy.

    d. have a good grasp of how the reproductive process works.

8. According to Alfie Kohn, competition gets in the way of real learning by making students anxious. It also makes them doubt their own abilities and become nasty towards losers, envious of winners, more prejudiced toward those

from other ethnic groups, and suspicious of just about everyone. In a book on competition, Kohn documented the case against competitive learning and asserted that we should move toward cooperative ventures to stimulate motivation and success.

(Lefton, *Psychology*, 5th ed., 367)

Pattern: _____

OPINION: _____ ventures are better than _____
learning in producing real learning.

Competition makes _____

Competition makes _____

Become _____ toward losers/ _____ of winners

Suspicious of _____

Cooperation stimulates motivation and success

8A. In Kohn's view, which of the following is NOT true of competition in learning?

   a. It can block real learning.
   b. It stimulates motivation and success.
   c. It can lead to a lack of self-confidence among students.
   d. It contributes to prejudice against ethnic groups.

8B. Students who are made to compete in learning

   a. may develop feelings of anxiety.
   b. may develop poor attitudes toward losers and winners.
   c. may lack trust in almost everyone.
   d. all of the above

Part B

Underline the main idea and identify the idea pattern of each paragraph, using the list in Part A. Then create your own umbrella, enumeration, or relationship map. Review the section on these maps to decide which type will best show the relationships in each paragraph.

1. The peripheral nervous system consists of the nerves that connect the central nervous system with sense organs, muscles, and glands. Nerves carry both incoming and outgoing information. The sense organs detect changes in the environment and send signals through the nerves to the muscles (causing behavior) and the glands (producing adjustments in internal physiological processes). Nerves are bundles of many thousands of individual fibers, all wrapped up in a tough protective membrane.

(Carlson and Buskist, *Psychology,* 5th ed., 87)

Pattern: _____

MAP

2. The horse's anatomy exhibits many adaptations to grassland not the least of which is in the dentition (teeth). After all, grasses are highly abrasive, and so eating them requires large, tough incisors for nipping and molars with broad, hardened surfaces for grinding. Of course, as the primitive horses left the forests in search of grass, predators followed. Because concealment was more difficult in the grassy, open spaces, natural selection favored "early warning systems" in the form of long necks and improved vision and hearing. It also favored the ability to respond with great speed—thus we see major changes in the lower legs and feet, particularly the consolidation of the toes into the hooved foot.

(Ferl and Wallace, *Biology,* 3rd ed., 288)

Pattern: _____

MAP

3. Words can be classified as function words or content words. Function words include determiners, quantifiers, prepositions, and words in similar categories: a, the, to, some, and, but, when, and so on. Content words include nouns, verbs, and most adjectives and adverbs: apple, rug, went, caught, heavy, mysterious, thoroughly, sadly. Content words express meaning; function words express the relations between content words and thus are very important syntactical cues. People with a particular type of brain damage lose the ability to comprehend syntax. Included with this deficit is the inability to understand function words or to use them correctly in speech.

(Carlson and Buskist, *Psychology,* 5th ed., 306)

Pattern: _____

MAP

4. During exercise, heat is produced as a by-product of muscular contractions. High-intensity exercise using large muscle groups produces more body heat than low-intensity exercise involving small muscle groups. Hence, during vigorous exercise using large muscle groups, the body must eliminate excess heat in order to prevent a dangerous rise in body temperature.

(Powers and Dodd, *Total Fitness: Exercise, Nutrition, and Wellness,* 2nd ed., 220)

Pattern: _____

MAP

5. The 1980s witnessed both advances and retreats for the American economy. A short but deep recession in 1981–1982 helped halt inflation and led to a seven-year boom. At the same time, however, a continuing decline in American manufacturing and a rising tide of imports led to a growing trade deficit and a steady fall in blue-collar jobs.

(Divine et. al, America, Past and Present, 5th ed., 1059)

Pattern: _____

MAP

6. The most striking change in the decade was the growing inequality of wealth in America. In the five income categories used by the Census Bureau, the poorest 20 percent of Americans fared badly, dropping 6 percent in pretax income in the 1980s. The three middle groups gained about 5 percent, largely as a result of the increased employment of women as middle-class families increasingly needed two wage earners to maintain their standard of living. The top fifth did far better, increasing their incomes by 20 percent over the decade. The top 1 percent, the truly rich, did best of all, doubling their after-tax income in ten years. By 1989, the top fifth made as much money as the other 80 percent combined, while the top 1 percent alone earned as much as the middle fifth of the population.

(Divine et al., America, Past and Present, 5th ed., 1050)

Pattern: _____

MAP

7. Pollination occurs when pollen is deposited on a receptive stigma, but fertilization occurs somewhat later. The events leading to fertilization begin when pollen on the stigma germinates (emerges from dormancy). After the hardcoat breaks open, a pollen tube emerges and grows through the stigma and down the style. During this growth the single generative cell nucleus undergoes one round of mitosis, producing two genetically identical, haploid sperm. Finally the pollen tube penetrates the ovule at a tiny opening, the micropyle. The two sperm then enter the embryo sac, and a double fertilization will occur.

(Ferl and Wallace, *Biology: The Realm of Life,* 3rd ed., 481)

Pattern: _____

MAP

8. In spite of wide public support, the policy of employee drug testing has its opponents. One criticism is that much of the evidence that supports drug testing is inaccurate. Statistics regarding lost productivity are often based on faulty methodology or interpretations. Chronic illegal drug use may adversely affect job performance, but critics insist that drug testing is unreasonable because heavy drug users can be easily spotted in the workplace or are not working in the types of jobs that are routinely tested. There is also concern about the unreliability of drug tests and the high rate of both false positives and false negatives. These types of errors could destroy an employee's reputation and chances for advancement or too quickly release a corporation from liability.

(Eshleman, Cashion, and Basirico, *Sociology: An Introduction,* 4th ed., 134–135)

Pattern: _____

MAP

◼ PARAGRAPHS AND IDEA UNITS

Reading might be a lot easier if all materials followed a simple "one idea equals one paragraph" formula with every paragraph controlled by a single topic or main idea. However, as experienced readers are well aware, paragraphs don't always follow the rules that traditionally have been used to define them. Thus, the effective reader must be constantly aware of the relationships between and among paragraphs as well as within paragraphs and must be able to recognize the signal words that are the key to understanding them.

SUBDIVIDED PARAGRAPH UNIT

A paragraph may be a logical unit but it is a visual one as well, and thus sometimes in making divisions, paragraphing becomes a matter of "paragraphics." Under some conditions, you will find that an idea that would fit in a standard paragraph unit may be subdivided. A **subdivided paragraph unit** may be created for emphasis but may also result from a visual factor. Many newspaper and magazine articles are written to be printed in narrow columns. As your eye drops down the page, it encounters many fewer words per line. To give the reader a sense of regular paragraph breaks, such articles are frequently printed with more indented units than would appear in an across-the-page format. When reprinted in a book, however, the paragraphs may look short and undeveloped. In such cases, you should be on the lookout for a subdivided unit. Here is a typical example from the beginning of a problem/solution article by Carolyn Kane, which originally appeared in *Newsweek* magazine.

> It is generally agreed that the American educational system is in deep trouble. Everyone is aware of the horrible facts: school systems are running out of money, teachers can't spell.
>
> Most of us know, or think we know, who is to blame: liberal courts, spineless school boards, government regulations. It's easy to select a villain.
>
> But possibly the problem lies not so much in our institutions as in our attitudes. It is sad that although most of us profess to believe in education, we place no value on intellectual activity.
>
> (Carolyn Kane, "Thinking: A Neglected Art,"
> *Newsweek,* 12/14/81, 19)

Obviously these three paragraphs function together as an introduction—a change of direction with the signal word *but* leading into the problem statement. However, trying to find a main idea for each of these subunits would be less useful than seeing them as a single, introductory unit. For some of the articles in this text that were originally printed in columns, you will be given an exercise in reorganizing subdivided paragraphs into larger units.

MULTIPARAGRAPH UNITS

Full-length articles and book chapters often contain groups of paragraphs that function together in developing part of the overall main idea. Thus, in these **multiparagraph units,** major and even minor details (for instance, a part of a narrative example) may occupy one or more paragraphs of their own.

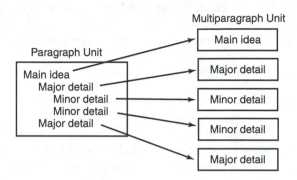

These units will be headed by their own main idea sentence or unified by an implied or divided main idea, and they frequently use listing phrases because of their multiple elements. As you read, look for signal words and phrases that show relationships between paragraphs or within larger passages. Words like *another, in addition, the second stage, a third type, similarly, in contrast,* or *for example* will, when occurring at the beginning of a paragraph, often signal that it is functioning as part of a multiparagraph unit. Multiparagraph units also do not always fall into perfect paragraph patterns. Two main points of support might follow a main idea, with the third in a new paragraph, or sometimes an example begins in one paragraph and runs into another. In these cases the unity of the ideas is not always clearly paralleled in the paragraph structure.

Exercise 4.2

For each multiparagraph unit below, identify the main pattern of organization and underline the sentence that contains the main idea for the entire passage. Circle key signal words or listing phrases that help with your analysis. Then answer the questions that follow. The last passage is a continuation of Carolyn Kane's article that began on p. 151.

Passage A

1   How often do we think that plants actually do anything impressive? Being mobile, intelligent, and emotional, we tend to be fascinated more with ourselves than immobile, expressionless plants. Yet plants don't just stand around soaking up sunlight. Consider a flytrap that evolved long before humans ever built one. The Venus flytrap, a native of North and South Carolina, has two-

lobed, spine-fringed leaves that open and close much like a steel trap. Like other organisms, this plant can't grow without nitrogen and other essential minerals. Certain minerals happen to be scarce in the soggy soils where the Venus flytrap lives. Ah, but insects flying in from nearby areas are abundant.

2   Sticky, sugary substances ooze out of leaf glands. The ooze is part bait, part snare. Insects enticed to land on it brush against tiny hairlike projections—triggers for the trap. If an insect touches two hairs at the same time, or even the same hair twice in rapid succession, the leaf snaps shut. Then digestive juices pour out from leaf cells, pool around the insect—and dissolve its minerals. The plant, in short, makes its own mineral-rich water!

(Starr, *Biology,* 2nd ed., 342)

Comprehension Questions

Circle the correct letter choice and fill in the blanks where indicated.

1. The unit begins with the strategy of asking a question. Complete the rephrasing of the question as a statement that will provide the main idea of the multiparagraph unit:

   "Plants actually do _____."

2. Which of the following is closest to expressing the main idea statement you completed above?

   a. We are more fascinated with ourselves than immobile, expressionless plants.

   b. Yet plants don't just stand around soaking up sunlight.

   c. Consider a flytrap that evolved long before humans ever built one.

   d. Like other organisms, this plant can't grow without nitrogen and other essential minerals.

3. Write the word from paragraph 1 that provides a change of direction signal.

   _____

4. Paragraph 2 relates to paragraph 1 by

   a. providing another example.

   b. giving a contrast.

   c. completing an example.

   d. giving reasons for an opinion.

5. Which sentence provides the main idea of paragraph 2?

   a. Sticky, sugary substances ooze out of leaf glands.

   b. The ooze is part bait, part snare.

    c. Insects enticed to land on it brush against tiny hairlike projections.

    d. The plant, in short, makes its own mineral-rich water!

6. Paragraph 2 is organized by the idea pattern of

    a. time sequence.

    b. classification.

    c. comparison/contrast.

    d. opinion/reason.

Passage B

1   The two most important groups of people who influence the social behavior of adolescents are parents and peers. There is no question that adolescents are responsive to parental influence and put up serious resistance to parental authority only in making life-altering decisions. Studies disagree on the influence of peers versus parents on academic achievement, but most indicate that adolescents' attitudes fall somewhere between those of their parents and those of their peers.

2   The influence of peer groups is formidable. Peer groups are people who identify with and compare themselves to one another. They often consist of people of the same age, gender, and race, although adolescents may change their peer group memberships and may belong to more than one group. As adolescents spend more time away from parents and home, they experience increasing pressure to conform to the values of their peer groups, especially same-sex peer groups.

3   Peer groups are sources of information about society, educational aspirations, and group activities. Peers sometimes praise, sometimes cajole, and constantly pressure one another to conform to behavioral standards, including standards for dress, social interaction, and forms of rebellion, such as shoplifting or drug taking. Most important, they influence the adolescent's developing self-concept.

(Lefton, *Psychology*, 5th ed., 319)

Comprehension Questions

Circle the correct letter choice and fill in the blanks where indicated.

1. Write the sentence that gives the main idea for the entire passage.

_____

2. The main pattern of development is

    a. time sequence.

b. cause/effect.

c. problem/solution.

d. whole/part.

3. Paragraph 1 mainly emphasizes the influence of

a. peers.

b. parents.

c. school authorities.

4. Paragraphs 2 and 3 form a unit within the passage. Write the sentence that provides its main idea. _____

_____

5. The second sentence of paragraph 2, "Peer groups are people who identify with and compare themselves to one another," is

a. an example.

b. a contrast.

c. a definition.

d. an effect.

6. The sentences of paragraph 3 describe the functions of peer groups. They are statements which illustrate

a. description.

b. contrast.

c. comparison.

d. time.

Passage C

1   It is easy to understand the causes of this prejudice against thinking. One problem is that to most of us, thinking looks suspiciously like loafing. *Homo sapiens* in deep thought is an uninspiring sight. He leans back in his chair, props up his feet, puffs on his pipe and stares into space. He gives every appearance of wasting time; he reminds us more of Dagwood and Beetle Bailey than of Shakespeare and Einstein. We wish he would get up and **do** something: mow the lawn, maybe, or wash the car. Our resentment is natural.

2   But thinking is far different from laziness. Thinking is one of the most productive activities a human being can undertake. Every beautiful and useful thing we have created—including democratic government and

freedom of religion—exists because somebody took the time and effort to think of it.

3   And thinking does require time and effort. It is a common misconception that if a person is "gifted" or "bright" or "talented," wonderful ideas will flash spontaneously into his mind. Unfortunately the intellect doesn't work this way. Even Einstein had to study and think for months before he could formulate his theory of relativity. Those of us who are less intelligent find it a struggle to conceive even a moderately good idea, let alone a brilliant one.

4   **Seclusion.** Another reason why we distrust thinking is that it seems unnatural. Human beings are a social species, but thinking is an activity that requires solitude. Consequently, we worry about people who like to think instead of going to a rodeo or a soccer match. We suspect that such a person needs counseling.

5   Our concern is misplaced. Intelligence is just as much a part of human nature as sociability. It would certainly be unnatural for a person to retreat into total seclusion. It would be equally unnatural for a person to allow his mind to die of neglect.

(Carolyn Kane, "Thinking: A Neglected Art," *Newsweek,* 12/14/81, 19)

Comprehension Questions

Circle the correct letter choice and fill in the blanks where indicated.

1. Write the sentence that gives the main idea for the entire passage. _____

   _____

2. The main pattern of development is

   a. time sequence.

   b. cause/effect.

   c. classification.

   d. comparison/contrast.

3. Write the main idea of paragraph 1. _____

   _____

4. Write the main idea of paragraph 2. _____

   _____

5. The pattern of development in paragraph 2 is

   a. time sequence.

   b. whole/part.

   c. cause/effect.

   d. comparison/contrast.

6. What two key signal words link paragraphs 2 and 3 to paragraph 1?

   _____   _____

7. Write the main idea of paragraph 3. _____

   _____

8. Paragraphs 1–3 form one of the two major elements of the multiparagraph unit. Which of the following would best complete the divided main idea of this section?

   "One problem is that to most of us, thinking looks suspiciously like loafing,…"

   a. and *Homo sapiens* in deep thought is an uninspiring sight.

   b. but thinking is far different from laziness and does require time and effort.

   c. so we wish he would get up and **do** something and our resentment is natural.

   d. and those of us who are less intelligent find it a struggle to conceive even a moderately good idea, let alone a brilliant one.

9. What key transition signal word in paragraph 4 introduces the second element of the multiparagraph unit? _____

10. Paragraphs 2 and 5 have a similar function in that both

   a. introduce a major pattern element.

   b. are organized by time sequence.

   c. give an opinion opposite to that in the previous paragraph.

   d. include a number of specific examples and statistical data.

SPECIALIZED PARAGRAPHS

There are a few **specialized paragraphs** that provide important functions. **Introductions** and **conclusions** quite obviously do what their names suggest. The form these paragraphs take varies with the pattern of organization of an article or chapter; therefore, they will be discussed in more detail in Parts II and III. Conclusions are often summaries, but **summary** paragraphs can appear at various places, not just the end, to summarize major sections or subsections. These paragraphs usually provide a reminder of the main points that have been covered. They appear most frequently in informational and topical writing. **Transition** paragraphs usually provide some summary material but they also look ahead to what is about to come. Notice how in the example below, an introduction to a unit in a biology text beginning with Chapter 20 points both backwards and forwards.

> Chapter 18 sprints through the spectrum of nearly 30,000 known plant species. Even that fleeting run through plant diversity reveals why no one species can be used as a typical example of plant body plans. However, when we hear the word "plant," we mostly think of gymnosperms (such as pine trees) and angiosperms (such as roses, apple trees, and corn).
>
> Angiosperms, recall, are the only plants that produce flowers. *And with more than 265,000 species, they dominate the plant kingdom.* We devote this chapter to the tissues and body plans of flowering plants. Chapter 21 explains how these plants take up water and nutrients, restrict water loss, and distribute organic substances through the plant body. Chapter 22 looks at key aspects of their growth, development, and reproduction.
>
> (Starr, *Biology,* 2nd ed., 327)

Transition paragraphs can be very helpful when material is lengthy and connections need to be kept clear.

METHODS OF DEVELOPMENT

In addition to using familiar thinking patterns to organize text, writers also use a variety of techniques to develop their materials fully. You have already seen how background information, including useful definitions, are included to make ideas clearer. Below are listed additional methods of development that appear often in textbook materials.

RESTATEMENT

Ideas may be restated in slightly different words, sometimes with the second statement being a little more specific. Authors often do this to gain emphasis for key concepts.

> One of the standard concerns about I.Q. tests is that they are biased towards or against members of different cultures. Critics have argued that group differences in I.Q. scores are caused by systematic bias in the test questions.
> (Carlson and Buskist, *Psychology: The Science of Behavior,* 5th ed., 615)

NEGATIVE/POSITIVE RESTATEMENT

One form of restatement repeats essentially the same idea in both a positive and a negative form.

> The powerful have not been munificent in giving a break to the power-
> less. <u>To the contrary</u>, much effort has been expended by the powerful to keep
> the powerless in that condition.
>
> (Eitzen and Zinn, *In Conflict and Order*, 7th ed., 67)

Here the writer restates a sentence with a negative (have <u>not</u> been) in a positive
form to emphasize the idea of the passage that the strong dominate the weak.

CLARIFICATION

Authors will also try to **clarify** abstract or difficult ideas—that is, they restate the
idea differently and more simply, with the result that second version is easier to
understand. Signal words and phrases like <u>in other words</u> or <u>indeed</u> may be used
to indicate a clarification.

> We must keep in mind that we are aware only a small part of our envi-
> ronment—that the world is far richer than we imagine. <u>Simply put</u>, we, too,
> know what we need to know.
>
> (Ferl and Wallace, *Biology: The Realm of Life* 3rd ed., 599)

ORDER OF IMPORTANCE

Writers often have a strategy for the order in which they arrange details. This
might be an order of familiarity—i.e., beginning with something very familiar to
the reader and then moving to the more difficult or unfamiliar. Another pattern
is the order of impact—an author might place the most striking examples in the
first and last positions, or save the strongest reason in an argument for the final
point. In the **order of importance,** the author uses key signal words to emphasize
a point that the reader should remember.

> Probably <u>the most important factor</u> unifying society is the phenomenon
> of functional integration.
>
> (Eitzen and Zinn, *In Conflict and Order*, 7th ed., 67)

Order of importance has a significant application for study techniques. This is
particularly true when the text lists a number of details and calls attention to one,
usually the last, as "most important" or words to that effect. These are details
that the student needs to mark and remember.

SUBPATTERNS

Occasionally another idea pattern will be used as support in developing the main
idea pattern. One common example in the description/support pattern is the use
of an extended narrative illustration (time sequence) to support the main idea.
Another commonly used subpattern is comparison/contrast.

I became increasingly frustrated at not being able to express what I wanted to convey in letters that I wrote, especially those to Mr. Elijah Muhammad. In the street, I had been the most articulate hustler out there—I had commanded attention when I said something. But now, trying to write simple English, I not only wasn't articulate, I wasn't even functional. How would I sound writing in slang, the way I would say it, something such as, "Look, daddy, let me pull your coat about a cat, Elijah Muhammad—"

(Malcolm X, *The Autobiography of Malcolm X, 1720*. Reprinted by permission of Alex Haley and Betty Shabazz, Castle Books, 1965)

The writer had the option here of developing the main idea of description by examples drawn from his current situation (he was in jail), but the strategy of using a subpattern of contrast allows introducing a specific example as well as indicating the source of his frustration.

Exercise 4.3

Part A

Identify each of the paragraphs as an illustration of one of the following methods of development:

A. simple restatement

B. negative/positive restatement

C. clarification

D. order of importance

List any words or phrases that signal a relationship between sentences.

1. _____ The body requires glucose to function normally. Indeed, the central nervous system uses glucose almost exclusively for its energy needs.
(Powers and Dodd, *Total Fitness,* 2nd ed., 153)

Signal word or phrase: _____

2. _____ If we want a listener to understand our speech, we must follow the "rules" of language. We must use words with which the listener is familiar and combine them in specific ways.
(Carlson and Buskist, *Psychology: The Science of Behavior* 5th ed., 304)

Signal word or phrase: _____

3. _____ Regardless of the specific reasons for relationships, the members of a social relationship are united at least in some minimal way with the others.

Most important, the members of a social relationship behave quite differently than they would as participants in a fleeting interaction

(Eitzen and Zinn, *In Conflict and Order,* 7th ed., 25)

Signal word or phrase: _____

4. _____   People with a language disorder known as conduction aphasia have difficulty repeating words and phrases, but they can understand them. In other words, they can retain the deep structure, but not surface structure, of other people's speech.

(Carlson and Buskist, *Psychology: The Science of Behavior,* 5th ed., 307)

Signal word or phrase: _____

5. _____   Riots, lynchings, and mob actions are not solely southern phenomena. Many people from other sections of the United States have used these techniques against various alien groups (usually Catholics and immigrants from non-Teutonic Europe) in order to maintain their superiority.

(Eitzen and Zinn, *In Conflict and Order,* 7th ed., 65–66)

Signal word or phrase: _____

6. _____   Humans are homeotherms, which means same temperature. That is, body temperature is regulated around a set point; humans regulate their body temperature around the set point of 98.6°F or 37°C.

(Powers and Dodd. *Total Fitness: Exercise, Nutrition, and Wellness,* 2nd ed., 220)

Signal word or phrase: _____

7. _____   The new science by no means swept away all other thought. Traditional beliefs and fears long retained their hold on the culture.

(Kagan, Ozment, and Turner, *Western Heritage,* Vol. I, 5th ed., 522)

Signal word or phrase: _____

8. _____   Throughout human history race has been used as a criterion for differentiation. If any factor makes a difference in the United states, it is race.

(Eitzen and Zinn, *In Conflict and Order,* 7th ed., 58)

Signal word or phrase: _____

9. _____   See if this statement rings true: "Facts crammed at examination time soon vanish if they are not sufficiently grounded by other study and later

subjected to a sufficient review." In other words, if you cram for a test, you're not likely to remember very much of it a few days later.

(Zimbardo and Gerrig, *Psychology and Life,* 15th ed., 268)

Signal word or phrase: _____

10. _____ Every moment of every day, we are involved in a steady aging process. Everything in the universe—animals, plants, mountain peaks, rivers, planets, even atoms—changes over time.

(Donatelle, *Access to Health,* 7th ed., 522)

Signal word or phrase: _____

Part B

The paragraphs below show ways in which subpatterns can be used in the development of a main pattern of organization. Analyze the paragraphs carefully (pay particular attention to signal words), and study the example, before deciding on patterns and subpatterns. Look back on the sections that explain and give examples of patterns, if you are unsure.

Example

White southerners beginning in about 1820 used violent means to preserve slavery. In the early stages this amounted to civil disobedience, and later it burst out into fighting in places like bleeding Kansas. Eventually the South seceded, and the Civil War was waged—a classic example of a minority group using violence to force a change and being suppressed by the power of the majority.

(Eitzen and Zinn, *In Conflict and Order,* 7th ed., 65)

Main pattern: _description_   Signal words: _none_

Subpattern: _time_   Signal words: _beginning in, later, in the early stages eventually_

---

1. It is important to understand that our intelligence has not evolved without costs. Like other mammals, we are born in a helpless state, but human infants seem to be particularly helpless, with fewer built-in adaptive responses than infants of many other species. A baby hare, for example, will lunge and hiss at an intruder. Newborn antelopes follow their mothers within minutes, and infant baboons quickly learn to ride on their mother's back. Virtually all baby primates will hold onto their mother's hair, so that she can move with ease. In comparison, our newborns seem witless and almost completely helpless. (And in what other species do

20-year-old offspring demand so much from their parents?) This early dependency of humans allows us time to learn all the things that will be important for living under the specific conditions in which our own complex culture exists.

(Ferl and Wallace, *Biology: The Realm of Life,* 3rd ed., 337)

Main pattern: _____   Signal words: _____

Subpattern: _____   Signal words: _____

2. Convective heat loss occurs only when the air or water molecules moving around the body are cooler than skin temperature, because the faster the flow of cool air or water around the body, the greater the heat loss. Minimal convective cooling occurs during exercise in a hot environment where there is limited air movement (riding a stationary exercise bicycle, for example). In contrast, bicycling outdoors on a cold day or swimming in cool water results in a large amount of convective cooling.

(Powers and Dodd, *Total Fitness: Exercise, Nutrition, and Wellness,* 2nd ed., 220)

Main pattern: _____   Signal words: _____

Subpattern: _____   Signal words: _____

3. There can be no doubt that Supreme Court Justice Thurgood Marshall's personal experience shaped his views of the law. He was born in Baltimore in 1908, when the city was as segregated as any in the deep South. Because the University of Maryland law school barred blacks, Marshall gave up hope of attending there. He went instead to the all-black law school at Howard University, which in the 1930's was being transformed under Vice-Dean Charles H. Houston into a training ground for lawyers who would challenge segregation in the courts. Houston became Marshall's mentor, firing the determination of the younger man to confront segregation head on. After graduation, Marshall worked as a lawyer for the Baltimore branch of the NAACP. One of his first major cases forced the integration of the same University of Maryland law school he had been unable to attend.

(Territo, Halsted, and Brimley, *Crime and Justice in America,* 4th ed., 40)

Main pattern: _____   Signal words: _____

Subpattern: _____   Signal words: _____

4. History is full of cases where dreams have been a pathway to creativity and discovery. A striking example is provided by Dr. Otto Loewi, a pharmacologist and winner of a Nobel Prize. Loewi had spent years studying the chemical

transmission of nerve impulses. A tremendous breakthrough in his research came when he dreamed of an experiment three nights in a row. The first two nights he woke up and scribbled the experiment on a pad. But the next morning, he couldn't tell what the notes meant. On the third night, he got up after having the dream. This time, instead of making notes he went straight to his laboratory and performed the crucial experiment. Loewi later said that if the experiment had occurred to him while awake he would have rejected it.

(Coon, *Introduction to Psychology,* 7th ed., 188)

Main pattern: _____   Signal words: _____

Subpattern: _____   Signal words: _____

5. For Durkheim, there are two types of societies, based on the way the members are bonded. In smaller, less complex societies, solidarity among members occurs through the collective holding of beliefs (ideologies, moral sentiments, traditions). Social interaction, therefore, occurs because the members are alike. Modern complex societies, in contrast, achieve social integration through differentiation. Society is based on division of labor, in which the members involved in specialized tasks are united by their dependence on others.

(Eitzen and Zinn, *In Conflict and Order,* 7th ed., 49)

Main pattern: _____   Signal words: _____

Subpattern: _____   Signal words: _____

CHAPTER REVIEW

1. Umbrella maps

    a. cannot be used to show supporting details.

    b. require details to be presented in a set order.

    c. show how a broad main idea is developed by supporting details.

2. The pattern of problem/solution can best be shown by using

    a. a relationship map.

    b. an umbrella map.

    c. an enumeration map.

3. "Carla is a very considerate worker. Whereas many clerks ignore older customers, Carla will hold open doors for them or assist them with their packages." These sentences shows a main pattern of

    a. description/support developed by a subpattern of comparison/contrast.

   b. description/support developed by a subpattern of time sequence.

   c. time sequence developed by a subpattern of cause/effect.

   d. comparison/contrast developed by a subpattern of classification.

Read the following passage and answer the questions that follow by circling the correct letter choice.

1   Many non-elderly poor have no access to government aid because they cannot afford it. Rapidly increasing costs are also making it difficult for businesses and middle-income people to cope. And even those covered by government programs find that they must pay for a large amount of their care themselves.

2   There seem to be two possible alternatives. One is to adopt a national health insurance system like all other industrial democracies have done. Traditionally, most medical interests, especially doctors and insurance companies, opposed such a system. Many still do today. However, as the system becomes more expensive and less accessible, pressures for making dramatic changes increase. The American Medical Association now has endorsed national health insurance. Seventy-five percent of the public favors a government-supported health insurance system.

3   The other alternative is to force private insurance companies to share the risk of insuring those most likely to be ill. Our existing system has been called "lemon socialism." Private enterprise insures those at least risk, the young, the well, and the well-off, while government—ultimately the taxpayer—pays for those most likely to be sick, the elderly and the poor. Such a system seems unlikely to last indefinitely.

(Welch et al., *American Government,* 4th ed., 500)

4. Paragraph 1 gives

   a. one example.

   b. an argument against the poor.

   c. a problem statement.

   d. a classification of health programs.

5. The sentence in paragraph 1, "Rapidly increasing costs are also making it difficult for businesses and middle-income people to cope," shows a pattern of

   a. cause/effect.

   b. comparison/contrast.

   c. whole/part.

   d. classification.

6. The first sentence of paragraph 2, "There seem to be two possible alternatives,"

   a. contains an example.

  b. gives a reason.

  c. states a problem.

  d. contains a listing phrase.

7. The first sentence of paragraph 2 also

  a. summarizes the points of paragraph 1.

  b. provides the main idea for paragraph 2 only.

  c. provides the main idea for a multiparagraph unit consisting of paragraphs 1–2.

  d. provides the main idea for a multiparagraph unit consisting of paragraphs 2–3.

8. The main idea for paragraph 2 is

  a. the first sentence.

  b. the second sentence.

  c. the last sentence.

9. The main idea for paragraph 3 is

  a. the first sentence.

  b. the second sentence.

  c. the last sentence.

10. The overall idea pattern for the passage is

  a. description/support.

  b. opinion/reason.

  c. problem/solution.

  d. cause/effect.

READING PORTFOLIO | Paragraphing and Methods of Development

Select a newspaper or magazine article that is written in narrow columns. Try to find examples of the following:

1. *Subdivided paragraphs.* Three or four short paragraphs often can be combined into a single introduction, conclusion, or main idea unit.

2. *Topical and main idea paragraphs or paragraph units.* Informational articles may have a number of the former. In editorial articles and featured columns, main idea paragraphs are the general rule. Develop a mind map for at least three paragraphs (or paragraph units) in the article.

3. *Methods of development.* Identify any examples of the following:

   a. restatement

   b. negative/positive restatement

   c. clarification

   d. order of importance

The Reader's Voice: Summary, Paraphrase, and Active Reading Strategies

CHAPTER

5

At its most basic level, reading involves the identification of important information—that is, the reader must locate and remember ideas that the author thinks are important. However, locating information does not always mean that we truly understand it. Only when we can restate what is said accurately, and can respond to it thoughtfully are we full partners in academic dialogue. Finding and using your own voice is essential in making summaries, using sources, and writing papers in your college classes.

■ CHAPTER PREVIEW

In this chapter, you will

- Discover how reading involves a dialogue with yourself
- Apply a five-step process to completing summaries
- Practice the technique of paraphrasing
- Learn what plagiarism is and how to avoid it
- Begin to use important prereading strategies that active readers practice

ACTIVE READING: A DIALOGUE WITH YOURSELF

The paragraph below contains a key definition for understanding the importance of becoming an active reader:

> One important aspect of cognitive development is metacognition: awareness and understanding of our own cognitive processes. Cognitive psychologists believe that in order to operate most effectively, cognitive systems such as our minds must be aware of themselves. They must be able to generate thoughts such as "I'd better read this paragraph again; I didn't understand it the first time," or "I'd better make a note of that information—it seems important, and I may want to use it later."
>
> (Robert Baron, *Essentials of Psychology,*
> 292–293. © 1996 Allyn and Bacon.)

Academic dialogue involves many reading strategies related to *metacognition,* or "thinking about thinking." Effective readers are engaged in an ongoing mental dialogue with themselves, as well as with the author. The reader moves through the text taking in information, but there is another "reader"—the little voice in the reader's head that keeps interrupting to ask questions:

- What does that mean? Where is the author going with this?
- How does that fit with what went before? Has the author changed direction?
- Is something left out? Or did I miss something?

Readers who think about what they are doing are **active readers**:

- They have a purpose and set goals when they read.
- They monitor their progress in reaching their reading goals.
- They don't read in a straight line, and only once. They look forward and check back to connect important information, and they reread difficult or confusing passages.
- They adjust their reading rate to the level of difficulty.
- They relate new information to their previous knowledge.

On the following page are the observations of a college philosophy professor on the processes that govern his reading. As you read, make a list of the ways in which he demonstrates the behaviors of active readers.

Kosta Bagakis from *Speaking of Reading*

1   I love reading. I think it's one of the most wonderful activities that human beings have developed. When I go on a vacation, the first thing I do is get my reading list together. Whenever I leave the house I take enough reading material with me to occupy myself during a five-hour traffic jam. I keep telling myself I should get a little flashlight so I could sit and read if I get stuck in an elevator.

2   As a Greek immigrant child I felt isolated from the world. Since I was the oldest child in my family, I lost out in terms of attention, so I decided to excel in school instead. The other members of my family were all nonreaders, but luckily I learned to read fairly rapidly since I was shut out from my family. I found my life in books. When my family went to an event, I sat at home and read. I got praise from them for reading and they often asked me what I read. Eventually, I gained a great amount of power in my family because they would ask me about issues and problems, and I'd tell them what I thought.

3   I was passive in school; teachers imposed readings on me and I accepted them. My school life was separate from my private life. When I read something that was directly related to my private life, I came alive, and I still do. Right now I'm reading about the Trojan War, and since I'm Greek, that era is part of my heritage. Those heroes are a part of me, and I want to make them clear in my mind so I can understand myself better.

4   I made sporadic attempts at being an active reader when I was in school, but I had decided that the reading I was supposed to do would not be interesting, so I wouldn't really read it, and there was no one in school to explain how it might be different. I never trusted adults because I felt they were always trying to manipulate me. For example, a high school teacher once tried to force me to read Silas Marner without first telling me how the book could possibly connect with my life, so of course I hated reading it. Reading can't be imposed without a context.

5   By this point in my life I've created my own context for my reading. I have a plan, a specific reason for everything I read: I want to understand my history, my heritage, my job, my worldview. I want to get it all clear and I believe everything is interconnected, so if I'm reading about math, for instance, I try to see how the major mathematical issues fit into my understanding of philosophy and history. All of my reading is focused on my attempt to understand the world.

6   I maintain that reading is a social act. A book won't stay in my head unless I tell a friend about it, so I like to find other people to read the books

Nadine Rosenthal, *Speaking of Reading,* (Nadine Rosenthal, 1995), 193–195. Reprinted by permission of the author.

I'm reading so we can talk about the ideas together. Sometimes, it's as if we've read different books, our ideas are so different. I have never read a book without sharing it with others—never.

7   I underline passages in my books that I want to share with others. Depending on my mood, and the book, I underline either a lot or just a little. Sometimes I put a number one in front of important parts; I may mark a reference or a nice phrase, but I only underline something if I expect I will go back and use it.

8   I used to have a different procedure when I picked up a book: First I would look at the cover and get whatever information I could from it. Then I looked at the table of contents to see if I liked the chapter titles. Next I looked at the references at the back to see what books the author had read before writing it. Then I would read the whole book cover to cover, every word. About seven or eight years ago I was talking to an old teacher about this method of reading and he said, "Just read the part of a book that tells the information you want. You don't have to read everything unless you have the time, or you like the author's style." I was amazed. I rarely read any book from cover to cover any longer.

9   Every book has its own language, its own vocabulary, its own set of assumptions. I may wonder why an author uses a particular word, but if I keep reading, I'll eventually understand it, and may even begin to use the word myself to express that certain thought. As long as I understand the language in a book, I can understand the material.

10   Reading passively without thinking about what I'm reading is a waste of my life force. If I want to be passive, I'll watch TV. Although it often exhausts me, reading can also make my energy extremely high. Sometimes I have to take a walk after I've read a book that is life-changing. An author can touch me most when he or she explains my connection to the world or expresses my feelings—those feelings I don't usually talk to other people about. A book won't touch me if it's too general.

11   Each book represents an individual's concentrated attempt at presenting his or her point of view. I can't think of anything else that human beings do that focuses their souls and their understanding of the world more than writing books. Books are intense, mini-human beings, and bookstores are the souls of humanity.

Exercise 5.1

Part A

Work in groups of three or four to answer the following questions. Numbers in parentheses refer to paragraph numbers.

1. What motivated Dr. Bagakas to do well in school (2)? _____

_____

_____

_____

2. Was he successful as an active reader in his early schooling (3–4)? Why or why not? _____

_____

_____

_____

3. "Reading can't be imposed without a context." (4) What does "context" mean here? What example is given earlier in the paragraph to illustrate this idea? _____

_____

_____

_____

4. Active readers have a goal behind their reading. What is the overall goal (5) behind Dr. Bagakis' reading? _____

_____

_____

_____

5. Active readers interact with the text by marking it. List the techniques (7) that Dr. Bagakis uses to annotate a text. _____

_____

_____

_____

6. Active reading involves prereading strategies—that is, techniques used before reading the entire text. What prereading strategies are noted in paragraph 8?

_____

_____

_____

_____

7. "As long as I understand the language in a book, I can understand the material." Do you agree that understanding all the vocabulary in a text will ensure comprehension? Explain your viewpoint and give any examples from your experience. _____

_____

_____

_____

8. What is the key difference (10) between active and passive reading? What judgment is made about the value of TV? _____

_____

_____

_____

9. "Books are intense, mini-human beings, and bookstores are the souls of humanity." (11) Explain. _____

_____

_____

_____

10. "When I go on a vacation, the first thing I do is get my reading list together. Whenever I leave the house I take enough reading material with me to occupy myself during a five-hour traffic jam." (1) How do you use your time in these kinds of situations? _____

_____

_____

_____

Part B

Paragraph 8 tells about one person's approach to a technique that experts agree is a must before you begin reading or studying anything: previewing the material. Whether it is a short article or a hefty textbook, you need to get a quick overview before you jump in. Select one of your college texts for this exercise. Use it to answer the following questions:

1. General information

Name of book: _____

Author: _____

Subject area: _____

Edition: _____

Date published: _____

2. Is there a table of contents? _____?

3. Is the book organized by units or chapters or a combination? _____

_____

4. Check the chapter features.

Is there a chapter preview? _____

Is there a chapter summary? _____

Is there a unit review or summary? _____

Is the specialized vocabulary defined? _____

5. Look in the back of the book.

Is there an index? _____

Is there a glossary? _____

Are there any useful appendices? _____

■ SAYING THINGS IN YOUR OWN WORDS

Only when we can explain to others, in our own words, what we have read do we truly understand it. Saying things "in other words" is a sign that we have found our own voice in our conversation with the author. The exercise below will give you some practice in restating ideas in your own voice.

Maxims and proverbs are short, striking sentences or phrases, which often use figurative comparisons. Through specific examples or clever comparisons, they express wise observations about life that can be applied to other situations. To demonstrate that we understand the point of these, we must restate the general idea in our own words.

Exercise 5.2

Work together in groups of 3–4 to complete this exercise. The pairs below contain proverbs that express general ideas. Discuss the meaning of that idea and then write it in your own words. Give any specific examples of situations that the proverb might apply to. The two proverbs in each pair express ideas or pieces of advice that are basically the same or the opposite of each other. Explain how they are alike or different.

Example}

"Let sleeping dogs lie."

The point this makes, in my words, is: ___*Don't stir things up. Leave*___ *problems alone if at all possible and maybe they'll go away.*

"Leave no stone unturned."

The point this makes, in my words, is: ___*To find the truth, don't hold back.*___ *Search every possible avenue.*

Alike or different? ___*Different*___   Explain: ___*They give opposite advice. One*___ *says avoid problems, the other says confront and pursue difficult situations.*

---

1. "A bird in the hand is worth two in the bush."

   The point this makes, in my words, is:_____

   _____

   "Nothing ventured, nothing gained."

   The point this makes, in my words, is:_____

   _____

   Alike or different?_____   Explain:_____

   _____

2. "The pen is mightier than the sword."

   The point this makes, in my words, is:_____

   _____

   "Actions speak louder than words."

   The point this makes, in my words, is:_____

   _____

   Alike or different?_____   Explain:_____

   _____

3. "After three days, fish and visitors begin to stink."

The point this makes, in my words, is:_____

_____

"Short visits make long friends."

The point this makes, in my words, is:_____

_____

Alike or different?_____   Explain:_____

_____

4. "Out of sight, out of mind."

The point this makes, in my words, is:_____

_____

"Absence makes the heart grow fonder."

The point this makes, in my words, is:_____

_____

Alike or different?_____   Explain:_____

_____

5. "A friend in need is a friend indeed."

The point this makes, in my words, is: _____

_____

"Lend your money and lose your friend."

The point this makes, in my words, is:_____

_____

Alike or different?_____   Explain:_____

_____

6. "Look before you leap."

The point this makes, in my words, is:_____

_____

"He who hesitates is lost."

The point this makes, in my words, is:_____

_____

Alike or different?_____   Explain:_____

_____

7. "The early bird catches the worm."

The point this makes, in my words, is:_____

_____

"Early to bed, early to rise, makes a man healthy, wealthy, and wise."

The point this makes, in my words, is:_____

_____

Alike or different?_____   Explain:_____

_____

8. "Marry in haste, repent in leisure."

The point this makes, in my words, is:_____

_____

"Faint heart never won a lady."

The point this makes, in my words, is:_____

_____

Alike or different?_____   Explain:_____

_____

9. "Many hands make light work."

The point this makes, in my words, is:_____

_____

"Too many cooks spoil the broth."

The point this makes, in my words, is:_____

_____

Alike or different?_____ Explain:_____

_____

10. "Like father, like son."

The point this makes, in my words, is:_____

_____

"The apple never falls very far from the tree."

The point this makes, in my words, is:_____

_____

Alike or different?_____ Explain:_____

_____

THE ART OF SUMMARIZING

Suppose, on returning to school in the fall, you run into a friend or teacher who casually asks about your summer. Your response to this question about a period of seventy-five days or so would probably be made in a few sentences and take no longer than a minute or two. Your reaction would be an example of a very important thinking process in communication, the ability to summarize. In many situations in life—at home, in school, on the job, in a court of law, at a public meeting—you will need this skill. A **summary** is simply a shortened version of an action or communication that still provides the key elements. When an instructor asks you to summarize a chapter or an article, you may be required to do so in a single page or less. And many times, when you are studying for an examination or preparing a report, you will find yourself needing to put lengthy material into a form you can manage. Before you attempt to write a summary, keep in mind some important guidelines.

1. Don't get the cart before the horse. You have probably been told that when you summarize, you should write down the most important points, but what makes a point important? The truth is you must determine the main idea and important details through careful reading and analysis *before* you ever attempt to write a summary. Summarizing will not lead you to discover the main idea; it will, however, make you sharpen your main idea statement, see more clearly the relationship among the parts, and better distinguish minor from major detail.

2. A summary does not require going line by line through a reading, shrinking the text equally in all places. Summarizing is more than a mechanical process of shortening; it requires thinking about and evaluating your material. Your sum-

mary must reduce the length of your source material, but it does so by retaining only the main idea and key pattern elements. This means that

- Some parts of the original may be shortened very little or not at all
- Some lengthy supporting examples or other detail may be shortened drastically or left out entirely
- The organization of your summary in the way points are taken up may be very different from the original

3. Remember: a summary must focus on the most important ideas in the text and must be written in your own words. Until you have fully mastered summarizing techniques, you should practice a very precise method to achieve these two objectives. The following diagram shows a sequence that takes you from the original text (A) to your analysis and annotation (B) through an outline/pattern map (C) and finally a summary in your own words (D).

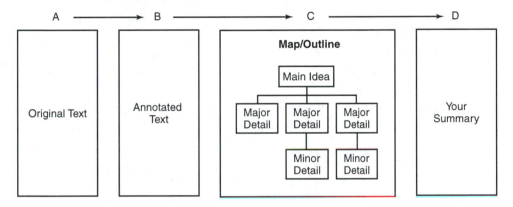

There are two keys in successfully following this process. First, follow the sequence from A through D. **Do not try to go directly from A, or even from B, to D.** If you summarize directly from the original, you will end up trying to summarize line by line and almost certainly, some of the original phrasing will end up in your summary. If you skip the map/outline stage C, you may fail to focus on the organizational pattern. In both instances, the original will dictate your organization. Second, make sure the phrasing in your annotations and on your map is in your own voice. When you are mapping, use your annotated notes rather than copying from the text; when writing your summary, use only the map, not the original text. If you must go back to the text to check a fact or reread a passage, make the changes on your map. Always put the original aside before you begin writing again.

4. Use your understanding of the main purpose or main idea to establish control over your materials. Readers of your summary should clearly hear your voice leading them through the main points. One effective strategy for

establishing control and voice is to begin by working in the name of the author and the title:

> In her article "Tasha's Story," Linda Ellerbe presents a sympathetic portrait of a family....

Other reminders of your control can come through phrases such as the following employed at intervals in your summary:

> Ellerbe maintains that....

> The author gives several examples of....

> Ellerbe sees a very bleak outlook for....

Below is a process that will help you focus on the purpose and method for writing summaries. The exercise in the section that follows will give you a chance to practice summarizing skills that you can apply to other college courses.

FIVE-STEP SUMMARY PROCESS

STEP 1 Determine the topic of the source material. Usually the title or a subheading gives a clear clue. If not, look for a word or phrase that seems to be frequently repeated.

STEP 2 Test to see whether the reading has a topical or main idea organization by determining whether the reading answers a central question about the topic.

- If the material has a topical organization, look for the major details that are given about the topic. Think how your source provides answers to the questions *Who? What? When? Where? Why? How?* Annotate your text using these questions as your guide.
- If the reading is organized around a main idea, formulate a main idea guess. Write the main idea in your own words in a complete sentence. Verify or adjust your hypothesis as you annotate your text.

STEP 3 Analyze and annotate key points in the text. Distinguish between what is major detail and minor detail in the supporting material included in the text: examples, statistics, historical data, expert opinion, studies, etc.

STEP 4 Create an outline or mind map to help you visualize the organization of the material. Decide how much minor detail you wish to include in your map; the length of your summary will depend on your purposes and/or the length requested by your instructor.

STEP 5 Write your summary. Your map—not the original text—determines the organization of your summary. Recheck the accuracy of your summary and determine whether any vital points have been left out. If any of your phrasing seems to be too close to the original, go back to the original text and think about the point being expressed; then look away from the source and rephrase the idea in your own words.

Deciding how much wording must be changed to "make it your own" can be difficult at times. There are instances where the wording need not be changed. Names of people, places, things, and organizations can be retained. Statistical data can sometimes be rounded off or made approximate: $487,345, for example, can become "nearly half a million dollars." Any short phrases from the source that you feel absolutely must be kept in their original forms must be enclosed in quotation marks exactly as in the original. It is also a wise practice to keep any such quotations to a minimum.

UTILIZING ACTIVE READING STRATEGIES IN SUMMARIZING

Your ultimate goal as an active reader is to make sense out of what you read. As you have seen above, active readers use a variety of strategies to direct and check on their reading progress. It is important, first of all, to recognize the writer's purpose in writing, because this will obviously partly shape your purpose and goal in reading. Authors sometimes write to entertain, for example, as in novels and short stories, but in academic work, the goal is more often to inform, explain, or persuade to belief and action. There are also some important **prereading strategies** that active readers practice that make reading the text more meaningful and promote real understanding. These strategies help readers predict what may lie ahead by (1) suggesting the topic and ideas that may be covered and (2) revealing the organization pattern through which ideas will be presented. Several special features will help you activate reading strategies for each particular reading.

Setting Your Reading Goals.   This section will help you focus on purposes—both yours and the writer's. It will help you to predict what is coming, and to adjust your strategies accordingly, by providing some prereading suggestions. These will direct you to do things like the following:

- Look at the title. You can usually determine the topic from the title, and sometimes you can infer the main idea.
- Read the first paragraph (or the first two or three, especially if they lead up to a heading) and the last paragraph. The reason for this is that the main idea is most often found in the first paragraph, and the final paragraph may provide a summary.
- Survey major and minor headings. It may be useful to skim through long sections that lack minor headings by reading the first sentence of some of the paragraphs.

Preview Vocabulary.   This will save you time by giving you the context meaning of unfamiliar words you will meet in the text. The paragraph number follows the word to help you locate it. For other words, there may be enough context clues to make a reasonable guess, or, if not, you will need to consult your dictionary.

Annotating As You Read. This section will help you establish a dialogue with the writer through suggestions on annotating the text. It will help you to test and revise your main idea guess to make it consistent with your prior knowledge and common sense. It will also help you to recognize patterns of organization and relate new information to old as you read. Annotating your text allows you to formulate questions as you go and to use inferences to make interpretations, clarify information, and draw conclusions. It also allows you to *evaluate* and *respond* to the author—to agree or disagree—as you work through the text. These personal kinds of notes will prove useful when you give a response to a reading, as, for example, in Reading Portfolio assignments.

The article below will provide you with an introductory example of the features listed above. It will also provide you practice in active reading strategies in analyzing, annotating, mapping, summarizing, and responding to text.

PREVIEWING *EATS OF EDEN*, BY DAVID E. GILBERT
Setting Your Reading Goals

Following the reading below, you will complete a summary and response. Complete the first two steps of the five-step process for summarizing before you read the entire text.

STEP 1 Determine the topic of the reading. The title is a play on words ("Eats" for "East") and involves an allusion (a reference to another source—here, to the biblical phrase "East of Eden.") In the space next to the title, annotate to indicate what this title suggests. Then look at the heading below the title. This should clearly indicate that the article will be about what topic?

Topic: _____

STEP 2 Determine if the article has a main idea. Read the first and last paragraphs. Recall that questions help us to focus on main ideas. Is there a broad question and answer that the text in general contributes to developing? Think about these questions: What, in your own words, is meant by "body and soul"? Who or what is being benefited by the markets and in what way? Write your main idea hypothesis in a complete sentence and in your own words:

Main idea hypothesis: _____

_____

Preview Vocabulary

subsistence (1)	means of support
agrarian (1)	relating to land and agriculture

condiments (1)	a seasoning or relish for foods—e.g. pepper, mustard, sauces, etc.
palate (1)	sense of taste (literally, the roof of the mouth)
corrugated (3)	shaped in parallel grooves, ridges, wrinkles, or furrows
canopy (3)	a roof structure, often of canvas or plastic, sheltering an area
artisan (3)	worker in a skilled trade; craftsman
tannin (4)	compound with a somewhat bitter, biting taste
cornucopia (5)	an overflowing abundance
pierogi (5)	small pastry turnover, filled with meat, cheeses, mashed potatoes, etc.
iridescent (5)	showing shifting changes in colors when viewed from different angles
magenta (5)	purplish red color
proletarian (7)	worker; member of the lower class
domestic (11)	of the home or household
culinary (12)	related to cooking and the kitchen

Annotating As You Read

STEP 3 This step of the summary process directs you to do the following:

Analyze and annotate key points in the text. Distinguish between what is major detail and minor detail in the supporting material included in the text.

As you read this article, you will want to mark the text and make notes on details that develop the main idea. Before you read the complete text, reread the first and last paragraphs and read the first sentence of paragraphs 2—11 to get an idea of major points that the article will deal with. List points here that seem to relate clearly to the main topic:

_____

_____

_____

_____

_____

Do these support your main idea guess? If not, you may want to revise your initial hypothesis. Highlight or underline these main points in the text—and any additional ones—and annotate key details in the margins. Mark any material that does not directly relate to the main idea as "background" or "definition."

Completing the above should prepare you to complete the other steps after you finish the reading. Flag any personal responses as "response" or keep a separate page with responses, additions, or criticisms that you may use later.

Eats of Eden

by David Gilbert

California Farmers' markets serve up nourishment for body and soul

1   "Cultivators of the earth are the most virtuous," wrote Thomas Jefferson, "furthering the principal subsistence of life." If the statesman were around today, he might be peddling the 250 varieties of herbs and vegetables he grew in his garden directly to the people at farmers' markets. Restoring the traditional link between the agrarian and urban communities, markets have become a means of survival for the small family farmer, with more than 350 certified farmers' markets in California, up from a handful in the late 1970s. For the consumer, they offer open-air therapy, serving up the freshest produce, condiments, flowers, entertainment, social contact—food for palate and soul.

2   Prime season runs from April through October, but many markets weather the elements all year, bringing you face-to-face with growers, like Ger Xiong, who cultivates Thai eggplant, cherry tomatoes, peas, and beans. Xiong drives four hours each way daily to market from his farm. What Xiong and his fellow farmers unload from their trucks—produce picked perfectly ripe but too delicate for conventional packing and shipping—cannot be had elsewhere.

3   Outdoor markets are movable feasts. "I love how a market transforms a street or lot for half a day, then tears down without a trace, save for a stray orange rind," says Meghan Askin, who manages the festive Jack London Square market in Oakland. Each market is as distinct as the community in which it resides. At the crossroads of agribusiness, under a green corrugated canopy, the year round Davis market enjoys a rural setting in the town square. Davis is where Les Portello sells the "AM-monds" he grows in Arbuckle, 40 miles north. ("To harvest them, we shake the tree so hard, we knock the 'L' out of them," Portello says.) One taste of his roasted almond butter is enough to make anyone forget about the grocery outlets.

4   Another virtue of the markets is having the chance to taste before you buy. A few tables down from the Portellos' almonds, Peggy and Michael Hen-

---

*David Gilbert, "Eats of Eden," (*VIA*, March/April 2000). Reprinted by permission of *VIA*.

wood of Henwood Estates encourage sampling of their artisan olive oils, made on their ranch near Marysville. Tidbits of bread saturated with green-golden oil, pressed days before, inspire wine-like descriptors: herbaceous and creamy, with slight tannin on the finish.

5   Farmers' markets serve as inspiration for home chefs and prominent chefs alike. Thursdays are market day for Bradley Ogden, chef/owner of Larkspur's Lark Creek Inn, who, in summer, spends $4,000 a week at market. Ogden has been frequenting the Marin market, located beside the Frank Lloyd Wright-designed Civic Center, since its founding in 1983. Surveying the market's cornucopia, he beholds a 1000-karat Hachiya persimmon and proclaims triumphantly, "A steamed pudding with a blood orange curd!"

6   Many markets combine old-world influences, like the one in Old Town Oakland. There you'll find everything from Russian pierogi to exotic Asian greens. The market's nestled between rows of Victorians and the revitalized Swan's, an old-style open market. A half-dozen languages meld with the calming notes of "Destiny the Harpist," who plucks her harp at many Bay Area markets. When Old Oakland comes alive at 8 a.m., so do the products. Indignant chickens and chukars (partridges) are extricated from cages while catfish are scooped from a tank on the back of a pickup. While fins and feathers fly, farmers stack salted duck eggs stained iridescent magenta, lest you confuse them with baluts (white fertile duck eggs).

7   Old Oak is "the proletarian market," says Sandro Rossi, who owns Caffe 817 around the corner, a popular retreat for farmers and shoppers. Rossi searches the stalls for a savoy cabbage for his Tuscan bean soup and dates to stuff with walnut meats for dessert. For the Florence native, markets are a way of life. Saturdays find Rossi at what he calls "the market of nobility— the social event of the week," the San Francisco Ferry Plaza market, on the Embarcadero.

8   On a typical Saturday at the Ferry Plaza gathering you might see the city's poet laureate Lawrence Ferlinghetti or symphony conductor Michael Tilson Thomas wandering among the fashionable throngs lined up for a bite at the Hayes Street Grill or Rose Pistola booths. From May through November, Ferry Plaza hosts free programs introducing consumers to farmers and chefs. One of those farmers is Art Lange of Honey Crisp Farm in Reedley, where he cultivates dwarf peaches, plums, and nectarines. As the fresh stone-fruit season is so fleeting. Lange has devised a sulfur-free method of preserving the summer sweetness in micro-thin slices, using honey and apple juice. His dried Snow Queen nectarines are so addictive that one customer thinks nothing of buying $150 worth at a pop.

9   Farmers' markets can sustain the vitality of city centers. Such is the case with San Luis Obispo's market, half a block from the mission founded by Father Junipero Serra. The evening market on Higuera Street is the centerpiece of an urban success story. During the 1970s, downtown business took

flight to suburban malls; the only action left on Thursday nights was cruising. The city tried holding volleyball tournaments, but it took someone setting up a barbecue in the street to get things cooking. Others followed suit, the downtown association invited the farmers, and the market was born in 1983.

10   Today on Thursday nights, the aroma of smoked meat and calzone wafts down five blocks of farmers and sundry merchants. The market transforms into one big street party, with bands battling for shoppers' attention. Under the lights, you can find sweet Chantenay carrots from Domingo Farm in Arroyo Grande and burdock root, which is good for ridding the body of excess fluid. To rehydrate yourself, there's apple zinfandel juice from Chadmark Farms. Mike Cirone trucks in Blenheim apricots and tiny lots of 50 heirloom apple varieties and tropical fruits adapted to the local clime, including the white sapote and cherimoya, from nearby See Canyon. No surprise, San Luis Obispo was honored by the National Trust for Historic Preservation for having one of the five best Main Streets in the nation.

11   The boast for the state's largest farmers' market goes to sunny downtown Santa Monica. Some 90 farmers gather there on Wednesday mornings. Professional chefs and their domestic counterparts wend their way along Arizona Street near the Third Street Promenade, pushing carts of ingredients for the evening meal. Chef Mark Peel of Campanile tracks down lamb's-quarters. Once a pesky weed, it now holds uncommon appeal. "We call it wild spinach; otherwise people expect a meat dish," says Peel. Bunches of arrow-headed leaves join lipstick peppers, squash blossoms, and sweet broccoli sprouts in Peel's cart.

12   At market, culinary trends evolve over casual conversation. Chefs track down heirloom seeds, farmers place them in the ground and bring the results to market, and consumers end up with a direct connection to the freshest produce and stories to be had. Jefferson would approve.

Exercise 5.3

Work together in small groups to compare your completion of steps 1 through 3 of the summary process. Reach a consensus on the following:

1. *Step 1* directed you to decide on the topic of the passage by looking at the title and at the phrase beneath the title. From this you should have determined that the topic of the article is:

   a. the story of Adam and Eve

   b. the body vs. the soul

   c. farmers' markets

2. *Step 2* suggested reading the first and last paragraphs in order to determine a general question and a main idea that answers it in the article. Which of the following best states the main idea of the article?

   a. Farmers' markets provide nutritious and delicious food, along with entertainment.

   b. Farmers' markets provide many features and benefits for individuals and society.

   c. Consumers end up with a direct connection to the freshest produce and stories.

   d. The many benefits of farmers' markets for consumers, farmers, chefs, and cities.

3A. In *step 3* of the summary process you were to analyze and annotate key points in the text and distinguish between major (important) and minor (less important) detail. Below is a sample annotation of the first three paragraphs of the article:

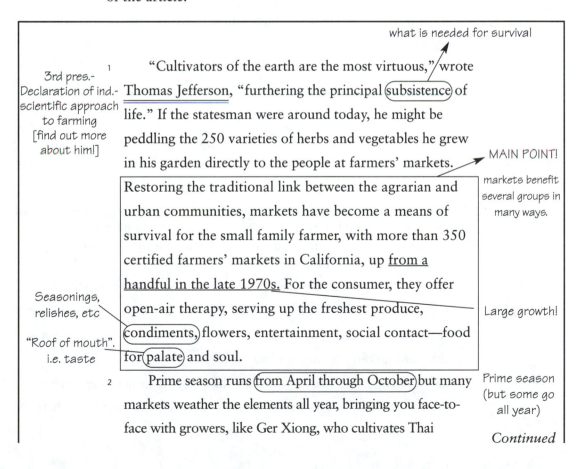

what is needed for survival

3rd pres.-
Declaration of ind.-
scientific approach
to farming
[find out more
about him!]

1   "Cultivators of the earth are the most virtuous," wrote Thomas Jefferson, "furthering the principal subsistence of life." If the statesman were around today, he might be peddling the 250 varieties of herbs and vegetables he grew in his garden directly to the people at farmers' markets.

MAIN POINT!

markets benefit
several groups in
many ways.

Restoring the traditional link between the agrarian and urban communities, markets have become a means of survival for the small family farmer, with more than 350 certified farmers' markets in California, up from a handful in the late 1970s. For the consumer, they offer open-air therapy, serving up the freshest produce, condiments, flowers, entertainment, social contact—food for palate and soul.

Seasonings,
relishes, etc

"Roof of mouth".
i.e. taste

Large growth!

2   Prime season runs from April through October but many markets weather the elements all year, bringing you face-to-face with growers, like Ger Xiong, who cultivates Thai

Prime season
(but some go
all year)

Continued

Example of farmer & produce

eggplant, cherry tomatoes, peas, and beans. Xiong drives four hours each way daily to market from his farm. What Xiong and his fellow farmers unload from their trucks—produce picked perfectly ripe but too delicate for conventional packing and shipping—cannot be had elsewhere.

Attractive feature: not permanent structures

3 Outdoor markets are movable feasts. "I love how a market transforms a street or lot for half a day, then tears down without a trace, save for a stray orange rind," says Meghan Askin, who manages the festive Jack London Square market in Oakland. Each market is as distinct as the community in which it resides. At the crossroads of agribusiness, under a green corrugated canopy, the year round Davis market enjoys a rural setting in the town square. Davis is where Les Portello sells the "AM-monds" he grows in Arbuckle, 40 miles north. ("To harvest them, we shake the tree so hard, we knock the 'L' out of them," Portello says.) One taste of his roasted almond butter is enough to make anyone forget about the grocery outlets.

feature: -variety in markets

"wrinkled, furrowed"

Typical example Davis market

3B. You were directed to reread paragraphs 1 and 12 and the first sentences of paragraphs 2–11 and list major details that seemed to support the main idea. Below are some of the points you should have annotated in your text and listed. Check your response with these.

Markets have become a means of survival for the small family farmer. (1)

For the consumer, they offer open-air therapy, entertainment, social contact—food for palate and soul. (1)

Outdoor markets are movable feasts. (3)

Another virtue of the markets is having the chance to taste before you buy. (4)

Farmers' markets serve as inspiration for home chefs and prominent chefs. (5)

Many markets combine old-world influences. (6)

Farmers' markets can sustain the vitality of city centers. (9)

The market transforms into one big street party. (10)

At market, culinary trends evolve over casual conversation. (12)

3C. You were also directed to look for background information and minor detail. Answer the following on the basis of your reading:

Which of the following paragraphs tells *when* the season runs?

    a. paragraph 2

    b. paragraph 3

    c. paragraph 5

    d. paragraph 10

Which of the following paragraphs tells which is the *largest* market?

    a. paragraph 3

    b. paragraph 6

    c. paragraph 9

    d. paragraph 11

Which paragraph tells of the growth in the number of markets?

    a. paragraph 1

    b. paragraph 4

    c. paragraph 7

    d. paragraph 12

Which paragraph is used wholly for giving or completing examples (minor details)?

    a. paragraph 7

    b. paragraph 8

    c. paragraph 10

    d. all three of the above

4. In *step 4*, you should work individually to create a map to guide your summary. Do that for the "Eats of Eden" article, using an umbrella map (main idea at the top) or a spider map (main idea in the center) to organize your details. Below are some suggested major categories for your main points. Use

the major points from the list you compiled and any others key points in the article that fall under these main areas.

Benefits for farmers

Benefits for consumers

Multicultural aspects

Benefits for chefs

Effect on city centers

Key features of markets

How much additional minor detail you include on your map is up to you. The amount of minor detail you use in a summary always depends on the length of the assignment.

MAP FOR "EATS OF EDEN"

5. Now you are ready for *step 5:* write the summary. Work individually to complete a summary of approximately 200 words (about one-third the length of the original). Remember to let the pattern map, not the article, determine the organization. For example, the article began with some quotes from, and ended with a reference to, Thomas Jefferson, who was the third President (1800–1808) of our country. That was an attention-getting device by the author, and appropriate because of Jefferson's great interest in and promotion of agriculture. Your summary, however, need not mention Jefferson at all—just stick to the main points regarding farmers' markets.

Also remember to gain control by establishing your voice in the summary. You can start that by beginning your summary with the name of the author and title of the passage.

> In the article "Eats of Eden," David E. Gilbert maintains that farmers' markets are …

As you write, look back at the article only to recheck the accuracy of details or to determine whether any vital points have been left out. When you are finished, exchange your summary with others in your group; evaluate them for accuracy, completeness, and acceptable paraphrasing. If any phrasing seems too close to the original, rephrase the idea in your own words without looking at the source.

Finally, in 75–100 words, respond to the article. Your response can include personal experience on the topic, additional information, criticism of the author's facts, or any other concern you have related to the topic and its presentation. Consult any personal "response" notes you made in the margins as you read.

PARAPHRASING AND PLAGIARISM

When you summarize, you shorten the original significantly by giving brief statements of the major points and excluding or compressing details. At times, however, you may find it necessary to **paraphrase** a paragraph or section, especially if it contains a main idea that is difficult or complex. A paraphrase differs from a summary in that it is generally as long as—or longer than—the original. It rephrases an idea in order to clarify the meaning. For example, paraphrasing can be helpful in the study of a poem by giving difficult parts a loose prose explanation. Paraphrasing is very important in note taking for projects like term papers which involve research. Failure to paraphrase correctly can subject you to the very serious charge of **plagiarism.** Most students are aware that plagiarism means the theft of someone's *ideas* and passing them off as their own. What they often don't realize is that plagiarism also applies to the *language* of the original as well.

Anything that appears in your paper that is not in quotation marks is presumed to be your own phrasing of the original source. Paraphrasing is not a simple or easy skill to master. It requires thinking about the *idea* being expressed by the language and then putting it into language of your own.

Sometimes paraphrasing is mistaken for a kind of patchwork rearranging of the original: a few words may be substituted, phrases rearranged, and parts of sentences stitched together. This kind of plagiarism of phrasing is often unintentional, but it is still unacceptable. Be careful that your paraphrases don't obscure the main idea or distort and misstate information. Compare, for instance, the three paraphrases that follow this passage.

> Most people in restricted environments find that they prefer non-interactive pastimes such as reading, listening to music, looking out windows, writing, and watching films or television. As much as anything, this preference may show again the need for privacy. A person can psychologically withdraw from the group by reading or listening to music. A good selection of passive entertainments looks like a must for any space station. Interestingly, Russian astronauts, who make much use of music, have also reacted with delight to grab bags containing unexpected toys or novelties.
>
> (Coon, *Introduction to Psychology*, 7th ed., 71)

Paraphrase A.   When people are in a restricted environment, most prefer passive pastimes such as listening to music, reading, watching films or television, or writing. A person who can psychologically withdraw from the group by reading or listening to music shows again the need for privacy. A must for any space station is a wide selection of passive entertainments. Russian astronauts have also reacted with delight to grab bags with toys and novelties, and they also make use of music.

Paraphrase B.   People who find themselves in confined situations often need to be entertained quietly and alone. That would be the case in a space station, as shown by Russian astronauts, who preferred listening to music and receiving surprise packages. The mental need to isolate oneself from others can also express itself in the desire to read, write, simply observe surroundings, or be entertained by visual media.

Paraphrase C.   Most people need to get away from others though private activities. By seeing movies or viewing television, people can mentally draw away from a group. Reading, writing, and music are also interesting activities. In fact, Russian astronauts on a space station make a lot of music. A space station must be stored with a number of surprises from Russia to be entertaining.

Paraphrase A quite obviously flunks the plagiarism test. Some changes have been made, but they are of the cut and patch variety. The synonyms *passive* and *non-interactive* have been switched. The beginning phrasing has been changed, but the author immediately picks the original phrasing up again with "restricted environment ..." and "prefer passive ..." For a good example of the technique of inverting clauses with only minor changes, compare the plagiarized version with the original.

Original: "A good selection of passive entertainments looks like a must for any space station."

Plagiarized: "A must for any space station is a wide selection of passive entertainments."

Paraphrase B represents an acceptable paraphrase. Ideas have been stated in the author's own phrasing. Certain inescapable words must appear—Russian astronauts, space station—and there is no real need to look for synonyms for basic words like "read" and "write." The paraphrase is slightly shorter than the original, but contains the essential details and examples.

Paraphrase C avoids the plagiarism problems of Paraphrase A but falls short in accuracy. The first sentence distorts the main idea—the paragraph is not talking about "most people" but rather about "most people in a restricted environment," a much smaller group. Sentence two picks up the wrong examples for "withdrawal" and fails to relate these activities to the "need for privacy." The paraphrase confuses the act of "making much of music" with actually "making music," and the final sentence clearly is a misstatement of the meaning of the original.

Exercise 5.4

The passage below on space habitats is followed by three paraphrases. Write acceptable *by the paraphrase that is accurate and uses its own phrasing. Write* inaccurate *by the one that misses or misstates the ideas of the passage, and explain under* Comments *where the inaccuracies are. Write* plagiarized *next to the one that is too close to the phrasing of the original, and put quotation marks around any sentences or phrases that are word for word from the original.*

1. Design of a space station as a living environment must take many human factors into consideration. For instance, researchers have learned that astronauts prefer rooms with clearly defined "up" and "down"—even in the weightlessness of space. Provisions must be made for regular exercise and full-body showers. As trivial as it might seem, a lack of showers was a major complaint among subjects in earlier confinement experiments.

(Coon, *Introduction to Psychology*, 7th ed., 712–713)

_____ **Paraphrase A.** Those who plan to make space station living comfortable need to keep certain considerations in mind. Astronauts will need rooms marked "up" and "down" because of the fact that they are weightless in space. They will need provisions, plenty of exercise, and showers, even though complaints about showers by people in cramped quarters in earlier experiments turned out to be trivial.

Comments: _____

_____

_____

_____

_____

_____ **Paraphrase B.** A number of human factors must be taken into account in the design of a space station as a living environment. For example, according to research, even in the weightlessness of space astronauts prefer rooms with clearly marked "up" and "down." They need to have regular exercise, and a lack of full-body showers was a big complaint of subjects in earlier experiments on confinement.

Comments: _____

_____

_____

_____

_____

_____ **Paraphrase** C. Despite being weightless, space inhabitants still want their quarters marked with the directions "up" and "down." Exercise opportunities must be provided, and prior research has shown that being able to take a complete shower is a priority for people living in cramped quarters. These are just some of the basic needs that must be met if planners are going to make a station crew comfortable in space.

Comments: _____

_____

_____

_____

_____

Create your own paraphrase for the following paragraph. Focus first on the main idea and determine how major details relate to it. Look away from the original as you write. Check your paraphrase carefully for accuracy and any phrasing that is too close to the original, and make any necessary changes. Then compare your version with those of two or three classmates.

2. Many studies of long-term isolation show steady declines in motivation. Most inhabitants intend to use their free time for creative pursuits. But in reality, they end up marking time and many become apathetic. Judging from submarine missions and Antarctic bases, as many as 5 percent of space inhabitants may experience some psychological disturbance. Most often the problem will be depression. However, in rare instances people have become paranoid, psychotic, suicidal, or uncontrollably aggressive. The risk of such problems may be minimized by carefully selecting personnel. Even so, it will be important to teach crew members basic counseling skills for solving conflicts.

(Coon, *Introduction to Psychology*, 7th ed., 712–713)

Paraphrase: _____

_____

_____

_____

_____

PREVIEWING *HOW THE WEB DESTROYS STUDENT RESEARCH PAPERS*, BY DAVID ROTHENBERG

Although technology provides great benefits, it has brought its own special problems, particularly in regard to the prevalence of plagiarism on campuses. Plagiarism is, of course, nothing new, but for some observers, such as the author of the article below, the problem is increasing in severity.

Setting Your Reading Goals

The title indicates that the topic of the article is:

Topic: _____

It also partly suggests the main idea. To clarify your main idea hypothesis, read the first paragraph and look for three questions the author writes. The answer is likely to be the main idea. Write it here:

Main idea hypothesis: _____

_____

Your goal as you read is to discover and evaluate the factors that the author maintains are having a negative effect on student research papers. In addition, continue to build on your understanding of plagiarism from the parts of the article that relate to it.

Preview Vocabulary

snippets (4)	bits and pieces
credibility (4)	trustworthiness, believability
neo-Luddite (5)	anyone opposed to technological change (originally, workers in early 19th century England who smashed labor-saving machinery that led to unemployment)
algorithms (6)	predetermined sets of instructions for solving problems in a series of steps
voila! (7) *(French)*	"there it is"
machinations (7)	actions as part of a plot or scheme
excerpt (8)	select, take out, or quote part of a source
montage (8)	a composite of parts that still remain distinct
ethereal (11)	heavenly, not earthly; unconnected to reality or reason

Annotating As You Read

The author indicates from the beginning that he feels that Web research fails to encourage the procedures of academic dialogue, and he suggests alternatives that should be taking place. As you read, mark the text and annotate the margins with notes related to procedures that encourage academic dialogue and those that do not. Be prepared to summarize these at the conclusion of your reading.

How the Web Destroys Student Research Papers

by David Rothenberg

1   Sometimes I look forward to the end-of-semester rush, when students' final papers come streaming into my office and mailbox. I could have hundreds of pages of original thought to read and evaluate. Once in a while, it is truly exciting, and brilliant words are typed across a page in response to a question I've asked the class to discuss. But this past semester was different. I noticed a disturbing decline in both the quality of the writing and the originality of the thoughts expressed. What had happened since last fall? Did I ask worse questions? Were my students unusually lazy? No. My class had fallen victim to the latest easy way of writing a paper: doing their research on the World Wide Web.

David Rothenberg, "How the Web Destroys Student Research Papers", *Chronicle of Higher Education*, 43 (August 15, 1997), A4. Reprinted by permission of the author.

2   It's easy to spot a research paper that is based primarily on information collected from the Web. First, the bibliography cites no books, just articles or pointers to places in that virtual land somewhere off any map: http://www.etc. Then a strange preponderance of material in the bibliography is curiously out of date. A lot of stuff on the Web that is advertised as timely is actually at least a few years old. (One student submitted a research paper last semester in which all of his sources were articles published between September and December 1995; that was probably the time span of the Web page on which he found them.)

3   Another clue is the beautiful pictures and graphs that are inserted neatly into the body of the student's text. They look impressive, as though they were the result of careful work and analysis, but actually they often bear little relation to the precise subject of the paper. Cut and pasted from the vast realm of what's out there for the taking, they masquerade as original work.

4   Accompanying them are unattributed quotes (in which one can't tell who made the statement or in what context) and curiously detailed references to the kinds of things that are easy to find on the Web (pages and pages of federal documents, corporate propaganda, or snippets of commentary by people whose credibility is difficult to assess). Sadly, one finds few references to careful, in-depth commentaries on the subject of the paper, the kind of analysis that requires a book, rather than an article, for its full development.

Only Advertising

5   Don't get me wrong. I'm no neo-Luddite. I am as enchanted as anyone else by the potential of this new technology to provide instant information. But too much of what passes for information these days is simply advertising for information. Screen after screen shows you where you can find out more, how you can connect to this place or that. The acts of linking and networking and randomly jumping from here to there become as exciting or rewarding as actually finding anything of intellectual value.

6   Search engines, with their half-baked algorithms, are closer to slot machines than to library catalogues. You throw your query to the wind, and who knows what will come back to you? You may get 234,468 supposed references to whatever you want to know. Perhaps one in a thousand might actually help you. But it's easy to be sidetracked or frustrated as you try to go through those Web pages one by one. Unfortunately, they're not arranged in order of importance. What I'm describing is the hunt-and-peck method of writing a paper.

7   We all know that word processing makes many first drafts look far more polished than they are. If the paper doesn't reach the assigned five pages, readjust the margin, change the font size, and ... voila! Of course, those machinations take up time that the student could have spent revising the paper. With programs to check one's spelling and grammar now standard

features on most computers, one wonders why students make any mistakes at all. But errors are as prevalent as ever, no matter how crisp the typeface. Instead of becoming perfectionists, too many students have become slackers, preferring to let the machine do their work for them.

8   What the Web adds to the shortcuts made possible by word processing is to make research look too easy. You toss a query to the machine, wait a few minutes, and suddenly a lot of possible sources of information appear on your screen. Instead of books that you have to check out of the library, read carefully, understand, synthesize, and then tactfully excerpt, these sources are quips, blips, pictures, and short summaries that may be downloaded magically to the dormroom computer screen. Fabulous! How simple! The only problem is that a paper consisting of summaries of summaries is bound to be fragmented and superficial, and to demonstrate more of a random montage than an ability to sustain an argument through 10 to 15 double-spaced pages.

Just Connect?

9   Of course, you can't blame the students for ignoring books. When college libraries are diverting funds from books to computer technology that will be obsolete in two years at most, they send a clear message to students: Don't read, just connect. Surf. Download. Cut and paste. Originality becomes hard to separate from plagiarism if no author is cited on a Web page. Clearly, the words are up for grabs, and students much prefer the fabulous jumble to the hard work of stopping to think and make sense of what they've read.

10   Libraries used to be repositories of words and ideas. Now they are seen as centers for the retrieval of information. Some of this information comes from other, bigger libraries, in the form of books that can take time to obtain through interlibrary loan. What happens to the many students (some things never change) who scramble to write a paper the night before it's due? The computer screen, the gateway to the world sitting right on their desks, promises instant access—but actually offers only a pale, two-dimensional version of a real library.

11   But it's also my fault. I take much of the blame for the decline in the quality of student research in my classes. I need to teach students how to read, to take time with language and ideas, to work through arguments, to synthesize disparate sources to come up with original thought. I need to help my students understand how to assess sources to determine their credibility, as well as to trust their own ideas more than snippets of thought that materialize on a screen. The placelessness of the Web leads to an ethereal randomness of thought. Gone are the pathways of logic and passion, the sense of the progress of an argument. Chance holds sway, and it more often misses than hits. Judgment must be taught, as well as the methods of exploration.

12   I'm seeing my students' attention spans wane and their ability to reason for themselves decline. I wish that the university's computer system would crash for a day, so that I could encourage them to go outside, sit under a tree, and read a really good book from start to finish. I'd like them to sit for awhile and ponder what it means to live in a world where some things get easier and easier so rapidly that we can hardly keep track of how easy they're getting, while other tasks remain as hard as ever-such as doing research and writing a good paper that teaches the writer something in the process. Knowledge does not emerge in a vacuum, but we do need silence and space for sustained thought. Next semester, I'm going to urge my students to turn off their glowing boxes and think, if only once in awhile.

Exercise 5.5

Vocabulary

Use the context to match the letters of the definitions on the right with the terms on the left. Numbers in parentheses refer to paragraph numbers.

1. _____ preponderance (2)	a. widely occurring; generally practiced
2. _____ masquerade (3)	b. out-of-date, no longer of use
3. _____ unattributed (4)	c. on the surface only; not profound
4. _____ prevalent (7)	d. the greater amount of material
5. _____ superficial (8)	e. bring parts together into a new whole
6. _____ repositories (8)	f. not identified or credited to
7. _____ obsolete (9)	g. decrease, grow less
8. _____ synthesize (11)	h. places where things are put for safekeeping
9. _____ disparate (11)	i. pretend to be what something isn't
10._____ wane (12)	j. varied, different

Comprehension Questions

Circle the correct letter choice and fill in the blanks where indicated.

1. Which sentence states the main idea for the multiparagraph unit 2–4?

   a. It's easy to spot a research paper based mainly on information collected from the Web.

   b. First, the bibliography cites no books, just articles or pointers to places.

     c. Another clue is the beautiful pictures and graphs that are inserted neatly into the body.

     d. Sadly, one finds few references to careful, in-depth commentaries on the subject.

2. Put a check in the blank next to the *five* words or phrases (paragraphs 2–4) that signal major details (i.e., the clues to spotting a Web-based research paper).

_____ first		_____ just
_____ then		_____ a lot of
_____ actually		_____ one
_____ another		_____ but actually
_____ accompanying		_____ and

3. The author feels that information on the Web is

     a. enchanting.

     b. advertising in disguise.

     c. exciting and rewarding.

     d. always of high intellectual value.

4. Search engines, according to the author,

     a. provide over a thousand pieces of useful information at many sites.

     b. should only be used in gambling casinos.

     c. can sidetrack and frustrate the user.

     d. all of the above

5. Word processing shortcuts may be harmful to a paper's quality if they

     a. make a shoddy first draft look far more polished than it is.

     b. disguise a paper's lack of proper length.

     c. cut into the time a student should spend revising the paper.

     d. all of the above

6. According to the author, the Web does all of the following EXCEPT

     a. make research look too easy.

     b. help the student understand, synthesize, and excerpt sources.

    c. result in disconnected summaries of summaries.

    d. discourage sustaining a lengthy written argument.

7. The article maintains that all of the following contribute to poor research practices EXCEPT

    a. the diverting of funds from books to soon-to-be-obsolete computer technology.

    b. surfing the Web and cutting and pasting.

    c. stopping to think and make sense of what's read.

    d. having no author cited on a Web page.

8. Paragraph 10 states that the Web is an inferior alternative to _____.

9. The author states that he needs to teach his students to do all of the following EXCEPT

    a. develop an ethereal randomness of thought.

    b. bring together different sources to come up with original thought.

    c. assess sources to determine their credibility.

    d. work through arguments.

10. The Web, in the eyes of the author,

    a. helps students to develop their attention spans.

    b. increases students' ability to reason for themselves.

    c. encourages students to read a really good book from start to finish.

    d. none of the above

Assessing the Characteristics of Academic Dialogue

*Below are some activities mentioned in the article related to the process of researching and writing a paper. The author believes some of these are appropriate and useful—that is, they are characteristic of academic dialogue—while others are not. Using your annotated notes, write **AD** (for academic dialogue) in the blank if the author seems to approve of an item. If not, leave the item blank.*

1. _____ including references to careful, in-depth commentaries

2. _____ turning in first drafts that look finished

3. _____ engaging in analysis that requires a book for its full development

4. _____ finding information that is really only advertising for information

5. _____ assessing sources to determine their credibility

6. _____ viewing libraries as centers for the retrieval of information

7. _____ linking, networking, and randomly jumping

8. _____ arranging in order of importance

9. _____ using the hunt-and-peck method

10. _____ preferring to let the machine do the work

11. _____ reading to understand, synthesizing, and tactfully excerpting

12. _____ downloading quips, blips, pictures, and short summaries

13. _____ compiling a paper consisting of summaries of summaries

14. _____ sustaining an argument through 10 to 15 double-spaced pages

15. _____ connecting, surfing, downloading, and cutting and pasting

16. _____ coming up with a fabulous jumble of words

17. _____ stopping to think and make sense of what's been read

18. _____ viewing libraries as repositories of words and ideas

19. _____ scrambling to write a paper the night before it's due

20. _____ synthesizing disparate sources to come up with original thought

21. _____ relying on snippets of thought that materialize on a screen

22. _____ working with logic, passion, judgment

23. _____ reading a really good book from start to finish

24. _____ writing a paper that teaches the writer something in the process

25. _____ turning off the glowing box and thinking

Questions for Discussion

Form groups of 4–5 to discuss the following.

1. Do you disagree with the authors assessment of any of the 25 items in the list above? If so, explain your views. _____

_____

_____

_____

2. Has the author exaggerated the dangers of researching on the Web? What benefits could it offer to students? _____

_____

_____

_____

3. What has been your experience with the Internet and World Wide Web? Would you rate it as positive, negative, or mixed? _____

_____

_____

_____

CHAPTER REVIEW

Answer T *for true or* F *for false to the following statements.*

_____ 1. Active readers never need to reread passages.

_____ 2. "Metacognition" refers to the action of "thinking about thinking."

_____ 3. We can truly understand what we read even if we can't explain it in our own words

_____ 4. The first place to start in a survey or preview is with the title.

_____ 5. The title will always suggest the main idea as well as the topic.

_____ 6. A summary must shrink all parts of the original in an equal ratio.

_____ 7. The organization of a summary may differ from the order of points in the original.

_____ 8. You should keep looking at the text frequently as you write a summary.

_____ 9. A paraphrase is often necessary for a difficult passage and may be as long or longer than the original.

_____ 10. To avoid plagiarism when you paraphrase, you need only change a few words or make minor rearrangements in sentence structure.

READING PORTFOLIO   An Information Article

1. *For this assignment you will need an article whose purpose is primarily to inform the reader with objective, factual information.* Look for a subject you are interested in, and try to find an article that will give you new information that you find valuable. If you have special interests—cars, physical fitness—try specialty magazines on those subjects.

2. *Practice the summary and paraphrase techniques you learned in this chapter,* going from text to map to summary. Map the main points of the article by answering basic questions: who, what, when, where, why, how. Look away as you write, in your own words, an accurate summary of about 175 words in length.

3. *Write a response of equal length in which you tell why you find the subject interesting or how the information you learned may be of use to you.* If you felt the article had inaccuracies or did not give a complete picture, you may wish to supply corrections or additional detail.

4. *Select five words from the selection that you are unsure of.* Use the dictionary to determine their meanings in the article. Then write a sentence for each, providing helpful context clues so that a person unfamiliar with the word would be able to guess its meaning.

5. *Decide under what category in your portfolio your article belongs and see if your instructor agrees.* File it in the appropriate category when your article is returned. If you think your article has a topical rather than an idea organization, label it so.

PART II

From Information to Proof

If all things were factual and informational, all in black and white, life might be easier and less stressful—although probably more boring. Fortunately or unfortunately, such is not the case, for truth often lies in areas of gray. We all face moments when, with whatever evidence we have at hand, we must make choices and arrive at decisions between competing versions of the truth.

When we move from purely informational writing to writing that must build a case in proving its view of the truth, academic dialogue shifts to questions of evidence and truth. The reader is in a much closer relationship with the writer, who no longer is an impersonal voice but instead often becomes an "I" with a definite viewpoint. We are apt to find ourselves actively responding, questioning, and disagreeing. For example, on a controversial issue such as the assassination of President John F. Kennedy, is it true that Lee Harvey Oswald was the lone assassin? Or did he have accomplices? Or is it the truth that some other individual or group was responsible? There are certain facts in the case, but the burden is on us to evaluate the evidence and to decide which view presents the most rational case.

In this unit, you will work in more detail with the first six idea patterns that you learned in Part I. Each chapter contains articles in which writers have brought evidence together to support their version of the truth. As you read, you should find yourself at times carrying on a running conversation with the author. This is a sign that the "inner worlds" of both writer and reader have now come into play—that part that is definitely *not* objective, that has been shaped by our personal histories and has helped to create our values and, unfortunately, our biases. For that reason there must be some ground rules in an honest search for the truth. We must adhere to the principles of academic dialogue. We must maintain an open mind and a willingness to look at all sides. We must carefully evaluate the evidence in order to reach a reasoned judgment, one as free as we can possibly make it of our personal feelings and emotions.

6

Evaluating What We Think: Facts, Opinions, and Beliefs

If you had been a typical person living a thousand years ago, would you have laughed at the idea that the earth was round, not flat? In the fifteenth century, would you have known for a fact that plague was spread by "bad air"? Or in seventeenth century New England, would you have agreed that the women of Salem were possessed by witches? The world of fact and information seems solid and comforting—until we run into facts that no longer seem to explain things, until we discover that the evidence of our senses cannot really be trusted, or until we find ourselves needing to make value judgments and interpretations. At that point we need some guidelines and ground rules if rational discussion is going to win out.

■ CHAPTER PREVIEW

In this chapter you will

- Distinguish among facts, opinions, and beliefs
- Find out how the denotations and connotations of words differ
- Examine how we determine and evaluate evidence
- Add purpose and tone to your critical reading vocabulary
- Discover how reference frameworks aid comprehension

If we were asked to describe a relative or an acquaintance, we might begin with physical facts about the person, gathered from our prior observations. However, we would most likely soon go beyond physical description to statements about personality traits. For example, which of the following descriptions of "Uncle Fred" would best give us a sense of what he is like?

tall and dark-haired

generous with his time and money

middle-aged

A specific statement like the first doesn't leave much room for further development. The third statement might invite a little more detail, but only the second would lead to a main idea about Uncle Fred that could be fully developed into an essay.

■ DISTINGUISHING FACT, OPINION, AND BELIEF

The difference between observations like the ones above illustrate some key distinctions you will need to learn to make between facts and opinions. Consider the following statements:

- A year on Venus is approximately 225 days.
- Last year the unemployment rate averaged over 9 percent.
- On clear days the sky appears blue.
- John F. Kennedy was assassinated in 1963.
- Last year there were 45,000 traffic fatalities in the United States.
- Water is composed of hydrogen and oxygen.
- Uncle Bob has red hair.

All of the above are facts because they can be verified by our senses, by scientific observation and analysis, from the historical record, or from statistical studies. It would also be useful to make a distinction between *fact* and *factual*. **Factual statements** are those that we agree can be proved to be either true or false. For example, "John F. Kennedy was assassinated in 1975" is a factual statement, not an opinion, because we can go to the historical record to prove it conclusively one way or another—in this case, it turns out to be false.

Opinions, on the other hand, are assertions that cannot now, or perhaps ever, be conclusively proved either true or false. Compare the following to the statements of fact above:

- Venus is a mysterious and forbidding planet.
- Last year was one of the most sluggish in the history of the American economy.

- Nothing is more beautiful than a blue sky on a clear day.
- Lee Harvey Oswald acted alone in Kennedy's assassination.
- We need to reduce speed limits to save lives on our highways.
- Athletes should replenish body fluids with water instead of sports drinks.
- Uncle Bob has ugly red hair.

With opinion, an opposite position can be held. For example, an astronomer may see nothing forbidding about Venus, an economist might interpret the data as showing a good deal of action in the economy, some athletes might prefer sports drinks over water, or Uncle Bob's wife might find his red hair quite attractive.

The examples above also show how opinions take a variety of forms. Statements like "We need to reduce speed limits" or "It is better to replenish body fluids with water" are generally followed by reasons intended to persuade the reader to action. This should be familiar to you as the opinion/reason pattern and will be dealt with at length in Chapter 13. This chapter will focus on two other kinds of opinions. As you move from straight information to questions of proof, you will often face uncertain situations where you must evaluate conflicting evidence to reach a reasonable conclusion. Statements like "Last year was one of the most sluggish" or "Lee Harvey Oswald acted alone" remain opinions because of insufficient or contradictory evidence.

A second common type of opinion statement involves value judgments. Sometimes these are directly indicated through value words like *excellent, good, bad, better, worst, right, wrong*. Which words mark these statements as opinions?

- Nothing is more beautiful than a blue sky.
- Uncle Bob has ugly red hair.

Words like *beautiful* and *ugly* clearly express value judgments. Many words, however, are less direct. Along with their literal meaning, some carry a kind of electrical charge, a positive or negative value judgment. For example, in the description of Venus, the words *mysterious* and *forbidding* do suggest some of the physical facts about the planet, but they also carry the feelings and attitudes of the viewer as well. Compare the following sentences:

- Senator Bowman is a statesman.
- Senator Bowman is a politician.

The words *statesman* and *politician* both have the meaning of "one who is involved in affairs of government." This is their **denotation**: the factual, literal reference of a word. But they vary greatly in their **connotations**: the feelings, emotions, or value judgments that a word may carry with it. The word *statesman* has a positive connotation, suggesting high-minded purpose and selfless commitment. *Politician,* on the other hand, has a negative connotation: lack of scruples and back room deals.

But there is only one Senator Bowman. Whether he is described as a statesman or politician depends on the opinion of the person giving the description.

For another example, analyze the following situation. Two observers are viewing Marie, a model, at a fashion show. She is 5'11" tall and weighs 106 pounds. Observer A comments that "Marie is slender and svelte." Observer B states that "Marie is scrawny and anorexic." What is the real truth? Is Marie slender and svelte? Or scrawny and anorexic? Who is right, observer A or observer B? The truth, of course, is that neither is right. There is only one certainty about Marie: she's 5'11" and weighs 106 pounds. Those are the only *facts* that we have. No matter how strongly they may feel, observers A and B are only expressing opinions.

Exercise 6.1

The following groups contain sentences that state facts, opinions, or a mixture of the two. If a sentence is all fact, write FACT. If it is all opinion, write OPINION. If it contains both fact and opinion, write MIXED, and underline the opinion part of the sentence. If a factual statement can be verified as untrue, write FALSE.

Examples:	FACT	The earth rotates on its axis once every 24 hours.
	OPINION	Earth is the most beautiful of all the planets.
	MIXED	The diameter of the earth is approximately 8,000 miles, the perfect size for a planet.
	FALSE	Earth is the largest of all the planets in our solar system.

Group 1

a. _____ American football is more exciting to watch than soccer.

b. _____ Advertisers may pay more than $1 million a minute on Super Bowl Sunday.

c. _____ The Denver Broncos were the Super Bowl champions in 2002.

Group 2

a. _____ Some movies are never released to theaters, but instead go directly to cable or video rental.

b. _____   Computer technology has created new special effects in fantasy and horror films, but the new movies just don't have the quality of the old classics.

c. _____   Westerns were Hollywood's greatest contribution to the art of the cinema in the 1950s.

Group 3

a. _____   Environmental pollution is the most pressing problem the world faces.

b. _____   The ozone layer consists of concentrated hydrogen ten to twenty miles above the Earth that absorbs solar radiation.

c. _____   The Earth has many natural resources, so we really don't need to worry so much about depleting its reserves.

Group 4

a. _____   Congress consists of the Senate, the House of Representatives, and the Supreme Court.

b. _____   The president is the country's chief executive officer, but the last thirty years have shown that he really has too much power for the nation's good.

c. _____   The vice president presides over the Senate but votes only in a tie.

Group 5

a. _____   Television was dominated in its beginnings by three major networks, CBS, NBC, and ABC.

b. _____   Television was invented in the early 1950s.

c. _____   Cable TV provides more choices today than early television did, but almost all shows on cable are of very low quality.

Group 6

a. _____   Some studies have maintained that links exist between high fat intake and increased health risks.

b. _____ Some people have become vegetarians in protest of the killing of animals; however, these people are uniformly weird or crazy.

c. _____ "Veggieburgers" are actually much more tasty than regular hamburgers.

Group 7

a. _____ The First Amendment deals with the right to bear arms.

b. _____ Some laws have been passed requiring a waiting period to buy some types of guns, an approach which is utterly wrong headed.

c. _____ Opponents of the right to carry concealed weapons are spineless traitors to the American ideals of freedom and self-rule.

Group 8

a. _____ Luxury cars today lack the pride of craftsmanship that went into the classic cars of yesteryear.

b. _____ The average car gets worse gas mileage today than twenty years ago.

c. _____ Some analysts feel that competition from Japan and other countries helped to steer American companies away from large, gas-guzzling cars.

Exercise 6.2

Two observers might choose very different words, positive or negative, to describe the same action. Below is a list of adjectives that relate to body movement and control. For those that carry positive connotations of "good coordination," put a plus sign (+); for those that have negative connotations of "poor coordination," put a minus sign (–). Look up the meanings of any words you are unsure of. The first two have been done for you.

1. ___+___ agile

2. ___–___ gawky

3. _____ skillful

4. _____ lumbering

5. _____ adept

6. _____ limber

7. _____ bungling

8. _____ dexterous

9. _____ ungainly

10. _____ supple

11. _____ lithe

12. _____ clumsy

13. _____ klutzy

14. _____ graceful

15. _____ smooth

16. _____ deft

17. _____ maladroit

18. _____ inept

19. _____ awkward

20. _____ gangling

The words *opinion* and *belief* are often used as interchangeable synonyms, but a useful distinction can be made between them. The dictionary defines the difference in this way:

> *Opinion* is applicable to any conclusion to which one adheres without ruling out the possibility of debate. *Belief* pertains to a conclusion, not necessarily derived firsthand, to which one subscribes strongly.
> (*American Heritage Dictionary*, 2nd College Ed.)

In this text, we will view *opinions* as **reasoned judgments** that may be changed or even given up after further debate and evaluation of evidence. *Beliefs* are more closed minded, concepts so necessary to us that we hold them with little or no factual evidence, or despite strong evidence to the contrary. For instance, despite the horrors of the Nazi occupations and the threat of death camp persecutions of World War II, many survivors continued to believe in the essential goodness of human nature. We also have many instances where family members or friends will continue to believe in the innocence of a convicted murderer despite overwhelming evidence or even a confession.

▨ EVALUATING EVIDENCE

To convince someone of the truth of their ideas, writers must of course provide support. For example, to support our earlier example of a main idea—Uncle Fred is generous with his time and money—we might provide this evidence:

■ He devotes many hours each month to programs of the Special Olympics.

■ His plumbing company provides two scholarships each year at the local college.

To support an idea, the writer needs to provide specific details such as facts, examples, anecdotes, statistical data, or expert testimony. As a reader, you must evaluate the evidence before agreeing or disagreeing with the writer's ideas. This is not an easy job, and may be complicated by what we see as acceptable evidence. One obvious problem is that even our most cherished facts can change. Consider the following:

■ The earth is flat.

■ The sun revolves around the earth.

■ The atom is the smallest unit of matter.

All of these factual statements have been proven false. Yet the average person a few hundred years ago would laugh at the idea that the earth is round or that the earth revolves around the sun, and with good reason. To our ordinary senses, it certainly does look like the earth is more flat than round and that the sun *rises* and *sets*.

Discovering new truths about our universe could not come about without a shift in what we call **evidence fields:** areas of experience we accept as valid authorities. We have had to acknowledge that the evidence of our senses is not always as reliable as the field of evidence that science and technology provide. Historically, another evidence field often on a collision course with the sciences, especially physics and astronomy, has been religion. The clash between religion and science is a good illustration that we can't get very far in any discussion unless we can agree on what kind of evidence we will accept as our authority. For example, while two archaeologists may disagree in interpreting findings, both accept the fossil record and certain scientific methods, such as age-dating techniques, used to establish the general outlines of their field. Likewise two debaters over religious doctrines may be very rational within the borders of their evidence field, which might include divine revelations. However, should an archeologist and a creationist join together to debate, say, the age and origin of the earth, sparks will fly. Since neither accepts the other's evidence field as the highest authority, they cannot debate reasonably. Often both sides will apply the label *belief* to any factual or opinion statement using support from an evidence field they cannot accept.

A similar situation exists in matters of strictly personal taste, where a confusion can occur between valuing—liking something—and evaluation—judging it good or bad against some standard. Compare the following statements:

- Ben and Jerry's vanilla ice cream is better than Breyer's vanilla.
- Vanilla is better than strawberry.

The first can be an evaluation. Expert taste testers could argue it rationally, once they agree on criteria about what is good: for example, texture, smoothness, aftertaste, nutritional value. The second, however, is a statement of personal value. "Vanilla and strawberry" are, as the saying goes, as different as apples and oranges. *Better* here really only means "I like it," and each of us is the sole expert on what we like. We can't debate statements like these because here the evidence field lies wholly *within* the individual. Too often arguments go nowhere because the participants confuse "I like it" with "It is good" statements.

Although it is upsetting to some people, most college and university courses lean heavily toward nonreligious and scientific evidence, and most assignments and tests will usually be evaluated on how well you follow standards of rational discussion. Within these boundaries, however, there may be a great deal of difference in the types and amount of evidence required. Facts, opinions, and beliefs form a continuum from the objective to the personal, and provide a framework for the variety of reading and writing assignments you will face in college.

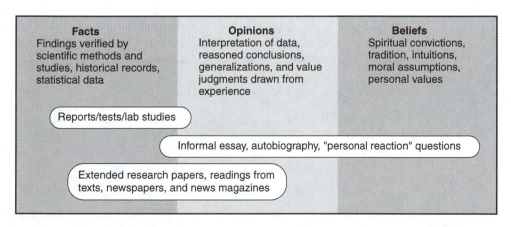

At one extreme, certain kinds of tests, factual reports, and lab studies require primarily informational writing, where the personal and subjective is not appropriate. At the other extreme, some writing assignments or group discussion questions may encourage you to share very personal experiences and convictions. Some short essays, such as Linda Ellerbee's "Tasha's Story" in Chapter 3, may get by without much hard evidence. The writer suggests generalizations that apply to society at large, but support is largely personal and anecdotal. Readers are invited to compare their own experiences to decide if the conclusions drawn are valid and/or typical.

In between, some assignments and readings may contain accounts of individual cases to help grab the reader's interest, but rely much more on public evidence to make their case. These may use individual stories as examples, but may also include historical background information, opinions of experts in the field, and studies or statistics reflecting national behaviors.

Exercise 6.3

In groups of four to five, review what you have learned so far in this chapter about

- *Facts, opinions, and beliefs*
- *How words suggest attitudes*
- *The authority of evidence fields*
- *Rational discussion in the college curriculum*
- *Confusing "I like it" with "it is good"*

Then discuss the two statements below, giving your reasons why you do or do not support them. Attempt to reach a consensus within your group, and write down your group's conclusions and the reasons for them. Then compare viewpoints with those of other groups in the class.

1. Statement: Everyone has a right to his or her opinion.

    Conclusion: _____

    _____

    _____

    _____

    Reasons: _____

    _____

    _____

    _____

2. Statement: My opinion is just as good as your opinion.

Conclusion: _____

_____

_____

_____

Reasons: _____

_____

_____

_____

GIVING SUPPORT TO OPINIONS

Despite its length and some difficult vocabulary, the following article has a fairly simple structure. The opinion is stated immediately; the support consists of illustrations, anecdotes, and quotations.

PREVIEWING *THE GREAT AMERICAN VANDAL* BY JOHN KEATS

Setting Your Reading Goals

Previewing the title and the first paragraph of the article will yield enough information to form a main idea hypothesis. We know from the title, "The Great American Vandal," that the article will deal with something about America, most likely the general public or some segment of it. The first three words of the introductory sentence, "The American tourist" confirm that guess and give us our topic. But how does *the American tourist* relate to *vandal*? We may have an idea what *vandalize* means but we need a reference framework for vandal. The dictionary gives these definitions:

> **Vandal** n. **1.** A member of a Germanic people that overran Gaul, Spain, and northern Africa in the fourth and fifth centuries A.D. and sacked Rome in A.D. 455. **2.** vandal. A person who maliciously defaces or destroys public or private property.
>
> (*American Heritage Dictionary*, 2nd College Ed.)

The first sentence of the paragraph helps make clear why *vandal* is an appropriate term: "The American tourist in full pursuit of life liberty and happiness may be less dangerous to the civilized world than Attila, but not much." Attila was King of the Huns, another group of fifth century barbarians noted for their ruthless destructiveness. The author's comparison of American tourists to these groups suggests that they share the same attributes. Therefore, to make your main idea guess, complete the following hypothesis.

The American Tourist is _____.

Preview Vocabulary

vacuous (3)	vacant, empty-headed
vulgarians (3)	unrefined, rude persons
presumably (4)	apparently, supposedly
spoor (5)	trail, track or scent left by a hunted animal
swinishness (7)	viciousness, boorishness
aplomb (7)	self-confidence, assurance
petrified (7)	turned to rock
depredation (13)	a plundering, ravaging, or despoiling
dowager (13)	elderly woman of upper classes
egocentrism (14)	selfishness, egotism
lugubrious (17)	woebegone, sad in an exaggerated manner
gaggle (18)	group of geese
irreverent (18)	disrespectful
Gothic (18)	pertaining to a style of architecture in Western Europe in the twelfth through fifteenth centuries
scourged (21)	tortured, tormented

Annotating as you Read

(1) Writers often use repetition to help the reader keep ideas in mind. In this article, the author uses over twenty different phrases to refer to the American tourist, some of which help to remind us of the main idea as well. For example, the title uses "Great American Vandal" as a synonym; at the end of the first paragraph, American tourists are referred to as "fun-loving friends and neighbors." Circle every instance in the article where the author uses a synonymous word or phrase to refer to American tourists or any part of that group. (2) As noted above, support in this article is mainly a series of short examples. Write EX in the margin next to each example that you find.

The Great American Vandal

by John Keats

1 The American tourist in full pursuit of life, liberty, and happiness may be less dangerous to the civilized world than Attila, but not much. The recent destruction at the John F. Kennedy Center for the Performing Arts in Washington, D.C., provides an example of what occurs, on only slightly less dramatic levels, everywhere else our fun-loving friends and neighbors go.

2 It was American visitors, and no one else, who ground out their cigarettes in the carpets, who dismantled the chandeliers, pried the faucets off the bathroom basins and the brass covers off the electric outlets, who stole the silverware from the restaurants and the paintings from the walls, who cut swatches out of the carpets and draperies to take them home for souvenirs. They took everything that was not nailed down and much else that was. It was again American visitors, and no one else, who stood around watching $1,500,000 worth of damage being done and did nothing to stop it.

3 The appalling thing was not that theft and wanton destruction were openly perpetrated and silently condoned by thousands of our countrymen. It was the vacuous stupidity of it. Apparently no one had the slightest consideration for, or interest in, anyone else. No one thought that everything taken or defaced made the Center that much less attractive for the next fellow. The fact that the Center was not theirs to wreck made no impression on our native vulgarians. They were merely doing what came natural to them.

4 They were, root and branch, of the same stock who think they can go barefoot into the shops of Orleans, Massachusetts, on Cape Cod, and steal from the counters. They do not go barefoot and steal because they are poor. Indeed, they are affluent. Presumably they do not go about in a state of undress committing crimes in their home towns, but they certainly do in towns like New Hope, Pennsylvania, where a family backed their station wagon to the entrance of the Playhouse Inn, the better to load it with all the fruit from a buffet table.

5 Our neighbors leave their spoor everywhere. In a national park in Utah, a vacationing family calmly tossed a large plastic bag of garbage onto the highway from their moving Cadillac, practically at the feet of an astonished National Park Service Ranger. At Perry's Victory Memorial on South Bass

Island in Lake Erie, freedom-loving vacationers customarily smash their whiskey bottles against the granite shaft. At the Lincoln Boyhood National Memorial there is a bronze cast of the hearthstone, and lower logs of the original cabin sitting in a slight depression in the ground. One group of patriots used it for a latrine, leaving it strewn with feces and toilet paper.

6   In Yellowstone Park, several geysers and the Morning Glory Pool have been irretrievably lost, because interested tourists could not resist the temptation to clog the vents with coins, stones, and logs. It was nature-loving Mom, Pop, and the kids who sprayed their names on rocks in the Grand Canyon with paint they had bought for the purpose, and when a Ranger protested, the father coolly replied, "We thought this was what everybody did. The rocks are for everybody, aren't they?"

7   More serious than this routine swinishness is the destruction our nature-loving countrymen visit upon everything that makes a park worth visiting. With an aplomb that can only be imagined, tourists in recent years have loaded literally tons of fossil wood into the trunks of their automobiles; each year, the Park Service says, there is less and less of Arizona's petrified forest to be seen.

8   It is American tourists, and no one else who, floating down the Colorado River, have turned it and Lake Mead into a sewer. Instead of availing themselves of the facilities that have been so expensively provided for their use, the happy boaters simply relieve themselves into the water, or along the banks of the river.

9   A possibly more disgusting, and certainly more pathetic, example of sheer poverty of mind and soul is the destruction of our rare petroglyphs. These are Indian paintings on rock faces. There are several in the western parks, most notably at Mesa Verde, Colorado, and Canyon de Chelly, Arizona. Not content to gaze with wonder upon these evidences of our vanished past, tourists have sought to improve upon them with aerosol paint sprays, knives, hatchets, sharp stones and, in one case, with rifle fire.

10   In addition to our national parks, historic sites and museums are particular targets of our touring barbarians—which accounts for the fact that so much of America's heritage is behind velvet ropes and iron bars or in glass cases, and is only to be seen through a screen of uniformed guards. It is not just for decorative effect that the Wright Brothers' airplane and Lindbergh's *Spirit of St. Louis* are suspended from the Smithsonian Institution's ceiling.

11   "There is almost nothing you can pick up and go away with now at our historical sites," a security officer at Independence Hall rather proudly said. "Of course, nobody can carry the Liberty Bell away, and they can't get close to the silver inkwells in the Assembly room because we won't let them inside there. We make sure they can't get close to anything that is movable. At the

same time, we give them something they can take away. If they touch the Liberty Bell, they get a certificate, suitable for framing, that says they have made a pilgrimage to the cradle of the nation's liberty, and this helps to keep them from trying to steal something else."

12   The cost of saving public treasures from the American public can sometimes be more than a city can bear. In Philadelphia, there are no longer sufficient funds to provide enough guards for the Museum of Art. As a result, on any given day only certain galleries are open.

13   Depredation is still largely a function of distance. The farther from home he is, the more oafish the American oaf dares to become. But it is all coming closer, and the thieves and vandals are increasingly those one might suspect of knowing better. A friend who had always opened his colonial mansion in Maryland to the local ladies' spring garden club tour, at so much per head for sweet charity, unwittingly donated more than $2,500 last year to the ladies— in the form of the books they took from his library, the Picasso ashtrays from his study, the antique flatware from his dining room. The gentlewomen also snipped flowers from his garden, and one charitable dowager apparently found the means and time to dig up and abscond with a small bush.

14   It is bad enough that American tourists foul their own nests, but worse, thanks to the creation of cheap jet travel, that our ill-mannered countrymen now commit their nuisances on a worldwide scale. They carve their initials and write their names in lipstick on the walls of the staircase inside St. Peter's Cathedral in Rome. They steal old Bibles from English country churches. Italian police lack courtroom evidence but have every reason to believe that certain American volunteers, helping with the work following the Florence flood, pocketed some of the irreplaceable artifacts they were supposed to be salvaging. A similar brutal egocentrism was displayed by four of our countrymen I found in the Academia in Florence. They were scratching on an early Sienese painting with their fingernails. Asked what the devil they thought they were doing, one of them explained that they were testing the paint.

15   It must be said that American tourists are not the only ones who do such things—they are merely the worst of the lot. The British contribute their share of those who should know better but act worse, of those like Byron, who carved his initials in a temple, of those like Elgin, who ran away with the marbles. It would seem there is something about tourism itself that brings out the barbarian in any people. The German yield to no one when it comes to oafishness, nor is the Belgian far behind. But American tourists are the worst of all, because they are particularly tactless, tasteless, and loudmouthed, and because there are so many of them and their numbers are increasing.

16   It is because of tourists' depredations that the great hotels of Europe and America have had to reduce their standards of comfort and elegance to cut their losses. Unmarked cheap napkins, sheets, towels, blankets, glassware, plates, and silverware have replaced the monogrammed linens, crystal, bone china, and silver of the pre-jet age. If there are still flowers in rooms, they are now apt to be plastic; where there used to be tasteful paintings hanging on the walls of opulent hotel suites, there are now cheap, rather ugly prints in frames screwed into the walls.

17   The pilfering and vandalism committed by American tourists are not, however, the most repellent of their activities. More obnoxious are the daily outrages they perpetrate against common decency wherever they go. They seem to think that being on vacation implies freedom and irresponsibility, and they express this notion in their dress and behavior. Getting themselves up in lugubrious costumes never worn in their home towns, they invade someone else's home town. Such behavior implies that tourists either think they are alone in the world, or they are ignorant of it.

18   For example, it seems not to occur to them that a foreign cathedral is a place for worship, not the fun house of an amusement park. I am not a Catholic, but I can certainly sympathize with any French priest who, trying to listen to a confession, also sees and hears a gaggle of irreverent know-nothings clattering and cackling, in the Gothic gloom, the bare heads and shoulders of the women an insult to his faith.

19   I am not a Communist, but I can understand the guards at Lenin's tomb who turned a couple away not because they were Americans, but because the woman was loud, low-bodiced, and miniskirted, while her husband was equally loud-mouthed, and clad in Bermuda shorts, a funny shirt, and a straw hat. Worse, such insensitive egocentrics resent a reprimand.

20   One future American wife and mother jittered in fury on the broad stairs of St. Peter's when refused admission because she was barefoot, wearing only a halter and hot pants. She cursed the nun who barred her way, then stripped off what little she wore, apparently thinking she was thereby making a gesture of righteous protest.

21   Badgered to despair by such barbarians, the Holy Synod of the Greek Orthodox Church has now asked its monks and nuns to recite, day and night, the following prayer: "Lord Jesus Christ, Son of God, have mercy on the cities, the islands, and the villages of our Orthodox fatherland ... which are scourged by the worldly touristic wave. Grace us with a solution of this dramatic problem and protect our brethren who are sorely tried by the modernistic spirit of these contemporary western invaders."

22   To which, civilized people everywhere can openly say "Amen."

Exercise 6.4

Vocabulary

Use the context to match the letters of the definitions on the right with the terms on the left.

1. _____ dismantled (2)   a. marred, scratched

2. _____ appalling (3)   b. uncontrolled

3. _____ wanton (3)   c. rebuke

4. _____ perpetrated (3)   d. unknowingly

5. _____ condoned (3)   e. luxurious

6. _____ defaced (3)   f. took apart

7. _____ affluent (4)   g. petty stealing

8. _____ unwittingly (13)   h. detestable

9. _____ oafishness (15   i. harassed

10. _____ opulent (16)   j. horrifying

11. _____ pilfering (17)   k. clumsiness

12. _____ repellent (17)   l. approved by not protesting

13. _____ obnoxious (17)   m. wealthy

14. _____ reprimand (19)   n. committed

15. _____ badgered (21)   o. offensive

Comprehension Questions

Circle the correct letter choice.

1. The main idea of this article ("The American tourist is a vandal") is developed by examples and supporting details showing behaviors and traits. That would indicate an idea pattern of

   a. description/support.

   b. comparison/contrast.

   c. opinion/reason.

   d. classification.

2. The example introduced in paragraph 1

    a. includes all its details in that paragraph.

    b. is concluded in paragraph 2 and not mentioned thereafter.

    c. is developed in detail in paragraph 2 and commented on in 3.

    d. occupies all of paragraphs 2, 3, and 4.

3. The sentence that best expresses the main idea of paragraph 3 is

    a. theft and wanton destruction were openly perpetrated.

    b. the vacuous stupidity of the action was appalling.

    c. the Center was not theirs to wreck.

    d. they were doing what came naturally to them.

4. In paragraph 4, the statement "they were, root and branch, of the same stock" means

    a. the exact same people who vandalized the Kennedy Center also stole on Cape Cod.

    b. the Kennedy Center vandals and the barefoot Cape Cod thieves are much alike.

    c. tourists at the Kennedy Center and in Orleans hold stock in the same companies.

    d. the Kennedy Center tourists also were barefoot.

Circle the one word that injects an opinion in each of the following phrases.

5. a vacationing family calmly tossed a large plastic bag of garbage

6. practically at the feet of an astonished National Park Service Ranger

7. when a Ranger protested, the father coolly replied

Circle the correct letter choice and fill in the blanks where indicated.

8. The main idea of paragraph 12 (the first sentence) is developed by a subpattern of

    a. comparison/contrast.

    b. time sequence.

    c. cause/effect.

    d. opinion/reason.

9. The last sentence of paragraph 15 begins by restating the main idea—"But American tourists are the worst of all"—and introduces two main details with the word "because" to form the pattern of

   a. description/support.

   b. comparison/contrast.

   c. opinion/reason.

   d. classification.

10. The main idea of paragraph 16 ("It is because …") is a cause/effect idea. The supporting details, however, are organized by what subpattern?

   a. description/support

   b. comparison/contrast

   c. opinion/reason

   d. classification

11. What phrase in paragraph 18 connects it to a multiparagraph unit that must include at least paragraph 17?_____

12. What two other paragraphs, each containing an example, belong in the multiparagraph unit that includes 17 and 18? _____   _____

Pattern Mapping

Complete the pattern map for paragraph 5:

Main Idea	

Support		
Example:	Example:	Example:

PURPOSE AND TONE

Two key terms help us define the relationship between writer and reader. **Purpose** refers to the author's intention or goal in writing. The three units of this textbook take you through three main outcomes a writer may have in mind: to inform, to prove (the present unit), and to persuade to action. You have, therefore, already been involved in determining purposes and will continue to do so throughout this text. **Tone** is a term we use to describe the writer's attitude, both toward his subject and his reader, and thus there are really as many tones as there are attitudes. The tone of an article, for example, can be light or serious, amused or angry, matter-of-fact or very impassioned, straightforward or ironic. The purpose an author has in mind also often determines the tone. For example, writing with a factual, informational purpose would usually be described as objective, neutral, straightforward, impersonal. Purposes which involve opinions and emotions have a much broader range of possible tones.

You are already probably an expert in recognizing tone; it's important in determining how people around us are feeling or how they are reacting to us. Most of us can recall a parent or other authority figure at some time telling us, "Don't use that tone of voice with me!" We also rely heavily on visual clues (for example, body language) to help determine tone. That's why we may experience difficulty in deciding someone's true message when visual clues are limited or absent (for example, in telephone conversations).

Since writers can't rely on visual clues, it is language alone that conveys (or in some cases betrays) their attitudes. That is possible because, as you learned in distinguishing between denotation and connotation, many words are not neutral. They carry positive or negative judgments, or imply good or bad motives. An author often has a number of word choices available; the words selected go a long way toward creating the tone of the work.

Because a writer's attitude can be complex, more than one word is often required to describe tone. To determine the tone of the author, think of tone in terms of some general categories that may or may not apply to a particular piece of writing. Figure 6.1 contains a sample list of common tone words showing a range of attitudes in several general areas. The tone of an essay might be located somewhere on one or more of the vertical scales—for example, humorous to serious, happy to sad, direct to indirect. Note that the horizontal list contains words in the middle that lean towards neither extremes. Writing which is essentially informational is generally described with words without any emotional coloring.

In determining the tone of "The Great American Vandal," we should observe that John Keats uses devices like repetition to draw attention to his criticism of the American tourist, as, for example, in these passages:

"It was the American visitors, and no one else ..."(2)

"It was again American visitors, and no one else ..."(3)

"It is American tourists, and no one else ..."(8)

Mainly, however, he relies on word choice to get his tone across, particularly the use of a variety of phrases to describe the American tourist. Many of these phrases—

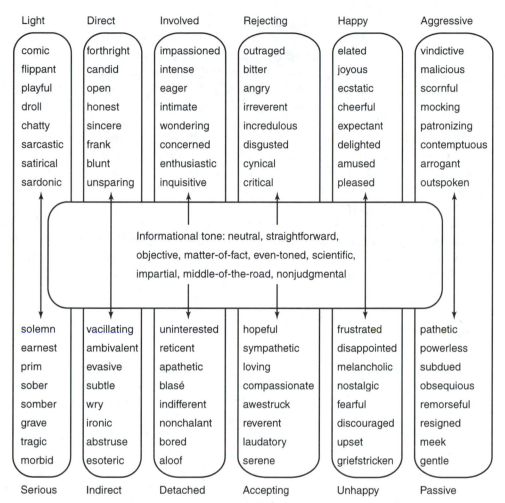

Light	Direct	Involved	Rejecting	Happy	Aggressive
comic	forthright	impassioned	outraged	elated	vindictive
flippant	candid	intense	bitter	joyous	malicious
playful	open	eager	angry	ecstatic	scornful
droll	honest	intimate	irreverent	cheerful	mocking
chatty	sincere	wondering	incredulous	expectant	patronizing
sarcastic	frank	concerned	disgusted	delighted	contemptuous
satirical	blunt	enthusiastic	cynical	amused	arrogant
sardonic	unsparing	inquisitive	critical	pleased	outspoken

Informational tone: neutral, straightforward, objective, matter-of-fact, even-toned, scientific, impartial, middle-of-the-road, nonjudgmental

solemn	vacillating	uninterested	hopeful	frustrated	pathetic
earnest	ambivalent	reticent	sympathetic	disappointed	powerless
prim	evasive	apathetic	loving	melancholic	subdued
sober	subtle	blasé	compassionate	nostalgic	obsequious
somber	wry	indifferent	awestruck	fearful	remorseful
grave	ironic	nonchalant	reverent	discouraged	resigned
tragic	abstruse	bored	laudatory	upset	meek
morbid	esoteric	aloof	serene	griefstricken	gentle

Serious	Indirect	Detached	Accepting	Unhappy	Passive

Figure 6.1   Some Categories of Tone

along with his anecdotes—amuse the reader, but Keats clearly feels he is dealing with an important problem. On the light/serious scale, therefore, we might locate his tone on the "light" side, but shading toward the "serious." In pinpointing his tone in this category, we should note that some of his descriptions are directly critical—*oafish, obnoxious, ill-mannered*—but others are less direct as, for instance, when he describes destructive tourists as "fun-loving friends and neighbors."

This mixture of words and their context results in a *sarcastic* tone. Sarcasm is form of verbal irony, which ridicules its subject by suggesting the opposite of its literal meaning. The context helps us to determine when a statement is sarcastic. For example, if a student flunks an exam after failing to study, a friend might comment "Wow! You really aced that test! Hard study sure pays off!" Someone overhearing the conversation might take the statement at face value, but the student who failed knows differently. On the surface Keat's phrase "fun-loving friends and neighbors" would appear to praise, but in the context of the rest of the article it obviously conveys a negative judgment—there is nothing "funny" or "loving" about destroying national treasures.

Sarcasm is an indirect device, but overall Keat's relentless attack on vandalism is certainly not subtle. On the direct/indirect scale, his tone is best described as "blunt" and "unsparing." He is clearly very caught up in his subject; in the involved/detached category, "intense" or "impassioned" would clearly apply. On the rejecting/accepting scale, Keats is clearly very mad—even outraged. This would suggest that his tone will belong on the aggressive side of the passive/aggressive scale: "scornful," "mocking," or perhaps even "vindictive" would fit as he heaps scorn upon polluters and despoilers. Since Keat's anger dominates, none of the words on the happy/sad scale would apply significantly in describing the tone of the article.

Exercise 6.5

Part A

As you read "The Great American Vandal," you were directed to circle all phrases that were used in place of "the American tourist." Compare your list to the one below. For each phrase write either N *for neutral,* C *for Critical (direct, negative connotation), or* S *for sarcastic (irony is intended). The first three have been done for you.*

1. ___C___ The Great American Vandal

2. ___N___ the American tourist

3. ___S___ fun-loving friends and neighbors

4. _____ American visitors

5. _____ our countrymen

6. _____ our native vulgarians

7. _____ our neighbors

8. _____ freedom-loving vacationers

9. _____ insensitive egocentrics

10. _____ nature-loving Mom, Pop, and the kids

11. _____ ill-mannered countrymen

12. _____ happy boaters

13. _____ our touring barbarians

14. _____ the American public

15. _____ the American oaf

16. _____ thieves and vandals

17. _____ nature-loving countrymen

18. _____ gaggle of irreverent geese

19. _____ one group of patriots

20. _____ contemporary Western invaders

Part B

Below are some articles you worked with earlier. Following each article are several tone categories and choices. If a category is applicable to the tone of the article, check either A or B (not both). If the tone words in neither A nor B seem to fit the selection, check C: "category does not apply." Definitions are given for the tone words in the exercise. For any other words on the lists in Figure 6.1, use your dictionary to learn their definitions.

Example

JOHN KEATS: "THE GREAT AMERICAN VANDAL"

Serious-Light

A. ___X___ sarcastic—ridiculing by suggesting the opposite of a literal meaning

satirical—attacking faults in a humorous way

B. _____ grave—dark, gloomy, dull

tragic—appropriate to the occurrence of a tragedy (disaster, sad event)

C. _____ category does not apply

Direct/Indirect

A. _____ subtle—sly, suggestive, not obvious

vacillating—not decisive, wavering

B. ___X___ blunt—direct, to the point without worrying about other's feelings

Continued

> unsparing—relentlessly attacking, never letting up on
>
> C. _____ category does not apply
>
> **Happy/Unhappy**
>
> A. _____ ecstatic—extremely joyful
>
> elated—greatly uplifted in spirit
>
> B. _____ melancholic—sad and depressed in spirit
>
> nostalgic—longing to return to something in the past or far away
>
> C. ___X___ category does not apply

1. LINDA ELLERBEE: "TASHA'S STORY"

Rejecting/Accepting

A. _____ compassionate—with concern and feeling for

sympathetic—sharing the feelings and emotions of another, esp. those of sorrow/loss

B. _____ incredulous—in a state of disbelief

irreverent—without awe or respect

C. _____ category does not apply

Happy/Unhappy

A. _____ frustrated—kept from achieving a desired end

discouraged—deprived of hope or confidence

B. _____ cheerful—filled with joy

pleased—happy about, satisfied

C. _____ category does not apply

Aggressive/Passive

A. _____ malicious—intending evil or harm

patronizing—helping or agreeing with, but in a snobbish, superior way

B. _____ obsequious—fawning, flattering

meek—mild; passive

C. _____ category does not apply

2. GARY SOTO: "FEAR"
Serious/Light

A. _____ earnest—sincere; not joking

somber—solemn, grave

B. _____ droll—humorous in an odd way

flippant—saucy, disrespectful

C. _____ category does not apply

Involved/Detached

A. _____ intense—having or showing strong emotion

intimate—relating to on a personal level; confiding in

B. _____ blasé—without any concern

apathetic—indifferent, not caring

C. _____ category does not apply

Aggressive/Passive

A. _____ resigned—yielding, submissive

powerless—unable to counter another's actions

B. _____ vindictive—mean, revengeful

arrogant—proud, haughty

C. _____ category does not apply

3. SUSAN SCHALLER: "ILDEFONSO"
Serious/Light

A. _____ prim—stiffly formal, proper, moralistic

morbid—dwelling on and fascinated by grim, grisly, horrible details

B. _____ chatty—breezy, talkative on light subjects

sardonic—bitterly sneering

C. _____ category does not apply

Direct/Indirect

A. _____ ambivalent—wavering, having contradictory feelings

abstruse—highly abstract and complex

B. _____ candid—truthful, holding nothing back
forthright—open, honest

C. _____ category does not apply

Involved/Detached

A. _____ inquisitive—probing, questioning
concerned—taking a deep interest in

B. _____ aloof—reserved, cool in manner, distant
nonchalant—casual, without any interest in

C. _____ category does not apply

FRAMES OF REFERENCE: A DIALOGUE WITH THE WORLD OUTSIDE

One problem developing readers face is lack of vocabulary; there may be simply too many unknown words in the text to allow full comprehension. Another serious difficulty—especially for students native to other cultures—is a lack of general background information. Writers often make reference to, or build conclusions on, information about the world at large that they assume readers will already have.

Such information groups itself in various fields into what are sometimes called "frames of reference"—connected guidelines of facts, concepts, and definitions in various fields that help you to understand new information by relating it to a larger context. In a previous passage, Dr. Kosta Bagakis addressed the importance of building larger connections in knowledge:

> I want to understand my history, my heritage, my job, my world view. I want to get it all clear and I believe everything is interconnected, so if I'm reading about math, for instance, I try to see how the major mathematical issues fit into my understanding of philosophy and history. All of my reading is focused on my attempt to understand the world.

Building frames of reference involves an important aspect of academic dialogue—an interaction with a world of information, past and present. A good example of a frame of reference is a timeline outlining an area of history. If a passage mentions Roman or Grecian or Mayan civilization, or refers to the Ottoman Turks, the Aztec empire, or the Crusades, you need to have an idea of at least approximate dates, and some notion of what cultures or events these terms refer to. All of the general education college courses you take are designed to help you build and internalize frames of reference that help you understand your world. Courses in history, political science, music, art, geography, or biology are not placed in your way as hurdles to be jumped over and forgotten. You will naturally forget many details, but if you pursue it seriously, your college education will provide a solid foundation for lifelong learning.

An African American writer who suffered severe discrimination and came to understand that knowledge is power was Richard Wright. Considered one of the foremost novelists of American literature, he vividly portrayed in his most famous novel, *Native Son,* the social and racial conditions that bred poverty, rage, and violence. In the following selection taken from his autobiography, *Black Boy (American Hunger),* Wright shows how—after he was able to borrow a library card when he was nineteen—his life changed radically.

PREVIEWING FROM *PART ONE: SOUTHERN NIGHT* BY RICHARD WRIGHT

Setting Your Reading Goals

Preview by reading the first and last paragraphs. The first begins with an incident; the last will give you more of a clue to the main idea. The passage is mainly concerned with a change that the author undergoes. Look for a sentence near the end that tells what has created the difference in his life and use it to complete the main idea hypothesis.

Richard Wright's reading _____

_____

_____

_____

Preview Vocabulary

passionately (6)	with great feeling
conviction (7)	strong belief
reveled (7)	took great pleasure in
steeped in (9)	engaged deeply in
Jim Crow (9)	subject to discrimination and segregation
buoying (10)	inspiring, cheering
preoccupation (12)	complete engagement of attention
naive (12)	simple, lacking in knowledge of the world
unlettered (12)	illiterate, not adept in reading and writing

Annotating as you Read

As you read, focus on the difference between Wright's situation in the world (his job, how he is treated) and what he is beginning to dare to hope for. Regarding the changes he is undergoing, think about what North and South represent to him, and make annotations in the margin accordingly.

From Part One: Southern Night

by Richard Wright

1   I entered the library as I had always done when on errands for whites, but I felt that I would somehow slip up and betray myself. I doffed my hat, stood a respectful distance from the desk, looked as unbookish as possible, and waited for the white patrons to be taken care of. When the desk was clear of people, I still waited. The white librarian looked at me.

2   "What do you want, boy?"

3   As though I did not possess the power of speech, I stepped forward and simply handed her the forged note, not parting my lips.

4   "What books by Mencken does he want?" she asked.

5   "I don't know, ma'am," I said, avoiding her eyes.

6   "Who gave you this card?"

7   "Mr. Falk," I said.

8   "Where is he?"

9   "He's at work, at the M—Optical Company," I said. "I've been in here for him before."

10   "I remember," the woman said. "But he never wrote notes like this."

11   Oh, God, she's suspicious. Perhaps she would not let me have the books? If she had turned her back at that moment, I would have ducked out the door and never gone back. Then I thought of a bold idea.

12   "You can call him up, ma'am," I said, my heart pounding.

13   "You're not using these books, are you?" she asked pointedly.

14   "Oh, no, ma'am. I can't read."

15   "I don't know what he wants by Mencken," she said under her breath.

16   I knew now that I had won; she was thinking of other things and the race question had gone out of her mind. She went to the shelves. Once or twice

---

she looked over her shoulder at me, as though she was still doubtful. Finally she came forward with two books in her hand.

17   "I'm sending him two books," she said. "But tell Mr. Falk to come in next time, or send me the names of the books he wants. I don't know what he wants to read...."

18   That night in my rented room, while letting the hot water run over my can of pork and beans in the sink, I opened *A Book of Prefaces* and began to read. I was jarred and shocked by the style, the clear, clean, sweeping sentences. Why did he write like that? And how did one write like that?... I stood up, trying to realize what reality lay behind the meaning of the words. Yes this man was fighting, fighting with words. He was using words as a weapon, using them as one would use a club. Could words be weapons? Well, yes, for here they were. Then, maybe, perhaps, I could use them as a weapon? No. It frightened me. I read on and what amazed me was not what he said, but how on earth anybody had the courage to say it.

19   Occasionally I glanced up to reassure myself that I was alone in the room. Who were these men about whom Mencken was talking so passionately? Who was Anatole France? Joseph Conrad? Sinclair Lewis, Sherwood Anderson, Dostoyevsky ... Nietzsche and scores of others? Were these men real? Did they exist or had they existed? And how did one pronounce their names?

20   I ran across many words whose meanings I did not know, and I either looked them up in a dictionary or, before I had a chance to do that, encountered the word in a context that made its meaning clear. But what strange world was this? I concluded the book with the conviction that I had somehow overlooked something terribly important in life. I had once tried to write, had once reveled in feeling, had let my crude imagination roam, but the impulse to dream had been slowly beaten out of me by experience. Now it surged up again and I hungered for books, new ways of looking and seeing. It was not a matter of believing or disbelieving what I read, but of feeling something new, of being affected by something that made the look of the world different....

21   I forged more notes and my trips to the library became frequent. Reading grew into a passion.... Reading was like a drug, a dope. The novels created moods in which I lived for days. But I could not conquer my sense of guilt, my feeling that the white men around me knew that I was changing, that I had begun to regard them differently....

22   Steeped in new moods and ideas, I bought a ream of paper and tried to write; but nothing would come, or what did come was flat beyond telling. I discovered that more than desire and feeling were necessary to write and I dropped the idea. Yet I still wondered how it was possible to

know people sufficiently to write about them? Could I ever learn about life and people? To me, with my vast ignorance, my Jim Crow station in life, it seemed a task impossible of achievement. I now knew what being a Negro meant. I could endure the hunger. I had learned to live with hate. But to feel that there were feelings denied me, that the very breath of life itself was beyond my reach, that more than anything else hurt, wounded me. I had a new hunger.

23   In buoying me up, reading also cast me down, made me see what was possible, what I had missed. My tension returned, new, terrible, bitter, surging, almost too great to be contained. I no longer *felt* that the world about me was hostile, killing; I *knew* it. A million times I asked myself what I could do to save myself, and there were no answers. I seemed forever condemned, ringed by walls....

24   If I went north, would it be possible for me to build a new life then? But how could a man build a life upon vague, unformed yearnings? I wanted to write and I did not even know the English language. I bought English grammars and found them dull. I felt that I was getting a better sense of the language from novels than from grammars.

25   I knew of no Negroes who read the books I liked and I wondered if any Negroes ever thought of them. I knew that there were Negro doctors, lawyers, newspapermen, but I never saw any of them. When I read a Negro newspaper I never caught the faintest echo of my preoccupation in its pages. I felt trapped and occasionally, for a few days, I would stop reading. But a vague hunger would come over me for books, books that opened up new avenues of feeling and seeing, and again I would read and wonder as only the naive and unlettered can read and wonder, feeling that I carried a secret, criminal burden about with me each day.... My reading had created a vast sense of distance between me and the world in which I lived and tried to make a living, and that sense of distance was increasing each day. My days and nights were one long, quiet, continuously contained dream of terror, tension, and anxiety. I wondered how long I could bear it.

Exercise 6.6

Comprehension Questions

Circle the correct letter choice and fill in the blanks where indicated.

1. Which of the following is the best statement of the main idea of this passage?

   a. The author feared that he would never be a successful writer.

b. The effect of Mencken's words on the author, his desire to be a writer and the many obstacles of discrimination in his path.

c. Reading opened a world of ideas and opportunities that had deliberately been denied the author because of his race.

d. People can overcome any obstacle if they put their mind to it.

2. What is the librarian's attitude toward the possibility that Richard might read the books?

a. mildly encouraging

b. suspiciously hostile

c. completely indifferent

d. highly supportive

3. Paragraphs 1—17 form a unit that is organized by the pattern of

a. time sequence.

b. cause/effect.

c. opinion/reason.

d. whole/part.

4. What is young Richard's reaction to Mencken's writings (paragraph 18)?

a. He is repelled by his ideas and rejects them.

b. He is awed by his ideas and his courage.

c. He is amused and entertained by his viewpoints.

d. He is angered and irritated by his opinions.

5. At one point in his reading (20) Richard wonders "But what strange world was this?" What world is he referring to? _____

_____

_____

6. Which of the following is the best statement of the divided main idea of paragraph 21?

a. I forged more notes and reading was like a drug, a dope.

b. My trips to the library became frequent and reading grew into a passion.

c. As my trips to the library became frequent, the white men around me knew that I was changing.

d. Reading grew into a passion, but I could not conquer my sense of guilt.

7. The main idea pattern of paragraph 21 is

    a. opinion/reason.

    b. comparison/contrast.

    c. problem/solution.

    d. classification.

What key signal word gave you the clue to this pattern?_____

8. Which of the following is true of Richard's early writing career?

    a. He was successful from the start.

    b. He lacked desire and feeling.

    c. He felt he needed to learn more about life and people.

    d. none of the above

9. What two methods did the author use to attack unfamiliar words?

    a. _____

    _____

    _____

    b. _____

    _____

    _____

10. What words best describe the tone of the author in this passage?

    a. neutral and scientific

    b. anxious and confused

    c. angry and bitter

    d. passive and submissive

Questions for Writing/Small-Group Discussion

1. An old adage says "Sticks and stones can hurt my bones, but words can never hurt me." Richard Wright asks, "Could words be weapons?" What is his conclusion? Do you think he is right?

2. Richard asks about the names he encountered (19), "Were these men real? Did they exist?" If so, what were they famous for?

CHAPTER REVIEW

Circle the correct letter choice for each of the following questions.

1. An author's tone
   a. is never neutral.
   b. may require more than one word to describe.
   c. has no relation to purpose.
   d. all of the above

2. Purpose refers to the author's intention
   a. to inform.
   b. to prove.
   c. to persuade to action.
   d. all of the above

3. "My son could never murder anyone" is a statement of
   a. fact.
   b. fact and opinion.
   c. opinion.
   d. belief.

4. An opinion
   a. is a reasoned judgment.
   b. might be modified after discussion.
   c. might be given up after evaluation.
   d. all of the above

5. "Secretary Davis is one of Washington's most shameless bureaucrats." In this sentence, the denotation of *bureaucrat* is
   a. a government official.
   b. a person who causes needless waste and delay.

6. In the above sentence, the connotation of *bureaucrat* is
    a. a government official.
    b. a person who causes needless waste and delay.

7. "Action movies are more fun than romantic movies" is a statement that really means
    a. "I like action movies better than romantic movies."
    b. "Action movies are of a higher quality than romantic movies."

8. "One of the Wilson children did not finish high school; the other completed college" is a statement of
    a. fact.
    b. opinion.
    c. fact and opinion.

9. "One of the Wilson children is a high school drop-out; the other somehow managed to slink his way through college" is a statement of
    a. fact.
    b. opinion.
    c. fact and opinion.

10. All of the following are examples of frames of reference *except*
    a. a timeline of the history of India.
    b. a wall chart showing the anatomy of the human body.
    c. a mystery novel set in an English mansion.
    d. a scale drawing of our solar system.

READING PORTFOLIO   *Evaluating Fact, Opinion, and Belief*

1. *One good source for finding writing that strongly expresses opinions and beliefs is the Letters to the Editor section of a newspaper's editorial page.* These often provoke lively discussion, showing a wide range from the factual and rational to the opinionated and emotional; letters can also express firmly held beliefs (often without much factual support) of the writers. Because of space considerations, editors limit the length of letters, so you should pick one that has as much meat to it as possible.

Option A

Find a factual, informational article. Then compare it to a letter on the same topic that seems to you to go well beyond fact into opinion and/or belief.

Summarize the facts presented in the factual article. Then summarize the main points of the letter. In your response, analyze carefully any emotional language or unsupported thinking and try to determine what "evidence field" the writer is using.

Option B

Find a letter that expresses opinions or beliefs that you find unacceptable or irrational. Write your own Letter to the Editor in response to that letter, in which you summarize the writer's position, identify unsupported opinions and beliefs, and respond by outlining what you consider to be your own reasonable viewpoint.

2. *File this Portfolio Article under the category of opinion/reason.*

Assessing Qualities and Functions: Description and Support

If you were asked to describe your personality or that of an acquaintance, what words would you choose? Actually you would have a lot of words to choose from—close to 20,000 English words refer to personal traits, adjectives such as *funny, cheerful, good-natured,* or nouns such as *optimist, prankster, couch potato.* Using words like these is one way we communicate our views about people and things around us. You were introduced to description/support—probably the most common of all idea patterns—at the sentence and paragraph level in Part I. Now you will examine in much more depth some different ways descriptive generalizations are made in writing.

▮ CHAPTER PREVIEW

In this chapter you will

- ▪ Observe how features of our language allow us to describe characteristics and traits
- ▪ Become familiar with other ways of describing
- ▪ Identify emotional appeals and logical fallacies related to description/support
- ▪ Analyze text selections and full-length articles in the description/support pattern
- ▪ Complete a profile assignment for your Reading Portfolio

We can move from a topic to an idea in description/support because our language has certain features that allow us to relate objects to their characteristics:

- The pencil is yellow.
- Ralph is a liar.
- The movie is highly suspenseful.

The difference between a topic—"the highly suspenseful movie"—and an idea—"The movie is highly suspenseful"—really lies in the way the word *is* lets us answer something *about* a topic, and in a complete sentence. A form of the verb *to be* like *is* lets us isolate and focus on specific traits as if they are separate from the object itself.

DESCRIPTIVE STATEMENTS

We describe traits, as in the examples above, through the use of adjectives and nouns. We can also use **verbs of action,** often accompanied by adverbs, to make general descriptive statements about behaviors, accomplishments, or functions. These statements can be similar to—or may lead directly to—statements about characteristics. For example, compare these pairs:

John **interrupts others** frequently.

John is **rude.**

State funding of road construction **has decreased markedly.**

State policy on funding road construction is becoming increasingly **tightfisted.**

The Pure Food and Drug Administration **controls** new products in the marketplace.

The Pure Food and Drug Administration is a **bureaucratic tyrant.**

Each statement helps to characterize a person, a policy, or an institution, and in each pair, the second is an opinion that could be inferred from the first. Note in the short essay below how the author uses statements about behaviors to convey the traits of successful students.

What Are the Characteristics of Successful Students?

by David Schultz

1   Not surprisingly, they attend classes—regularly. Moreover, they are on time. If they miss a session, they feel obligated to let the instructor know why, and their excuses seem legitimate and reasonable. They make sure they get all assignments they missed and understand specifically what was covered in class.

2   They take advantage of extra credit opportunities if they are offered. They demonstrate that they care about their grades and are willing to work to improve them. They often do the optional (and frequently challenging) assignments that many students pass up, such as giving a five-minute presentation that substitutes for an essay.

3   Successful students speak in class, even if their attempts are a bit clumsy and difficult. They ask the questions that the instructor knows many in the class are bound to have, provided they are listening.

4   They see the instructor before or after class about grades, comments made on their papers, and upcoming tests. Sometimes they just want to ask a question or make a comment relative to the class discussion.

5   Successful students turn in assignments that look neat and sharp. They take the time to produce a final product that looks good, a reflection of a caring attitude and pride in their work.

6   They are attentive in class. They don't chat, read, or stare out of windows. In other words, they are polite and graceful, even if they get a little bored.

7   Almost all work and assignments are turned in, even if every one of them is not brilliant. Successful students seem driven to complete all work.

8   The most successful students may well end up at the instructor's office door at least once during the semester. They'll go out of their way to find the instructor and engage him/her in meaningful conversation.

*David Schultz, "What Are the Characteristics of Successful Students?", (*Innovation Abstracts,* Vol. X, no. 17.). Reprinted by permission of Innovation Abstracts and National Institute Staff and Organizational Development, University of Texas at Austin, Austin, TX 78712.

Exercise 7.1

Comprehension Questions

Circle the correct letter choice.

1. The information in paragraphs 1 and 7 shows that successful students are
   a. all brilliant.
   b. full of excuses.
   c. perfectionists.
   d. highly responsible.

2. From paragraphs 2 and 5 we can conclude that successful students are
   a. neat and sharp dressers.
   b. conscientious.
   c. sneaky.
   d. manipulative.

3. Paragraph 3 shows that successful students
   a. provide verbal input in class.
   b. are often difficult to understand.
   c. ask unnecessary questions.
   d. only ask questions they know the instructor can answer.

4. From the behaviors of good students in paragraphs 4 and 8, they would best
   be described as
   a. frequent complainers.
   b. nuisances to their instructors.
   c. interactive with instructors.
   d. constant flatterers.

5. Paragraph 6 states that successful students are all of the following EXCEPT
   a. attentive.
   b. polite.
   c. graceful.
   d. boring.

Questions for Writing/Small-Group Discussion

1. Rate yourself on a scale of 1 (low) to 5 (high) on each of the points that the author makes about successful students. What do you think you can do to improve?

2. Does the author anywhere in the article say that successful students are smarter or more talented than unsuccessful ones? What viewpoint toward success in school is indicated by your answer? Do you agree?

3. Can you think of any other attitudes or behaviors characteristic of good students?

REFERENCE FRAMEWORKS: THE ACADEMIC CONNECTION 1

Many general education courses in college that center on people and their accomplishments must rely on the idea pattern of description/support. Courses in history, for example, obviously deal with time, but at the same time they must assess the characteristics and actions of the actors on the historical stage. History must attempt to answer questions like "What kind of personal qualities account for the successes and failures of Napoleon, Hitler, or Winston Churchill?" or "What were the strengths and weaknesses of Roosevelt's New Deal?" Courses in political science and sociology will likewise involve issues and ideas that require description with supporting statements about social or institutional relationships.

Being able to recognize the structure of description/support is particularly important in the study of literature. Students frequently have trouble with such courses because they require skill in making inferences about a character's personal traits. Particularly in modern short stories, novels, and plays, authors don't often give direct statements about characters or themes. We draw our conclusions from what characters say and do, what others say of them, how they interact with each other, and what their fates tell us about the qualities or conditions of life.

As you read in your college course work about historical or fictional characters, the role of government in people's lives, and the social structures and relationships in various cultural and ethnic groups, try to come up with words or phrases that summarize traits, features, and attitudes. You may also find it helpful to utilize description/support pattern maps when you study and when you organize notes in preparation for taking exams or writing reports.

▨ EMOTIONAL APPEALS AND LOGICAL FALLACIES

Although most of us would agree that reaching a sound judgment should be the goal of discussion, debate is often undermined by emotional appeals or by some classic **logical fallacies:** errors in reasoning and inference. This section will introduce you to some of the appeals and fallacies that are common to certain idea patterns.

NAME-CALLING

When we make judgments through value words, we must give enough evidence to justify our word selection. Recalling a previous example, if I describe Senator Bowman as a *politician* instead of a *statesman,* I must be prepared to provide statements by the senator, or other facts regarding his conduct, to justify my views. Unfortunately, however, people sometimes resort to a technique that instead tries to attach an unfavorable label or a name to a person or an idea. This technique, name-calling, may also be referred to as "mudslinging," "poisoning the well" or, more formally, *argument ad hominem* (argument against the man). During the 1950s, for example, many politicians tried to hang the labels *commie* or *pinko* on the opposition to suggest a lack of patriotism. In our own era, Republicans and Democrats attack each other with words like *liberal, free spenders,* and *fat cats.* Opponents in debates on abortion and gun control all too frequently fail to focus on rational issues and sink to the level of name-calling.

GLITTERING GENERALITIES

An opposite technique, but one also aimed at feelings rather than thinking, is the use of statements that sound great but on closer examination are just giving vague opinions. "All that glitters is not gold" is certainly true of glittering generalities; they are particularly common in politics and advertising. A classic example a few years back was the slogan for Coca-Cola: "It's the Real Thing."

HASTY GENERALIZATION

Also called sweeping generalization, this is the fallacy of making a very broad statement with too little evidence. This fallacy is always a danger when we present an inference based on our observations. "All immigrants nowadays are lazy and dependent" is a sweeping statement that is impossible to prove. "Many immigrants today are lazy and dependent" may sound more logical, but not if it is supported only by statements like "I know this family that lives on our street and they're that way." In such cases there is too little evidence to justify the broad conclusion.

Exercise 7.2

Identify the following statements as NC *for name-calling,* GG *for glittering generality, or* HG *for hasty generalization.*

1. _____ . Americans today have simply lost the work ethic. My brother-in-law would rather draw unemployment than get a job.

2. _____ "Lexus: The Relentless Pursuit of Perfection"

3. _____ Watching the drivel that passes for television is a pastime proper only for pathetic, unimaginative creatures devoid of interest in life.

4. _____ It's time for a return to traditional American values, the spirit of our forefathers.

5. _____ "When guns are outlawed, only outlaws will have guns."

6. _____ Women are just unable to compete with men. None of the girls at our school could play successfully on the boy's team.

7. _____ Welfare cheating is everywhere. A woman down the street has a new car and color TV, and she gets a check in the mail every month.

8. _____ Gun control is a crackpot idea cooked up by a bunch of soft-headed liberals.

9. _____ Only a fanatic skinhead with the IQ of a rock would oppose thoughtful legislation to limit the ownership of guns.

10. _____ "Wheaties, Breakfast of Champions!"

■ DESCRIPTION AND SUPPORT IN TEXTBOOKS

Analyzing qualities, traits, and functions occurs across many disciplines, especially in the humanities and social sciences. The selection below from a psychology textbook illustrates a typical use of the pattern by outlining the characteristics associated with a significant psychological disorder.

PREVIEWING *ANTISOCIAL PERSONALITY DISORDER* BY NEIL R. CARLSON AND WILLIAM BUSKIST

Setting Your Reading Goals

Your objective in this kind of textual material is to bring together the various traits and/or functions being discussed to get a complete picture of the whole. A preview of the title and first paragraph should provide a clear focus for the topic being developed.

Preview Vocabulary

DSM-IV (1)   most recent *Diagnostic and Statistical Manual;* widely used by psychiatrists and psychologists for classifying psychological disorders

perverted (2)   deviating from the correct or normal

depraved (2)   corrupt; characterized by bad habits

prevalence (4)   extent to which something exists

Annotating As You Read
Highlight text and make brief notes in the margins regarding the qualities and characteristic behaviors of antisocial personality types. The selection also contains some definitions of key terms that should be underlined or highlighted and summarized.

Antisocial Personality Disorder

by Neil R. Carlson and William Buskist

1   The DSM-IV classifies abnormalities in behavior that impair social or occupational functioning—personality disorders. Although there are several types of personality disorders, the one discussed here has the most impact on society: antisocial personality disorder. Figure 7.1 provides a description of several other personality disorders.

2   People have used many different terms to label what we now call **antisocial personality disorder,** which is characterized by a failure to conform to standards of decency, repeated lying and stealing, a failure to sustain long-lasting and loving relationships, low tolerance of boredom, and a complete lack of guilt. Prichard (1835) used the term *moral insanity* to describe people whose intellect was normal but in whom the "moral and active principles of the mind are strongly perverted and depraved ... and the individual is found to be incapable ... of conducting himself with decency and propriety." Koch (1889) introduced the term *psychopathic inferiority,* which soon became simply *psychopathy* (pronounced *sy-**kop**-a-thee*); a person who displayed the disorder was called a *psychopath*. The first version of the DSM (the DSM-I) used the term *sociopathic personality disturbance,* which was subsequently replaced by the present term, *antisocial personality disorder*. Most clinicians still refer to such people as *psychopaths* or *sociopaths*.

Description

3   People with antisocial personality disorder cause a considerable amount of distress in society. Many criminals can be diagnosed as psychopaths, and most psychopaths have a record of criminal behavior. The diagnostic criteria of the DSM-IV include evidence of at least three types of antisocial behavior before age fifteen and at least four after age eighteen. The adult forms of antisocial behavior include inability to sustain consistent work behavior; lack of ability to function as a responsible parent; repeated criminal

Neil Carlson and William Buskist, *Psychology: The Science of Behavior,* 5th ed.

TABLE 17.4

Descriptions of Various Personality Disorders*

Personality Disorder	Description
Paranoid	Suspiciousness and extreme mistrust of others; enhanced perception of being under attack by others.
Schizoid	Difficulty in social functioning—poor ability and little desire to become attached to others.
Schizotypal	Unusual thought patterns and perceptions; poor communication and social skills.
Histrionic	Attention-seeking; preoccupation with personal attractiveness; prone to anger when attempts at attracting attention fail.
Narcissistic	Self-promoting; lack of empathy for others; attention-seeking; grandiosity.
Borderline	Lack of impulse control; drastic mood swings; inappropriate anger; becomes bored easily and for prolonged periods; suicidal.
Avoidant	Oversensitivity to rejection; little confidence in initiating or maintaining social relationships.
Dependent	Uncomfortable being alone or in terminating relationships; places others' needs above one's own in order to preserve the relationship; indecisive.
Obsessive-compulsive	Preoccupation with rules and order; tendency toward perfectionism; difficulty relaxing or enjoying life.
Passive-aggressive	Negative attitudes; negativity is expressed through passive means: complaining, expressing envy and resentment toward others who are more fortunate.
Depressive	Pervasive depressive cognitions and self-criticism; persistent unhappiness; feelings of guilt and inadequacy.

Source: Adapted from Carson, R.C., Butcher, J. N., and Mineka, S. *Abnormal Psychology and Modern Life,* 10th ed. New York: HarperCollins, 1996, p.317; from Carlson and Buskist, *Psychology: Science and Behavior,* 5th ed., 580.

Figure 7.1   Descriptions of Various Personality Disorders*
* The antisocial personality disorder, not listed here, is described in detail in the text

activity, such as theft, pimping, or prostitution; inability to maintain enduring attachment to a sexual partner; irritability and aggressiveness, including fights or assault; failure to honor financial obligations; impulsiveness and failure to plan ahead; habitual lying or use of aliases; and consistently reckless or drunken driving. In addition to meeting at least four of these criteria, the person must have displayed a "pattern of continuous antisocial behavior in which the rights of others are violated, with no intervening period of at least five years without antisocial behavior." Clearly, these are people most of us do not want to be around.

4   The lifetime prevalence rate for antisocial personality disorder is estimated to be about 3.5 percent, although estimates of prevalence reported in the DSM-IV are lower: about 3 percent for men and less than 1 percent for women. However, we cannot be sure that any of these figures are accurate because psychopaths do not voluntarily visit mental health professionals for help with their "problem." Indeed, most of them feel no need to change their ways. Psychopaths who are indicted for serious crimes will often be seen by psychiatrists in order to determine whether they are "sane," and some will feign some other mental illness so that they will be committed to a mental institution rather than to a prison. Once they reach the institution, they will quickly "recover" so that they can be released

5   Cleckley, one of the most prominent experts on psychopathy, has listed sixteen characteristics of antisocial personality disorder. Cleckley's list of features provides a good picture of what most psychopaths are like. They are unconcerned for other people's feelings and suffer no remorse or guilt if their actions hurt others. Although they may be superficially charming, they do not form real friendships; thus, they often become swindlers or confidence artists. Both male and female psychopaths are sexually promiscuous from an early age, but these encounters do not seem to mean much to them. Female psychopaths tend to marry early, to be unfaithful to their husbands, and to soon become separated or divorced. They tend to marry other psychopaths, so their husbands' behavior is often similar to their own. Psychopaths habitually tell lies, even when there is no apparent reason for doing so and even when the lie is likely to be discovered. They steal things they do not need or even appear to want. When confronted with evidence of having lied or cheated, psychopaths do not act ashamed or embarrassed and usually shrug the incident off as a joke.

6   Psychopaths do not easily learn from experience; they tend to continue committing behaviors that get them into trouble. They also do not appear to be driven to perform their antisocial behaviors; instead, they usually give the impression that they are acting on whims. When someone commits a heinous crime such as a brutal murder, normal people expect that the criminal had a reason for doing so. However, criminal psychopaths are typically unable to supply a reason more compelling than "I just felt like it." They do not show much excitement or enthusiasm about what they are doing and do not appear to derive much pleasure from life.

7   Psychopaths tend not to become emotionally involved with other people. The following report illustrates this lack of attachment:

> I can remember the first time in my life when I began to suspect I was a little different from most people. When I was in high school my best friend got leukemia and died and I went to his funeral. Everybody else was crying and feeling sorry for themselves and as they were praying to get him into heaven I suddenly realized that I wasn't feeling anything at all. He was a nice guy but what the hell. That night I thought about it some more and found that I wouldn't miss my mother and father if they died and that I wasn't too nuts about my brothers and sisters for that matter. I figured there wasn't anybody I really cared for but, then, I didn't need any of them anyway so I rolled over and went to sleep.
> (Carlson and Buskist, *Psychology: The Science of Behavior,*
> 5th ed., 579–581)

Exercise 7.3

Vocabulary

Use the context in the text selection to match the letters of the definitions on the right with the correct terms on the left.

1. _____ criteria (3)
2. _____ aliases (3)
3. _____ intervening (3)
4. _____ indicted (4)
5. _____ feign (4)

6. _____ remorse (5)
7. _____ superficially (5)
8. _____ confidence artists (5)
9. _____ promiscuous (5)
10. _____ heinous (6)

a. only on the surface; only appearing to be
b. fake, pretend
c. outrageously evil or wicked; abominable
d. a standard by which something is judged
e. engaging casually in sex with many persons
f. phony names
g. experts at swindling and fraud
h. coming in between
i. formally charged with a crime
j. shame, deep guilt felt over one's actions

Mapping

The text included a graphic (not reprinted here) which worked as a kind of map by listing the characteristics of antisocial personality disorder. Create your own checklist graphic to summarize the chief traits associated with the disorder. Below are twenty statements regarding traits and actions. Consult your text marking and notes to decide on which ten accurately describe this personality type. Then write them in the box below.

demonstrate a very poor work ethic

avoid engaging in theft or prostitution

are good at laying long-range plans

feel need to change their ways, but can't

are unconcerned for other people's feelings

are very charming and form real friendships

are sexually promiscuous from an early age

generally avoid marrying other psychopaths

steal even when they don't need to

do not easily learn from experience

are usually fairly responsible parents

show irritability and aggressiveness

habitually lie and use aliases

feel no remorse if they hurt others

commit crimes because of mental illness

often become swindlers or con men

soon become separated or divorced

only lie when there is a reason to

get great pleasure from life

have usually been forced into criminal acts

**Primary Characteristics of
Antisocial Personality Disorder**

1. _____

2. _____

3. _____

4. _____

5. _____

6. _____

7. _____

8. _____

9. _____

10. _____

Comprehension Questions

Circle the correct letter choice and fill in the blanks where indicated.

1. Antisocial personality disorder is characterized by all of the following EXCEPT

    a. failure to conform to standards of decency.

    b. repeated lying and stealing.

    c. ability to sustain long-lasting and loving relationships.

    d. low tolerance to boredom.

2. Sociopaths are also known as

    a. psychopaths.

    b. sycophants.

    c. psychiatrists.

    d. all of the above

3. The minimum number of antisocial behaviors required by the DSM-IV for an adult to be classified as an antisocial personality would be

    a. three.

    b. four.

    c. nine.

    d. forty.

4. A diagnosis of antisocial personality disorder might NOT be made if the person

    a. has displayed a pattern of continuous antisocial behavior.

    b. continuously violates the rights of others.

    c. has had an intervening period of at least five years without antisocial behavior.

    d. none of the above

5. Determining the number of persons with the disorder is difficult because

    a. the DSM-IV is a very unreliable testing mechanism.

    b. women are more prone to give dishonest responses than men.

    c. psychiatrists often misdiagnose psychopaths as insane.

    d. psychopaths do not voluntarily visit mental health professionals for help.

Determine whether, according to the text, the following are (True) or (False):

6. _____ Estimates suggest that men are more likely to be psychopaths than women are.

7. _____ Criminal psychopaths deemed insane recover quickly in institutions because of the exceptional care they receive.

8. _____ Cleckley, a famous psychopath, had sixteen characteristics of antisocial personality disorder.

9. _____ Psychopaths are generally in a state of high emotion and excitement when they commit major crimes such as murder.

Using Figure 7.1, write the name of a personality disorder in the blank next to the description that best illustrates it.

10. _____ Amanda is abused by her husband, but won't criticize or report his behavior to the authorities for fear he will leave her.

11. _____ When nobody would pay attention to him, Alfredo finally jumped up on his chair and began to give a very theatrical and rambling speech.

12. _____ The owner of the pizza parlor is convinced that hundreds of foreign agents are engaged in a conspiracy to murder him.

13. _____ After some early unsatisfactory experiences, Melvin refuses to attend any more social gatherings.

14. _____ Though she could be attractive, Samantha continually belittles herself, and has convinced herself that she isn't worthy of anyone's friendship.

15. _____ Lowell washes his hands continually all day, and always taps on his desk three times before he opens it.

▪ DESCRIPTION AND SUPPORT: THE PROFILE

Reading longer passages, articles, or chapters organized by description/support can be fairly simple. Once you have grasped the main idea (it is often restated more than once), the support can be a straightforward list of facts and illustrations, or one or more long narrative examples. A good example in the last chapter was "The Great American Vandal." This pattern often lends itself to speed reading or quick review by skimming, and pattern mapping of even a very long article can be done quickly.

However, even though description/support may have fewer elements than some of the other patterns, you need to pay careful attention to the ways in which the central idea and the support may be distributed in longer passages. The pattern map model below will help you visualize how the ideas of a single paragraph might be expanded into a six-paragraph article.

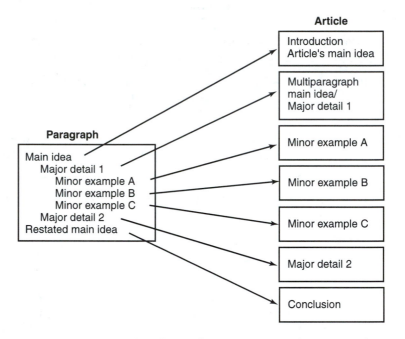

As you can see, a major detail may form its own multiparagraph unit; minor details such as narrative examples often occupy a paragraph or more. The pattern can also have a divided main idea combining a series of qualities or actions describing the subject. Also, support may come in the form of patterns within patterns—for instance, examples organized by time sequence or comparison/contrast. Paragraphs are not isolated units. You must continue to pay attention to how a single paragraph relates to paragraphs that precede it and those that follow, and how each contributes to the overall main idea pattern.

The next reading is a good example of a very common type of description/support article called a **profile**. Its purpose is to focus squarely on the traits and/or accomplishments of a person, place, or object, to give us an understanding of the essential nature of the subject. In this profile, the authors describe the traits they think made their subject an influential personality of the time. By bringing together facts, anecdotes, and opinions regarding their subject, they hope to convince you to share their evaluation.

PREVIEWING *MADAME C.J. WALKER* BY ROBERT A. DIVINE, T.H. BREEN, GEORGE M. FREDRICKSON, AND R. HAL WILLIAMS

Setting Your Reading Goals

Your aim in reading a profile is not just to get biographical information, but to determine the qualities and characteristics of subjects and to understand the forces that shaped them. Preview by reading the title and the first and last paragraphs. The title and first paragraph give us the subject and an approximate date:

Subject: _____   Time: _____

The last paragraph is a better clue to the characteristics that make the subject of importance to history. Construct a tentative main idea hypothesis from the information given there:

Main idea hypothesis: _____

_____

_____

Preview Vocabulary

sharecropper (3)   one who works the land of another for a share of the crop

militant (10)   ready and willing to fight for a cause

hygiene (11)   sanitary practices, cleanliness

Annotating As You Read

Highlight or underline key statements by the authors, including comments cited from others, that reveal important traits of Madam Walker. Make notes in the margins regarding any inferences you can draw based upon her actions, accomplishments, and words.

Madame C.J. Walker

by Robert A. Divine, T.H. Breen, George M. Fredrickson,
and R. Hal Williams

1   At the 1912 convention of the National Negro Business League, a group devoted to promoting African American businesses, a 45-year-old woman, Madam C.J. Walker, tried again and again to catch the eye of Booker T. Washington, the League's founder and head. But Washington ignored her until finally, her patience gone, she sprang to her feet and said, "Surely you are not going to shut the door in my face. I feel that I am in a business that is a credit to the womanhood of our race."

2   "I ... came from the cotton fields of the South," she went on, "I was promoted from there to the wash-tub; then I was promoted to the cook kitchen, and from there *I promoted myself* into the business of manufacturing hair goods and preparations…. I have built my own factory on my own ground." Captivated, League members invited her back the next year to speak.

3   Had Washington listened, Madam Walker had a remarkable story to tell. She was born Sarah Breedlove in 1867 on a plantation in Delta, Louisiana, the first in her sharecropper family born free. Orphaned at age 7, she married at 14 to escape a cruel brother-in-law and find a home. Her husband died when she was 20, leaving her with a young daughter and a back already aching from years of picking cotton and doing laundry. Looking for a better life, she moved to St. Louis and then to Denver, working as a cook and laundress. In Denver she married Charies J. Walker and began calling herself "Madam," a title that lent prestige to a new business she had just begun.

4   For years, Walker had had trouble with her hair. It came out in bunches, partly because of the painful "wrap and twist" method that was popular for styling African American hair. After trying various remedies, she developed her own formula she said came to her in a dream, "I tried it on my friends," she said; "it helped them. I made up my mind to begin to sell it." Filling jars of the mixture in the attic of her home, she sold it door-to-door. Starting in 1905, Madam Walker promoted the Walker system of hair care, designed to foster hair growth and improve personal appearance. The Walker system called for women to first wash their hair with Madam Walker's Vegetable Shampoo, then apply her Wonderful Hair Grower, add a light oil called Glossine, and finally press and relax the hair with a wide-toothed "hot comb."

5   Advertising in the African American press, Walker saw her business grow. She opened schools to teach her system, hired thousands of African American women as sales agents, and in 1910 moved her factory to Indianapolis

Robert A. Divine et al, *America Past and Present*, 5th ed., (Addison-Wesley Educational Publishers Inc, 1999), 684–685. Reprinted by permission of Pearson Education, Inc.

for its central location. Knowing that white stores would not stock her products, she relied on churches and women's clubs, two of the key institutions of the black community. Sales soon extended throughout the United States, Central America, and the Caribbean; Josephine Baker, the famous dancer, used Walker's products in Paris.

6   Dressed in white shirts and long black skirts, Walker agents became a familiar sight in African American neighborhoods everywhere. There were twenty thousand agents by 1916, most of them former maids, laundresses, and farm workers. "I have made it possible for many colored women to abandon the wash-tub for more pleasant and profitable occupation," she said.

7   As her income grew, Walker gave generously to various causes, including the YMCA, Mary McLeod Bethune's Educational and Industrial Institute for Negro Girls (now Bethune-Cookman College), the Tuskegee Institute, and the NAACP. "Lady Bountiful," she was called, and she encouraged her agents to contribute to charity, too. "I love to use a part of what I make in trying to help others," she said.

8   When the country entered World War I, Walker helped sell war bonds and joined the many black leaders who encouraged African Americans to aid in the war effort, hoping that contributions to victory abroad "would improve race relations at home." But she grew impatient as lynchings and other racial incidents continued. Angered by a race riot in East St. Louis, Missouri, in 1917, she supported the Negro Silent Protest Parade, in which ten thousand black New Yorkers marched in silence down Fifth Avenue while another twenty thousand African Americans looked on.

9   Walker went to Washington to ask President Woodrow Wilson to support legislation making lynching a federal crime, but Wilson was too "busy" to see her. Refusing to give up, Walker donated $5000 to the NAACP's anti-lynching campaign and defended the rights of returning war veterans. In 1918, Walker built Villa Lewaro, a mansion overlooking the Hudson River above New York City, near the estate of John D. Rockefeller. Vertner W. Tandy, the first African American architect registered in New York, designed it. Walker called it a symbol, to show "young Negroes what a lone woman accomplished and to inspire them to do big things." Madam Walker died at the villa in 1919, aged 51. At her death, *The Crisis,* the journal of the NAACP, said she had "revolutionized the personal habits and appearance of millions of human beings."

10   According to the *Guinness Book of World Records,* Madam Walker was the first self-made woman millionaire. What she did, said Ida B. Wells-Barnett, the militant black leader, "made me take pride anew in Negro womanhood." Mary McLeod Bethune, the black educator, said, "She has gone, but her work still lives and shall live as an inspiration to not only her race but to the world." Walker bequeathed her company to her daughter—asking that a woman always serve at the head—but it began to fail during the

Great Depression. Housed in the Walker Building, a National Historic Landmark, the Madam Walker Theatre Center today serves as a cultural center for the performing arts in downtown Indianapolis.

11   Even at the height of Madam Walker's business, "hot combs" and hair straighteners were controversial. Some black leaders (Booker T. Washington among them) denounced them as attempts to imitate whites, but many African American women straightened their hair anyway, prodded by a cultural style and popular songs in which black men sang lovingly of "long-haired babes." Walker herself argued that she had no interest in straightening hair, only in boosting confidence and personal hygiene.

12   Walker's business dwindled, but the debate over hair continued, carrying important economic as well as social dimensions. In 1992, African Americans spent three times more per person than other consumer groups on hair-care products, cosmetics, toiletries, and other grooming aids.

13   Famous African American singers, actresses, and television personalities, including Oprah Winfrey, relax their hair. Others object. Alice Walker, an African American and one of the nation's foremost authors, calls hair straightening a form of oppression, a "ceiling on the brain" that keeps people from fulfillment. Hip-hop music reinforces the message, taking hair, as one music magazine has said, "back to its African roots. From dreads, cornrows, and braids to twists, coils to 'fros, hip-hop is keeping it real'... natural. For many, hair is more than just a style—it's a statement."

14   Madam Walker agreed. Hair care, she thought, involved more than hair; it meant pride, better health, and new opportunities for black women everywhere. When she went back to that convention of the Negro Business League in 1913, she talked about economic independence for African American women. "The girls and women of our race," she said, "must not be afraid to take hold of business endeavor and wring success out of a number of business opportunities that lie at their very doors. I want to say to every Negro woman present, don't sit down and wait for the opportunities to come ... Get up and make them!"

Exercise 7.4

Context Vocabulary

Use the context to match the definitions on the right with the words in the left column.

1. _____ captivated (2)   a. attempt to

2. _____ prestige (2)   b. most important

3. _____ abandon (6)   c. captured the attention of, fascinated

4. _____ revolutionized (9)   d. get something from

5. _____ bequeathed (9)   e. give up

6. _____ controversial (11)   f. changed significantly

7. _____ dwindled (12)   g. reputation based on high achievement

8. _____ endeavor (14)   h. left as an inheritance

9. _____ wring (14)   i. causing sharp disagreement

10. _____ foremost (14)   j. got smaller

Comprehension Questions

Circle the correct letter choice and fill in the blanks where indicated.

1. The National Negro Business League

    a. was founded by Booker T. Washington.
    b. was devoted to promoting African American businesses.
    c. was led by Booker T. Washington.
    d. all of the above

2. In 1912, Madam Walker

    a. came from the cotton fields of the South and promoted herself.
    b. delivered a formal speech at the request of National Negro Business League leaders.
    c. finally caught the eye of Booker T. Washington and was encouraged to speak.
    d. none of the above

3. Sarah Breedlove was later known as

    a. Mrs. Charles J. Walker.
    b. Madam C. J. Walker.
    c. Lady Bountiful.
    d. all of the above

4. The text mentions all of the following as users of Madam Walker's products EXCEPT

    a. African-American women.

    b. women in the Caribbean.

    c. Josephine Baker.

    d. Alice Walker.

5. Walker invented her new product because

    a. her friends asked her to.

    b. she had trouble with her own hair.

    c. she was having bad dreams.

    d. none of the above

6. Paragraph 4 is organized by the pattern of

    a. comparison/contrast.

    b. cause/effect.

    c. classification.

    d. time sequence.

    List three signals words in the paragraph that give clues to its pattern:

    _____   _____   _____

7. The Walker system of hair care

    a. aimed at improving personal appearance.

    b. was designed to help hair to grow.

    c. involved a four-step process.

    d. all of the above

8. In selling her products Madam Walker utilized all of the following EXCEPT

    a. African American women as sales agents.

    b. white stores that stocked her products.

    c. churches.

    d. women's clubs.

9. Walker's mansion, Villa Lewaro

    a. was where she died in 1951.

    b. was purchased from the estate of John D. Rockefeller.

c. was viewed as a symbol of accomplishment and inspiration by Walker.

d. all of the above

10. Hair straighteners

a. became controversial only after Walker's death.

b. were endorsed and promoted by black leaders like Booker T. Washington.

c. are seen by some as a form of oppression.

d. are used to create hairstyles like dreadlocks and cornrows.

Evaluating Descriptive Statements

We decide on the qualities of people on the basis of what they say and do and on what others say about them. The exercise below contains descriptive statements that may or may not be accurate representations of Madam Walker. For each statement, check <u>one</u> of the following:

_____   "Directly mentioned"—if the statement can be located in the text.

_____   "Can be inferred"—if there is information from which a solid inference can be drawn.

_____   "Contradicted in the text"—if a statement to the opposite occurs or can be inferred.

Then list the evidence and/or locations that support your decision. Use paragraph numbers if appropriate.

If a statement does not appear in the text, cannot be inferred, or is not contradicted, check

_____   "Not enough evidence/not mentioned"

1. Madam Walker was timid and not capable of standing up for herself.

_____   Directly mentioned

_____   Can be inferred

_____   Contradicted in the text

Evidence/location: _____

_____

_____

_____   Not enough evidence/not mentioned

2. Walker was innovative and opportunistic in her business.

_____ Directly mentioned

_____ Can be inferred

_____ Contradicted in the text

Evidence/location: _____

_____

_____

_____ Not enough evidence/not mentioned

3. Walker had a poor personal relationship with her daughter.

_____ Directly mentioned

_____ Can be inferred

_____ Contradicted in the text

Evidence/location: _____

_____

_____

_____ Not enough evidence/not mentioned

4. Madam Walker's achievements made her a role model for African-American women.

_____ Directly mentioned

_____ Can be inferred

_____ Contradicted in the text

Evidence/location: _____

_____

_____

_____ Not enough evidence/not mentioned

5. Walker gave generously to various causes, including education.

_____ Directly mentioned

_____ Can be inferred

_____ Contradicted in the text

Evidence/location: _____

_____

_____

_____ Not enough evidence/not mentioned

6. Walker worked against the reelection of Woodrow Wilson.

_____ Directly mentioned

_____ Can be inferred

_____ Contradicted in the text

Evidence/location: _____

_____

_____

_____ Not enough evidence/not mentioned

7. Walker was an anti-war activist in World War I.

_____ Directly mentioned

_____ Can be inferred

_____ Contradicted in the text

Evidence/location: _____

_____

_____

_____ Not enough evidence/not mentioned

8. Walker was strongly opposed to social injustice and was active in fighting it.

_____ Directly mentioned

_____ Can be inferred

_____ Contradicted in the text

Evidence/location: _____

_____

_____

_____ Not enough evidence/not mentioned

9. Through her business, Walker helped change the way many people acted and looked.

_____ Directly mentioned

_____ Can be inferred

_____ Contradicted in the text

Evidence/location: _____

_____

_____

_____ Not enough evidence/not mentioned

10. Madam Walker was the first self-made woman millionaire.

_____ Directly mentioned

_____ Can be inferred

_____ Contradicted in the text

Evidence/location: _____

_____

_____

_____ Not enough evidence/not mentioned

Mapping and Summarizing

Use your annotated text and valid statements about Madam Walker from the exercise above to create a descriptive umbrella map that summarizes her qualities and accomplishments. Select the main idea from the choices below. Add additional lines or more minor detail to the map as needed.

Main idea:

a. Madam Walker was generous and she had a strong concern for justice, but she couldn't get along with leaders like Washington and Wilson.

b. Madam Walker's early struggles against poverty, a success in business, and her concern with social and political issues of the day.

c. Madam Walker's life and work demonstrated what African Americans, especially women, could achieve.

d. Madam Walker's business succeeded at first, but dwindled and eventually failed when her daughter took over.

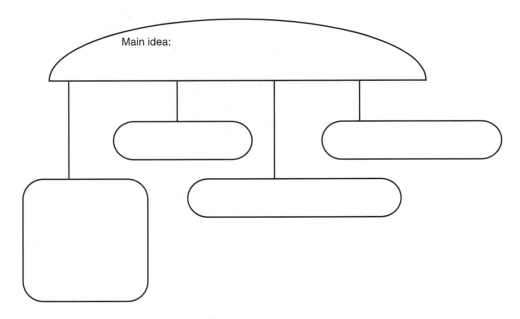

Main idea:

Using your map as a guide, write a summary of approximately 250 words.

In the following article, Neil Henry, who teaches writing and reporting at University of California at Berkeley, profiles a group who suffered one of the great injustices in American history. During World War II, over 100,000 American residents, legal aliens and citizens alike, were forced into U.S. government detention camps solely on the basis of race. In the article, descriptive statements detailing the response to that action develop the main idea.

PREVIEWING *THEIR FIGHT FOR FREEDOM AT HOME* BY NEIL HENRY

Setting Your Reading Goals

From the title and the subtitle, "For Japanese American Veterans, WWII Was the Ultimate Proving Ground," the topic of the article is clearly "the Japanese American veteran." The subtitle provides a good starting place for a main idea hypothesis. The first and last paragraphs give illustrations; therefore, previewing them will not help greatly in sharpening your thesis.

Preview Vocabulary

amiable (1)   friendly, sociable

interrogators (7)   questioners, as in an investigation

mosaic (10)	a composite of different elements
curator (12)	director of a museum collection or a library
Jim Crow laws (14)	laws systematically discriminating against and segregating blacks
unprecedented (22)	having no previous example
reparations (23)	compensation made for damage or injury

Annotating As You Read

The article begins with an introductory illustration. After its conclusion, look for a main idea statement that is broad enough to include all of the accomplishments attributed to the Japanese American veterans. Also, the article provides a good deal of background information on this aspect of World War II. Look up any historical references and make short notes in the margins. Try to make this a part of your own "reference framework" for American history; you will very likely encounter this subject again in your college course work. If you are interested in one family's experience in the relocation camps, read *Farewell to Manzanar* by Jeanne Wakatsuke Houston and James Houston.

Their Fight for Freedom at Home
For Japanese American Veterans, WWII
Was the Ultimate Proving Ground

by Neil Henry

1   Lean and amiable Harry Akune always saw himself as just an ordinary American guy. He grew up in rural California in the 1930s, picked grapes and peaches to help support his family, and like many young men hoped to go to college one day and earn a share of the American Dream.

2   But then came Pearl Harbor. Promptly picked by the FBI—like 110,000 other Japanese Americans who were branded aliens of questionable loyalty solely because of the color of their skin—Akune was put behind barbed wire in a makeshift detention camp in Granada, Colo. He was 19 years old, cutting sugar beets to get by, and angry as hell.

3   Then one day he and the other young men at Amache Relocation Camp heard a U.S. Army recruiter was coming by soon to ask for volunteers. "At first, nobody wanted to do it," recalls Akune, a 74-year old retired Gardena,

---

*Neil Henry, "Their Fight for Freedom at Home," (the *Washington Post Weekly Edition,* June 5–11, 1995). Neil Henry teaches writing and reporting at University of California at Berkeley.

Calif., aerospace engineer. "The feeling was, 'Look at how they treat us! Now they expect us to fight?' It didn't make sense."

4   But as the talks went on, someone asked an important question: "What's going to happen to us if we don't join up? Will our children live like the Indians, on a reservation somewhere? Will we be treated forever like third-class citizens like the blacks? Will they send us back to Japan?"

5   By the end, the answer for many was clear. They *had* to fight.

6   Today, more than 50 years later, the wartime achievements of Japanese Americans like Akune and his detention camp comrades are the stuff of legend. In the face of repression, racism, and outright hostility, more than 33,000 Japanese Americans joined the Army during World War II and became the most highly decorated servicemen in U.S. military history.

> Do you think you have located a broad enough main idea statement by this point? Before you decide for sure, read the next two paragraphs.

7   Nearly 10,000 fought in North Africa, Italy, and France with the Army's 442nd Regimental Combat Team and 100th Infantry Battalion, all-Japanese units that earned more than 18,000 individual citations in battles such as Anzio, Salerno, Cassino, and the Vosges Mountains. Others, like Akune, served in the Pacific as fighters, translators, and interrogators with the Army's Military Intelligence Services.

8   But what these veterans accomplished when they returned to the United States after the war was arguably just as profound. With new determination and far less tolerance for ignorance, discrimination, and bigotry, many went to school on the GI Bill and forged successful careers in fields long largely off-limits to Japanese Americans—law, politics, engineering, education. For all of them, World War II was not just a fight for a new order overseas, but for freedom at home.

9   "They called us gooks and dirty Japs, but we knew no other country but America. This was our home," says Kiyoshi Yoshii, 76, a retired San Francisco postal worker who lost his left arm to a mortar round in France in 1944. "We lost many friends. But in the end, we accomplished much more for our kids than we ever thought possible."

10   In the Japanese language, this remarkable generation of Japanese Americans is known as the Nisei or *second,* a term of admiration and respect. California, Oregon, Washington, and Hawaii are home to more than three-fourths of the nearly 1 million Japanese American population, and it is here that the lives and experiences of the Nisei form a significant part of the social and cultural mosaic.

11   In coming months, Nisei veterans will be honored at numerous gatherings throughout the West. In Los Angeles, a new exhibit has opened at the Japanese American National Museum detailing the experiences of the all-Japanese

522nd Field Artillery Battalion, whose soldiers were among the first to rescue survivors at the Dachau concentration camp in Germany 50 years ago.

12   "The greatest legacy of the Nisei veterans is that they proved they were as good as anybody," says Kaoru Oguri, curator of the Japanese American National Museum. "They had all the reason in the world not to fight, but many of them did. When they came back, they knew they weren't going to take any sort of subjugation anymore."

13   In many ways, the experiences of Japanese Americans mirrored those of black Americans. Both enjoyed limited rights in American society and had to serve in either menial capacities in the armed services or fight in racially segregated units.

14   Like blacks, Japanese Americans suffered systematic discrimination in employment and education and were barred from most public swimming pools in California and other western states. A network of Jim Crow laws worked just as effectively to repress Asians in the west as they did to repress blacks in the South.

15   But it was World War II that triggered the greatest injustices and humiliation for Japanese Americans, a horrific period that saw them rounded up from their homes and workplaces and their property confiscated under Franklin D. Roosevelt's infamous Executive Order 9066. Placed in detention at 21 camps around the United States, they were branded aliens of questionable loyalty to the only country many had ever known.

16   "It makes me mad just remembering those questions they asked us," says Rudy Tokiwa, 71, a San Jose nursery owner and a winner of the Silver Star for valor in Italy and France, recalling the "loyalty test" that all detainees were ordered to answer by the War Relocation Authority after they were interned. Among the questions:

> Do you believe in the divine origin of the Japanese race?
>
> Can you furnish any proof that you have always been loyal to the United States?
>
> Do you forswear any allegiance or obedience to the Japanese emperor?
>
> Are you willing to serve in the armed forces of the United States on combat duty wherever ordered?

17   "They didn't ask the Italians or the Germans. They didn't put them in camps and take away their property," says Tokiwa, who was born and reared in California. "You tell me it wasn't racist."

18   Some Japanese Americans resisted, claiming the questioning was illegal and offensive, and riots broke out at several camps. Other Japanese Americans filed suits against the government for wrongful imprisonment and confiscation of property. But many young Nisei men decided the only way out was to join the Army and fight.

19   The Army used the Nisei's battlefield successes for propaganda and recruitment, widely issuing a photograph at one point depicting Rudy Tokiwa, a carbine in his hand and a cigarette in his mouth, leading a dozen captured German soldiers from a battlefield in Italy. The government also extolled the Nisei servicemen in the Pacific who helped break codes and translate battle plans that were instrumental in victories from Midway to Okinawa.

20   Such feats were so widely known and celebrated after the war that even Hollywood got in on the act, with a movie about the men of the 442nd RCT titled *Go for Broke!*—with Van Johnson in the leading role as a white officer.

21   But it was President Harry S. Truman who perhaps summed up the lessons of the Nisei veterans best in a ceremony on the White House lawn in 1945 when he told them, "You fought not only the enemy, you fought prejudice, and you have won. Keep up that fight, and continue to win.... Bring forward the colors."

22   In Hawaii, where Japanese Americans had been the largest racial minority, returning veterans became active in Democratic Party politics and gradually rose to positions of unprecedented power in industry and commerce. Hawaii elected a Nisei veteran to the U.S. Senate, Daniel K. Inouye, followed by another, Spark Matsunaga.

23   Nisei veterans also fueled the drive to attain a formal apology and $1.5 billion in reparations from the U.S. government for their detention and loss of property during the war, legislation that finally came about in 1988.

24   But it was in smaller and more personal ways, perhaps, that greater gains were made. Harry Akune returned to the states, got a bachelor's degree in engineering and eventually went to work for McDonnell Douglas Corp. in Los Angeles. "Before the war, practically the only thing open to us was warehouse or gardening work," he says. "But we showed what we could do during the war and the companies couldn't ignore us."

25   Often these changes came in fits and starts. Rudy Tokiwa, the Silver Star winner who suffered wounds to his legs and back in France, recalls his return to San Jose. With crutches under his arms, he stood in a line at a cafeteria and got to talking about his Army experiences with another veteran, a young white man.

26   "We don't serve you folks here," says the woman behind the counter when Tokiwa reached the front. His face trembling with rage, he was about to shout at her—but his new friend spoke first.

27   "He said, 'This man has done more for this country than you'll ever know, lady,'" Tokiwa remembers. "'And you'll treat him with respect.'"

28   Tokiwa pauses and smiles at the memory. "It was good to know we had people on our side for a change."

Exercise 7.5

Vocabulary

Use the context to match up the definitions on the right with the words in the left column.

1. _____ makeshift (2)   a. detestable
2. _____ repression (6)   b. terrifying
3. _____ citation (7)   c. praised highly
4. _____ bigotry (8)   d. control by external force
5. _____ subjugation (12)   e. bravery
6. _____ horrific (15)   f. quickly made
7. _____ confiscated (15)   g. intolerance
8. _____ infamous (15)   h. being held back
9. _____ valor (16)   i. commendation for brave action
10. _____ extolled (19)   j. seized by authorities

Comprehension Questions

Circle the correct letter choice and fill in the blanks where indicated.

1. The article begins with an introductory subdivided unit that includes paragraphs

   a. 1–2.
   b. 1–3.
   c. 1–4.
   d. 1–5.

2. The introductory words and phrases in some of the paragraphs in the unit above show that it is organized by the idea pattern of

   a. comparison/contrast.
   b. classification.
   c. time sequence.
   d. whole/part.

3. Write three of those signal words or other clues that led you to your answer to question 2.

   _____   _____   _____

4. Which of the following is the best statement of the main idea of the article?

    a. Today, more than 50 years later, the wartime achievements of Japanese Americans like Akune and his detention camp comrades are the stuff of legend.

    b. More than 33,000 Japanese Americans joined the Army during World War II, and became the most highly decorated servicemen in American history.

    c. Many went to school on the GI Bill and forged successful careers in fields long largely off limits to Japanese Americans.

    d. For all of the Nisei, World War II was not just a fight for a new order overseas, but for freedom at home.

5. Paragraphs 6 and 7 form a multiparagraph unit of description/support. Complete the pattern map for them.

Main Idea

Support

Example (6):	Example (7):	Example (7):

6. Paragraph 10 is an informational, topically organized paragraph. The topic is

    a. the Japanese language.

    b. the Nisei.

    c. the Japanese American culture.

    d. the population and geographical distribution of Japanese Americans.

7. Paragraphs 13 and 14 form a subdivided unit of comparison. What two groups are being compared? _____

_____

_____

Write the sentence that expresses the main idea of this unit. _____

_____

_____

8. Which of the following is the best statement of the implied main idea of paragraph 18?

   a. Many Japanese Americans did not resist.

   b. Japanese Americans responded in a variety of ways.

   c. All Japanese Americans should have resisted.

   d. Riots at the camps were justified.

9. Paragraphs 19–20 form a multiparagraph unit with a divided main idea. Which of the statements below best goes with the following to complete the main idea "The Army used the Nisei's battlefield successes for propaganda and recruitment":

   a. and also extolled the Nisei servicemen in the Pacific who helped break codes.

   b. that were instrumental in victories from Midway to Okinawa.

   c. and such feats were widely known and celebrated after the war.

   d. and Hollywood made a movie, *Go for Broke*.

10. Which statement of Harry S. Truman bests restates the article's main idea?

    a. "Go for broke!"

    b. "You fought not only the enemy, you fought prejudice, and you have won."

    c. "Keep up that fight, and continue to win."

    d. "Bring forward the colors."

11. Write the main idea sentence of paragraph 24. _____

    _____

    _____

12. The main idea of paragraph 24 is supported by

    a. statistics.

    b. a quotation from a government official.

    c. an example involving a veteran.

    d. a number of examples.

13. Paragraphs 25–28 make up a subdivided paragraph of conclusion. Write the main idea sentence for this unit. _____

    _____

    _____

14. The main idea of the concluding unit (25–28) is supported by

    a. statistics.

    b. a quotation from a government study.

    c. one example involving a veteran.

    d. more than one example.

15. The author's tone in this selection could best be described as

    a. neutral.

    b. sarcastic

    c. admiring.

    d. condescending.

Questions for Writing/Small-Group Discussion

1. One question on the loyalty test the Japanese Americans had to take was "Can you furnish any proof that you have always been loyal to the United States?" What sort of proof do you think the government would accept? If you were asked that question today, what sort of evidence could you produce?

2. "'They didn't ask the Italians or the Germans. They didn't put them in camps and take away their property,' says Tokiwa, who was born and reared in California." The United States was also at war with Italy and Germany but, as Tokiwa observes, these groups were not sent to camps. What reasons can you think of for the difference in treatment?

3. Watch the movie *Go for Broke!* Decide if it is historically accurate or a whitewash of the entire incident. Does it reflect the point of view of the establishment, does it sympathize with the Japanese Americans, or is it possible that it can do both?

WORD PARTS 1: UNLOCKING THE MEANING OF WORDS

English has a core vocabulary of words that has its origin in the Germanic language family. But, due to heavy borrowing during its history, English has many words of Greek and Latin origin and from the Romance languages, especially French, that descended from Latin. Many of our vocabulary words, both native and borrowed, are themselves made up of smaller meaningful units of one or more syllables.

Roots are the base part of a word. A word may combine two or more roots ("phonograph") or have a single root ("happy").

Prefixes are word parts that we add before roots and that generally make a big change in the meaning. For instance, if we add the prefix *un* to "happy," we have made the antonym "<u>un</u>happy."

Suffixes are word parts that follow roots and are used mainly to change the part of speech of a word. For example, if we wanted to talk about the condition of being unhappy, we would have to add the suffix *ness* to create the noun form "unhapp<u>iness.</u>"

Many of the words you know and use daily contain these word parts, though you might not recognize them or know their meaning if they stood alone. You might, for example, say that you like an "automatic transmission" better than a "manual transmission" without knowing that *auto* means "self," *matic* signifies "action," *trans* means "across," *miss* means "send," and that *manual* is from the Latin for "hand." However, if you know that *mal* means "bad," you would have a better chance of guessing—and remembering—the meaning of words like these:

malicious	maladroit
malevolent	malfunction
malaise	malpractice
malcontent	malefactor

From the meanings of word parts in words you already know, and by adding a short list of new word parts, you will be able to unlock, connect, and remember the meaning of hundreds of unfamiliar words that you will meet in college reading. Combining what you know of word parts with using context clues can give you a powerful one-two punch for vocabulary. For example, look at this sentence: "I thought the crowd would be excited, but instead an air of *apathy* seemed to hang over it." Here the contrast word *but* signals that "apathy" means the opposite of "excited." Even without that clue, however, knowing that *a* means "without" and *pathy* has to do with "feeling" will get you close to the meaning and save you the time of going to a dictionary.

To learn and remember word parts, you will need to link the word part with a word you know or want to learn. Some common examples will be given to you, but you should start making a list of your own. In working with word parts, remember these points:

1. The modern meaning of a word may not be an exact translation of its words parts. For example, we use the word *preamble* to refer to an introductory statement; the literal meaning of its word parts is "to walk before."

2. The spelling of a word part may vary when used with other word parts. For example, all the following forms have the meaning "yield, go": re<u>cede</u>, ex<u>ceed</u>, pro<u>cession</u>.

3. You can't trust spelling alone to identify a word part. *Mis* means "wrongly, incorrectly" in the word *misspelled,* but it is just one syllable of the entire root in *mister. Unit* does not mean "not it." The *un* in this case is part of *uni,* meaning "one."

<u>Word Part</u>	<u>Meanings</u>	<u>Word Examples</u>	<u>Your Examples</u>
act	do, move	actor, react	
anthrop	man	anthropology, misanthrope	
aqua/aque	water	aqueduct, aquarium	
aud	hear	audit, auditorium	
bell/bel	war	bellicose, rebellion	
bene	well, good	benevolent, benefit	
bio	life	biology, antibiotics	
cis/cide	cut/kill	genocide, incision	
crat/cracy	rule	aristocracy, democracy	
dem	people	democratic, demotic	
dict	say, tell	dictator, predict	
gen	origin, kind	gender, genetic	
graph/gram	write, record	graphic, polygraph	
logy	study of	demonology, criminology	
jus/jud/jur	law, right	jurisdiction, judicial	
mal	bad	malignant, dismal	
nov	new	novel, innovative	
ortho	correct, straight	orthodontist, orthodox	
ped/pod	foot, child	tripod, pedal, pediatrician	
phobia	fear	hydrophobia, claustrophobia	
phil	love	Anglophile, philanthropy	
psych	mind	psychoanalysis, psychotic	

scrib/script	write	inscribe, prescription
soph	wise	sophisticated, philosophy
theo, thei	god	polytheism, theology
therm	heat	thermal, thermos
ver	true	verify, veritable
vis/vid	see	invisible, video
vit/viv	life	vitality, revive
voc/voke	voice, call	vocation, revoke

Exercise 7.6

Vocabulary

Each of the following words are composed of two of the word parts listed on pages 283–284. Write the meanings you think the words might have, without consulting a dictionary.

1. biography _____

_____

_____

2. philosophy _____

_____

_____

3. theocracy _____

_____

_____

4. genocide _____

_____

_____

5. anthropology _____

_____

_____

6. orthopedic _____

_____

_____

7. thermograph _____

_____

_____

8. psychoactive _____

_____

_____

9. jurisdiction _____

_____

_____

Use the meaning of the word part to make an educated guess on the following:

10. Someone described as *vivacious* would be _____.

11. Someone with a *belligerent* attitude would be likely during a discussion to

_____

_____.

12. *Xeno* means "stranger"; what would a *xenophobic* person's viewpoint toward immigration most likely be? _____

_____

_____.

13. *Aquatic* sporting events would be held in _____.

14. If you were hired for a job, why would a *novice* not likely be your supervisor?

_____

_____

15. If a situation *evokes* memories, that means that those memories have been

_____

_____.

16. If a perfume is *malodorous,* would it be likely to attract or repel? _____

_____

_____

17. *Pre* means "before"; a *prescription* would be _____

_____

_____.

18. A *malediction* is a curse; a *benediction* would be a _____.

19. A person with a reputation for *veracity* would be one who _____

_____

_____.

20. Someone who is believes in *democracy* would favor rule by _____

_____

_____.

CHAPTER REVIEW

Circle the correct letter choice and fill in the blanks where indicated.

1. Descriptive statements may be made by using
   a. nouns.
   b. adjectives.
   c. verbs.
   d. all of the above

2. Descriptive statements
   a. tell about traits and characteristics.
   b. can be made about people, organizations, or institutions.
   c. tell us about actions or functions that recur.
   d. all of the above

3. Fill in the blank in the sentence below with either the word *adjective* or *verb.*

   _____ are used to describe traits.

4. Which of the following is a statement of description?
   a. The budget bill should be vetoed for several good reasons.
   b. The Congress is more to blame in the budget mess than the president.

   c. In the recent budget battle, the president has been wise and restrained.

   d. The foolish, rash, disastrous actions of the president in the budget battle.

5. Which of the following is a statement of description?

   a. Campaign financing limitations should be enacted for several good reasons.

   b. The president has consistently supported campaign financing legislation.

   c. In campaign reform, the Senate has acted more responsibly than the House.

   d. The wise, restrained actions of our president on the campaign reform issue.

6. *Logical fallacies* are

   a. classical logical arguments.

   b. errors in reasoning and inference.

   c. always deliberate.

   d. statements of scientific fact.

7. *Name-calling* may also be referred to as

   a. mudslinging.

   b. poisoning the well.

   c. *argument ad hominem* (argument against the man).

   d. all of the above

8. The statement that the Dallas Cowboys are "America's Team" is an example of

   a. glittering generality.

   b. hasty generalization.

   c. name-calling.

   d. mudslinging.

9. "Robert got a D on his first history test. He just isn't going to make it in college." This statement is an example of

   a. glittering generality.

   b. hasty generalization.

   c. name-calling.

   d. mudslinging.

10. "It's about time those lazy welfare cheats were driven away from feeding at the public trough." This statement is an example of

   a. glittering generality.

   b. hasty generalization.

   c. name-calling.

   d. sarcasm.

READING PORTFOLIO   A Profile Article

1. *Look for an article that does more than describe an action that a person participated in.* Remember: the purpose of a profile is to focus squarely on the traits and accomplishments of a subject to help us understand it. Often the subjects of profiles are people "in the public eye"—sports and entertainment celebrities, politicians, world figures—but articles may be about ordinary people who have made notable achievements.

2. *As you read the article, compile a list of key descriptive statements made about your subject.* These will include adjectives and other descriptive phrases, and statements regarding behaviors and accomplishments. When you are ready to write your summary (about 175 words), ask yourself "What picture do all of these add up to?" Try to find adjectives of your own to describe the subject's most important personality traits. Paraphrase carefully any accomplishments that need to be mentioned; be sure to begin with enough identifying information so that your reader can place the subject in a clear context.

3. *Write a response of equal length in which, first of all, you assess the* tone *of the author of the article.* Is the profile favorable? Or is the author—perhaps slyly or ironically—taking some jabs at the person being profiled? Express your own view of the subject. Do you agree with the author's attitude toward the subject? If you were familiar with the subject prior to reading the article, have your views changed in any way?

4. *Select five words from the article that you are unsure of.* Use the dictionary to determine their meanings in the article. Then write a sentence for each, providing helpful context clues.

5. *Profiles can be done on **places** and **objects** as well as on people.* Check with your instructor to see if an article on one of these is an acceptable alternative.

6. *Before you submit your articles, meet in small groups of 3–4 and exchange papers.* Evaluate papers on the following:

- Does the summary provide framing information and deliver a clear main impression of the subject?
- Is the summary accurate, and does it avoid the phrasing of the original?
- Does the response evaluate the tone of the article and present its own views?

Revise your paper by using any suggestions that you think will strengthen it.

7. *File your article in the Profile category of your portfolio when it is returned by your instructor.*

8

Recognizing the Order of Events: Time Sequence

Clocks and calendars are an inescapable part of our existence. We see our lives as a series of personal events, flowing in one direction from a start to a finish. Marriage and divorce, births and deaths, graduating or dropping out, promotions or sudden unemployment, becoming a grandparent, retiring—we mark such divisions based on biological changes, calculated decisions, or chance occurrences. In the selections in this chapter, you will work with a number of variations in time sequence, the pattern through which we answer the fundamental human questions of **when** and **how**.

CHAPTER PREVIEW

In this chapter you will

- Read a narrative history organized by time sequence
- Trace the origins of events in explanations of "how things came about"
- Learn word parts that indicate time
- Summarize and respond to a time sequence article for your Reading Portfolio

A student is given an assignment, to be completed in the space of a single class hour, to write an autobiographical essay. Suppose the essay began like this:

> It was a very rainy day when they took my mother to the hospital. Then they took her to the delivery room. After two hours, I was delivered. Then they put me in room with the other babies and my dad looked at me through the window. Then …

The student should realize quickly that the essay is headed for trouble. It won't be finished in an hour; in fact, it's likely to take as long to write it as it did to live it. "And then … and then … and then" certainly creates a time sequence. But, although time does pass in a series of equal ticks on the clock, we really see our lives more in terms of **important** chunks of time. We don't see all actions in our lives as equally important. An assignment to write about the four most significant turning points in your life would be better because it requires **selection** and **summary**.

◼ TIME SEQUENCE IN TEXTBOOKS

Time sequence deals with a series of actions, but the pattern involves more than just a list of separate events. When we read a story or study an historical event, we expect the author to group actions in chunks or segments. To understand connections fully, we need a framework that provides a sense of a beginning situation, followed by developments and changes, and a final resolution of the action. In tracking the main lines of a sequence of events, effective readers make use of various signals that good writers provide. Earlier you were given a select list of common pattern words of time.

stage	first	before	since
phase	next	after	until
era	then	during	at last
step	now	earlier	finally
while	later	at the beginning	

Words for time periods (*day, month, century*) and dates also help keep time sequences clear.

The basis for making divisions in time depends upon our interests and our point of view. In a history text, for example, eras might correspond to

- ◼ a leader (The Kennedy Years)
- ◼ a scientific event (The Atomic Age)
- ◼ an economic occurrence (The Great Depression)
- ◼ a social upheaval (The Roaring Twenties)

Other history texts are likely to have very different divisions for the same time periods.

In the selection below from a history text, the authors outline the stages of development of an institution that has played a profoundly important role in shaping American history.

PREVIEWING *A LESS PARTISAN PRESS* BY KAREN O'CONNOR AND LARRY J. SABATO

Setting Your Reading Goals

Imagine that your goal here is preparation for a test that will include questions over material which is typical of texts appropriate for a college course in American history. You will want to focus on retaining facts, but also on understanding the overall process of development and change. Preview the material by reading the title and the first and last paragraphs. The title tells you clearly what the topic of the passage is:

Topic: _____.

The first and last paragraphs spell out the early and later developments, but do not contain a main idea statement for the overall development of the press. Preview further by reading the first sentences of paragraphs 2–6. Then construct a tentative main idea hypothesis that is broad enough to account for the stages you were able to identify in your prereading.

Main idea hypothesis: _____

_____

_____

Preview Vocabulary

partisan (1)   favoring one side over another; not objective or fair-minded

sordid (2)   low, immoral, squalid

fabulously (2)   in an unbelievable way

intrusive (3)   pushy, nosy

burgeoning (3)   growing rapidly

exceedingly (5)   extremely

alienating (6)   causing to be unfriendly or opposed to

pillars of (6)   key elements of

insurgents (6)   rebels

of yore (6)   formerly

Annotating As You Read

Writing organized by time contains dates and other words or phrases (e.g., "during this decade," "later") to keep sequences clear. As you read, circle or highlight all dates and phrases that indicate stages or changes, and write summary notes in the margin for key milestones in the development of the press. Make any necessary revisions in your main idea guess.

A Less Partisan Press

by Karen O'Connor and Larry J. Sabato

1   The partisan press eventually gave way to the penny press. In 1833 Benjamin Day founded the *New York Sun,* which cost a penny at the newsstand. Because it was not tied to one party, it was politically more independent than the party papers. The *Sun* was the forerunner of the modern press built on mass circulation and commercial advertising to produce profit. By 1861 the penny press had so supplanted partisan papers that President Abraham Lincoln (who succeeded Buchanan) announced that his administration would have no favored or sponsored newspaper.

2   The press thus became markedly less partisan but not necessarily more respectable. Mass-circulation dailies sought wide readerships, and readers were clearly attracted to the sensational and the scandalous. The sordid side of politics became the entertainment of the times. One of the best-known examples occurred in the presidential campaign of 1884, when the *Buffalo Evening Telegraph* headlined "A Terrible Tale" about Grover Cleveland, the Democratic nominee. In 1871, while sheriff of Buffalo, the bachelor Cleveland had allegedly fathered a child. Even though the woman in question had been seeing other men, Cleveland willingly accepted responsibility since all the other men were married, and he had dutifully paid child support for years. Fortunately for Cleveland, another newspaper, the *Democratic Sentinel,* broke a story that helped to offset this scandal: Republican presidential nominee James G. Blaine and his wife had had their first child just three months after their wedding. There is a lesson for politicians in this double-edged morality tale. Cleveland acknowledged his responsibility forthrightly and took his lumps, whereas Blaine told a fabulously elaborate, completely unbelievable story about having had two marriage ceremonies six months apart. Cleveland won the election (although other factors also played a role in his victory).

O'Connor and Sabato, *American Government: Continuity and Change,* 1997 ed., 577–579.

3   In the late 1800s and early 1900s, the era of the intrusive press was in full flower. First yellow journalism and then muckraking were in fashion. Pioneered by prominent publishers such as William Randolph Hearst and Joseph Pulitzer, **yellow journalism** featured pictures, comics, and color designed to capture a share of the burgeoning immigrant population market. These newspapers also oversimplified and sensationalized many news developments. The front-page editorial crusade became common, the motto for which frequently seemed to be, "Damn the truth, full speed ahead."

4   After the turn of the century, the muckrakers—so named by President Theodore Roosevelt after a special rake designed to collect manure—took charge of a number of newspapers and nationally circulated magazines. **Muckraking** journalists such as Upton Sinclair and David Graham Phillips searched out and exposed real and apparent misconduct by government, business, and politicians in order to stimulate reform. There was no shortage of corruption to reveal, of course, and much good came from these efforts. But an unfortunate side effect of the emphasis on crusades and investigations was the frequent publication of gossip and rumor without sufficient proof.

5   The modern press corps may also be guilty of this offense, but it has achieved great progress on another front. Throughout the nineteenth century, payoffs to the press were not uncommon. Andrew Jackson, for instance, gave one in ten of his early appointments to loyal reporters; and during the 1872 presidential campaign, the Republicans slipped cash to about 300 newsmen. Wealthy industrialists also sometimes purchased editorial peace or investigative cease-fire for tens of thousands of dollars. Examples of such press corruption are exceedingly rare today, and not even the most extreme of the modern media's critics believe otherwise.

6   As the news business grew, its focus gradually shifted from passionate opinion to corporate profit. Newspapers, hoping to maximize profit, were more careful to avoid alienating the advertisers and readers who produced their revenues, and the result was less harsh, more objective reporting. Meanwhile, media barons became pillars of the establishment; for the most part, they were no longer the anti-establishment insurgents of yore.

7   Technological advances had a major impact on this transformation in journalism. High-speed presses and more cheaply produced paper made mass-circulation dailies possible. The telegraph and then the telephone made news gathering easier and much faster, and nothing could compare to the invention of radio and television. When radio became widely available in the 1920s, millions of Americans could hear national politicians instead of merely reading about them. With television—first introduced in the late 1940s, and nearly a universal fixture in U.S. homes by the mid-1950s—citizens could see and hear candidates and presidents.

Exercise 8.1

Mapping Time Sequence

The annotations you made in your text will help you complete the time sequence map below with these events:

   a. readers attracted to the sensational, scandalous

   b. payoffs to the press not uncommon

   c. technological inventions transform journalism

   d. the press partisan, party-dominated, opinionated

   e. the era of the intrusive press

   f. the penny press supplanted partisan papers

   g. first penny press—politically more independent

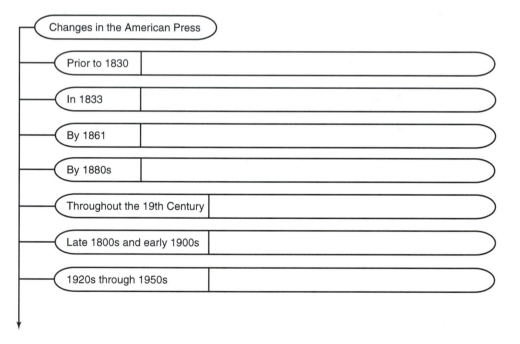

Changes in the American Press

Prior to 1830

In 1833

By 1861

By 1880s

Throughout the 19th Century

Late 1800s and early 1900s

1920s through 1950s

Comprehension Questions

Circle the correct letter choice and fill in the blanks where indicated.

  1. Which of the following best summarizes the main idea of the passage:

    a. The American press became much less partisan, but as mass-circulation dailies sought wide readerships, readers were attracted to the sensational and the scandalous.

b. Overcoming its partisan beginnings, the press grew less corrupt and more objective, but was often scandal-oriented and later more aligned to corporate interests.

c. Changes in the partisan press, the Harding-Blaine scandals, a decline in corruption, important technological changes, and ultimately the influence of corporate America.

d. Technological advances (1920s–50s) had a major impact on the transformation in journalism from passionate opinion to corporate profit.

2. All of the following have a main idea that is best stated in the first sentence EXCEPT

a. paragraph 1

b. paragraph 2

c. paragraph 3

d. paragraph 5

e. paragraph 7

Write the main idea sentence of the paragraph you selected in question 2:

_____

_____

3. Which is the best statement of the main idea of paragraph 4?

a. The muckrakers were named by President Theodore Roosevelt after a manure rake.

b. Muckrakers exposed government and business misconduct to stimulate reform.

c. An unfortunate side effect of muckraking was the publication of unsupported rumors.

d. Muckraking had positive reform results, but it also had some negative side effects.

4. Which of the following best states the main idea of paragraph 6?

a. As the news business grew, it changed its focus from partisan opinion to profit.

b. To maximize profit, newspapers tried not to alienate advertisers and readers.

c. As the news business grew, it underwent some significant changes.

d. Media barons were no longer rebels but key members of the establishment.

5. All of the following are stated as facts regarding the penny press EXCEPT

    a. The *New York Sun*'s cost at the newsstand was only a penny per copy.

    b. It eventually replaced the partisan press.

    c. Abraham Lincoln's favorite paper was the *Sun*.

    d. The *Sun* derived profits through mass circulation and advertising.

6. Which of the following can we most clearly infer from the Blaine-Cleveland campaign?

    a. Most political campaigns are marred by scandals from the past.

    b. Acknowledging misbehavior has better political results than trying to hide the truth.

    c. Politicians who are involved in scandals usually win their elections anyway.

    d. Blaine was more at fault than Cleveland was.

7. We can infer from paragraph 5 that

    a. Republicans were the most corrupt political party in the nineteenth century.

    b. Most wealthy industrialists try to manipulate the press.

    c. Not all payoffs are in the form of direct cash payments.

    d. Critics believe the modern media is still corrupt.

8. Muckraking journalism and yellow press journalism were similar in that they both

    a. stressed features designed to capture a share of the growing immigrant population.

    b. were concerned with generating real reform.

    c. helped to generate many positive social changes.

    d. were not always careful enough in separating truth from fiction or rumor.

9. The authors' purpose in this selection is to

    a. criticize the activities of the modern press in America.

    b. provide an informational summary of the development of the press.

    c. entertain the reader with historical examples like the Blaine-Cleveland scandals.

    d. complain about the corruption initiated by politicians and media tycoons.

10. The authors' tone in the passage is best described as

    a. matter-of-fact, straightforward

    b. grave, intense

    c. bitter, aloof

    d. flippant, ironic

Questions for Discussion

1. "These newspapers also oversimplified and sensationalized many news developments. The front-page editorial crusade became common, the motto for which frequently seemed to be, 'Damn the truth, full speed ahead.'" Does that still seem true of newspapers and television? Can you give any examples from the modern age?

2. Would the actions of Blaine and Cleveland still be considered "scandals" today? How would today's press react? The voters?

■ TIME SEQUENCE: NARRATIVE HISTORY

Biographical and autobiographical writing relies on time sequence as a natural and dramatic idea pattern. Mary Crow Dog, a member of the Brule Tribe of the Lakota Sioux, grew up on a South Dakota reservation and later, alongside her husband, Leonard Crow Dog, became an activist in the American Indian Movement in the 1960s and 1970s. A selection from her autobiography, *Lakota Woman*, shows how time sequence provides organizational unity.

PREVIEWING *CIVILIZE THEM WITH A STICK* BY MARY CROW DOG
Setting Your Reading Goals

Preview the selection by reading the title, introductory quotation, the first two sentences of the introduction, and the last sentence of the article. From this you should be able to gather that the author's purpose is to relate her experiences at

_____.

Your focus should be on the sequence of the author's experiences and her reactions to them.

Preview Vocabulary

wickiup (introductory quote)	frame hut covered with matting, used by nomadic Indians
cajolery (introductory quote)	persistent coaxing

induced (introductory quote)	persuaded
bewildered (1)	confused
instinctively (1)	without thought
Nazi (1)	German political party under Hitler, responsible for death camps of World War II
tolerable (1)	adequate, passable
tiyospaye (2)	extended family and hunting group of Sioux society
enveloped (2)	surrounded, enclosed
impersonality (3)	a lack of emotion or feeling
sterile (3)	devoid of life or feeling
doodling (8)	drawing aimlessly
venom (9)	poison, spite
orthography (18)	study of correct spelling, according to established usage

Annotating as You Read

The author presents background information and does make statements about the institution (the location of the action) and the people involved. However, description/support is subordinated to the main idea structure of time sequence. As you read, consider how you might organize a summary of the selection. What would fit logically in the beginning, middle, and end? Mark these sections in the margins of the text. Try to frame an implied main idea statement that covers the sequence of events from the author's entrance at the institution to her exit.

Civilize Them with a Stick

by Mary Crow Dog

Gathered from the cabin, the wickiup, and the tepee, partly by cajolery and partly by threats, partly by bribery and partly by force, they are induced to leave their kindred to enter these schools and take upon themselves the outward appearance of civilized life.

(*Annual report of the Department of Interior,* 1901)

1   It is almost impossible to explain to a sympathetic white person what a typical old Indian boarding school was like; how it affected the Indian child

Mary Crow Dog with Richard Erdoes, excerpts from "Civilize Them with a Stick," from *Lakota Woman.* Copyright © 1990 by Mary Crow Dog and Richard Erdoes. Used by permission of Grove/Atlantic, Inc.

suddenly dumped into it like a small creature from another world, helpless, defenseless, bewildered, trying desperately and instinctively to survive and sometimes not surviving at all. I think such children were like the victims of Nazi concentration camps trying to tell average, middle-class Americans what their experience had been like. Even now, when these schools are much improved, when buildings are new, all gleaming steel and glass, the food tolerable, the teachers well-trained and well-intentioned, even trained in child psychology—unfortunately, the psychology of white children, which is different from ours—the shock to the child upon arrival is still tremendous. Some just seem to shrivel up, don't speak for days on end, and have an empty look in their eyes. I know of an eleven-year-old on another reservation who hanged herself, and in our school, while I was there, a girl jumped out of the window, trying to kill herself to escape an unbearable situation. That first shock is always there.

2   Although the old tiyospaye has been destroyed, in the traditional Sioux families, especially in those where there is no drinking, the child is never left alone. It is always surrounded by relatives, carried around, enveloped in warmth. It is treated with the respect due to any human being, even a small one. It is seldom forced to do anything against its will, seldom screamed at, and never beaten. That much, at least, is left of the old family group among full-bloods. And then suddenly a bus or car arrives, full of strangers, usually white strangers, who yank the child out of the arms of those who love it, taking it screaming to the boarding school. The only word I can think of for what is done to these children is kidnapping.

3   Even now, in a good school, there is impersonality instead of close human contact; a sterile, cold atmosphere, an unfamiliar routine, language problems, and above all the maza-skan-skan, that damn clock—white man's time as opposed to Indian time, which is natural time. Like eating when you are hungry and sleeping when you are tired, not when that damn clock says you must. But I was not taken to one of the better, modern schools. I was taken to the old-fashioned mission school at St. Francis, run by the nuns and Catholic fathers, built sometime around the turn of the century and not improved a bit when I arrived, not improved as far as the buildings, the food, the teachers, or their methods were concerned....

4   The mission school at St. Francis was a curse for our family for generations. My grandmother went there, then my mother, then my sisters and I. At one time or another every one of us tried to run away. Grandma told me once about the bad times she had experienced at St. Francis. In those days they let students go home only for one week every year. Two days were used up for transportation, which meant spending just five days out of three hundred and sixty-five with her family. And that was an improvement. Before grandma's time, on many reservations they did not let the students go home

at all until they had finished school. Anybody who disobeyed the nuns was severely punished. The building in which my grandmother stayed had three floors, for girls only. Way up in the attic were little cells, about five by five by ten feet. One time she was in church and instead of praying she was playing jacks. As punishment they took her to one of those little cubicles where she stayed in darkness because the windows had been boarded up. They left her there for a whole week with only bread and water for nourishment. After she came out she promptly ran away, together with three other girls. They were found and brought back. The nuns stripped them naked and whipped them. They used a horse buggy whip on my grandmother. Then she was put back into the attic—for two weeks.

5   My mother had much the same experiences but never wanted to talk about them, and then there I was, in the same place. The school is now run by the BIA—the Bureau of Indian Affairs—but only since about fifteen years ago. When I was there, during the 1960s, it was still run by the Church. The Jesuit fathers ran the boys' wing and the Sisters of the Sacred Heart ran us—with the help of the strap....

6   The girls' wing was built like an F and was run like a penal institution. Every morning at five o'clock the sisters would come into our large dormitory to wake us up, and immediately we had to kneel down at the sides of our beds and recite the prayers. At six o'clock we were herded into the church for more of the same. I did not take kindly to the discipline and to marching by the clock, left-right, left-right. I was never one to like being forced to do something. I do something because I feel like doing it. I felt this way always, as far as I can remember, and my sister Barbara felt the same way. An old medicine man once told me: "Us Lakotas are not like dogs who can be trained, who can be beaten and keep on wagging their tail, licking the hand that whipped them. We are like cats, little cats, big cats, wildcats, bobcats, mountain lions. It doesn't matter what kind, but cats who can't be tamed, who scratch if you step on their tails." But I was only a kitten and my claws were still small....

7   I did not escape my share of the strap. Once, when I was thirteen years old, I refused to go to Mass. I did not want to go to church because I did not feel well. A nun grabbed me by the hair, dragged me upstairs, made me stoop over, pulled my dress up (we were not allowed at the time to wear jeans), pulled my panties down, and gave me what they called "swats"—twenty five swats with a board around which Scotch tape had been wound. She hurt me badly....

8   The routine at St. Francis was dreary. Six a.m., kneeling in church for an hour or so; seven o'clock, breakfast; eight o'clock, scrub the floor, peel spuds, make classes. We had to mop the dining room twice every day and scrub the tables. If you were caught taking a rest, doodling on the bench with a fingernail or knife, or just rapping, the nun would come up with a dish towel and

just slap it across your face, saying, "You're not supposed to be talking, you're supposed to be working!" Monday mornings we had cornmeal mush, Tuesday oatmeal, Wednesday rice and raisins, Thursday cornflakes, and Friday all the leftovers mixed together or sometimes fish. Frequently the food had bugs or rocks in it. We were eating hot dogs that were weeks old, while the nuns were dining on ham, whipped potatoes, sweet peas, and cranberry sauce. In winter our dorm was icy cold while the nuns' rooms were always warm....

9   Charlene Left Hand Bull and Gina One Star were two full-blood girls I used to hang out with. We did everything together. They were willing to join me in a Sioux uprising. We put together a newspaper which we called the *Red Panther*. In it we wrote how bad the school was, what kind of slop we had to eat—slimy, rotten, blackened potatoes for two weeks—the way we were beaten. I think I was the one who wrote the worst article about our principal of the moment, Father Keeler. I put all my anger and venom into it. I called him a wasicun son of a bitch. I wrote that he knew nothing about Indians and should go back to where he came from, teaching white children whom he could relate to. I wrote that we knew which priests slept with which nuns and that all they ever could think about was filling their bellies and buying a new car. It was the kind of writing which foamed at the mouth, but which also lifted a great deal of weight from one's soul.

10   On Saint Patrick's Day, when everybody was at the big powwow, we distributed our newspapers. We put them on windshields, and bulletin boards, in desks and pews, in dorms and toilets. But someone saw us and snitched on us. The shit hit the fan. The three of us were taken before a board meeting. Our parents, in my case my mother, had to come. They were told that ours was a most serious matter, the worst thing that had ever happened in the school's long history. One of the nuns told my mother, "Your daughter really needs to be talked to." "What's wrong with my daughter?" my mother asked. She was given one of our *Red Panther* newspapers. The nun pointed out its name to her and then my piece, waiting for mom's reaction. After a while she asked, "Well, what have you got to say to this? What do you think?"

11   My mother said, "Well, when I went to school here, some years back, I was treated a lot worse than these kids are. I really can't see how they can have any complaints, because we was treated a lot stricter. We could not even wear skirts halfway up our knee. These girls have it made. But you should forgive them because they are young. And it's supposed to be a free country, free speech and all that. I don't believe what they done is wrong." So all I got out of it was scrubbing six flights of stairs on my hands and knees, every day....

12   We got a new priest in English. During one of his first classes he asked one of the boys a certain question. The boy was shy. He spoke poor English, but he had the right answer. The priest told him, "You did not say it right. Correct yourself. Say it over again." The boy got flustered and stammered. He could

hardly get out a word. But the priest kept after him: "Didn't you hear? I told you to do the whole thing over. Get it right this time." He kept on and on.

13   I stood up and said, "Father, don't be doing that. If you go into an Indian's home and try to talk Indian, they might laugh at you and say, 'Do it over correctly. Get it right this time!'"

14   He shouted at me, "Mary, you stay after class. Sit down right now!"

15   I stayed after the class, until after the bell. He told me, "Get over here!" He grabbed me by the arm, pushing me against the blackboard, shouting, "Why are you always mocking us? You have no reason to do this."

16   I said, "Sure I do. You were making fun of him. You embarrassed him. He needs strengthening, not weakening. You hurt him. I did not hurt you."

17   He twisted my arm and pushed real hard. I turned around and hit him in the face, giving him a bloody nose. After that I ran out of the room, slamming the door behind me. He and I went to Sister Bernard's office. I told her, "Today I quit school. I'm not taking any more of this, none of this shit anymore. None of this treatment. Better give me my diploma. I can't waste any more time on you people."

18   Sister Bernard looked at me for a long, long time. She said, "All right, Mary Ellen, go home today. Come back in a few days and get your diploma." And that was that. Oddly enough, that priest turned out okay. He taught a class in grammar, orthography, composition, things like that. I think he wanted more respect in class. He was still young and unsure of himself. But I was in there too long. I didn't feel like hearing it. Later he became a good friend of the Indians, a personal friend of myself and my husband. He stood up for us during Wounded Knee and after. He stood up to his superiors, stuck his neck way out, became a real people's priest. He even learned our language. He died prematurely of cancer. It is not only the good Indians who die young, but the good whites, too. It is the timid ones who know how to take care of themselves who grow old. I am still grateful to that priest for what he did for us later and for the quarrel he picked with me—or did I pick it with him?—because it ended a situation which had become unendurable for me. The day of my fight with him was my last day in school.

Exercise 8.2

Comprehension Questions

Circle the correct letter choice and fill in the blanks where indicated.

1. What is the best statement of the implied main idea of the article?

   a. Many generations of women in Mary Crow Dog's family had attended boarding school.

    b. Mary Crow Dog was justified in her reaction to the treatment of her schoolmate.

    c. The story of Mary Crow Dog at the Indian boarding school, her family's experience, getting in trouble writing a newspaper with her friends, and why she left.

    d. Mary Crow Dog endured a number of disturbing learning experiences in the Indian boarding school before abruptly leaving.

2. The author supports the statement in paragraph 1 that "the shock to the child upon arrival is still tremendous" with

    a. one specific example.

    b. two specific examples.

    c. testimony of experts.

    d. statistics.

3. The last two sentences in paragraph 2 ("And then suddenly a bus or car arrives ...") relate to the rest of the paragraph by presenting

    a. a contrast to what went before.

    b. a part of a whole.

    c. a good solution to a problem.

    d. a reason for an opinion.

4. What change of direction signal word in paragraph 3 shifts the reader's attention from schools in general to Mary Crow Dog's personal narrative?

    _____

5. The main idea of paragraph 4, "The mission school at St. Francis was a curse for our family for generations," is supported *mainly* by specific experiences of

    a. the author's mother.

    b. the author's sister.

    c. the author's grandmother.

    d. the author herself.

6. "But I was only a kitten and my claws were still small." (6) This comparison suggests that in the future the author will

    a. learn to conform to authority.

    b. become just like the people she now dislikes.

    c. be even more rebellious against unjust authority.

    d. decide to become a veterinarian.

7. Paragraph 7 is organized by time sequence. What is the topic sentence?

    a. I did not escape my share of the strap.

    b. When I was thirteen years old, I refused to go to Mass.

    c. I did not want to go to church because I did not feel well.

    d. She [a nun] hurt me badly.

8. In paragraph 8, time sequence is used as a subpattern to develop a main idea of description/support. What is the topic sentence?

    a. The routine at St. Francis was dreary.

    b. We had to mop the dining room twice every day and scrub the tables.

    c. Frequently the food had bugs or rocks in it.

    d. In winter our dorm was icy cold while the nuns' rooms were always warm.

9. In the last two sentences of paragraph 8, which subpattern does the author use to illustrate the idea that the young boarders received substandard food and housing?

    a. cause/effect

    b. comparison/contrast

    c. classification

    d. opinion/reason

10. The following passage appears in paragraph 9:

> We put together a newspaper which we called the *Red Panther*. In it we wrote how bad the school was, what kind of slop we had to eat—slimy, rotten, blackened potatoes for two weeks—the way we were beaten. I think I was the one who wrote the worst article about our principal of the moment, Father Keeler.

Rewrite the passage to make it completely factual. Leave out value statement words and use neutral words to replace any words with emotional connotations. How did your revision affect the ideas and intent of the original?

_____

_____

_____

_____

_____

_____

Inference and Evidence

Narrators of a story, like characters in a novel, do and say things that lead read-ers to draw conclusions about their personal traits. Put a check next to each of the words and phrases below that accurately describes the narrator. For each that you check, give one piece of evidence from the narrative (an action or a state-ment) that would support your inference.

<u>Support</u>

1. _____   impulsive   _____

2. _____   indifferent to others   _____

3. _____   capable of violence   _____

4. _____   timid   _____

5. _____   dishonest   _____

6. _____   independent   _____

7. _____   sensitive to injustice   _____

8. _____   highly self-critical   _____

9. _____   rebellious   _____

10. _____   inclined to compromise   _____

Vocabulary in Context

Circle the correct letter choice.

1. The Indian child is described as being "suddenly dumped into [boarding school] like a small creature from another world, helpless, defenseless, bewil-dered." (1) From this description we would imagine that *bewildered* means

   a. unimpressed.

   b. very confused.

   c. angry.

   d. contented.

2. "It is always surrounded by relatives, carried around, enveloped in warmth." (2) From this context, *enveloped* means

    a. rejected.

    b. enclosed.

    c. spoiled.

    d. crying.

3. "Even now, in a good school, there is impersonality instead of close human contact; a sterile, cold atmosphere." (3) From the signal words "instead of," we can guess that *impersonality* means

    a. lack of emotion or feeling.

    b. liveliness.

    c. respect.

    d. discussion.

4. Which of the possible meanings of *sterile* best fits the context of the quotation in question 3?

    a. producing little or no vegetation

    b. incapable of reproduction

    c. without feeling or imagination

    d. free from bacteria

5. "I put all my anger and venom into it." (9) From the words the author uses to describe her principal, *venom* must mean

    a. energy.

    b. knowledge.

    c. vanity.

    d. spite.

Questions for Writing/Small-Group Discussion

1. Paragraphs 9–11 relate the incident where the author and her friends get in trouble for producing an unauthorized newspaper. The items below tell the action in chronological order. Without looking back, use two lines to separate the sequence into a beginning situation, the developing action, and the conclusion.

    The three girls join in a "Sioux uprising."

    They create a paper with critical articles.

They distribute the papers.

Someone snitches on them.

The staff presents charges.

Mary's mother defends her.

Mary receives her punishment.

Now look back at the original paragraphs. Do your three divisions correspond exactly with the three paragraphs of the text? If not, what would account for the difference?

2. At the beginning of the selection, the author states that one girl attempted to kill herself by jumping out of a window. The author herself experienced and observed beatings and harassment. According to the staff, however, "the worst thing that had ever happened in the school's long history" was that three girls put out a newspaper. Why was this act so threatening?

3. The author complains about the "maza-skan-skan, that damn clock—white man's time as opposed to Indian time, which is natural time." Is this distinction valid? Can you give some further examples of "natural time"?

◼ TIME SEQUENCE: ORIGINS AND DEVELOPMENT

Like stories and biographical narratives, writing that traces the origin and development of objects or customs relies mainly on time sequence as its organizational pattern. Usually, however, the reader will have a more obvious timeline to follow—a sequence divided into clearly defined periods or marked by stages or phases with dates. Writers must be very selective in creating these kinds of histories, picking out from the day-to-day details only the most important highlights. Thus a reader will find that not all moments in the history are treated equally. There may be large gaps of time where nothing important happens; then again, a very short period may see a number of key developments.

PREVIEWING *THE BIG DICTIONARY CONCEIVED* BY SIMON WINCHESTER
Setting Your Reading Goals

This selection is taken from a best-selling book that tells two interrelated stories. One is of a nineteenth century physician whose mental illness led him to commit murder. The other—the story that this selection focuses on—deals with the very important project to which the doctor, while in prison, contributed greatly. Keep in mind that your purpose is not only to understand the sequence of events, but the significance of the project.

From the title, you can gather what the topic of the section is:

Topic: _____

Preview to determine the main idea by reading the first and last paragraphs. Which one gives you the best overall idea of what the selection is about? _____. Use the information in that paragraph to construct a tentative main idea hypothesis.

Main idea hypothesis: _____

_____

_____

Preview Vocabulary

prodigious (1)	very large, great
sheer (1)	complete, absolute
lexicographical (2)	relating to dictionary work
the Great Cham (2)	(Cham, a variation of Khan, a ruler in the Middle East); applied to Dr. Johnson (1709–84), a ruler of the literary scene in eighteenth century England
impertinence (4)	overstepping the bounds of what is considered proper or appropriate
nuance (4)	shade or variation in meaning or tone
etymology (4)	the tracing of the origins of words or word parts
grandiosity (5)	characterized by grandness of scale, often to the point of being showy
intractable (6)	not capable of being managed or solved
self-effacing (7)	modest, tending to stay in the background
quintessential (7)	of a perfect or most characteristic type or example
remit (8)	area of responsibility or authority
autocratic (15)	having absolute power to decide
eccentricity (15)	oddness in thought or behavior
astrakhan (15)	a loosely curled fur, from lambs originally bred in Astrakhan, Russia
paragon (16)	the perfect model
lingua franca (16)	the common or dominant language of the time
apotheosis (17)	a glorified ideal

Annotating As You Read

Track the development of the project by marking and taking notes on key stages and participants in its development. Circle or highlight dates and other words or phrases that keep sequences clear. Look for places where the text discusses the important features and methods of the dictionary; highlight these and make notes in the margins. Make necessary additions or changes to your main idea guess as your read. The language is difficult in places, so look back when necessary to the preview vocabulary and reread carefully any paragraphs whose meaning seems unclear.

The Big Dictionary Conceived

by Simon Winchester

1   The achievements of the great dictionary makers of England's seventeenth and eighteenth centuries were prodigious indeed. Their learning was unrivaled, their scholarship sheer genius, their contributions to literary history profound. All this is undeniable—and yet, cruel though it seems even to venture to inquire: Who now really remembers their dictionaries, and who today makes use of all that they achieved?

2   The question begs an inescapably poignant truth, of the kind that dims so many other pioneering achievements in fields that extend beyond and are quite unrelated to this one. The reality, as seen from today's perspective, is simply: However distinguished the lexicographical works of Thomas Elyot, Robert Cawdrey, Henry Cockeram, and Nathaniel Bailey, and however masterly and pivotal the creation of the Great Cham, Samuel Johnson himself, their achievements seem nowadays to have been only stepping-stones, and their magnificent volumes of work very little more than curios to be traded, hoarded, and forgotten.

3   And the reason for this is principally that in 1857, just over a century after the publication of the first edition of Johnson's *Dictionary,* there came a formal proposal for the making of a brand-new work of stellar ambition, a lexicographical project that could be of far, far greater breadth and complexity than anything attempted before.

4   It had as its goal a quite elegantly simple impertinence: While Johnson had presented a selection of the language—and an enormous selection at that, brilliantly fashioned—this new project would present *all of it*; every word,

Simon Winchester, *The Professor and the Madman: A Tale of Murder, Insanity, and the Making of the Oxford English Dictionary* (HarperCollins Publishers, Inc., 1998), 25-26, 101–106.

every nuance, every shading of meaning and spelling and pronunciation, every twist of etymology, every possible illustrative citation from every English author.

5   It was referred to simply as the "big dictionary".... Victorian England was, after all, a time of great men, great vision, great achievement. Perhaps no time in modem history was more suited to the launching of a project of such grandiosity; which is perhaps why duly, and ponderously, it got under way. Grave problems and seemingly intractable crises threatened more than once to wreck it. Disputations and delays surrounded it. But eventually—by which time many of those great and complicated men who first had the vision were long in their graves—the goal of which Johnson himself might have dreamed was duly attained. And while Samuel Johnson and his team had taken six years to create their triumph, those involved in making what was to be, and still is, the ultimate English dictionary took seventy years almost to the day.

6   The big dictionary's making began with the speech at the London Library, on Guy Fawkes Day, 1857. Richard Chenevix Trench was officially designated by his contemporary obituarists as "a divine," a term that is rarely used today but that embraced all manner of good and eminent Victorians who pursued all kinds of callings and who wore the cloth while doing so. At the time of his death in 1886, Trench was still regarded more as a divine than anything else—he had had a glittering ecclesiastical career that culminated in his being made dean of Westminster and then archbishop of Dublin.

7   His theme on that lexicographically famous evening was intriguing. Advertised on handbills and in flyers posted around London's West End, it was "On Some Deficiencies in Our English Dictionaries." By today's standards the title seems self-effacing, but given the imperial temper of the time and the firm belief that English was the quintessential imperial language and that any books that dealt with it were important tools for the maintenance of the empire, the title offered an amply understandable hint of the impact that Doctor Trench would be likely to have.

8   He identified seven principal ways in which the dictionaries then available were to be found wanting—most of them are technical and should not concern us here. But his underlying theme was profoundly simple: It was an essential credo for any future dictionary maker, he said, to realize that a dictionary was simply "an inventory of the language" and decidedly not a guide to proper usage. Its assembler had no business selecting words for inclusion on the basis of whether they were good or bad. Yet all of the craft's earlier practitioners, Samuel Johnson included, had been guilty of doing just that. The lexicographer, Trench pointed out, was "an historian...not a critic." It was not within the remit of one dictator—"or Forty" he added, with a cheeky nod at Paris—to determine which words should be used and which should

not. A dictionary should be a record of all words that enjoy any recognized life span in the standard language.

9   And the heart of such a dictionary, he went on, should be history of the life span of each and every word. Some words are ancient and exist still. Others are new and vanish like mayflies. Still others emerge in one lifetime, continue to exist through the next and the next, and look set to endure forever. Others deserve a less optimistic prognosis. Yet all these types of words are valid parts of the English language, no matter that they are old and obsolete or new and with questionable futures. Consider the golden question, said Trench: If someone needs to look up any word, then it should be there—for if not, the work of reference that book purports to be becomes a nonsense, something to which one cannot refer.

10   Now he was warming to his theme: To chart the life of each word, he continued, to offer its biography, as it were, it is important to know just when the word was born, to have a record of the register of its birth. Not in the sense of when it was first spoken, of course—that, until the advent of the tape-recorder, could never be known—but when it was first written down. Any dictionary that was to be based on the historical principles that, Trench insisted, were the only truly valid ones had to have, for every word, a passage quoted from literature that showed where each word was used first.

11   And after that, and also for each word, there should be sentences that show the twists and turns of meanings—the way almost every word slips in its silvery, fishlike way, weaving this way and that, adding subtleties of nuance to itself, and then perhaps shedding them as the public mood dictates. "A Dictionary," Trench said, "is an historical monument, the history of a nation contemplated from one point of view, and the wrong ways into which a language has wandered ... may be nearly as instructive as the right ones."

12   Johnson's dictionary may have been among the pioneers in presenting quotations (an Italian, for example, claimed that his dictionary had already done so in 1598), but they were there only to illustrate meaning. The new venture that Trench seemed now to be proposing would demonstrate not merely meaning but the history of meaning, the life story of each word. And that would mean the reading of everything and the quoting of everything that showed anything of the history of the words that were to be cited. The task would be gigantic, monumental, and—according to the conventional thinking of the times—impossible.

13   Except that here Trench presented an idea that—to those ranks of conservative and frock-coated men who sat silently in the library on that dank and foggy evening—was potentially dangerous and revolutionary. But it was the idea that in the end made the whole venture possible. The undertaking of the scheme, he said, was beyond the ability of any one man. To peruse all of English literature—and to comb the London and New York newspapers and

the most literate of the magazines and journals—must be instead "the combined action of many." It would be necessary to recruit a team—moreover, a huge one—probably comprising hundreds and hundreds of unpaid amateurs, all of them working as volunteers.

14   The audience murmured with surprise. Such an idea, obvious though it may sound today, had never been put forward before. But then, some members said as the meeting was breaking up, it did have some real merit. It had a rough, rather democratic appeal. It was an idea consonant with Trench's underlying thought, that any grand new dictionary ought to be itself a democratic product, a book that demonstrated the primacy of individual freedoms, of the notion that one could use words freely, as one liked, without hard and fast rules of lexical conduct.

15   Any such dictionary certainly should not be an absolutist, autocratic product, such as the French had in mind: The English raised eccentricity and poor organization to a high art, and placed the scatterbrain on a pedestal, loathed such Middle European things as rules, conventions, and dictatorships. They abhorred the idea of diktats—about the language, for Heaven's sake!—emanating from some secretive body of unaccountable immortals. Yes, nodded a number of members of the Philological Society, as they gathered up their astrakhan-collared coats and white silk scarves and top hats that night and strolled out into the yellowish November fog: Dean Trench's notion of calling for volunteers was a good one, a worthy and really rather noble idea.... (101–106)

16   It took more than seventy years to create the twelve tombstone-size volumes that made up the first edition of what was to become the great *Oxford English Dictionary*. This heroic, royally dedicated literary masterpiece—which was first called the *New English Dictionary,* but eventually became the *Oxford* ditto, and thence forward was known familiarly by its initials as the *OED*—was completed in 1928; over the following years there were five supplements and then, half a century later, a second edition that integrated the first and all the subsequent supplementary volumes into one new twenty-volume whole. The book remains in all senses a truly monumental work—and with very little serious argument is still regarded as a paragon, the most definitive of all guides to the language that, for good or ill, has become the lingua franca of the civilized modern world.

17   Just as English is a very large and complex language, so the *OED* is a very large and complex book. It defines well over half a million words. It contains scores of millions of characters, and, at least in its early versions, many miles of hand-set type. Its enormous—and enormously heavy—volumes are bound in dark blue cloth: Printers and designers and bookbinders worldwide see it as an apotheosis of their art, a handsome and elegant creation that looks and feels more than amply suited to its lexical thoroughness and accuracy....

18   The aims of those who began the project, back in the 1850s, were bold and laudable, but there were distinct commercial disadvantages to their methods: It took an immense amount of time to construct a dictionary on this basis, it was too time-consuming to keep up with the evolution of the language it sought to catalog, the work that finally resulted was uncommonly vast and needed to be kept updated with almost equally vast additions, and it remains to this day for all of these reasons a hugely expensive book both to produce and to buy.

19   But withal it is widely accepted that the *OED* has a value far beyond its price; it remains in print, and it still sells well. It is the unrivaled cornerstone of any good library, an essential work for any reference collection. And it is still cited as a matter of course—"the *OED* says"—in parliaments, courtrooms, schools, and lecture halls in every corner of the English-speaking world, and probably in countless others beyond. (25–26).

Exercise 8.3

Vocabulary in Context

Use the context to match the meanings on the right with the words on the left.

1. _____ profound (1)   a. no longer in use

2. _____ poignant (2)   b. arguments

3. _____ stellar (3)   c. hated

4. _____ duly (5)   d. deep, important

5. _____ ponderously (5)   e. worthy of praise

6. _____ disputations (6)   f. felt very strongly

7. _____ eminent (6)   g. look through, survey

8. _____ prognosis (9)   h. on schedule

9. _____ obsolete (9)   i. coming from

10. _____ peruse (13)   j. very high, lofty

11. _____ absolutist (15)   k. slowly, awkwardly

12. _____ abhorred (2)   l. orders, rules given without discussion

13. _____ diktats (15)   m. of highly respected standing, important

14. _____ emanating from (15) n. rigid, unyielding

15. _____ laudable (18)   o. prediction

Mapping

Use the items below to complete the timeline map.

   a. *OED* completed after 70 years

   b. second edition integrating all supplements.

   c. remains in print, and it still sells well.

   d. italian dictionary claiming to present quotations

   e. making of dictionaries leading to *OED*

   f. new massive project began with Trench's speech

   g. five supplements and updates

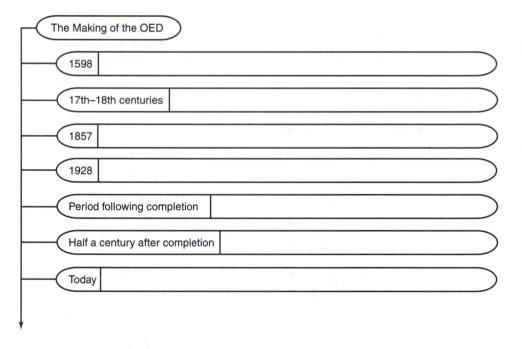

Comprehension Questions

Circle the correct letter choice and fill in the blanks where indicated.

   1. Which of the following best summarizes the main idea of the selection?

      a. The achievements of the great dictionary makers of England's seventeenth and eighteenth centuries were great, but they were only stepping stones to the *OED*.

      b. The aims of those who began the project, back in the 1850s, were bold and laudable, but there were distinct commercial disadvantages to their methods.

    c. The *OED* was a monumental and innovative achievement that retains its popularity, usefulness, and position as the final authority on words to this day.

    d. The first important dictionary makers, the history of the *OED,* its achievements and methods, along with its importance and usefulness today.

2. Which of the following states the main idea of paragraphs 1–2, taken as a unit?

    a. The achievements of the great dictionary makers of England's seventeenth and eighteenth centuries were prodigious indeed.

    b. The learning, scholarship, and genius of the early dictionary makers such as Samuel Johnson was unrivaled.

    c. The contributions of early dictionary makers to literary history were profound, and their lexicographical works were distinguished and masterly.

    d. The achievements of the early dictionary makers seem today only stepping-stones, and their magnificent work little more than curios to be traded, hoarded, and forgotten.

3. Early dictionaries became less important because they were

    a. overshadowed by the OED.

    b. totally inaccurate.

    c. far too complex.

    d. too broad in scope.

4. Which paraphrase gives the best clarification of the meaning of paragraph 7? (Remember: a paraphrase must be *in one's own words.*)

    a. Trench was an intriguing but modest person who believed that the English language had some deficiencies that needed to be worked on if England's empire and language were to maintain their high positions.

    b. Trench's intriguing title seems self-effacing, but because English was the quintessential imperial language, any book that dealt with it would have high impact and be important for the maintenance of the empire.

    c. Discussing "deficiencies" in English dictionaries marked Trench's speech as very important, because people believed that English was the ruling language in the world and a dictionary would have a significant effect on the way it kept up its empire.

5. The information in which paragraph below would be the LEAST important to annotate or include in a summary?

    a. paragraph 6

    b. paragraph 7

c. paragraph 8

d. paragraph 9

Why? _____

_____

_____

6. We can infer from paragraph 8 that

   a. none of the technical problems noted by Trench were important.

   b. most dictionary makers had a background in history.

   c. the French held a view of dictionary making that was the opposite of Trench's.

   d. words that imply judgments like *good* or *bad* should not be included in the dictionary.

7. Which of the following statements contains an opinion?

   a. "…in 1857…. there came a formal proposal for the making of a brand-new work."

   b. "If someone needs to look up any word, then it should be there."

   c. "[The *OED*] defines well over half a million words."

   d. "…the *OED* was completed in 1928; … there were five supplements."

8. "Any such dictionary certainly should not be an absolutist, autocratic product, such as the French had in mind." (15) This sentence is expressing the the viewpoint of

   a. Dr. Johnson.

   b. the French.

   c. the members of the philological society

   d. none of the above

9. The author's purpose is to

   a. relate a fascinating historical achievement that both informs and entertains the reader.

   b. list facts and dates about the *OED*, without giving judgments or opinions.

   c. persuade the reader that English lexicographers are superior to the French.

   d. promote the sale and use of the *Oxford English Dictionary*.

10. The author's tone in the selection is best described as

    a. earnest, enthusiastic, laudatory.

    b. matter-of-fact, indifferent, aloof.

    c. cynical, patronizing, incredulous.

    d. somber, evasive, resigned.

Based on the reading, mark the following True (T) or False (F):

1. _____ Johnson's dictionary included every English word, though not all had quotations.

2. _____ The development of the big dictionary over the years was nearly trouble-free.

3. _____ All early dictionary makers thought a dictionary should be a guide to proper usage.

4. _____ Words are included in the *OED* only if they are still being used.

5. _____ The *OED* includes an historical record of every English word.

6. _____ Trench felt that word meanings through time can change and be hard to pinpoint.

7. _____ Johnson was a pioneer in using quotations to show the history of meaning.

8. _____ A little over half of all workers on the *OED* were paid.

9. _____ The first edition of the *OED* contained twelve very large volumes.

10. _____ The *OED* is a complex book that defines scores of millions of words.

Dictionary Exercise

Use the OED in your library or go online to do the following:
Look up two of the following words and answer the questions below:

    confetti

    lament

    jaunty

    squelch

    volunteer

Word 1: _____

What is the earliest quotation cited? _____

_____

_____

What is the name of the source? _____

What is the date? _____

What did the word mean in that quotation? _____

Word 2: _____

What is the earliest quotation cited? _____

_____

_____

What is the name of the source? _____

What is the date? _____

What did the word mean in that quotation? _____

Questions for Discussion

1. The author says of Samuel Johnson and others that "their achievements seem nowadays to have been only stepping-stones, and their magnificent volumes of work very little more than curios to be traded, hoarded, and forgotten." Ask one or more instructors of English literature on your campus whether they agree with this assessment, and share your findings with the class.

2. Some people in the past have maintained that a word like "ain't" should not be in the dictionary. How would they justify their view? Do you agree? Why or why not?

▉ WORD PARTS 2: TIME INDICATORS

The list of word parts indicating time is short, but some occur with very high frequency. *Pre* and *post,* for example, combine with a great number of words and can be freely attached to many new words, events, or personages (for example, the post-Reagan years). Word parts like *neo* are used frequently to mark eras and epochs in history and science. Your knowledge of these word parts, together with your recognition of transition words of time, will help you to organize sequences clearly as you read.

Word Part	Meanings	Word Examples	Your Examples
ann/enn	year	annuity, biennial	
dec	ten	decade, decameter	
cent	one hundred	centenarian, century	
mill	one thousand	millenium, millisecond	
meso	middle	Mesolithic, Mesozoic	
neo	new	neolithic, neologism	
paleo	ancient	Paleolithic, Paleozoic	
post	after	postwar, posthypnotic	
pre	before	predetermined, preview	
prim	first	primary, primeval	
proto	first	prototype, protozoa	
chron	time	chronology, chronometer	
tempor	time	temporary, temporal	
re	back, again	remission, recession	
retro	backward	retrofit, retroactive	

Exercise 8.4

Complete the sentences below without using a dictionary.

1. A *chronic* infection would be one that _____

   _____

   _____.

2. *Mort* means "dead"; a *postmortem* investigation would be conducted

   _____

   _____.

3. The Nazis ruled a fascist government under Adolph Hitler in World War II.
   A *neo-Nazi* would be someone who _____

   _____.

4. Fabricate means "to construct"; someone who *prefabricates* trial testimony
   is _____

   _____.

5. The word part *ordi* means "to begin"; a *primordial* creature would be one that _____

_____.

6. To say that Roosevelt and Churchill were *contemporaries* would mean that they _____

_____.

7. *Spect* means "see, look"; a *retrospective* of an artist's life would be an exhibit that _____

_____.

8. A *centennial* celebration of an event would be held on _____

_____.

9. *Gress* comes from a word part meaning "to step, go"; a child who *regresses* in behavior may act like _____

_____.

10. History usually means a written record of events; a *protohistory* would refer to _____

_____.

CHAPTER REVIEW

Circle the correct letter choice and fill in the blanks where indicated.

1. Which word does *not* signal a time sequence?
    a. next
    b. although
    c. before
    d. later

2. Which "how to" topic would most likely be developed in a strict time sequence?
    a. investing in the stock market
    b. being a good listener
    c. handling a grumpy boss
    d. changing the oil on a car

Throughout the ages and in every culture, human beings have rendered their thoughts into language and have employed words to order their thoughts. Tens of thousands of years ago, our cave-dwelling ancestors put their thoughts into words to organize hunting parties. Several millennia later, Egyptian scribes used hieroglyphics (writing in pictorial characters) to represent the written word. Still later, Socrates was sentenced to drink hemlock for preaching corrupting ideas to the youth of ancient Greece. Today, world leaders employ oratory to rouse their constituencies to moral behavior and social progress, professors verbally instruct students in the various fields of human knowledge, and people from all walks of life use language to exchange ideas with others or to mentally solve problems.

(Lefton, *Psychology*, 5th ed., 263)

3. The main idea of the preceding paragraph is

    a. stated in the first sentence.

    b. stated in the last sentence.

    c. divided.

    d. implied.

4. The main idea makes a general statement about what people have done. The rest of the paragraph gives examples. The idea pattern, therefore, is

    a. opinion/reason.

    b. cause/effect.

    c. description/support.

    d. problem/solution.

5. How many different examples are given to support the main idea?

    a. 3

    b. 4

    c. 5

    d. 6

6. The examples used to support the main idea are organized by which idea subpattern?

    a. comparison/contrast

    b. cause/effect

    c. time sequence

    d. whole/part

7. Three time signal transitions introduce specific examples. Which one does *not?*

   a. throughout the ages

   b. tens of thousands of years ago

   c. still later

   d. today

8. "Several millennia later, Egyptian scribes used hieroglyphics (writing in pictorial characters) to represent the written word." This sentence

   a. gives one example to help develop the main idea.

   b. begins with a transitional signal phrase.

   c. contains a definition.

   d. all of the above

9. *Post*-game activities are those that would be held

   a. during a game.

   b. before a game.

   c. after a game.

   d. away from a game.

10. *Pre*-game activities are those that would be held

   a. during a game.

   b. before a game.

   c. after a game.

   d. away from a game.

READING PORTFOLIO   *A Time Sequence Article*

1. *For this assignment you will need to find a magazine or newspaper article dealing with time sequence.* There are two types of articles in this area.

OPTION A: Origins or Stages.   You want something more than just a story here. Look for an article that traces a topic from its origins to the present and/or gives stages by which something developed.

OPTION B: "How to" Process.   These articles are very common, particularly in speciality magazines on topics like woodworking, auto mechanics, weight training, and crafts. The danger here is using an article that may be too short or really too mechanical to interest the general reader. The content may be easy, but trying to summarize an article with, say, 20 different steps can be very difficult. You must be selective and be able to lump steps into larger phases. Also, summarizing short steps *in your own words* can be difficult.

2. *Your summary should be 150–175 words.* Try to come up with a pattern map like the samples in this chapter. For a time sequence, use a timeline and organize steps or stages into three sections: beginning, middle, and end. Use your own phrasing in your outline or map. That way you can write your summary directly from it.

3. *Your response should be of equal length.* How you respond really depends a lot on which option you are trying. For articles about origins and developments, do you have a new or better understanding? Has reading the article changed your attitude toward the topic, for better or worse? For "how to" articles, you might evaluate the usefulness of the information. Will the process work? Is the sequence correctly ordered? Or is there a better way? Your personal experience is very relevant here.

4. *Select five words from the article that you are unsure of.* Use the dictionary to determine their meanings in the article. Then write a sentence for each, providing helpful context clues.

Seeing Connections in Events: Cause and Effect

CHAPTER

9

Who is responsible for the budget mess in Washington? What explains the acts of terrorists? Why were you not invited to a friend's wedding? In dealing with events, we often find that knowing *when* they happened is not enough. Questions that spring from our need to know *why* things are the way they are—whether trivial or profound, private or personal—lead us into cause/effect ideas. You will now become more familiar with this very important pattern that helps us to take some control over our destiny.

▉ CHAPTER PREVIEW

In this chapter you will

- ▪ Examine variations of cause/effect in a textbook passage
- ▪ Analyze articles concerned with offering answers to the question *why*
- ▪ Identify a logical fallacy common to cause/effect
- ▪ Work with a sample "how to" advice article
- ▪ Summarize and respond to a cause/effect article for your Reading Portfolio

At a very basic level, the cause and effect pattern involves a simple equation: **X causes Y.** A number of verbs and signal words indicate cause and effect relationships.

influence	because	so
contribute to	for	thus
create	so that	therefore
determine	since	if ... then
result in	consequently	in order for

Although cause/effect might seem easy to diagram, the pattern is usually a lot more complex. There may be multiple causes or effects, and main ideas in this pattern are often implied or divided.

ANALYZING CAUSE AND EFFECT: TEXTBOOK PASSAGE

Most people do not read textbooks for fun or by choice. Texts are clearly designed for learning situations, primarily the classroom, and are usually an important part of the requirements for passing a course. As practice for answering questions from texts in college courses, read the selection below as if you were preparing to take a test.

PREVIEWING *EXERCISE IN THE ENVIRONMENT* BY SCOTT K. POWERS AND STEPHEN L. DODD

Setting Your Reading Goals

The selection below comes from a chapter in a health text. Preview by reading the title selection and the first paragraph. According to paragraph 1, what are the author's goals in this chapter?

_____

_____

_____

Look for and write the heading in boldface that tells you what this part of the chapter will focus on: _____. Read the sentence at the end of paragraph 3 that precedes the second heading. Together, this information should help you decide on what points you need to locate and remember. Read carefully as though preparing for a test on this material.

Preview Vocabulary

impair (1)	damage, make worse
contractions (2)	the shortening or thickening of a muscle in action
stationary (4)	fixed, not moving
saturated (6)	filled to capacity, having absorbed all that can be taken in
retarded (8)	slowed down
ambient (8)	that which surrounds

Annotating As You Read

To increase your awareness of cause/effect, circle any words that indicate causal relationships. Some of these stand out clearly—because, therefore, etc.—but others are less obvious. In paragraph 1, for example, the verbs *affect, elevate, promote,* and *impair* all link cause with effect. To anticipate possible test questions, formulate and write in the margins questions regarding causes that the text answers: e.g., "Why does…?" "Under what conditions will…?" etc. One helpful feature of texts is the inclusion of definitions directly in the text. As you read, look for and mark the definitions located in the text for five key technical terms.

Exercise in the Environment

by Scott K. Powers and Stephen L. Dodd

1   Most of us know from personal experience that environmental factors can affect exercise performance. For example, hot environments, high altitude, and air pollution can elevate exercise heart rates, promote labored breathing, and impair exercise tolerance. A general understanding of how environmental factors can influence exercise performance is important for the physically active individual. In this chapter we discuss common environmental hazards that should be considered when planning workouts and outline ways to cope with environmental stress. In particular, we focus on the following environmental concerns: heat and humidity, cold, altitude, and air pollution. Let's begin with a discussion of exercise in a hot environment.

Powers and Dodd, *Total Fitness: Exercise, Nutrition, and Wellness,* 2nd ed., 168.

Exercise in the Heat

2   Humans are **homeotherms,** which means same temperature. That is, body temperature is regulated around a set point; humans regulate their body temperature around the set point of 98.6°F or 37°C. Variations in body temperature can result in serious bodily injury. Indeed, heat illness can occur when body temperature rises above 105°F (41°C). Cramps, dizziness, nausea, lack of sweat production, and dry, hot skin are all indications of impending heat illness. Therefore, the body must maintain precise control over temperature to avoid a life-threatening situation.

3   During exercise, heat is produced as a by-product of muscular contractions. High-intensity exercise using large muscle groups produces more body heat than low-intensity exercise involving small muscle groups. Hence, during vigorous exercise using large muscle groups, the body must eliminate excess heat in order to prevent a dangerous rise in body temperature. In the next several paragraphs we discuss heat loss during exercise and outline key factors to consider when exercising in a hot environment.

Heat Loss during Exercise

4   The primary means of heat loss during exercise are convection and evaporation. Convection is heat loss by the movement of air (or water) around the body. Evaporative heat loss occurs due to the conversion of sweat (water) to a gas (water vapor). Let's discuss each of these methods individually.

5   Convective heat loss occurs only when the air or water molecules moving around the body are cooler than skin temperature, because the faster the flow of cool air or water around the body, the greater the heat loss. Minimal convective cooling occurs during exercise in a hot environment where there is limited air movement (riding a stationary exercise bicycle, for example). In contrast, bicycling outdoors on a cold day or swimming in cool water results in a large amount of convective cooling.

6   On a warm day with limited air movement around the body, evaporation is the most important means of body heat loss. The evaporation of sweat on the skin's surface removes heat from the body, even if the air temperature is higher than body temperature, as long as the air is dry. However, if the humidity is high, meaning the air is relatively saturated with water, and the air temperature is high, evaporation is retarded and body heat loss is drastically decreased. Under these conditions, heat produced by the contracting muscles is retained and body temperature increases gradually throughout the exercise session. Prolonged exercise in a hot and humid environment can result in a dangerously high increase in body temperature. Figure 9.1 (page 322) illustrates the differences in body heat gain during exercise in a high-temperature/high-humidity environment, a high-temperature/low-humidity environment, and a low-temperature/low-humidity environment.

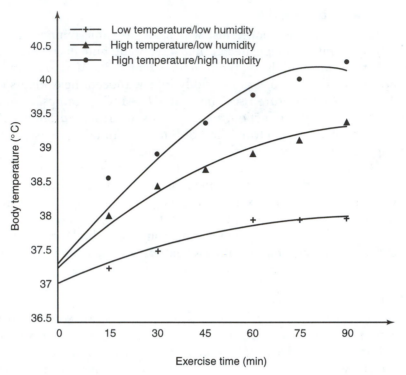

FIGURE 9.1 Body temperature responses to prolonged exercise in a high-temperature/high-humidity environment, a high-temperature/low-humidity environment, and a low-temperature/low-humidity environment. (Source: Powers and Dodd, *Total Fitness*, 2nd ed., 222)

Guidelines for Exercise in the Heat

7   Short-term exposure (30 to 60 min.) to an extremely hot environment is sufficient heat stress to cause heat illness in some people. This is especially true for people at high risk for heat illness (the elderly and those with low cardiovascular fitness levels are most susceptible). Even those individuals who are physically fit and accustomed to the heat are at risk if they exercise in a hot environment.

8   Heat stress on the body is not simply a function of the air temperature; both the heat and humidity must be considered. The higher the humidity, the higher the "effective" temperature. The effective temperature can be defined as the temperature that the body senses. At high levels of humidity, evaporation is retarded and the body cannot get rid of the heat normally lost through evaporative processes. This causes the temperature in the body to increase above what it would normally be on a less humid day at the same ambient temperature.

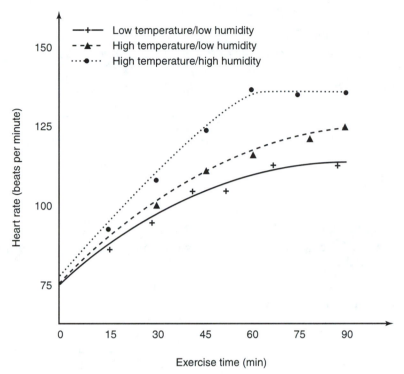

FIGURE 9.2   Heart rate responses to prolonged exercise in a high-temperature, high-humidity environment and a low-temperature, low-humidity environment. (Source: Powers and Dodd, *Total Fitness*, 2nd ed., 224)

9   Although it is obvious that it is extremely dangerous to exercise at high air temperatures (130°F, 55°C), it may not be obvious to most people that the body undergoes the same heat stress at only 85°F (29.5°C) when the humidity is high (~100%). In other words, the effective temperature remains at 130°F. Thus, high humidity causes a moderately high ambient temperature to be sensed by the body as extremely hot.

10   The best way to determine if the environmental conditions are imposing a heat load on your body is to monitor your heart rate. An increase in body temperature during exercise in a hot environment will result in large increases in heart rate compared with exercise in a cool environment. This point is illustrated in Figure 9.2, which shows the large differences in heart rate responses to exercise in the three different conditions. A temperature-induced increase in exercise heart rate is significant because it increases the difficulty of staying within your target heart rate zone.

Exercise 9.1

Definitions in the Text
Write a definition for each of the following, based on information in the selection.

1. homeotherms: _____

2. convection: _____

3. evaporation: _____

4. humidity: _____

5. "effective" temperature: _____

Mapping Cause and Effect Relationships

1. Paragraph 1 contains a section showing multiple causes and multiple effects. Fill in the map with the items below

   elevate exercise heart rates   impair exercise tolerance

   hot environments   high altitude

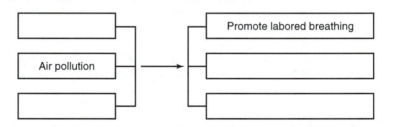

2. The elements below form a chain of cause and effect in paragraph 3. Put them in correct order in the map.

   rise in body temperature

   high-intensity exercise

   excessive body heat

3. Make and label your own map of paragraph 6, using the elements below. Your map should be somewhat similar to one of the two maps above.

decrease in heat loss   high humidity

evaporation slowed down   increase in body temperature

high air temperature

Asking Questions About the Text

Below are samples of questions you may have written in the margins. Write short answers in your own words. If you can't recall the answer, look back into the text to locate the information.

1. What can be done to prevent a dangerous rise in body temperature during vigorous exercise?

   _____

   _____

2. Under what conditions does convective heat loss occur?

   _____

   _____

3. Why is riding a bike outside on a cold day better rather than riding an exercise bike in a hot room?

   _____

   _____

4. Under what conditions is evaporation not effective?

   _____

   _____

5. What factors combine to cause heat stress?

   _____

   _____

Understanding Graphics

Below are questions on the graphics that appeared in the text. Study them carefully before answering the questions.

Figure 9.1 Body Temperature Responses

1. How many environments does the graphic show?

   a. 2

   b. 3

   c. 6

   d. none of the above

2. The word *temperature* in "high temperature/low humidity" means

   a. air temperature.

   b. body temperature.

   c. both.

   d. neither.

3. Exercising at high temperature/low humidity will cause a body temperature of about 38.5°C after

   a. 15 minutes.

   b. 45 minutes.

   c. 75 minutes.

   d. none of the above

4. After how many minutes will a person's temperature in low-temperature/low-humidity exercise be about the same as it would be if exercising for 15 minutes in high temperature/low humidity?

   a. 30

   b. 45

   c. 60

   d. none of the above

5. Exercising in which of the following would result in the least variation in body temperature?

   a. High temperature/high humidity for 45–75 minutes

   b. High temperature/low humidity for 30–60 minutes

   c. High temperature/low humidity for 60–90 minutes

   d. Low temperature/low humidity for 60–90 minutes

Figure 9.2 Heart Rate Responses

1. Heart rate is measured in

    a. beats per minute.

    b. time of exercise.

    c. degree of humidity.

    d. none of the above

2. The highest heart rate recorded on the chart for the low-temperature/ low-humidity environment differs approximately how much from the highest for high temperature/high humidity?

    a. 25 beats lower

    b. 50 beats lower

    c. 112 beats lower

    d. 50 beats higher

3. The biggest difference in heart rate between high temperature/high humidity and high temperature/low humidity occurs at approximately

    a. 40 minutes.

    b. 60 minutes.

    c. 75 minutes.

    d. 90 minutes.

4. The heart rate for high temperature/low humidity after 45 minutes is about the same as that for

    a. High temperature/high humidity after 20 minutes.

    b. High temperature/high humidity after 50 minutes.

    c. Low temperature/low humidity after 55 minutes.

    d. Low temperature/low humidity after 75 minutes.

5. We can determine from the graph that

    a. women's heart rates would probably be lower than men's in all environments.

    b. exercise after 75 minutes in all environments has little additional effect on heart rate.

    c. exercising more than 40 minutes in high temperature/low humidity is very dangerous.

    d. only professional athletes should exercise more than 60 minutes in high humidity.

Putting It to the Test

Imagine that you are in a test situation. Below are objective and short essay questions typical of those you might find on a test of this kind of material. Do not look back at the text to answer these; from your annotated reading and the exercises above you should be able to answer most of them correctly.

1. A sign of heat illness might be

   a. cramps.

   b. dizziness and nausea.

   c. dry, hot skin.

   d. all of the above

2. The most amount of heat would be produced by

   a. high-intensity exercise using small muscle groups.

   b. low-intensity exercise involving large muscle groups.

   c. high-intensity exercise using large muscle groups.

   d. low-intensity exercise involving small muscle groups.

3. The best way to determine if the environmental conditions are imposing a heat load on your body is to monitor your

   a. temperature.

   b. breathing.

   c. water intake.

   d. heart rate.

Write T for True or F for False next to the statements.

4. _____   Heat illness will occur when body temperature rises above 98°F.

5. _____   The faster the flow of cool air or water around the body, the greater the heat loss.

6. _____   Riding a stationary bike in a hot room causes more convective cooling than swimming in cool water.

7. _____   Evaporation of sweat will remove heat from the body, even in conditions of very high temperature and humidity.

8. _____   Those most at risk for heat illness are the elderly and those with low cardiovascular fitness.

9. _____   Heat stress is a variable of humidity and temperature.

10. _____   The higher the humidity, the higher the temperature that the body senses.

Write a short essay on each of the following:

1. Explain the difference between convective and evaporative heat loss.

2. The text states that the body might undergo the same heat stress when the air temperature is only 85°F as when it is 130°F. Explain how and under what conditions this would be true.

CAUSE AND EFFECT: MAGAZINE AND NEWSPAPER ARTICLES

It is human nature to feel uncomfortable or even unsafe when we are unsure of why things are happening. Many newspaper and magazine articles are therefore directed at giving explanations for events or trends that the public finds both disturbing and fascinating. Depending on the source, treatment of such issues in the popular press can range from serious, objective analyses to articles that tend to sensationalize and exploit an issue in order to increase circulation.

PREVIEWING *SEXY ADS TARGET KIDS* BY TOM REICHERT

Setting Your Reading Goals

This article, written by a professor of advertising, appeared in a popular magazine, aimed at the general population. Your goal in reading this kind of article is to become more knowledgeable about an emotionally charged issue of concern to society at large. The title states the topic:

Topic:_____

It also suggests main a main idea. Read the first paragraph and write the sentence that can best serve as a beginning main idea statement:

Main idea:_____

_____

_____

Preview Vocabulary

explicit (1)	clearly shown or directly stated
innuendo (1)	a remark or image suggesting something negative
allude (2)	make a reference to
demeanor (8)	outward behavior, conduct
influx (11)	a continual, often increasing coming in of persons or things

entendre (12)	suggested meaning
uninitiated (13)	without experience
culmination (13)	highest point or most important stage
salient (14)	noticeable, obvious
albeit (15)	although
double entendre (15)	statement open to two interpretations, often suggestive
pedophilia (15)	an abnormal condition in which an adult has sexual feelings for children
implicitly (21)	in a way that is clearly understood though not directly stated or shown

Annotating As You Read

In presenting his viewpoint, the author concentrates on three areas. Look carefully for these and annotate your findings as you go.

1. To prove that ads are doing what he says they are, the author includes a number of striking examples. Mark these as you go.

2. The author analyzes reasons why such ads are effective. Look for a listing phrase and signal words that will help you locate and mark these.

3. The author lists ways that ads with strong sexual content influence young people. Find and mark these. Look for signals in the text to guide you in your annotation.

You may experience some personal reactions—agreement, disagreement, recollections of personal experience with the issue—as you read. Make personal notes in the margin, or record these in a separate reading journal.

Sexy Ads Target Kids

by Tom Reichert

1   The Justice Department's report that movie studios market adult-oriented films to young people was a hot topic during the 2000 presidential campaign. If officials had examined the use of sexually explicit ads, the same might have been true for the advertising industry. Increasingly, sexual content in the form of innuendo, nudity, and sexual situations and behavior is being used to sell products to teenagers and young adults.

Tom Reichert, "Sexy Ads Target Young Adults" (*USA Today Magazine,* May 2001), 50–52. Reprinted by permission of The Society for the Advancement of Education.

2   The results of a 2000 study suggest that advertisers' sexy messages are getting through. More than 200 young adults, ages 18–25, demonstrated no hesitation when asked to name an ad they considered "really sexy." Over 60 ads were mentioned, and those cited most frequently were for Calvin Klein, Victoria's Secret, Clairol's Herbal Essences, Candie's, and Levi's. These, and many others like them, depict or allude to sexual behavior which is often more explicit than that found in movies. Unlike movies, however, these ads contain no ratings.

3   Consider, for instance, a commercial for Candie's fragrances that was popular among young people in the study. The ad featured actress Alyssa Milano writhing longingly on a bed as her boxers-clad male friend searched for something in the bathroom, seemingly for condoms. During his search, the camera cuts intermittently to provocative shots of her as she sprays perfume on herself. The viewer soon discovers it's cologne he is looking for, which he sprays on himself, including a quick spray in his boxer shorts. The last scene is a close-up of the fragrance bottles rocking back and forth on the sheets of the bed.

4   Although this commercial is clearly targeted toward young people, some sexual ads are not. All of them, though, appear in mainstream consumer media like prime-time television programs, billboards, and magazines. As such, they are seen and absorbed by a diverse audience that includes young adults, teenagers, and children.

5   By the time a youngster turns 14, he or she has been exposed to more than 350,000 television commercials. The average viewer watches at least six hours of commercial television messages a week. These estimates of media exposure do not include the countless print ads and promotional messages seen in other places. In all likelihood, sexy ads can be viewed by children watching programming during prime time or simply leafing through their brother's or sister's magazines.

6   What did the young adults involved in this study find sexy about the ads they identified? A 20-year-old male, describing another Candie's ad, said what he found sexy was "a partially naked Alyssa Milano [who is] surrounded by condoms and has her skirt hiked way up." Ads for Clairol Herbal Essences shampoo featuring women making orgasmic sounds prompted another 20-year-old male to say, "If I didn't see the TV, I might have thought it was a porno."

7   An 18-year-old female described a more recent Herbal Essences ad by saying, "The three men in black make the ad sexy. They are attractive and muscular, and the camera sometimes focuses on their hands touching the woman's body. It makes me, as the consumer, want to open the bottle of shampoo and have three strong, handsome men wash me." The ad she was describing features a woman in a courtroom being attended to by three men.

At the end of the commercial, celebrity sex therapist Dr. Ruth Westheimer makes a reference to a full-body wash. This ad, which has run on many networks, including MTV, is part of a long campaign that has featured women making orgasmic sounds while washing their hair in out-of-the-ordinary places, such as an airplane lavatory and a service station restroom. The tag line of the campaign is a true play on words—"A totally organic experience."

8   In 1995, CBS refused to let a Victoria's Secret commercial air during early prime time. The ad featured model Claudia Schiffer dancing "seductively" in her underwear. In 2000, the Schiffer commercial seems mild when compared to the ads mentioned by the respondents. Most young adults rated what the models were (or were not) wearing and their physiques as top reasons they found ads to be sexy. Others included the models' demeanor or behavior, sexual behavior between models, and some aspect of each ad's production value (for example, commercials filmed in black and white). Frequently, all of these elements are used by advertisers to create a sexy spot.

9   In all fairness, sexy ads aren't prevalent for all brands and services. The technique typically is used to market mainstream brands associated with social interaction and attractiveness, such as clothing, health and beauty aids, fragrances, and alcohol. Recently, however, sexual themes have been used to sell coffee, tea, computers, watches, cigarette lighters, and lollipops. If you peruse magazines read by teenagers, you will see that sex is used for a wide range of products.

10   Why do advertisers use sex when advertising to young adults? One answer is novelty. Remember your first kiss? Chances are you do. For young people just discovering romance and crushes, venturing into the realm of sexuality is new and exciting, as well as laden with anxiety and danger if their parents should ever find out what they're up to.

11   Research in psychology has shown that novel, emotion-evoking stimuli attract a person's attention. It has the same effect for advertising. Provocative images and words are more likely to be noticed by a potential consumer. Subsequently, the attention directed toward the ad may enhance the probability the ad's message is processed. Given the saturation and proliferation of commercial messages and ads in the media market, any edge an advertiser can use to grab consumers' attention in the battle for their dollars is considered. The influx of hormones caused by adolescence amplifies the effect.

12   Another reason sexy ads are effective is that young people are more susceptible to advertising's promises. Young boys are more apt to believe a particular cologne really does attract women and that a certain brand of athletic shoe just may make them irresistible. Consider ads mentioned by several young people involved in the study. They identified ads in a recent campaign for Lucky brand cologne that are notable for their unmistakable use of sexual entendre. One magazine ad features an interaction between a young cou-

ple. The man is ogling the woman's breasts. He's looking at her; she's looking at the viewer; and the tagline reads, "Get Lucky." The implication is that, if you wear Lucky, you just might "get lucky."

13   Whether people refuse to accept such a premise or not, it's true that advertising appeals are more believable to the uninitiated. In an attempt to sell Chupa Chups lollipops, an advertising agency in Texas developed a campaign titled "Oral Pleasure." The thrust of the campaign was to emphasize the fun of having a sucker in your mouth. The culmination of this campaign was a commercial titled "Here Kitty, Kitty." The ad featured a woman seductively licking a lollipop, much to the delight of male actors who were obviously aroused by her actions. The campaign and this commercial were targeted at the 14–24 age group. To reach the target, ads were scheduled to run on "The Simpsons," "Friends," and "South Park," programs that also are popular with young people under the age of 14.

14   Sexy ads are important to consider because they can influence young people in several ways. For one, they provide a highly salient behavioral model for young people. Most of these ads indicate, "If you do this or say this, you'll be more sexually attractive." That is a powerful promise for those experiencing sexual feelings for the first time. This effect is compounded when viewers are able to identify with the models in the commercials. Because humans constantly compare themselves to those around them and to those in the media, advertisers want to cast people similar in some respects to the target audience. Frequently, the point of comparison is age. All things being equal, young people are more apt to identify and subsequently compare themselves to those who are similar in age.

15   The use of young models in sexually provocative advertising is not new. In 1980, 15-year-old starlet/model Brooke Shields was cast in several provocative Calvin Klein jeans ads. In one commercial that was particularly memorable, albeit controversial, Shields uttered the now-famous line, "Do you want to know what comes between me and my Calvins? Nothing." The impact of the double entendre was enhanced by the way in which the camera slowly panned across her body. The ad created a flap and was eventually pulled. Fifteen years later, Calvin Klein pulled yet another campaign because of criticism that the ads portrayed young models in inappropriate situations. Some even likened the campaign to mass-market pedophilia. Klein and others have been criticized for sexualizing young people to sell their brands.

16   One obvious reason for the criticism is that, for young people, these images are instructive. They see images of people like themselves dressing in a sexually provocative manner and receiving attention. They see images of their peers acting in certain ways and being rewarded with intimacy and romance. In a sense, sexually provocative advertising serves to teach young adults that sex is a prize and that they need only to behave in certain ways

to be rewarded. It teaches them what and whom are valued. At the very least, these images and portrayals are an area of concern because they serve as role models for young people. Young people want to believe that wearing fragrances and certain styles of clothing will help them achieve intimacy by being popular with the opposite sex. For example, an 18-year-old female described the effect Victoria's Secret commercials have on her: "[It] makes me want to go out and buy the product: if these women look good wearing it, so will I." A 21-year-old female who identified a Tommy Hilfiger ad in which a young woman dances seductively in a photo booth, said, "It just put the thought in my mind that it would be fun to dance with my boyfriend like that."

17   Research also shows that sexual ads are titillating. Ads with sexual information encourage thoughts about sex and about sexual situations. A 20-year-old female, for example, described the effect of a Trojan condom radio ad of a car motor varying at different speeds: "It makes you think about sexual activities and sexual thoughts. With the way the motor sounds, it makes you imagine the different ways and speeds of sexual intercourse."

18   A 20-year-old male described his reaction to an ad for Wilson's leather goods featuring a female model with her thumbs in the belt loops of her pants: "Just imagining how far she will pull her pants down is a real turn-on."

19   One female described the mental story she created in response to a Calvin Klein ad: "The wet shiny bodies are very sensual. The hair in the face makes you envision that they just got done with the best lovemaking of their lives and they are so worn out that they don't have enough energy to kiss or put their clothes back on."

Sexy Is Sexist

20   Another area of concern is that these ads, as a whole, are sexist. In reality, the vast majority of sexual appeals use images of women to provoke desire. "So what?" a few of my students ask. "Women are naturally more beautiful than men." It may be acceptable for a few isolated incidents, I say, but the cumulative effect of a fairly excessive diet of sexually provocative images of women has been shown to have detrimental effects in regard to attitudes and behaviors about and toward women.

21   By sexist, it's meant that these images foster stereotypes of social roles based on gender. What stereotypes do these images reinforce? One is that a primary trait or purpose of women is sexual attraction and sexual satisfaction. In these ads, women are present merely to look good and fulfill sexual needs. They also implicitly state that real men have worth when they snare a physically attractive woman. As a whole, these ads devalue vital aspects of the female persona such as personality and intellect.

22   The message being sent to women is: "You must look like this. You must act like this. You must dress like this. If you want to attract a man or achieve

some level of relational 'success' with a man, you need to follow these rules." Similarly, an unspoken set of rules is provided to men: "You need to look for women who look like and behave like this." Are these the scripts we want to instill in our young people?

23   All this makes sense when you consider that ads for Victoria's Secret were the overall runner-up according to the young adults in the study. Respondents identified Body by Victoria commercials as well as Angel ads. Interestingly, ads for the Desire campaign by Victoria's Secret were not mentioned. In the ads, Victoria's Secret models Stephanie Seymour and others offer their definitions of "desire." One of them giggles while she says. "Wanting something you can't have," as the camera cuts to a close-up of her breasts. Young people picked up on these types of images in Victoria's Secret commercials. According to a 20-year-old female, Victoria's Secret ads are sexy because the models are "hot in nothing but bra and panties." A 20-year-old male said he found Victoria's Secret ads sexy because they contained "half-naked women prancing around."

24   Obviously, most underwear ads these days tend to show a lot of skin. It is important to remember, though, that they reinforce the sense of implicit sexism discussed above. As argued by feminists and media scholars, these portrayals can influence perceptions of what a woman is, how people behave toward her, and how she perceives of herself. Consider how a 20-year-old male described an ad for Trojan condoms: "The body of an [apparently] athletic woman with skimpy underwear on and the condom is held up by one of the strings on her panties." Here's why he found the ad to be sexy: "It would have to be a combination of the quite large breasts, toned stomach, and other nice curves without much to cover them up. And when you add the condom, it's like letting you know."

25   It can work the other way, however. For example, one 19-year-old female described what she found sexy in a commercial for Dentyne's Ice gum: "muscular man—no shirt and tight jeans." One Diet Coke commercial is famous for its role reversal, showing women gawking at a construction worker who sheds his shirt and drinks a Diet Coke during his break. These commercials were created to poke fun at traditional sexist ads, especially those that are sexually oriented.

26   Although truthfulness and substantiation of advertising claims are regulated by law, the "nature" of advertising content is regulated by self-discipline on the part of the ad creator or self-regulated by the advertising profession and media industry. This means that people involved in the process make decisions about what is acceptable based on personal moral considerations, long-term brand positioning considerations, and the desire to avoid negative press and consumer reaction. As a result, brand managers often "kill" ads deemed too risky or provocative. In some instances, networks and local stations refuse to run appeals they consider inappropriate for their viewers or that may violate community standards.

27   Recently, the publisher of Dallas' *D* magazine reprinted 70,000 issues without a Gucci ad he discovered after the initial press run. In the publisher's opinion, the ad crossed the line of acceptability with regard to blatant sexual imagery. Consumer backlash can also result in sexual appeals being pulled. One need only think of the Calvin Klein jeans ads, featuring underage models in sexual situations, that were voluntarily pulled after an intense public backlash. Overall, ad professionals claim to have little respect for sexual appeals when used to get attention. To quote one executive, "Whoever created the ad is lazy. Anyone can do it." On the other hand, most agree that, if sex is used in a novel or creative way to communicate brand benefits, or if partnered with humor, it can be very effective.

28   With their tails tucked between their legs, Jack Valenti, president of the Motion Picture Association of America, and others in the movie industry recently admitted that the practice of promoting films with questionable content to young people is wrong. When one considers reports that consistently show young adults are exposed to thousands of promotional messages every day, many of them containing explicit sexual imagery and innuendo, it is clear that another culprit may be the messenger. Sexual information will be used to sell products as long as people aspire to be sexually attractive to others. Nevertheless, advertisers should be called to task for targeting young people with sexual appeals. Just because it's effective doesn't mean it's right.

Exercise 9.2

Vocabulary

Use the context to match the letters of the definitions on the right with the terms on the left. (continued on page 337)

1. _____	explicit (1)	a.	loaded with
2. _____	allude (2)	b.	erotically stimulating
3. _____	intermittently (3)	c.	proof, validation
4. _____	provocative (3)	d.	clearly stated or shown
5. _____	mainstream (4)	e.	liable to be affected by
6. _____	prevalent (9)	f.	shamelessly obvious
7. _____	peruse (9)	g.	make a reference to
8. _____	laden with (10)	h.	excessive increase
9. _____	proliferation (11)	i.	harmful
10. _____	amplifies (11)	j.	look through

11. _____ susceptible (12)   k. major, at the center of

12. _____ titillating (17)   l. increases

13. _____ detrimental (20)   m. dominant, most common

14. _____ substantiation (26)   n. at different, often irregular times

15. _____ blatant (27)   o. exciting, stimulating

True or False

Mark the following T *for True or* F *for False according to the information in the article:*

1. _____ The content of ads aimed at young people was a hot topic in 2000.

2. _____ Sexual behavior in popular ads is often more explicit than that found in movies.

3. _____ Though ads, like movies, carry ratings, the system has not been well enforced.

4. _____ All sexual ads are targeted at young adults, teenagers, and children.

5. _____ The average 14-year old has been exposed to more than 350,000 television commercials.

6. _____ The average viewer watches six commercial television messages a week.

7. _____ Sexy ads market mainstream brands showing social activity and attractiveness.

8. _____ The Calvin Klein ad with Brooke Shields was pulled after it ran for 15 years.

9. _____ Shields' ad for Klein jeans was provocative and memorable but not controversial.

10. _____ In identifying with models, young viewers feel product use makes them attractive.

Comprehension Questions

Circle the correct letter choice and fill in the blanks where indicated.

1. Youngsters are exposed to sexy media through

   a. print ads in magazines.

   b. television commercials.

    c. promotional messages.

    d. all of the above

2. The function of paragraph 7 is to

    a. introduce the main idea of the article.

    b. argue that the Herbal Essence ad should be banned.

    c. give another example of how young people are aware of the sexual message of ads.

    d. all of the above

Questions 3–5 deal with a multiparagraph unit beginning with paragraph 10.

3. Paragraph 10 begins with a question that is answered in a unit composed of paragraphs

    a. 10 and 11.

    b. 10 through 12.

    c. 10 through 13.

    d. 10 through 14.

4. Which is the best statement of the implied main idea of the unit identified above?

    a. The realm of sexuality is new, exciting, stimulating, and attention-grabbing.

    b. The uses of advertising, how young people react and the susceptibility to advertising.

    c. Young people—especially boys—and the uninitiated are very susceptible to advertising.

    d. Two reasons help explain why advertisers use sex in advertising to young adults.

5. What two signal words or phrases are used to introduce the major details of that unit?

    _____   _____

6. In paragraph 13, what evidence shows that sexy ads intentionally target young people?

    _____

    _____

Questions 7–9 below deal with a lengthy unit, beginning with paragraph 14, that analyzes negative effects of sexy ads.

7. Write the main idea of that section:

_____

_____

_____

8. Check any signal that helped to lead you to your choice:

a. _____ It answered a question stated in the unit.

b. _____ It contained a broad listing phrase.

c. _____ It had a change of direction signal.

d. _____ It was followed by a "first item in a list" signal.

e. _____ It has a summary or conclusion signal word.

9. Circle the three signal words or phrases that introduce the three major reasons that are discussed and supported by examples:

for one	also
frequently	one female
for example	another area

10. Paragraphs 18 and 19 are similar in that they both

a. give examples of titillating ads.

b. introduce new major details.

c. report on the experiences of females.

d. all of the above

11. By sexist, the author means that sexually explicit ads do all of the following EXCEPT

a. prove that women are naturally more beautiful than men.

b. foster the stereotype that women's main role is sexual attraction and sexual satisfaction.

c. imply real men have worth when they snare a physically attractive woman.

d. devalue vital aspects of the female persona such as personality and intellect.

12. The author suggests in paragraph 28 that

    a. the movie industry shares responsibility for negative advertising practices.

    b. the thousands of promotional messages seen every day are not really a problem.

    c. the movie industry is on the defensive regarding promoting adult-themed films to young people.

    d. sexual information is a natural consequence of human nature, so we really can't and shouldn't waste time trying to change things.

13. The author mentions (first and last paragraphs) the marketing of adult films to kids to

    a. show what silly issues the candidates in 2000 were concerned about.

    b. convince the reader that targeting kids with sexy ads is an equally serious issue.

    c. argue that advertising of adult-themed films should be banned.

    d. praise the actions of the Justice Department and Jack Valenti.

14. The author's main purpose in the article is to

    a. present a scientific survey of evidence on the effects of sexually explicit advertising on young people.

    b. show that sexy ads aimed at the young have such negatives effects that the issue should be recognized as a social problem in need of a solution.

    c. argue that both adult-themed movies and sexual explicit ads should be banned or censored in order to protect the young.

    d. point out that though movies and ads emphasizing sexuality may have some negative effects on young people, it's all just part of human nature and must be tolerated.

15. The author's tone could best be described as

    a. intense, blunt, and concerned.

    b. mocking, ironic, and amused.

    c. nonchalant, subtle, and resigned.

    d. matter-of-fact, scientific, and nonjudgmental.

Questions and Activities for Discussion and Writing

1. Do you think the issue of sexual exploitation of youth is as serious for ads as movies?

2. A headnote to this selection included this statement: "… treatment of issues in the popular press can range from serious, objective analyses to articles that tend to sensationalize and exploit an issue in order to increase circulation." How would you rate this article on a scale from serious analysis to sensationalizing?

3. Write your own response to the selection. Include any personal reactions to these or other advertisements. Use personal notes to agree/disagree or make additional points.

REFERENCE FRAMEWORKS: THE ACADEMIC CONNECTION 2

In regard to course work that involves time sequence, the most obvious example would probably be history: U.S. history, European history, African history, Latin American history, etc. Textbooks for these and other history courses usually are organized in a time sequence pattern with divisions into periods, eras, and ages. However, many other courses have a strong time element as well. Archeology and anthropology both trace human life and development through time. Sciences like geology and biology are concerned with groups and structures, but also with the historical development of the physical world and the plants and creatures that inhabit it. A very clear example of time sequence in science would be Darwin's theories of evolution and natural selection. In addition, you will find specialized history courses in many fields, such as the histories of art, music, or languages.

Cause/effect analysis is important in every field. Its use is obvious in sciences like physics and chemistry, but social science courses in economics, psychology, geography, sociology, and political science also must use cause and effect in analyzing human relationships and motivations. Literature courses require students to summarize and discuss plot, not just the story. The story tells what happened. Analyzing plot makes us see structure—beginning, development, conclusion—by leading us to questions of not just what happened but why.

Many professions and vocations center on cause and effect. The practice of medicine and medical research involve a constant search to establish causation—why a patient is ill, what will combat the AIDS virus. Law enforcement officers at the scenes of crimes and accidents must piece together chains of events to establish guilt and responsibility. Mechanics of all types constantly deal with what makes engines go—and what stops them. For example, after the Challenger disaster in 1986, scientists spent thousands of hours sifting though data before pinpointing the final cause: O-ring seals that failed. No matter what the field, most employers rate the ability to be a trouble shooter or problem solver at the top of their list of the desired abilities of an employee. The time and trouble spent in learning to analyze cause and effect relationships will pay off not only in college course work, but in later life as well.

■ THE FAULTY CAUSATION FALLACY

In cause and effect, the cause comes first, and the effect follows, but problems occur when we assume that a causal relationship exists simply because one thing comes after another. Take, for example, some of our superstitions. Having a black cat cross your path or walking under a ladder will cause bad luck. Coaches wear lucky ties or socks; athletes insist on wearing the same number or go through elaborate rituals before a game. Faulty causation can also be a source of intentional humor. A friend might comment, "We're not taking Jim to the Packers' games with us any more; every time he goes with us, they lose!" The Latin phrase *post hoc ergo propter hoc*—"after this, therefore caused by this" (*post hoc* in its short form)—is often used to identify faulty causation.

There are many times, of course, where our analysis of cause and effect is wrong simply because we can't determine the facts. If your car occasionally stalls or misses, does it only do it in the morning? Only when you use a certain kind of gasoline? Or does it indicate a need for new spark plugs? If your guesses don't solve the problem, you'll end up having to take the car to a mechanic who has more scientific ways of finding the cause of the problem. In other areas of life, we find faulty causation used deliberately to mislead, or it results from snap judgments or irresponsible research. This is particularly so in politics. The crime rate drops or rises, interests rates go up or down, a recession or recovery occurs—and whoever is in office gets the blame or grabs the credit, even though the true causes may reach back far into the past. Because of these dangers in determining causes, scientists and statisticians tend to talk more of **correlation** than causation. Events can show a high or low correlation depending on the frequency with which they are found to occur together. We might wish to say cigarette smoking results in a number of bad health effects. Researchers in the past have been more cautious, more likely to report that a high correlation exists between cigarette smoking and the incidence of lung cancer and heart disease.

In your college course work, pay particular attention to the support that is given to claims about cause and effect. If an article deals with a factual, scientific topic, is there enough hard data to back up cause/effect claims? In more informal essay writing, look to see if the author is going too far out on a limb by making very broad or unsupported statements. One way writers avoid such problems is by using qualifiers. Words like *probably, possibly, perhaps, appears,* or *seems* allow an author to suggest the possibility of a cause and effect relationship without the risk of faulty causation.

■ "HOW TO": ADVICE

A common type of "how to" article follows a strict time sequence: a series of steps are given in chronological order, and only in that order will the process work. A second type of "how to" follows a cause/effect pattern. Advice is given; if the advice is followed, a goal will be reached—the advised action will *cause* the desired result. In this case there is no set chronological sequence. For instance, here is some advice on how to make your study time more effective:

- Keep lighting at an adequate level.
- Have supplies you need with you: pens, paper, etc.
- Make sure your study place is quiet.
- Play soft, soothing music if it seems to help you.

These could obviously be listed in a different order without confusion, since all might occur at the same time. They are means to a goal. If all are done, they will cause the goal—effective studying—to be reached. Advice articles are probably the most frequent of any type in popular magazines and specialty sections of newspapers. A typical example is an article from *Parade Magazine*.

PREVIEWING *DOES YOUR BODY-TALK DO YOU IN?* BY DIANNE HALES AND DR. ROBERT HALES

Setting Your Reading Goals

The title asks a question. Turning it into a statement is a good way to form a main idea hypothesis:

Your body-talk _____.

How many paragraphs make up the introduction? _____ Write the section heading that indicates where the introduction ends and the body of the article begins.

_____

Preview Vocabulary

discrepancy (5)	difference or disagreement of facts or claims; inconsistency
manipulated (5)	used to advantage
garble (14)	distort or scramble so as to be not understandable
fluid (14)	smooth and effortless
torso (14)	human body exclusive of head, arms, and legs
collegial (14)	relating to colleagues or coworkers
straitjacket (14)	restrain or restrict (as if in a restraining device like a straitjacket)

Annotating As You Read

Subdivided paragraphing is typical of articles written in column format. As you read, pay special attention to short paragraphs and think about how they might be combined into larger paragraph units. Mark possible block combinations in the margin of your text.

Does Your Body-Talk Do You In?

by Dianne Hales and Dr. Robert Hales

1   She extends only her fingers for a limp handshake. His grip could shatter bones. She looks down as she talks. His eyes lock onto the interviewer's unflinchingly.

2   Even though the two applicants are highly qualified, neither lands the job—not because of what they say but because of what they *do*. Her body language says she's timid; his says he's arrogant. "As much as 95 percent of communication is nonverbal," says Marilyn Maple, a professor of education at the University of Florida. "Body language is the oldest, most trusted language in the world."

3   **What body language can tell you.** Most nonverbal communication on the job centers on power. "In our culture, someone in power appears large, strong, with a relaxed posture," says Albert Mehrabian, a psychology professor at UCLA and author of *Silent Messages*. "People lower down look stiff and symmetrical."

4   Leaders signal superiority by sitting while others stand, leaning back in chairs and gesturing expansively. They also talk more, in louder voices, and interrupt others. Subordinates may lean forward and nod in agreement. Others may scratch their legs, twitch watchbands—idiosyncratic ways of saying they're nervous or not interested.

5   Often there's a discrepancy between what someone says—that your job is secure, for instance—and what he or she does—jiggles a foot, perhaps, or avoids looking you in the eye. Which should you believe? What you see, not what you hear. While words can be manipulated, gestures are a lot harder to control. Also be suspicious of a speaker who barely moves. "People generally freeze up when they're lying," says Mehrabian.

6   **"Saying" it right.** "People can't see your credentials—they can only see you," says Lynn Pearl, the president of Executive Communication Inc., a consulting company in Chicago. "That's why awareness of the nonverbal signals you send gives you a leg up."

---

7   One key to positive responses is posture. "Good posture identifies you as someone with something to say," Pearl explains. Stand tall, with flexed knees, and pull your rib cage up out of your waist.

8   Look directly at the people you address, no matter how many. "Eye contact is the most remembered element in forming an impression," says Nancy Austin of Capitola, Calif., a management consultant and co-author of *A Passion for Excellence*. But don't stare—five to seven seconds is maximum for a meeting of the eyes.

9   For women, the greatest nonverbal challenge is demonstrating that they should be taken seriously. "Women in business have to appear more assertive just to be heard," says Donna Chevrier, an image consultant in Toronto. "Unfortunately, the body language they learn while growing up is almost apologetic. I tell women to try this assertiveness exercise in private: standing as if they owned a big mountain, with their legs open a bit, and their hands on their hips."

10   In the workplace, a woman should put her hands on the arm rests of her chair rather than in her lap and not "glue" her arms together. Large gestures from the elbow also are effective in projecting authority. If challenged, she should train herself not to back away but to hold her ground and maintain eye contact.

11   In today's sexually sensitive workplace, women should check their innocent actions—such as "preening" moves, like brushing back hair, or "nervous" moves, like crossing and uncrossing legs—that can be misinterpreted as provocative.

12   And "a lot of good-hearted men are realizing that their old behavior isn't appropriate anymore," says Julian Fast, the author of *Subtexts: Making Body Language Work in the Workplace*. Pats, hugs, and neck rubs are out. Similarly, a man shouldn't shake a woman's hand for more than a few seconds.

13   Any touching, by men or women, should be light, brief and in a neutral zone: the elbow or shoulder. Touching superiors of either sex is always taboo.

14   **Dos and don'ts.** Just as the right body language can make your words more effective, the wrong gestures can garble the message. Here are some nonverbal no-nos and their alternatives:

- *The Fig Leaf.* Speakers who clasp their hands in front of their groins look insecure. To project confidence, keep your arms loosely at your sides and use fluid gestures for emphasis.

- *The Terminator.* An unforgivably brutal handshake can crush any hope of a good impression. Also, avoid The Fish Hand—a lifeless palm dangling from a limp wrist. To put your best hand forward, hold your fingers and thumb vertically, extend them directly, clasp well, then release.

- *The Space Invasion.* Americans feel most comfortable with a 3- to 6-foot "bubble" of space around them. Getting closer puts the other person on the defensive. Show respect for invisible personal boundaries.

- *The Roadblock.* Physical barriers—like folding your arms across your chest—indicate resistance. "Open" positions, with the torso exposed, convey a receptive attitude. Sit down and lean forward to give a kind impression.

- *The Pickpocket.* A man who keeps his hands in his pockets looks like he's hiding something. "After a while," observes Lynn Pearl, "people start to wonder what he's doing in there." To avoid such musings, keep your hands in sight.

- *The Pat on the Back.* It may seem to say "good job," but in fact it's patronizing. Better is a collegial squeeze of the upper arm at shoulder level.

- *The Fidgets.* "Comfort" gestures—rocking, stroking your leg, tugging on your ear—increase with stress. While you should try to control such nonverbal "noise," you don't have to straitjacket yourself. "Just make sure not to do anything in excess," says Pearl.

Exercise 9.3

Comprehension Questions

Circle the correct letter choice and fill in the blanks where indicated.

1. Which of the following is the best statement of the implied main idea of the article?

    a. The importance of body language, particularly on the job, the advice of experts on how to use body language, and several dos and don'ts.

    b. There are seven dos and don'ts for body language.

    c. The ability to use body language and gestures effectively comes naturally to most people.

    d. Following some tips can help you learn to use body language to your advantage.

2. The function of paragraph 1 is to

    a. suggest the topic of body language.

    b. give examples of negative body language.

    c. grab the reader's attention.

    d. all of the above

3. Paragraph 4 could be combined with paragraph 3 into one paragraph because it

    a. provides a contrast to paragraph 3.

    b. gives the solution to a problem stated in paragraph 3.

    c. gives specific examples that further develop the main idea of paragraph 3.

    d. provides the reasons for an opinion stated in paragraph 3.

4. "Often there's a discrepancy between what someone says—that your job is secure, for instance—and what he or she does—jiggles a foot, perhaps, or avoids looking you in the eye." (5) This sentence uses examples to support an idea of

    a. comparison/contrast.

    b. time sequence.

    c. cause/effect.

    d. problem/solution.

5. Which of the following is the best statement of the main idea of paragraph 5?

    a. Never trust what anyone tells you.

    b. Believe what you see, not what you hear.

    c. Don't trust people who barely move.

    d. People who freeze up are lying.

6. The relationship between the two sentences in paragraph 6 is one of cause/effect: "People can't see your credentials—they can only see you" is the _____. "[A]wareness of the nonverbal signals you send gives you a leg up" is the _____.

From the information given in paragraphs 8 and 14, we can infer that the applicants described in paragraph 1 each committed what two body language errors?

7. the "timid" woman _____ (8)

                  _____ (14)

8. the "arrogant" man _____ (8)

                  _____ (14)

9. The subdivided paragraphs 9–13 could be combined into two larger paragraph units. Would paragraph 11 belong with the unit 9–10 or with the unit 12–13? Explain your reasoning. _____

_____

_____

_____

10. The section on The Terminator contains both types of "how to" patterns: process (time sequence) and advice (causation).

The first two sentences are _____.

The last sentence is_____.

Fact and Opinion

Label the statements below with F *for fact and* O *for opinion.*

1. _____ Body language is the oldest, most trusted language in the world.

2. _____ While words can be manipulated, gestures are a lot harder to control.

3. _____ Which should you believe? What you see, not what you hear.

4. _____ But don't stare—five to seven seconds is maximum for a meeting of the eyes.

5. _____ Unfortunately, the body language they learn … is almost apologetic.

6. _____ Similarly, a man shouldn't shake a woman's hand for more than a few seconds.

7. _____ A man who keeps his hands in his pockets looks like he's hiding something.

8. _____ People generally freeze up when they're lying.

9. Based on your answers above, circle which of the following you think the article is.

   a. mostly fact
   b. mostly opinion
   c. a fairly balanced mixture of fact and opinion

Mapping Exercise

Paragraph 14 is much longer than the others, with a number of subpatterns. The main two patterns it uses to present its list are comparison/contrast (the "dos and don'ts") and classification (the various types of "no-nos"). Complete the pattern map.

Divided Main Idea	To avoid wrong gestures that can garble the message, _____ _____ .

Type	Do	Don't
Fig leaf		Clasp hands in front of groin
Terminator	Shake hands by extending, clasping well, releasing	
Pickpocket		

Questions for Writing/Small-Group Discussion

1. a. "Also be suspicious of a speaker who barely moves. 'People generally freeze up when they're lying,' says Mehrabian (5)."

    b. "A man who keeps his hands in his pockets looks like he's hiding something." (14)

    Are these judgments fair? What other explanations could be given that would make these behaviors reasonable and justified?

2. Athletes frequently declare that they "gave 110 percent" in effort. One baseball legend once commented that "50 percent of this game is 90 percent mental." The author here quotes an expert as saying "As much as 95 percent of communication is nonverbal." What does a statement like that mean? How do you arrive at a specific percentage like "95"? Are any of these statistics really factual?

3. In our dealings with others, the article states that "Physical barriers—like folding your arms across your chest—indicate resistance." "Open" positions, with the torso exposed, convey a receptive attitude. Sit down and lean forward to give a kind impression." Suppose, however, you intend to fire someone and are happy to do it, or someone is trying to convince you to do something you're strongly opposed to. Should you "lean forward to give a kind impression"? Is this article giving good practical advice or is it encouraging us to be phony actors? Should we be putting this much emphasis on body language?

Working with Word Parts

Use context and the meanings of the word parts below to answer the following. Do not use the dictionary.

1. "People lower down look stiff and *symmetrical*." (3) *Sym* means "like," *metri* comes from the Greek root *metron,* meaning "measure." What sort of posture is being described here? _____

   _____

   _____

2. "Leaders signal superiority by sitting while others stand, leaning back in chairs and gesturing *expansively*." (4) *Ex* means "out," *pansive* comes from the Latin root *pandere,* meaning "to spread." The leaders described here would be doing what with their hands? _____

   _____

   _____

3. "Others may scratch their legs, twitch watchbands—*idiosyncratic* ways of saying they're nervous or not interested." (4) *Idiosyncratic* is a combination of two word parts meaning "own" and "temperament or mixture." The word therefore describes what about individual behavior? _____

   _____

   _____

4. "… 'preening' moves, like brushing back hair, or 'nervous' moves, like crossing and uncrossing legs … can be misinterpreted as *provocative*." (11) The word part *pro* means "forth"; you were given the meaning of *voc* in Chapter 7. The word is used here to describe what kind of action? _____

   _____

   _____

5. "*The Pat on the Back*. It may seem to say 'good job,' but in fact it's *patronizing*." (14) *Patron* means "father." If you *patronize* someone, you are treating them like what? _____

_____

_____

CHAPTER REVIEW

Match the statements with the letter of the correct pattern listed below:

a. multiple causes/one effect

b. one cause/multiple effects

c. chain of cause/effect

d. cause and effect statement/example

e. divided cause/effect idea

1. _____ Because Bob forgot to set the alarm on his clock, he got to the airport late. As a result, he missed his flight to Phoenix, thus losing out on a chance to interview for a great job.

2. _____ A balanced, low-fat diet, moderate exercise, and reduction of stress will lead to safe and permanent weight loss.

3. _____ Anna prepared very carefully for the final exam. Consequently, she passed the test with flying colors.

4. _____ As a result of losing his job, Paul's wife left him, his car was repossessed, and he lacked the funds to continue his education at night school.

5. _____ Smoking has been linked to many health problems. Many Americans, for instance, die of lung cancer each year.

Applied psychologists claim that simply maintaining a positive attitude can have beneficial effects on coping with stress and reducing its physical symptoms. People who believe they have control over their lives, health, and well-being are more relaxed than those who do not. An upbeat mood, a positive sense of personal control, and even a self-serving bias can facilitate such behaviors as helping others and evaluating people favorably. Some researchers suggest that people who have positive attitudes may even live longer.

(Lefton, *Psychology,* 5th ed., 486)

Based on the paragraph on the previous page, label the following as cause *or* effect.

6. _____ a positive attitude

7. _____ being relaxed

8. _____ sense of personal control

9. _____ living longer

10. Circle the statement that is an example of faulty causation.

    a. The Democrats controlled the presidency when the Vietnam War started.

    b. Perhaps your stress may be due to your recent change of jobs.

    c. Ever since your mother came to stay here, we've had nothing but bad luck.

    d. Many psychiatrists are pushy incompetents who should keep their greedy noses out of other people's business.

READING PORTFOLIO   A Cause/Effect Article

1. *For this assignment you will need to find a magazine or newspaper article organized by cause/effect.* There are two choices in this area.

OPTION A: Cause/Effect

The key here is answering the question **why.** Titles often contain a causation word: *cause, effect, result.* For this assignment look for an article that is concerned only with *explanations,* not *solutions.* (The problem/solution pattern contains cause and effect elements; you will have a chance to do this pattern later.)

OPTION B: "How To": Advice

This is one of the easiest of all articles to find. Look for one that has general interest. Articles such as those giving advice on money, on marriage or dating, about jobs or school, etc., will give you interesting ideas to react to in a thoughtful response section.

2. *Your summary should be 150–175 words.* Try to come up with a pattern map like the samples in this chapter, with boxes and arrows to show cause and effect relationships. Use your own phrasing in your outline or map. That way you can write your summary directly from it.

3. *Your response should be of equal length.* How you respond really depends a lot on which option you are trying. Has reading the article changed your attitude toward the topic, for better or worse? For cause/effect articles, is the author's evidence convincing? Is there perhaps faulty causation (the *post hoc* fallacy) at work? Is there possibly a different cause or projected effect? For a "how to" article, you might evaluate the usefulness of the information. Will the advice achieve its end or is there a better way? Your personal experience is very relevant here.

4. *Select five words from the article that you are unsure of.* Use the dictionary to determine their meanings in the article. Then write a sentence for each, providing helpful context clues.

Grouping and Dividing: Classification and Whole/Part Analysis

CHAPTER

10

By this point you have learned that reading requires a lot more than running your eyes over lines of print or following a simple story line. You have begun to "see things differently" through recognizing the patterns we use to make sense of the world around us, and you have found that doing this is hard work indeed, but also very rewarding. Now you are ready to examine in depth two thinking patterns that underlie many courses in the physical and social sciences.

■ CHAPTER PREVIEW

In this chapter you will

- Distinguish between classification and whole/part analysis
- Read articles that illustrate approaches to classification
- Learn about fallacies and emotional appeals related to classification
- Analyze articles on physical and nonphysical whole/part structures
- Increase your list of word parts with those of space and structure
- Add an article of classification or whole/part structure to your Reading Portfolio

Classification and **whole/part** patterns are sometimes confused because the word *division* is used both for creating subclasses and breaking wholes into parts. You can keep the difference between classification and structure analysis clear by asking the question "What is being divided?"

■ CLASSIFICATION VS. WHOLE/PART ANALYSIS

One aspect of classification involves beginning with a plural—a "bunch of things"—and sorting them into smaller groups. You begin with apples, or students, or coaches, and you create groupings based on a **sorting factor:**

- ■ apples by *color:* red, yellow, green
- ■ students by *class standing:* freshman, sophomore, junior, senior
- ■ coaches by *personality traits:* neurotic coach, bully coach, fatherly

In whole/part analysis, you begin with a singular—one thing—and break it down into parts:

- ■ Our country is divided into *states.*
- ■ States are divided into *counties.*
- ■ Our federal government is divided into *three branches.*
- ■ The human body or an automobile can be divided into its *parts.*

   You will find yourself classified by nationality, race, religion, age, gender, profession, economic standing, marital status, and many other factors throughout your life. Classification helps to show relationships and create definitions in many fields. For example, psychologists will often distinguish between different types of love, an abstract category, though no two psychologists are likely to agree on exactly how many different types of love there are. One question we must ask is, how "real" are classifications like these? For instance, are there "really" three or five or seven kinds of love? Many classifications made by society that determine minimum ages for voting rights, the draft, drinking, or marriage may seem very artificial. Yet even if classifications are more in our heads than in any natural order of things, they are very real in the effects they have in our everyday lives. In Nazi Germany, for example, having one Jewish great-grandparent in your ancestry would be enough to be classified as Jewish—and face the possibility of a sentence to a death camp.

   We don't have very far to look for whole/part structures; our entire world is a whole, and everything in it is a part. These terms are also relative. Each of us is a part of the world, but we are also each a whole in relationship to the parts of our bodies, which are themselves both parts and wholes. A hand is composed of various parts, but the hand itself is part of the arm, itself a part of the upper body, and so forth. Our world is part of something larger, the solar system, which is in turn part of the universe.

Sometimes the distinction between classification and whole/part analysis depends on our purposes. Take, for example, a deck of cards. *Deck* is singular; we can think of it as a whole, with 52 separate cards. But the word *cards* is plural. A deck of cards is also "a bunch of things" that can be divided into classes. We can form four groups based on suit; we can form thirteen groups based on designation (four threes, four jacks); or we can form two groups, number cards and face cards. Similarly, we sometimes speak of society as singular and a person as a *part* of society. Yet we also belong to different social *groups* and *classes*, formed on the basis of sorting factors such as age, race, gender, religion, or profession. The human body can be divided into parts, but once divided, those parts can be seen as forming groups: fingers and toes into *appendages*, for example, or heart, lungs, and liver into the class *internal organs*. Whether we are classifying or breaking a whole into parts can thus depend on our purposes and interests at the time.

REFERENCE FRAMEWORKS: THE ACADEMIC CONNECTION 3

Classification is clearly at work in the division of the college curriculum into major areas—for example, physical and biological sciences, social and behavioral sciences, arts and humanities—and into specialized fields within these areas. Regarding individual courses, it is difficult to think of any that do not involve a good deal of classification, whole/part structure, or both. In biology, for example, the development of life forms is paralleled by their movement into more and more specific classifications—for example, from *phylum, class,* and *order* through *genus* and *species.* Concerns with types and kinds runs through other physical sciences like geology and through the social sciences and humanities as well. Courses in political science explore types of government and class arrangements. Sociology examines various kinds of groupings within family and society. Psychology groups people according to such things as living styles, parenting styles, or coping styles; it divides the population on the basis of personality characteristics; it classifies the kinds of mental illnesses people may suffer from. Literature is divided into genres such as drama, the novel, poetry—and recognizes different types within these groupings. Other categories like *comedy* and *tragedy* cut across the entire field. The study of music or art likewise involves many different classes of musical compositions or styles of painting.

Whole/part patterns are very obvious in mechanics and in the physical sciences. Anatomy and physiology deal with parts that make up life structures. Chemistry analyzes the elements that combine to form the physical universe;

geology focuses on the structure of the earth and on the component parts of specific regions on its surface. Other sciences center on spatial relationships. Astronomy gives us a map of the universe. Geography gives us a map of our physical world, but also deals with divisions based on human activity and political concerns. Changes in the political geography of the earth—in national boundaries, for example—often parallel historical actions. During the course of their histories, many countries (Poland is a good example) have been divided up, have virtually disappeared, and, in some cases, have reemerged. Germany became a national power in the nineteenth century, was separated into East and West following World War II, and after fifty years was at last reunited.

Psychology is concerned with physical parts that control perception (the eye, the ear, the brain) but also with more abstract structures like the components of personality or Freud's division of the mind into the id, ego, and super-ego. Political science breaks down governmental structures into their components; sociology does likewise for social institutions and familial structures. Whole/part structures in the arts and humanities are not so obvious but still very important. Linguistics and the study of foreign languages, courses in composition or in the structure of novels, art, and poetry—all of these clearly require an ability to analyze relationship between parts and wholes.

All such courses can require a good deal of memorization, or they at least assume that you have a basic reference framework for the main classifications or whole/part relationships in the field. Using outlines or mind maps is therefore especially recommended as a means to effective studying. Texts for these courses, especially in the sciences, often utilize many charts, graphs, and other visual aids as supplements, and these help the student to keep the essentials in memory. Where these aids are minimal or not provided, students need to create their own.

ANALYTICAL PATTERNS IN TEXTBOOK MATERIALS

As you have seen, depending on our interests, classification and whole/part analysis can be directed at the same topic. In textbooks, authors frequently intermingle classification and whole/part analysis in their presentation of a a subject, as the selection below illustrates.

PREVIEWING *THE SOLAR SYSTEM* BY JAMES B. KALER

Setting Your Reading Goals

The selection below, from a textbook in astronomy, analyzes relationships in the physical world. Your objective in this kind of textual material is to grasp the general outlines of the topics under construction—their major groups and subgroups (classification) and/or systems and components (whole/part). A preview of the title and first paragraph should give you a clear idea of the general topic and organization of the selection. Also, note the headings of any graphics that accompany the text.

Preview Vocabulary
    elongated (2)   lengthened; stretched out

Annotating As You Read

The selection contains examples of both classification and whole/part analysis, in both text and graphics. Sharpen your ability to distinguish between the two as you read by using the following markings. For analytical processes involving classification, write <u>class</u> for groups or types; write <u>member</u> for the elements that make up a classification. For statements involving whole/part relationships, use <u>whole</u> for the main or overall structure (words like *organization* and *structure* usually refer to a single whole made of component parts). Write <u>part</u> for any components that help to create it.

As this selection illustrates, most texts contain definitions of important terms, either directly or indirectly. Look for and mark definitions of key terms as you read; in some case you may need to put together definitions from what goes before and after the term.

The Solar System

by James B. Kaler

1   Many celestial bodies (*celestial* means "pertaining to the sky") orbit the Sun, the whole collection making up the **Solar System.** Among them is a family of nine traditional planets [Figures 10.1 and 10.2], of which the Earth is the third one out. All the planets orbit in the same direction, in nearly circular paths, and in nearly the same plane. Six of the nine spin in the same direction. All shine by reflected sunlight. Yet each has its own special characteristics and each is a different world to explore.

2   The planets are divided into two main groups. The inner four, all within 1.5 AU of the Sun [one AU equals 93 million miles, the distance from the Sun to Earth], are called the **terrestrial planets** because they are constructed of rock like the Earth, the largest of the four. (*Terrestrial,* from *Terra,* the Roman goddess of Earth, means "Earthlike.") The next four, orbiting between 5 and 30 AU from the Sun, are much larger than Earth, are made partly or mostly of hydrogen and helium, and are commonly called the Jovian planets after

Kaler, *Astronomy: A Brief Edition,* 7–10.

TABLE 1.3

The Planets

Planet	Average Distance from the Sun (AU)	Characteristics
		Terrestrial[a]
Mercury	0.4	Second smallest
Venus	0.7	Brightest; just smaller than Earth
Earth	1.0	Carries life
Mars	1.4	Red color
		Jovian[b]
Jupiter	5.2	Largest; prominent cloud belts; four bright satellites
Saturn	9.5	Surrounded by bright rings
Uranus	19.2	Tipped on it's side; nearly featureless
Neptune	30.1	Blue-green clouds
		Neither Class
Pluto	39.4	Smallest

[a]Like Earth.   [b]Like Jupiter.

Source: Kaler: *Astronomy, A Brief Edition*, p.7

FIGURE 10.1

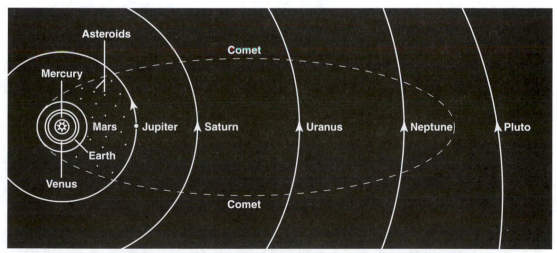

FIGURE 10.2   The Solar System and portions of the orbital paths of the planets around the Sun are drawn to scale. The Sun, on this scale only 0.04 mm in diameter, is at the center of the orbits. Jupiter is 10 times smaller and the Earth 10 times smaller yet. The dot that represents Jupiter encompasses the diameter of its whole satellite system. Most of the asteroids orbit between Mars and Jupiter. The dashed curve shows the path of a comet; most comets have orbits tilted out of the Solar System's plane. (Source: Kaler, *Astronomy: A Brief Edition*, 8).

Jupiter, the biggest of them. Jupiter, however, is still only 0.001 AU across, and on the scale of Figure 10.2 would be invisible to the eye. The last planet is tiny Pluto. Only 2400 km across, and on average 39 AU from the Sun, it fits into neither of the two categories, a modern view removing it from the class of planets altogether. On the scale of a basketball Earth 3km out from the Sun, Pluto would be about 110 km (75 miles) away.

3   The terrestrial planets have few satellites: Mercury and Venus have none, the Earth one, and Mars only two tiny ones. In contrast, the Jovian planets have extensive satellite systems. Jupiter has 16 known satellites, 4 of them easily visible in binoculars. Saturn has at least 18, Uranus 15, and Neptune 8. Pluto has a companion half as big as itself.

4   Minor bodies throng the Solar System. The asteroids are small chunks of rock or metal that orbit the sun in paths that lie largely, but not exclusively, between Mars and Jupiter [see Figure 10.2]. Thousands have been catalogued, and we know that there are countless more. The largest, Ceres, has a diameter only a quarter that of the Moon, and the smallest are mere pebbles. **Comets,** made of dusty ice, are typically a few kilograms in diameter and orbit the Sun on highly elongated paths. As a comet approaches the warmth of the Sun, the ice turns into gas that streams out in one or more *tails* that can be millions of kilometers long. We believe there are trillions of comets in clouds that extend perhaps as far as 100,000 AU from the Sun. Only a tiny fraction ever comes close enough to the Sun for us to see them.

5   Comets steadily disintegrate under the action of sunlight. As the Earth orbits, it continually collides with pieces of cometary debris and stray asteroids that heat up in our atmosphere and streak brilliantly across the sky as **meteors.** The cometary dust all burns up in the air, but asteroids more than about a centimeter or so across can survive to strike the ground to become **meteorites.**

Exercise 10.1

Definitions in the Text

Definitions for the six terms below were provided in the text. Use your notes to match the letter of each definition on the right with the correct term on the left.

_____ 1. celestial	a. small chunks of rock or metal that orbit the sun
_____ 2. solar system	b. asteroids more than a centimeter across that survive to strike the ground.
_____ 3. terrestrial	c. pieces of cometary debris and stray asteroids that heat up and streak across the sky

_____ 4. the asteroids   d. pertaining to the sky

_____ 5. meteors   e. earthlike

_____ 6. meteorites   f. the sun and all the heavenly bodies that
                                       orbit it

Identifying Patterns of Analysis

Use your annotations in the text as a guide to filling in the blanks in the statements below. For an analytical process involving classification, fill in the blank with one of the following:

class   member

classes   members

For statements illustrating whole/part relationships, fill in the blanks with one of the following:

whole   part   parts

Any of the words above may be used more than once.

The Solar System is a _____ whose _____ consist of the sun and the objects that orbit it. The nine planets form a traditional _____. The planets are subdivided into two _____. The terrestrial planets form a _____, which includes four _____. Jupiter is a _____ of the solar system, and is the largest _____ of the _____ known as the Jovian planets. Pluto fits into neither of the two _____ of planets; still, it is a _____ of the solar system. Jupiter's satellite system has 16 _____. A tail is a large _____ of a comet.

Comprehension Questions

Circle the correct letter choice.

1. Which of the following is a characteristic that is NOT shared by all of the nine planets?

    a. They orbit in the same direction.

    b. They orbit in nearly circular paths.

    c. They spin in the same direction.

    d. They shine by reflected sunlight.

2. Use Figure 10.1 and the text in paragraph 2 to decide which of these statements is true:

    a. Jupiter and Earth are the two largest planets in the solar system.

    b. Venus is larger than Neptune but smaller than Pluto.

    c. The smallest Jovian planet is bigger than the largest terrestrial planet.

    d. Except for Neptune, Mercury is the smallest planet.

3. The Jovian planets

    a. are divided into two groups.

    b. are all larger than Earth.

    c. are made partly or mostly of hydrogen and oxygen.

    d. are mostly made of rock.

4. The number of confirmed satellites in the Solar System at present is

    a. 3.

    b. 61.

    c. 64.

    d. 65.

5. Which of the following is the most comprehensive statement of the main idea of paragraph 3?

    a. The terrestrial planets have few satellites, but Mars has two.

    b. Jovian planets have extensive satellite systems.

    c. The terrestrial and Jovian planets differ greatly in the number of their satellites.

    d. Earth has only one satellite, whereas Jupiter has 16 satellites.

6. Minor bodies in the Solar System would include all of the following EXCEPT

    a. asteroids.

    b. comets.

    c. small planets.

    d. meteorites.

7. Which of the following is true of comets?

    a. They are small chunks of rock or metal that orbit the Sun.

   b. The largest recorded comet was named Ceres.

   c. They have been known to have trillions of tails.

   d. Their tails are created by the conversion of ice into gas.

8. Meteorites are created by a process which may include all of the following EXCEPT

   a. asteroids more than a centimeter long entering the atmosphere.

   b. cometary dust entering the earth's atmosphere.

   c. a meteor only partially burning in the earth's atmosphere.

   d. a meteor in the form of rock or metal striking the earth.

9. The main purpose of Figure 10.2 is to show

   a. the parts that make up a whole.

   b. the members that form a class.

   c. both of the above

   d. neither *a* nor *b*

10. We could infer, from the text and the graphics, that it is generally true that

   a. the closer planets are to the Sun, the closer they tend to be to each other.

   b. planets get progressively larger as their distance from the sun increases.

   c. the farther planets are from the sun, the smaller they become.

   d. the smaller the planet, the more likely it is to have satellites.

Short Essay Question

Explain the difference between meteors and meteorites.

◼ CLASSIFICATION: IDENTIFYING A NEW TYPE

One process in classification involves identifying a single group with shared characteristics. This process occurs often in social groups, when we see a segment of society that appears to share important traits. Names are often invented for a new group. For example, in the sixties, the name *hippies* designated the so-called "flower children" of the counterculture. In recent decades, *baby boomers* (the generation born after 1945) and *Generation X* have been identified as special groups. Often acronyms designate new classes: *WASP* for "White, Anglo-Saxon Protestant" or *yuppy* for "young urban professional." Occasionally our interest may be struck by other types of new categories—for example, a new type of matter or energy discovered in physics or astronomy, or a very different music form, like *rapping*.

PREVIEWING *THE THIRD CULTURE* BY KEVIN KELLY
Setting Your Reading Goals

The title suggests that the author intends to identify something not widely recognized before—a "third culture." That indicates that there are also two other cultures that the reader needs to be aware of. Your first objective, therefore, is to identify these three "cultures" as soon as possible. Preview by reading the first and last paragraphs. Which paragraph, first or last, gives the clearest indication of the cultures the author will discuss? _____

List the the three cultures that the article will deal with: _____

_____   _____

Preview Vocabulary

anointed (2)	appointed, chosen, as though in ceremony of holy dedication
laureate (2)	a person who is given honor or distinction
mediated (3)	saturated with media
supernova (6)	a star that increases tremendously in brightness; something growing rapidly
trump (9)	to surpass, outdo
lay (10)	ordinary, not a part of the clergy or of a particular profession
mandarin class (11)	a special or elite class, as in China
procreate (13)	reproduce
mutate (13)	to change in form or quality
evolve (13)	to grow into a higher or more complex form
paleontologist (14)	one who studies prehistoric man
posit (17)	put forward as an hypothesis
vernacular (19)	ordinary or common language

Annotating As You Read

The author's purpose is to identify a new class and add it to two already existing classes. Classification is often closely aligned to comparison and contrast. That is, the various classes show some similarity in their characteristics (they are all cultures) but they show enough differences to put them into different subcategories as well. As you read, annotate your text to note similarities and differences (there will obviously be more of the latter). Highlight or underline the special characteristics of each culture and write "art," "science," and "nerd" or "technology" to indicate to which classification each belongs.

The Third Culture

by Kevin Kelly

1   "Science" is a lofty term. The word suggests a process of uncommon rationality, inspired observation, and near-saintly tolerance for failure. More often than not, that's what we get from science. The term "science" also entails people aiming high. Science has traditionally accepted the smartest students, the most committed and self-sacrificing researchers, and the cleanest money—that is, money with the fewest political strings attached. In both theory and practice, science in this century has been perceived as a noble endeavor.

2   Yet science has always been a bit outside society's inner circle. The cultural center of Western civilization has pivoted around the arts, with science orbiting at a safe distance. When we say "culture," we think of books, music, or painting. Since 1937 the United States has anointed a national poet laureate but never a scientist laureate. Popular opinion has held that our era will be remembered for great art, such as jazz. Therefore, musicians are esteemed. Novelists are hip. Film directors are cool. Scientists, on the other hand, are nerds.

3   How ironic, then, that while science sat in the cultural backseat, its steady output of wonderful products—radio, TV, and computer chips—furiously bred a pop culture based on the arts. The more science succeeded in creating an intensely mediated environment, the more it receded culturally.

4   The only reason to drag up this old rivalry between the two cultures is that recently something surprising happened: A third culture emerged. It's hard to pinpoint exactly when it happened, but it's clear that computers had a lot to do with it. What's not clear yet is what this new culture means to the original two.

5   This new third culture is an offspring of science. It's a pop culture based in technology, for technology. Call it nerd culture. For the last two decades, as technology supersaturated our cultural environment, the gravity of technology simply became too hard to ignore. For this current generation of Nintendo kids, their technology is their culture. When they reached the point (as every generation of youth does) of creating the current fads, the next funny thing happened: Nerds became cool.

6   Nerds now grace the cover of *Time* and *Newsweek*. They are heroes in movies and Man of the Year. Indeed, more people wanna be Bill Gates than wanna be Bill Clinton. Publishers have discovered that cool nerds and cool science can sell magazines to a jaded and weary audience. Sometimes it seems as if technology itself is the star, as it is in many special-effects movies. There's jargon, too. Cultural centers radiate new language; technology is a supernova

K. Kelly, "The Third Culture", (*Science,* vol. 279, 1998), 992–993. Reprinted with permission by the American Association for the Advancement of Science.

of slang and idioms swelling the English language. Nerds have contributed so many new words—most originating in science—that dictionaries can't track them fast enough.

7   This cultural realignment is more than the wisp of fashion, and it is more than a mere celebration of engineering. How is it different? The purpose of science is to pursue the truth of the universe. Likewise, the aim of the arts is to express the human condition. (Yes, there's plenty of overlap.) Nerd culture strays from both of these. While nerd culture deeply honors the rigor of the scientific method, its thrust is not pursuing truth, but pursuing novelty. "New," "improved," "different" are key attributes for this technological culture. At the same time, while nerd culture acknowledges the starting point of the human condition, its hope is not expression, but experience. For the new culture, a trip into virtual reality is far more significant than remembering Proust.

8   Outlined in the same broad strokes, we can say that the purpose of nerdism, then, is to create novelties as a means to truth and experience. In the third culture, the way to settle the question of how the mind works is to build a working mind. Scientists would measure and test a mind; artists would contemplate and abstract it. Nerds would manufacture one. Creation, rather than creativity, is the preferred mode of action. One would expect to see frenzied, messianic attempts to make stuff, to have creation race ahead of understanding, and this we see already. In the emerging nerd culture a question is framed so that the answer will usually be a new technology.

9   The third culture creates new tools faster than new theories, because tools lead to novel discoveries quicker than theories do. The third culture has little respect for scientific credentials because while credentials may imply greater understanding, they don't imply greater innovation. The third culture will favor the irrational if it brings options and possibilities, because new experiences trump rational proof.

10   If this sounds like the worst of pop science, in many ways it is. But it is also worth noting how deeply traditional science swirls through this breed. A lot of first-class peer-reviewed science supports nerdism. The term "third culture" was first coined by science historian C. P. Snow. Snow originated the concept of dueling cultures in his famous book, *The Two Cultures*. But in an overlooked second edition to the book published in 1964, he introduced the notion of a "third culture." Snow imagined a culture where literary intellectuals conversed directly with scientists. This never really happened. John Brockman, a literary agent to many bright scientists, resurrected and amended Snow's term. Brockman's third culture meant a streetwise science culture, one where working scientists communicated directly with lay people, and the lay challenged them back. This was a peerage culture, a peerage that network technology encouraged.

11   But the most striking aspect of this new culture was its immediacy. "Unlike previous intellectual pursuits," Brockman writes, "the achievements

of the third culture are not the marginal disputes of a quarrelsome mandarin class. They will affect the lives of everybody on the planet." Technology is simply more relevant than footnotes.

12   There are other reasons why technology has seized control of the culture. First, the complexity of off-the-shelf discount computers has reached a point where we can ask interesting questions such as: What is reality? What is life? What is consciousness? and get answers we've never heard before. These questions, of course, are the same ones that natural philosophers and scientists of the first two cultures have been asking for centuries. Nerds get new answers to these ancient and compelling questions not by rehashing Plato or by carefully setting up controlled experiments but by trying to create an artificial reality, an artificial life, an artificial consciousness—and then plunging themselves into it.

13   Despite the cartoon rendition I've just sketched, the nerd way is a third way of doing science. Classical science is a conversation between theory and experiment. A scientist can stand at either end—with theory or experiment—but progress usually demands the union of both a theory to make sense of the experiments and data to verify the theory. Technological novelties such as computer models are neither here nor there. A really good dynamic computer model—of the global atmosphere, for example—is like a theory that throws off data, or data with a built-in theory. It's easy to see why such technological worlds are regarded with such wariness by science—they seem corrupted coming and going. But in fact, these models yield a third kind of truth, an experiential synthesis—a parallel existence, so to speak. A few years ago when Tom Ray, a biologist turned nerd, created a digital habitat in a small computer and then loosed simple digital organisms in it to procreate, mutate, and evolve, he was no longer merely modeling evolution or collecting data. Instead, Ray had created a wholly new and novel example of real evolution. That's nerd science. As models and networked simulations take on further complexity and presence, their role in science will likewise expand and the influence of their nerd creators increase.

14   Not the least because technological novelty is readily accessible to everyone. Any motivated 19-year-old can buy a PC that is fast enough to create something we have not seen before. The nerds who lovingly rendered the virtual dinosaurs in the movie *Jurassic Park,* by creating a complete muscle-clad skeleton moving beneath virtual skin, discovered a few things about dinosaur locomotion and visualized dinosaurs in motion in a way no paleontologist had done before. It is this easy, noncertified expertise and the unbelievably cheap access to increasingly powerful technology that is also driving nerd science.

15   Thomas Edison, the founder of *Science* magazine, was a nerd if ever there was one. Edison—lacking any formal degree, hankering to make his own tools, and possessing a "just do it" attitude—fits the profile of a nerd. Edison held brave, if not cranky, theories, yet nothing was as valuable to him as a working "demo" of an invention. He commonly stayed up all night to hack

together contraptions, powered by grand entrepreneurial visions (another hallmark of nerds), yet he didn't shirk from doing systematic scientific research. One feels certain that Edison would have been at home with computers and the Web and all the other techno-paraphernalia now crowding the labs of science.

16   Techno-culture is not just an American phenomenon, either. The third culture is as international as science. As large numbers of the world's population move into the global middle class, they share the ingredients needed for the third culture: science in schools; access to cheap, hi-tech goods; media saturation; and most important, familiarity with other nerds and nerd culture. I've met Polish nerds, Indian nerds, Norwegian nerds, and Brazilian nerds. Not one of them would have thought of themselves as "scientists." Yet each of them was actively engaged in the systematic discovery of our universe.

17   As nerds flourish, science may still not get the respect it deserves. But clearly, classical science will have to thrive in order for the third culture to thrive, since technology is so derivative of the scientific process. The question I would like to posit is: If the culture of technology should dominate our era, how do we pay attention to science? For although science may feed technology, technology is steadily changing how we do science, how we think of science, and what it means to be a scientist. Tools have always done this, but in the last few decades our tools have taken over. The status of the technologist is ascending because for now, and for the foreseeable future, we have more to learn from making new tools than we do from making new concepts or new measurements. As the eminent physicist Freeman Dyson points out, "The effect of concept-driven revolution is to explain old things in new ways. The effect of tool-driven revolution is to discover new things that have to be explained." We are solidly in the tool-making era of endlessly creating new things to explain.

18   While science and art generate truth and beauty, technology generates opportunities: new things to explain; new ways of expression; new media of communications; and, if we are honest, new forms of destruction. Indeed, raw opportunity may be the only thing of lasting value that technology provides us. It's not going to solve our social ills, or bring meaning to our lives. For those, we need the other two cultures. What it does bring us—and this is sufficient—are possibilities.

19   Technology now has its own culture, the third culture, the possibility culture, the culture of nerds—a culture that is starting to go global and mainstream simultaneously. The culture of science, so long in the shadow of the culture of art, now has another orientation to contend with, one grown from its own rib. It remains to be seen how the lofty, noble endeavor of science deals with the rogue vernacular of technology, but for the moment, the nerds of the third culture are rising.

Exercise 10.2

Vocabulary

Matching: Use the context to match the words on the left with the meanings on the right.

1. _____	endeavor (1)	a. brought back to life
2. _____	receded (2)	b. natural environment
3. _____	supersaturated (5)	c. something slight or flimsy
4. _____	jaded (6)	d. an earnest attempt or effort
5. _____	jargon (6)	e. acting in defiance of established custom
6. _____	wisp (7)	f. the creation of new methods or products
7. _____	messianic (8)	g. so full nothing more can be taken in
8. _____	innovation (9)	h. collection of technical equipment and products
9. _____	resurrected (10)	i. moved back, lost power
10. _____	amended (10)	j. convinced of carrying out a divine mission
11. _____	rendition (13)	k. desire for
12. _____	habitat (13)	l. dulled in appetite from overindulgence
13. _____	hankering (15)	m. changed or corrected
14. _____	techno-paraphernalia (15)	n. a specialized language
15. _____	rogue (19)	o. a particular version or performance

Words with multiple meanings: The two words below can have several, very different, meanings. Study the sentences below carefully before circling the letter with the meaning that best fits the context.

1. "For the last two decades, as technology supersaturated our cultural environment, the **gravity** of technology simply became too hard to ignore. For this current generation of Nintendo kids, their technology is their culture." (5) In this context, **gravity** means

   a. seriousness.

   b. danger or threat.

   c. physical force that draws bodies to the earth.

   d. attraction or pull.

2. "Unlike previous intellectual pursuits," Brockman writes, "the achievements of the third culture are not the **marginal** disputes of a quarrelsome mandarin class: They will affect the lives of everybody on the planet." (11) In this context, **marginal** means

    a. not in the mainstream.

    b. close to a lower limit.

    c. written or printed in the margins of a paper.

    d. on the border between profitable and unprofitable.

Mapping

Use the annotations in the text to decide which culture each of the statements below describes. In the blank write:

    AC for the culture of art

    NC for nerd culture

    SC for the culture of science

Purpose:

1. _____ generate beauty

2. _____ pursue the truth of universe

3. _____ express the human condition

4. _____ create new opportunities

5. _____ explain old things in new ways

6. _____ discover/explain new things

To find how the mind works:

7. _____ measure/test one

8. _____ contemplate one

9. _____ manufacture one

To answer old questions:

10. _____ study philosophers of the past

11. _____ set up controlled experiments

12. _____ create/plunge into artificial reality

Other characteristics:

13. _____   rational, high-minded endeavor

14. _____   derives from/dependent on another culture

15. _____   in popular opinion, most memorable for our era

16. _____   products bred pop culture based on the arts

17. _____   most likely to have a laureate

18. _____   concerned with "new," "improved," "different"

19. _____   prefers new theories to new tools

20. _____   most associated with "culture"

21. _____   going global/mainstream at the same time

Use your answers to fill in the classification grid below.

	Art Culture	Science Culture	Nerd Culture
Purpose			
How Mind Works?			
Answer Questions			
Other			

Comprehension Questions

Circle the correct letter choice and fill in the blanks where indicated.

1. Which of the following is the best statement of the main idea of this article?

    a. The emergence of a new culture, the goals of art culture and the culture of science, recent technological innovations, and the current threat to science.

    b. The cultural center of Western civilization has revolved around the arts, with science, though productive, remaining on the outskirts.

    c. The technology of nerd culture, in its creation of new possibilities, opportunities, and tools, is challenging the traditional cultures of science and art.

    d. The culture of technology is not just an American phenomenon but as international as science, with "nerds" networking around the world.

2. The purpose of paragraphs 1–4 is to

    a. give a brief history of the background of the issue of cultures.

    b. note the preference in popular opinion for art culture over the culture of science.

    c. introduce the topic.

    d. all of the above

3. The main purpose of paragraph 6 is to

    a. compare the accomplishment of Bill Gates and Bill Clinton.

    b. give examples of the changing image and importance of nerds.

    c. give a brief survey of new special effects in movies.

    d. survey the harmful effects of technology on language.

4. "Science has traditionally accepted the smartest students, the most committed and self-sacrificing researchers, and the cleanest money—that is, money with the fewest political strings attached." (1) Which technique of development is illustrated by this passage?

    a. simple restatement.

    b. positive/negative restatement.

    c. clarification.

    d. order of importance.

5. "How ironic, then, that while science sat in the cultural backseat, its steady output of wonderful products—radio, TV, and computer chips—furiously bred a pop culture based on the arts. The more science succeeded in creating an intensely mediated environment, the more it receded culturally." (3) Which of the following best states the irony that the author refers to?

    a. Science is responsible for creating a culture that is pushing science into the background.

    b. Radio, television, and computer chips are important components of the arts.

    c. Science deals objectively with facts, but yet is very creative.

    d. Science was in the back seat because it achieved more during this period than the arts.

6. Tom Ray's experiment illustrates a new way of doing science in that it

    a. put live animals into a computer for the first time.

    b. provided a means for collecting new data.

    c. created a conversation between theory and experiment.

    d. created a new, complex example of real evolution.

7. The author maintains that an essential component of the third culture is the

    a. existence of science in schools.

    b. availability of cheap, hi-tech goods.

    c. establishment of a network of nerds.

    d. all of the above

8. We can conclude from the information in the article that the term "third culture"

    a. was first used by the author of this article.

    b. was introduced by C. P. Snow in the second edition of *The Two Cultures*.

    c. was actually created by John Brockman.

    d. none of the above

9. The author feels that traditional science is now threatened because

    a. it is dependent upon the third culture.

    b. we currently can learn more from new tools than from new concepts.

    c. science feeds technology.

    d. all of the above

10. Technology's greatest contribution, according to the author, may be

    a. the generating of beauty and truth.

    b. creating new means of mass destruction.

    c. creating raw opportunities and new possibilities.

    d. helping to create a bright generation of Nintendo kids.

11. We can infer from the reading that art culture

    a. will soon disappear as a force in our society.

b. is morally superior to nerd culture and the culture of science.

c. only appeals to snobbish intellectuals and artsy types.

d. is the culture most independent of any other culture.

12. According to the author, the essential attribute that marks one as a scientist is

a. having the proper credentials from a major university.

b. being actively engaged in the systematic discovery of our universe.

c. creating opportunities and possibilities.

d. staying up all night to put weird contraptions together.

13. The author adds status to nerd culture by characterizing all of the following as nerds EXCEPT

a. Bill Gates.

b. Bill Clinton.

c. Thomas Edison.

d. John Ray.

14. The author's intended audience for this article would most likely be

a. only scientists with high credentials and degrees.

b. "nerds" and other people highly supportive of technology.

c. both scientists and the educated public.

d. readers of scandal sheets like *The National Inquirer* and *The Star*.

15. Write the one word of opinion/judgment that occurs in the following mainly factual statement:

> As the eminent physicist Freeman Dyson points out, "The effect of concept-driven revolution is to explain old things in new ways. The effect of tool-driven revolution is to discover new things that have to be explained." _____

Questions for Group Discussion

1. "In the last few decades our tools have taken over." (17) In what way, over the past ten years, have new "tools" like the computer affected the way education is delivered, in the traditional classroom and through distance education? Give examples from your own experience and observation that would help to illustrate your viewpoint.

2. "For this current generation of Nintendo kids, their technology is their culture." (5) Explain what this statement means. Do you agree or disagree? Give some examples to back up your viewpoint.

◼ FALLACIES RELATED TO CLASSIFICATION

Logic—the structure, method, and validity of reasoning—is a very complex subject that requires formal study to master. Understanding some basic concepts can help you avoid some errors in thinking. Two kinds of reasoning are generally identified.

Inductive Reasoning.   Most main ideas in reading result from this process wherein we infer general statements from particular facts and events. For example, one experience with a stove or furnace would probably be enough to lead a child to this inference: "Things called stoves are hot."

Deductive Reasoning.   Starting with a generalization like the one above, deductive reasoning draws a particular conclusion. The result is a three-part argument, called a *syllogism,* which gives a formula for checking how valid our reasoning is. It consists of two statements (the major and minor *premises*), followed by a conclusion. Extending our example above would lead to this simple deduction:

> All stoves are hot.
> This object is a stove.
> Therefore, this object is hot.

HASTY GENERALIZATION

A hasty generalization can be a product of inductive reasoning. For example, is it really true that "All stoves are hot"? With further experience a child learns that stoves are not hot all of the time. To be accurate, the statement would have to be changed to something like "Stoves may become hot when they have been turned on."

FAULTY DEDUCTION

Faulty deduction occurs when the premises do not lead to a valid conclusion. Deductive reasoning is often explained through classification; using circles for terms that represent classes is helpful in spotting errors in thinking. For example, the argument above could be represented in this way:

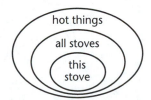

We would call this argument valid because it reflects what the circles show: if all stoves belong to the larger class of "hot things," and this particular object *is* a stove, then it too has to have the properties of the larger class: hotness. But compare the argument above to this:

All stoves are hot.

This object is hot.

Therefore, this object is a stove.

This argument is not valid: the first premise does not state that everything that is hot is a stove. The object may be a stove, but it could also be anything that is hot. The fact that "this object" is not necessarily in the class "stoves" is clearly shown by classification:

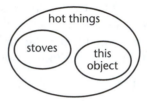

This fallacy becomes obvious when the conclusion is ridiculous. Here is a classic example:

All men are mortal.

My dog is mortal.

Therefore, my dog is a man.

GUILT BY ASSOCIATION

Faulty deduction may be obvious in examples like the above, but it can easily creep into many arguments or everyday observations. When it does, it can some-times result in what is called guilt by association. Take, for example, a statement like the following: "Robert supports gun control; wimpy liberals like him make me sick." Part of the syllogism is only implied; in its complete form, we can see the argument is invalid:

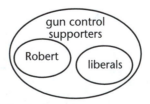

It assumes that because an object (Robert) shares one trait with others (support-ers of gun control), it must belong in the same class (liberals). As a result, Robert is associated with a group that he may have no connection with at all.

Two other fallacies result from our desire to be a part of or identify with special groups.

BANDWAGON TECHNIQUES

They urge us to join with the "in" group or the majority. "Join the Pepsi Generation" was a classic advertisement that used this technique.

PLAIN FOLKS

As its name suggests, this fallacy plays on our belief in the wisdom of the common man and our suspicion of elitists or "eggheads." This technique is a favorite of advertisers and politicians. For instance, during election time, candidates try to portray themselves as political outsiders, just ordinary folks, as opposed to "professional politicians" or "Washington insiders."

CROSS-CLASSIFICATION

Another problem in logic happens when we use sorting factors that overlap. For example, we cannot sort apples into four groups of "red apples, green apples, large apples, small apples." The first two deal with color; the last two, size. A large green apple would therefore cross over into two categories at the same time. If we wished to use two sorting factors here, we would have to include both in each category: large red apples, small red apples, large green apples, small green apples.

Exercise 10.3

If a statement below shows sound reasoning, write valid. *If it confuses categories, write* cross-classification. *If a statement contains fallacies, identify it as one of the following:* bandwagon, plain folks, guilt by association.

_____ 1. When Roger rolled up his shirt sleeve, a tattoo on his right arm was revealed. I would never have suspected that he was a gang member.

_____ 2. Carlos wants to become a Highway Patrol field officer. That's a little odd, considering he's always expressed a real dislike for uniforms.

_____ 3. Vote for Senator Billings. He supports raising the minimum wage.

_____ 4. Vote for Senator Billings. He'll stand up for the little guy.

_____   5. In a census in the late 1800s, the categories included "white" and "Irish."

_____   6. In the 1790 census, the four categories were white woman, white man, free black, slave.

_____   7. "You've come a long way, baby!" (Virginia Slims cigarettes)

_____   8. Professor Jameson says he's an atheist. I'm surprised that they would let a Communist teach here.

_____   9. "We make money the old-fashioned way. We earn it." (investment firm)

_____   10. Vote for the Republican revolution—a movement whose time has come!

■ WHOLE/PART: NONPHYSICAL STRUCTURE

The mind, the extended family, religious or governmental institutions—although we can't touch these or put them under a microscope, we still think of such things as whole systems involving a relationship between parts. Each of us, for example, plays many different parts in the course of our lives. At any one point of time, we are each a significant part of our family structure or of the social unit in which we function. The reading below from *What Will My Mother Say*—an autobiography with the subtitle "A Tribal African Girl Comes of Age in America"—deals with social relationships from the perspective of a different culture. The author, Dympna Ugwu-Oju, balances her role as an English professor at an American community college with that of a wife and mother within the Nigerian Ibo culture.

PREVIEWING *MARRIAGE AS A GROUP EFFORT* BY DYMPNA UGWU-OJU

Setting Your Reading Goals

The article's first clause ("Marriage among Ibos is a community venture") turns the chapter title into a sentence. Use it as a main idea hypothesis and focus on the way in which "community venture" is illustrated in the text.

Preview Vocabulary

novenas (3)	prayers for special purposes, repeated nine days (Roman Catholic Church)
privy (5)	given access to
condiments (6)	seasonings, spices
sanction (11)	approve
impulsiveness (13)	action without thinking
titular (16)	having the title of
consummate (17)	to bring to completion
entailed (25)	involved
temper (26)	tone down, soften

Annotating as you Read

Background knowledge of history, geography, and culture helps us greatly to understand readings that deal with a particular country. Nigeria is located on the coast of West Central Africa. At the time described in this selection, the country was recovering from a devastating civil war. This short passage from an earlier section of *What Will My Mother Say?* will give you a reference frame-work for the make-up of the country.

> The Nigerian-Biafran war was long in the making. It resulted from tribal politics and inexcusably bad government. When Nigeria got its independence from Britain in October 1960, the country was divided into four regions, representing the dominant tribes and language groups: North, Hausas and Fulanis; East, Ibos; West, Yorubas; Midwest, a number of small minority groups....
>
> The eastern Ibos were the most embracing of Western culture and were comprised of the largest number of Christians. With their formal education, they occupied key positions in the civil service and wielded a lot of bureaucratic power. Ibos are the most outgoing of Nigeria's peoples and even early in Nigeria's history, they refused to allow regional boundaries to dictate the scope of their lives. By the beginning of the civil strife, as many Ibos lived outside the boundaries of Eastern Nigeria as lived within them. While the Hausas/Fulanis had the numbers and Yorubas had their money, Ibos had nothing more than ingenuity and hard work. Consequently, they were in the forefront of the fight for Nigeria's independence and, had it not been for tribal politics, would have taken over power from the British....(174–175)

The action in the selection below hinges upon relationships in the social structure of the Ibo culture. As you read, pay special attention to the power structure of the community and especially to the roles the bride-to-be plays before and after her marriage. Mark these in the text and make clarifying notes in the margins where needed.

Marriage as a Group Effort

by Dympna Ugwu-Oju

1   Marriage among Ibos is a community venture, so a married woman is referred to by her husband's entire clan as *Nwunye Anyi* (Our Wife). The woman is married to the entire community of men, women, and children. She treats them all as she would her husband, and any one of them has a right to rebuke her, punish her, even influence her relationship with her actual husband. A married woman wields more power in her father's village than she does in her husband's. In the village of her birth, she's *nwada* (daughter of the land), and she joins the group of *umuada* (daughters of the land). As a group, the *umuada* of any Ibo village is a power to be reckoned with, often more powerful than most male groups. They are primarily entrusted with maintaining social order and ensuring that men and women, husbands and wives, stay within their prescribed roles. *Umuada* could find that their "brother" was mistreating his wife and send a warning to him to cease and desist or incur their wrath. They could equally send a wife (who's also a *nwada* but only in her father's village) packing if they felt she was mistreating her husband. But the same *nwada* who leads the females in her father's village would crawl on her hands and knees before the *umuada* of her husband's village. A woman's daughter, by implication, can throw her own mother out of her father's home. The daughter is a *nwada* in her father's home, but the mother is merely a wife.

2   So marriage extends beyond the immediate and extended family.... Mama was determined to make the best of my situation, and not just for my benefit but for everything our family could gain from it. Marriages were often made for political reasons, for uniting two powerful families. In spite of my father's early death and the hardships my family endured afterwards, there was not a better family in everyone's opinion than ours. The number of suitors and marriage proposals I received is evidence of that....

3   The Ugwu-Ojus had pressures that originated from me, as well as Mama, concerning their first son's marriage. They settled on me soon after I was

Dympna Ugwu-Oju, "Marriage as a Group Effort," from *What Will My Mother Say?* (Dympna Ugwu-Oju Bonus Books, Inc., 160 East Illinois Street, Chicago, 1995), 230–237.

born, and they never wavered. They were pleased with my physical and academic development; nothing out of the ordinary happened along the way. There were a few nervous moments involving how tall I would grow. My two sisters grew to be five-nine, "too tall for boys." Members of Charles' family, on the other hand, are on the short side; he's five-seven. I remained smallish, shorter than normal, through adolescence, but then I had a growth spurt, and everyone held their breath, hoping I wouldn't grow as tall as my sisters. That would have been disastrous, for I would have towered over him. I wasn't aware of it then, but they held novenas and offered gifts to the poor; God must have heard their prayers for I stopped growing short of five-six.

4   Finally, my future parents-in-law believed that if Charles made a good marriage, so would his three brothers. The first son's is the most crucial, because it is to him that the responsibilities of the household fall after his father is gone. It is he who guarantees that the family succeeds. My mother-in-law confided in me that they couldn't trust their future to anyone other than someone they had known all her life, someone like me. "You will hold our family together, like your mother did your father's family."

5   The first official pronouncement of my future in-laws' intentions was made in December 1973 when I was 17 and had just graduated from high school. My oldest brother John was visiting home from New York, where he was doing his surgical residency at Roosevelt Hospital. I was not privy to the exchange until years after it happened.

6   On the Sunday before John's planned departure, the Ugwu-Ojus paid him a visit befitting of a dignitary. If I had been more aware, I would have suspected that it was more than a visit, for they came laden with gifts traditionally recognized as those made to one's in-laws. All eight of their children at that time (my future mother-in-law was pregnant with her ninth), dressed in finery, graced the occasion. A live goat, three large hens, a fifty-kilogram bag of rice, twelve tubers of yam, more smoked fish and dried meat than I had ever seen, plus other condiments were laid out on the floor of the verandah and presented to John as gifts.

7   Later, according to John, my future parents-in-law, Mama, and John engaged in a somewhat secretive discussion about Charles and me. Felix Ugwu-Oju, an acclaimed orator, presented his case so convincingly that even John was wowed by it. "We're here to ask you, since you're Dympna's father by our tradition, to permit us to continue to hope that if it is the Lord's will, that Charles and Dympna will be married in the future."

8   John says that in his American way of looking at things then, he was not aware that a request had been made of him, or that he was expected to provide an answer. He continued to listen for more, but nothing more was said. An uncomfortable silence ensued until Mama nudged him. John spoke, saying that he had known the Ugwu-Ojus well and that Mr. Ugwu-Oju had been

very generous with him, but he felt thrown back in time and forced to address an issue that wasn't his in the first place.

9   "Thanks for your interest in my sister, but the little I've seen of Dympna suggests that she still has far to go in her education. Let's postpone this discussion until a time when she's ready to think about marriage, and even then, it should be her decision, not mine."

10   "We're not asking that anything be finalized right away, for our son is only in his first year of a pre-med program. We only seek an understanding between us, so we can all have peace of mind, knowing that their union is guaranteed," Charles' father said. But John, in his new American liberalism and convictions, refused to yield.

11   "Nothing can be guaranteed without the approval of the two involved. I cannot in good conscience commit my sister to a relationship that she may not sanction. Everything just has to wait until she's ready."

12   Which is when Mama intervened. Her first son, her "husband," was taking the discussion in a direction that she did not wish it to go. It was she, after all, who encouraged the Ugwu-Ojus to make the presentation while John was there; it was Mama who thought that with John's seal of approval, I would go along. John's answer took her completely by surprise and she sought a quick way to contain the damage that was being done.

13   "John has been gone a long time and is quite rusty in our ways; please forgive his impulsiveness."

14   The Ugwu-Ojus chuckled, which eased some of the tension.

15   "John," Mama turned her full attention to her first living son, her eyes begging, pleading for his support, as she'd done when he was a child. "There's nothing wrong with what Charles' parents are asking. They're not asking that your sister be handed over to them today. They desire as much as we do that she be well educated, for that would benefit them as much as us. The ultimate decision, of course, would be Dympna's and Charles'."

16   Put that way, John found little objection to it, and nodded his head in agreement. A bottle of schnapps, which sat on a small table in the center of the room, was opened and poured into four glasses that appeared instantly. Unknown to Charles and me, his parents, my mother, and my titular father drank to our life together. On that Sunday afternoon in December 1973 our fate was sealed. They convinced John that it would be better if neither Charles nor I was made aware of the discussion. My official father-in-law-to-be insisted, "It could distract them from their studies, which should be foremost in their lives now."

17   John now says that the exchange that afternoon made up his mind about me. It reminded him of the inequitable traditions in our culture. If he desired a better life for me, it would not be attained if I were left to pursue my higher education in Nigeria. He felt that I would be married off in the church before

I completed my education "just to secure the relationship," and that I would be compelled to begin to have children "just to consummate the deal." He decided then and there that he would not leave me in Nigeria. When he returned to America, he would prepare to bring me over. But he dared not bring that issue up with Mama for fear that she'd discourage him.

18   I stayed in the dark about my impending marriage, while John enlightened Mama about his plans for my education. He wasted no time in processing my papers after he went back to New York. Mama was reluctant to let me go. She used one argument after another. "She's too young and naive about a lot of things," she responded to John's initial letter on the subject of my education abroad. John reminded her that at my age, she herself was married and had four children. Then she raised the issue of my future. "She'll be too old when she returns."

19   "Too old for what?" inquired John, who continued with his plans.

20   I knew that Mama was uncomfortable with the path my brother wanted my life to take, and her discomfort, for a reason I didn't know then, pleased me immensely. When she seemed to stall the processing of the papers from her side, I wrote my brother for his intervention, and he came to my rescue. When it was evident to Mama that I would go to America with or without her support, she began to reveal the real reasons for her hesitation. It was during one of these conversations, one that I remember distinctly, that she told me about my impending marriage for the first time, though she did not reveal the identity of my intended....

21   "Who is it?" I asked her then, my eyes locking with hers in a rare challenge of wills.

22   "The particular man in question isn't as important as what agreeing to his proposal would represent," she said, trying to evade the subject.

23   "Mama, how can I agree to a proposal without knowing who the man is?" I knew that I was out of line, but something kept me going.

24   "Do you trust me?"

25   "Yes, Mama."

26   "Have I ever steered you wrong?"

27   "No."

28   "Why would I mislead you now? Why would I settle for someone who isn't the best possible choice for you?"

29   I said nothing, for I'd already said more than I should. She begged me to trust her and to give my consent to the union. Mama could certainly have proceeded with or without my consent had she had John's approval. However, she felt that since John was opposed, she needed me not only to agree, but also to help convince my brother that I approved of the plan.

30   "It could do no harm," she said, her eyes begging me. When she thought I was nearly convinced, she progressed, "We can say yes to them now, and

everything can wait until you return. This way, your suitor will wait for you. He won't propose to another girl until you return."

31   I agreed to consider it, but in the meantime, I dashed off an SOS to John to intervene.

32   I pondered the implications of whatever decision I made on the matter. Both entailed immense risks, but if I were really my mother's daughter, the Ibo girl I was raised to be, I would take the safer course and agree to the arrangement. If nothing out of the ordinary happened, I would be guaranteed a husband when I returned from America, spared the fate of an old maid. On the other hand, my intuition cautioned me to hold out, to delay my agreement. Who knew how I would be a few years later. "What if something changes and I don't like him when I come back or he doesn't like me?" I asked Mama over and over.

33   My brother's letter settled the issue. It arrived via express one afternoon in Mama's absence. I suspected it contained the news I awaited and felt relieved, but also panicked that she would be angry with me. I waited for her return, knowing that she would ask me to read the letter for her as I had others before. It took me a second to skim the letter; I'd already decided that I would temper the harsh words that my brother John would surely use in it. In place of John's "If you don't stop harassing Dympna about marriage, you'll alienate her and possibly lose her forever," I said, "Leave Dympna alone; I do not want her married until she's done with her education. I want to make sure she has a choice about what she does in her life."

34   Still, Mama felt I had betrayed her. She switched tactics, and for the rest of my stay with her (two weeks), she resorted to telling me more stories about unmarried Ibo women. She had dozens of them, each a variation on the same theme: Ibo women who wait too long invite a life of misery.

Exercise 10.4

Comprehension Questions

Circle the correct letter choice and fill in the blanks where indicated.

1. According to paragraph 1, which name and/or title would a married Ibo woman have?

   a. *Nwunye Anyi*

   b. *nwada*

   c. wife

   d. all of the above

2. The descriptive statement in paragraph 1 that "the *umuada* of any Ibo village is a power to be reckoned with" is supported by all of the following EXCEPT

  a. personal examples from the author's family.

  b. a statement of specific powers of the *umuada*.

  c. examples of typical decisions that might be made.

  d. analysis of the dual role of *nwada* and wife.

3. The first sentence of paragraph 2

  a. adds another example.

  b. summarizes the main idea of paragraph 1.

  c. provides a contrast to paragraph 1.

  d. all of the above

4. Two patterns combined in paragraph 3 are

  a. cause/effect with whole/part.

  b. time sequence with comparison/contrast.

  c. comparison/contrast with classification.

  d. classification with description/support.

5. At one point in the engagement discussion (6–16), Mama's eyes are described as "begging, pleading." Yet the author was not present to make this observation or others regarding her mother's feelings and motivations during this time. Who was most likely her source for this portrayal? Explain your reasoning.

  _____

  _____

  _____

  _____

  _____

6. What is mentioned in paragraphs 8 and 10 that helps to explain John's opposition to the proceedings?

  _____

  _____

  _____

  _____

  _____

7. The main idea pattern of paragraph 17 is opinion/reason. Write the opinion below and the main reason given for it.

Opinion: _____

Reason: _____

8. Which of the following is true according to paragraph 29?

a. The Ibo bride-to-be has a veto power over the arrangement of a marriage.

b. The mother of the bride may make decisions wholly on her own.

c. The mother must have the father's and the bride's approval to succeed.

d. none of the above

9. Two patterns combined in paragraph 32 are

a. cause/effect with whole/part.

b. time sequence with comparison/contrast.

c. comparison/contrast with opinion/reason.

d. classification with description/support.

10. The role of the bride-to-be is a passive one, but the author found ways to protect her interests. Cite one piece of evidence of this from paragraphs 20–34.

_____

_____

_____

Inference

Put INF *for inference for any of the statements below that would be strongly probable based on the evidence in the reading. Be prepared to defend your choices.*

1. _____   Dympna and Charles were playmates as children.

2. _____   Most Ibo women marry for love.

3. _____   Women hold most of the power in Ibo marriages.

4. _____   Mama must have been 14 or younger when she was married.

5. _____   The author usually did not oppose her mother's wishes.

6. _____   Mama reads English poorly or not at all.

7. _____ Physical appearance is of no concern in Ibo marriages.

8. _____ The Ugwu-Ojus are Catholics.

9. _____ The Ibo culture puts a minor value on education.

10. _____ Arranging Ibo marriages is an uncomplicated process.

Mapping Exercise

Paragraph 1 helps the reader to visualize the dual position of a married Ibo woman in the structure of that culture. Place the following in the pattern map below (one term is used twice):

- *nwada*
- *umuada*
- *wife*
- *Nwunye Anyi*

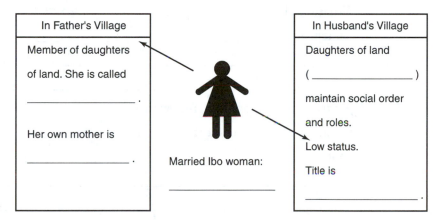

In Father's Village	In Husband's Village
Member of daughters of land. She is called _____ .	Daughters of land (_____) maintain social order and roles.
Her own mother is _____ .	Low status. Title is _____ .

Married Ibo woman: _____

Writing Context Sentences

Use the definitions and the general situation clues below to write context sentences of your own. Remember: your goal is to give enough specific clues so that someone unfamiliar with the word could guess its meaning from your sentence.

1. *pondered:* thought about, went over mentally

   Situation clue: someone considering a course of action

   Sentence: _____

   _____

   _____

2. *alienated:* isolated, no longer friendly

    Situation clue: person becomes angry over treatment by others

    Sentence: _____

    _____

    _____

3. *rebuke:* reprimand; criticize sharply

    Situation clue: a child misbehaves

    Sentence: _____

    _____

    _____

4. *laden:* burdened; weighted down by a load

    Situation clue: people shopping

    Sentence: _____

    _____

    _____

5. *dignitary:* a person of note, importance

    Situation clue: city dedicating a new structure

    Sentence: _____

    _____

    _____

WORD PARTS 3: SPACE AND STRUCTURE RELATIONSHIPS

There are quite a few word parts that can indicate shape, structure, and spatial relationships. Familiarity with these can add to your skill in unlocking the meanings of words that frequently appear in writing that deals with wholes and parts.

Word Part	Meanings	Word Examples	Your Examples
alt	high	alto, altimeter	
angle/angul	angle	angular, triangulate	

ante	in front of	antecedent, anteroom
bi	two	biped, binary
cata	down	cataract, catatonia
circum	around	circumscribe circumspect
cycle	circle	tricycle, cyclone
de	down, from	deport, deduction
di/du	two	duo, duet
dia	through/across	diagonal, dialogue
endo	within/inside	endemic, endodermis
epi	upon/outer	epidemic, epiglottis
ex/e	out/beyond	exceed, exclude
extra/extro	beyond/ouside	extraordinary extravagant
im/in	in/into (also "not")	inspect, impression
hypo	under/less	hypocrisy hypoglycemia
inter	between	interrupt, intercede
intra/intro	within	intramural introspective
junct	join	junction, adjunct
later	side	bilateral, collateral
meso	middle	mesolithic, mesomorph
morph	form/shape	morphology, amorphous
poly	many	polygon, polytechnical
se	apart	separate, secede
semi	half/part	semicircle, semester
sub	under	subordinate, submarine
super/supr	over, above	supervise, superfluous
tele	far	television, telepathy
trans	across	transpose, transport
ultra	beyond	ultraviolet ultramicroscopic
vacu	empty	vacuous, vacant

Exercise 10.5

The word parts in pairs below are often used to indicate contrasts or opposites. Use the meanings of the word parts to answer the questions by circling the correct word. Do not use the dictionary in this exercise.

1. *epidermis/endodermis*   Which word denotes the outer layer of the skin?
2. *imports/exports*   Which word do we use for goods coming into our country?
3. *intrastate/interstate*   Which word would describe travel between states?
4. *introvert/extrovert*   *Vert* means "to turn." Which of these words would be used to describe someone very shy?
5. *substructure/superstructure*   The foundation of a house would be a
6. *deplane/enplane*   Which word describes boarding a plane?

Use the meaning of the word part to make an educated guess on the following:

7. Magellan was the first to *circumnagivate* the globe. What did he do?

_____

_____

8. Why is the *cyclone* so named?   _____

_____

9. Why could a brawl involving a number of people not be termed a *duel?*

_____

_____

10. *Terra* means "earth"; from where would an *extraterrestrial* come?

_____

_____

The following words occurred in the selection "Marriage as a Group Effort." Combine your knowledge of word parts, from the list above and from earlier lessons, with the clues below to unlock the meaning of each word.

11. The word part *pon* means "to put or place." To *postpone* a vacation would mean that you _____.

12. The word part *ven* means "to come"; if someone *intervened* in a fight, what would he do? _____

13. You have been given both word parts for *prescribed*. What is the literal meaning of the word? _____

14. The word part *in* can mean "in" or "not"; *equi* means "equal." What meaning would "in" have in the word *inequitable* in the following: "The living conditions of the rich and poor are inequitable"? _____

15. The word part *pend* means "to hang"; to say that one's doom is *impending* would mean _____.

CHAPTER REVIEW

Analyze the following statements about love and identify their main idea patterns. Circle the correct letter choice and fill in the blanks where indicated.

1. "Love's ingredients include sexual desire, commitment, and a need for closeness" is an idea statement of
   a. description.
   b. classification.
   c. comparison/contrast.
   d. whole/part.

2. Deciding that there are four different types of love illustrates the thinking process of
   a. description.
   b. classification.
   c. comparison/contrast.
   d. whole/part.

3. Statements such as "Their relationship is very intimate" or "Their relationship is highly passionate" are examples of
   a. description.
   b. classification.
   c. comparison/contrast.
   d. whole/part.

4. Asking how one kind of love might differ from another involves us in the idea pattern of
   a. description.
   b. classification.
   c. comparison/contrast.
   d. whole/part.

5. Circle the letter below that describes relationships *between* people:
   a. intrapersonal
   b. interpersonal

6. Body types have been classified into three groups: *mesomorph, endomorph,* and *ectomorph*. Which falls between the two extremes of thin/muscular and fat/soft? _____

Identify the following as bandwagon, plain folks, *or* guilt by association:

7. _____ A school dress code will free our kids from those outlandish styles dictated by slick big city advertising types. Kids will look like kids again.

8. _____ At the last board meeting, a number of people supported school uniforms. Where do these skinhead fascists come from?

9. _____ Schools all over the country are turning to school uniforms. Everyone is recognizing that they're the best solution to a difficult situation.

10. Does list *A* or *B* (below) create the error of cross-classification? _____

A. Students will be placed in one of four groups:
   1. Students with GPAs of 3.0 or more
   2. Students with GPAs below 3.0
   3. Students with 12.0 or more units
   4. Students receiving financial aid

B. Students will be placed in one of four groups:
   1. Student-athletes with GPAs of 3.0 or more
   2. Student-athletes with GPAs below 3.0
   3. Student-nonathletes with GPAs of 3.0 or more
   4. Student-nonathletes with GPAs below 3.0

1. *For this assignment you will need to find a magazine or newspaper article dealing with either classification or whole/part structure.* Avoid articles that are heavily technical or mechanical in favor of articles that have more of a human interest angle. In newspapers, look for these especially in feature sections.

<u>Option A: Classification</u>

A number of various approaches to classification were mentioned in this chapter. Look for an article that

1. Breaks a large group into subtypes
2. Identifies a special or new type/class(model: "The Third Culture")
3. Places someone or something in a class they have not previously been linked with

Pay particular attention to the sorting factors in your article: what traits, uses, or other features form the basis for the classification? Classifications are often humorous or critical, so you should consider the writer's tone as well as the content.

<u>Option B: Whole/Part Structure Analysis</u>

You were given models of whole/part structures both physical ("The Solar System") and nonphysical ("Marriage as a Group Effort"). Articles about physical structures (a new weapon or vehicle, for example) are easy to find but run the danger of being overly technical. Summarizing this kind of article can be difficult. Nonphysical structure articles (for instance, those about human organizations and institutions) occur less frequently but can be good choices for this assignment. The inclusion of human relationships (on the job, in school, in families, etc.) will give you more to react to in your response section.

2. *If your article does not include graphic aids, you may want to create a pattern map or drawing for your summary.* Be sure to explain or define key terms and references.

3. *Your summary and response section together should be about 350 words.* When your article is returned, be sure to file it in the correct category.

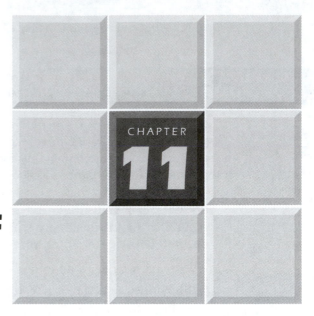

Recognizing Similarities and Differences: Comparison and Contrast

CHAPTER

11

The physical, the mental, the emotional—all alike can involve thinking that requires us to observe similarities and differences. We can compare past and present, present and future, what is with what might have been, the bad with the good, and the good with the best. In the pages that follow, you will work with a few examples of the many varieties of this universal pattern.

▓ CHAPTER PREVIEW

In this chapter you will

- ▪ Discover the versatility of comparison/contrast
- ▪ Read comparison/contrast articles showing a variety of approaches
- ▪ Complete your word parts with comparison/contrast
- ▪ Be introduced to figurative language that involves comparison/contrast
- ▪ Learn about fallacies and emotional appeals related to the pattern of comparison/contrast
- ▪ Find an article of comparison/contrast for your Reading Portfolio

Of all idea patterns, comparison/contrast is the most versatile. For example, as you saw in the last chapter, we use comparison and contrast to classify things based on their traits, functions, or structure. Comparison/contrast is also commonly used as a pattern in support of other main idea patterns. By its very nature, comparison/contrast has no choice; it *must* use elements from other patterns to create ideas of similarity and difference. The following examples illustrate how the seven other idea patterns can incorporate comparison/contrast.

Description (Characteristics)	Pedro is very outgoing, whereas his brother Tomas is extremely shy.
Description (Actions)	Just like his father before him, Martin has broken many school records in track and field.
Time Sequence	Selena always prefers to eat before she exercises; Helena, in contrast, would rather wait until after her workout.
Cause/Effect	Some people feel that success in school is the result of superior intelligence, but others think that high motivation and effective organization are better explanations of why students succeed.
Classification	Today the Democrat and Republican parties have more viewpoints in common than one would suspect.
Whole/Part	For reasons of economy, many compact cars have four-cylinder engines; larger luxury cars, on the other hand, require engines with six to eight cylinders.
Problem/Solution	A decline in the use of tobacco products by young people will only come about through education; a similar approach is needed for the problem of drug abuse.
Opinion/Reason	Some people argue for capital punishment as morally defensible and an effective deterrent to crime; however, others maintain it is barbaric and lacks a clear deterrent effect.

COMPARISON AND CONTRAST: FACT AND OPINION

By showing how things are alike or unlike, comparison/contrast generates factual information. However, it also may be used to express opinions and value judgments.

1. Ernest is quite tall, whereas Brad is of average height.
2. Ernest is very moody; Brad, on the other hand, is genuinely pleasant to everyone.
3. Community college is a better deal than a four-year college. It's less expensive, more personal, and less stressful.

Statement 1 is factual and informational. Provided we agree on a cutoff for *tall* and a range for *average,* we can measure and decide on these labels objectively. Statement 2 requires supporting details such as illustrations and examples. However, no matter what support is given, the statement will remain an opinion because the descriptive words contain value judgments: *moody* carries a negative connotation, whereas *genuinely pleasant* would be considered a compliment. Statement 3 is persuasive, with an implied call for action; articles in which comparison/contrast combine with opinion/reason are dealt with in Part 3. The article below follows the pattern of statement 2 above. It details differences between a younger and an older generation but also develops a judgment about the values underlying their lifestyles.

PREVIEWING *STOP THE CLOCK* BY AMY WU

Setting Your Reading Goals

The title of the article suggests a concern about what? _____

Does the title alone suggest a clear topic or main idea? _____

Preview further by reading the first two paragraphs and the concluding paragraph. Decide on a sentence among these three that would clarify what the title means and write it here:

_____

_____

_____

Preview Vocabulary

scallions (2)	young onions, before the bulbs enlarge
inept (3)	clumsy, incompetent
domestic (13)	relating to the family and home
tedious (9)	tiresome, boring due to length or slowness

rite of passage (10)	significant event marking a movement from one stage to another
lavish (13)	abundant; extravagant
slather (15)	spread thickly on

Annotating as you Read

From your preview, you should have picked up that the main contrast in the article will be between the generation of the author and that of her _____.

Track that contrast as you read. What traits and actions characterize the two sides? Mark these in the text and margin, and make a pattern map to help you visualize their differences.

Stop the Clock

by Amy Wu

1   My aunt tends to her house as if it were her child. The rooms are spotless, the windows squeak, the kitchen counter is so shiny that I can see my reflection and the floors are so finely waxed that my sister and I sometimes slide across in socks and pretend that we are skating.

2   Smells of soy sauce, scallions, and red bean soup drift from the kitchen whenever I visit. The hum of the washing machine lulls me to sleep. In season, there are roses in the garden, and vases hold flowers arranged like those in a painting. My aunt enjoys keeping house, although she's wealthy enough to hire someone to do it.

> The first two paragraphs deal only with the author's aunt. If you picked a sentence from these two paragraphs as your hypothesis, reread the concluding paragraph and revise your guess.

3   I'm a failure at housework. I've chosen to be inept and unlearn what my aunt has spent so much time perfecting. At 13, I avoided domestic chores as my contribution to the women's movement. Up to now, I've thought there were more important things to do.

4   I am a member of a generation that is very concerned with saving time but often unaware of why we're doing it. Like many, I'm nervous and jittery without a wristwatch and a daily planner. I am one of a growing number of students who are completing college in three years instead of four—cramming credits in the summer. We're living life on fast-forward without a pause button.

5   In my freshman year, my roommates and I survived on Chinese takeout, express pizzas, and taco take-home dinners. Every day seemed an endless picnic as we ate with plastic utensils and paper plates. It was fast and easy—no washing up. My girlfriends and I talked about our mothers and grandmothers, models of domesticity, and pitied them. We didn't see the benefits of staying at home, ironing clothes and making spaghetti sauce when canned sauces were almost as good and cleaning services were so convenient. A nearby store even sold throwaway underwear. "Save time," the package read. "No laundry."

6   We baked brownies in 10 minutes in the microwave and ate the frosting from the can because we were too impatient to wait for the brownies to cool. For a while we thought about chipping in and buying a funky contraption that makes toast, coffee, and eggs. All you had to do was put in the raw ingredients the night before and wake up to the smell of sizzling eggs, crispy toast, and rich coffee.

7   My aunt was silent when I told her about plastic utensils, microwave meals, and disposable underwear. "It's a waste of money," she finally said. I was angry as I stared at her perfect garden, freshly ironed laundry, and handmade curtains. "Well, you're wasting your time," I said defensively. But I wasn't so sure.

8   It seems that all the kids I know are time-saving addicts. Everyone on campus prefers e-mail to snail mail. The art of letter writing is long gone. I know classmates who have forgotten how to write in script, and print like 5-year-olds. More of us are listening to books instead of reading them. My roommate last year jogged while plugged in. She told me she'd listened to John Grisham's *The Client*. "You mean read," I corrected. "I didn't read a word," she said with pride.

9   My nearsighted friends opt for throwaway contacts and think the usual lenses are tedious. A roommate prefers a sleeping bag so she doesn't have to make her bed. Instead of going to the library to do research we cruise the Internet and log on to the Library of Congress.

10 School kids take trips to the White House via Internet and Mosaic. I heard that one school even considered canceling the eighth-grade Washington trip, a traditional rite of passage, because it's so easy to visit the capital on the Information Highway. I remember how excited my eighth-grade classmates and I were about being away from home for the first time. We stayed up late, ate Oreos in bed, and roamed around the Lincoln Memorial, unsupervised by adults.

11 It isn't as if we're using the time we save for worthwhile pursuits like volunteering at a soup kitchen. Most of my friends spend the extra minutes watching TV, listening to stereos, shopping, hanging out, chatting on the phone, or snoozing.

12 When I visited my aunt last summer, I saw how happy she was after baking bread or a cake, how proud she seemed whenever she made a salad with

her homegrown tomatoes and cucumbers. Why bother when there are ready-made salads, ready-peeled-and-cut fruit, and five-minute frosting?

13   Once, when I went shopping with her, she bought ingredients to make a birthday cake for her daughter. I pointed to a lavish-looking cake covered with pink roses. "Why don't you just buy one," I asked. "A cake is more than a cake," she replied. "It's the giving of energy, the thought behind it. You'll grow to understand."

14   Slowly, I am beginning to appreciate why my aunt takes pleasure in cooking for her family, why the woman down the street made her daughter's wedding gown instead of opting for Vera Wang, why the old man next door spends so much time tending his garden. He offered me a bag of his fresh-grown tomatoes. "They're good," he said. "Not like the ones at the supermarket." He was right.

15   Not long ago, I spent a day making a meal for my family. As the pasta boiled and the red peppers sizzled, I wrote a letter to my cousin in Canada. At first the pen felt strange, then reassuring. I hand-washed my favorite skirt and made chocolate cake for my younger sister's 13th birthday. It took great self-control not to slather on the icing before the cake cooled.

16   That night I grinned as my father and sister dug into the pasta, then the cake, licking their lips in appreciation. It had been a long time since I'd felt so proud. A week later my cousin called and thanked me for my letter, the first handwritten correspondence she'd received in two years.

17   Sure, my generation has all the technological advances at our fingertips. We're computer savvy, and we have more time. But what are we really saving for? In the end, we may lose more than we've gained by forgetting the important things in life.

Exercise 11.1

Comprehension Questions

Circle the correct letter choice and fill in the blanks where indicated.

1. Which of the following is the best statement of the main idea of the article?

    a. The younger generation understands and uses technology, thus saving valuable time.

    b. The difference in values between the author's generation and her aunt's, showing up in important areas like housework, cooking, and gardening.

    c. The new generation has the means to save time but lacks a sense of values in using it wisely.

    d. We should reject all modern technology and return to a simple way of life.

2. In paragraph 3, the author states that "I'm a failure at housework." The rest of the paragraph suggests what reason for that?

   a. The author is naturally clumsy.
   b. The author is a slow learner.
   c. The author deliberately decided to fail.
   d. all of the above

3. The main idea of paragraph 4 is that

   a. the author's generation wants to save time but often doesn't know why.
   b. many rely on wristwatches and daily planners.
   c. increasingly, students are completing college in three years instead of four.
   d. the author's generation is living life on fast-forward without a pause button.

4. Paragraph 9 forms a multiparagraph unit with paragraph 8. Its function is to

   a. provide additional examples to support the main idea.
   b. provide the main reasons for an opinion.
   c. provide possible solutions to a problem.
   d. list the steps in a sequence of events.

5. The details in paragraph 11 are included to show that

   a. students need time off to avoid stress.
   b. more volunteers are needed at local soup kitchens.
   c. the time young people save is wasted.
   d. all of the above

6. Paragraphs 15 and 16 form a unit in which the author describes changes she is beginning to make in her lifestyle. The details are organized in the pattern of

   a. comparison/contrast.
   b. whole/part.
   c. opinion/reason.
   d. time sequence.

   List some of the transition words that led you to your answer. _____

   _____

   _____

7. Examples regarding her aunt's activities include all of the following EXCEPT:

   a. drawing.

  b. cooking.

  c. cleaning.

  d. ironing.

8. Authors sometimes use the technique of foreshadowing to give the reader a clue about what is to come. Find one example in each of the following paragraphs where the author foreshadows her eventual change of view:

  Paragraph 3: _____

  Paragraph 7: _____

9. Most of the evidence for the author's main idea comes from

  a. published studies regarding behavior of the present college-age generation.

  b. formal interviews with students and parents.

  c. comments of experts in sociology.

  d. personal observation and experience.

  e. all of the above

10. The author's tone in the article could best be described as

  a. comic and slightly sarcastic.

  b. thoughtful and self-critical.

  c. angry and defensive.

  d. mean and nasty.

Mapping Exercises

1. Paragraph 2 is organized in the idea pattern of description/support. Complete the pattern map with the choices below:

  ■ smells of cooking in the kitchen

  ■ my aunt enjoys keeping house

  ■ flowers in garden and vases

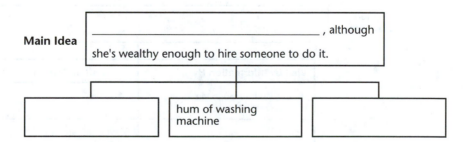

2. Multiparagraph unit 8–9 and paragraph 10 are examples of two very common patterns in comparison/contrast: point-by-point development and block development. In the first, two subjects are paired regarding their similarities and/or differences on various points. In block development, first one element is developed completely and then the other is developed.

In the exercise below, match the implied main ideas with the correct map. Then identify the pattern of the map as block or point by point and complete the map with the choices that follow each map.

Implied main ideas:

- Students prefer a fast electronic simulation to the real thing.
- Young people are time-saving addicts who choose the fastest way.

Implied Main Idea		

Faster	Slower
E-mail	
	Reading books
Throwaway contacts	
	Making a bed
Cruising Internet/logging on Library of Congress	

Pattern: block or point by point? _____

- using a sleeping bag
- regular lenses
- going to library to do research
- writing letters
- listening to books

Implied Main Idea		

Visit by Information Hwy.	Visit in Person
Visited White House via Internet and Mosaic	
	Stayed up late, ate Oreos, roamed unsupervised

Pattern: block or point by point? _____

■ author's eighth-grade trip with classmates

■ school nearly canceled visit in favor of Information Highway

Fact, Opinion, and Belief

On the line below, place an X *where you think Amy Wu's article would fall on the fact to belief scale, and explain your choice. Given the subject matter and the conclusions she draws, is there enough evidence to persuade you to her viewpoint?*

FACT   OPINION   BELIEF

Questions for Writing/Small-Group Discussion

1. At the time of writing this article as a "My Turn" feature in *Newsweek,* the author was a 20-year-old history major at New York University. Do you think she is headed in the right direction? Why? Is the change likely to be permanent or only temporary? Why or why not?

2. The article gives some specific examples of our fixation with saving time. Does the speedy lifestyle show up in other areas—for example, our driving habits or our preferences in entertainment? Can you think of other examples that support the author's portrait of the habits of the college-age generation?

▦ FIGURATIVE LANGUAGE

Look at the following sentences from the "Stop the Clock":

> "Like many, I'm nervous and jittery without a wristwatch and a daily planner."

> "More of us are listening to books rather than reading them."

> "We didn't see the benefits of … making spaghetti sauce when canned sauces were almost as good."

In literal statements like these, the comparison or contrast itself is the main point. Our attention is directed equally to both sides involved in *either/or* or *like/unlike* comparisons and contrasts: the author and her generation, books read or books listened to, homemade spaghetti sauce versus canned sauces. Now compare these statements with others from the article, and you will notice that something is different:

> "My aunt tends to her house as if it were her child."

> "Every day seemed an endless picnic as we ate with plastic utensils and paper plates."

Figurative statements like these are not literally true: the house is not her child, every day was not really a picnic. Nor is the point to inform us equally about both sides of the comparison—the author is not out to tell us about children or picnics. We use figurative comparisons like these to emphasize a single point of connection about the one we are concerned with: the house receives *immaculate care;* the students' meals have a *haphazard and casual atmosphere.* Some special terms—simile, metaphor, and analogy—have been used for figures of speech like these.

SIMILE

Simile is applied to comparisons using *like* or *as:* "My aunt tends to her house *as if* it were her child."

METAPHOR

Metaphor applies to figurative comparisons made directly by the verb *to be* or some other linking verb: "Every day *seemed* an endless picnic." Metaphors are also often indirectly stated.

> The lumberjack held out a paw.
>
> The angry old woman stuck her beak in the salesman's face and pecked away at him.
>
> The wrestler waddled across the gym floor to the drinking fountain.

These statements show vividly a similarity between isolated traits in things that are otherwise unlike:

> A man's hand and a bear's paw share the traits of being huge (and perhaps hairy).
>
> A pecking bird and an angry woman both move quickly and aggressively.
>
> The wrestler and a duck share a distinctive way of moving.

ANALOGY

Analogy is a highly analytical comparison. It connects things that may not seem even remotely related. Underlying analogy is a kind of mathematical formula: A is to B as C is to D.

Questions on college entrance tests like the SAT often test a student's ability to do this kind of reasoning. These can range from the fairly simple:

sheep is to lamb   a. claws

      as   b. den

bear is to _____   c. cub

                                        d. wild

to the very difficult:

persecution is to amnesty   a. execution

       as   b. veracity

mendacity is to _____   c. revenge

                                 d. freedom

Our experience helps us to detect the relationship in the first example—parent to offspring—and so select *cub* as the correct answer. It's somewhat harder to recognize *veracity* as the correct response to complete pairs of antonyms (opposites), especially if one is unsure of the definitions of one or more of the terms.

As with metaphors and similes, analogies are aimed at only one side of the comparison. Their purpose is to use the more familiar to explain the unfamiliar. Suppose a group of young fathers is taking a class in infant care. The instructor might choose to approach the subject with an analogy: "Taking care of a baby is like taking care of your car." The instructor intends for the young men to apply their knowledge of car care to a new subject, babies: both need to be kept clean, both have to have things changed (diapers/filters), both have to be fed (food, water/oil, gas). Of course, the situation could be the opposite. In a class on car care for women, the instructor might reverse the analogy with the focus on the car: "Taking care of a car is like taking care of a baby."

Analogies are often given in a kind of shorthand; it's left to the reader to fill out the full terms. For example, look at the following sentence taken from "Stop the Clock": "We're living life on fast-forward without a pause button." (4) What in the world does a malfunctioning VCR possibly have to do with today's generation of college students? We can answer that by following the formula above:

a program stuck on fast-   the college generations's
forward is to a program   as   lifestyle is to the older
at regular speed   generation's lifestyle

The younger generation's lifestyle and a program on fast-forward are connected only by the opinion that both are out of control and going too fast to be enjoyed.

Analogy also differs from metaphor and simile in that it may be extended much further. In an analogy relating to government, for instance, the nation might be compared to a ship, the president to a captain, government officials to the crew, and the general population to the passengers; an international threat might be likened to a storm, and so forth. The reader's job with analogies is to look for the key point of connection and see how it applies.

Exercise 11.2

Part A

Below are figurative comparisons from the two stories you read in Chapter 3, "Fear" by Gary Soto and "The Penny" by Dorothy West. Identify figurative language as either simile *or* metaphor. *If the sentence presents a nonfigurative comparison or contrast, write* C/C.

1. _____ The boy whimpered like a whipped puppy.

2. _____ Miss Halsey was purring softly.

3. _____ I stared at his face, shaped like the sole of a shoe.

4. _____ No two people were happier than Miss Halsey and the little boy.

5. _____ His teeth were green like the underside of a rock.

6. _____ The gnome who clutched the penny had turned into a child.

7. _____ The little boy's head was in the clouds.

8. _____ His breath was sour as meat left out in the sun.

9. _____ But just as he had not felt the cold, now he did not feel the pain.

10. _____ He was not walking on earth anyway. He was walking on air.

Part B

Identify the examples of figurative language below as simile, metaphor, *or* analogy. *If the sentence presents a straightforward comparison or contrast, write* C/C.

1. _____ "Everyone on campus prefers e-mail to snail mail."

2. _____ Life is like a box of chocolates. You can never be sure of what the future may hold, so you may be disappointed or pleasantly surprised.

3. _____ The motorcycle gang sliced through the crowd as if it were cheese.

4. _____ Community colleges, like universities, offer general education courses, but they also provide extensive remedial services.

5. _____ Going to college is a lot like hitting yourself over the head with a hammer. It feels so good when you stop.

6. _____ The new Toyota Corolla is very similar to last year's model.

7. _____ Joe performs high dives as gracefully as an eagle.

8. _____   No man is an island. We are all a part of the mainland. If any part is washed away, we are all lessened by it.

9. _____   "Put a tiger in your tank." (gasoline ad)

10. _____   At the interview, he was a bowl full of Jell-O in a room full of spoons.

ANALYZING COMPARISON AND CONTRAST IN TEXTBOOKS

Comparison and contrast is a common pattern of organization in many fields that seek to show similarities and to draw clear distinctions regarding groups, trends, and concepts. The selection below provides a typical example of how text and graphics combine to convey the complex attitudes and positions involved in various topics in a field of study.

PREVIEWING *INEQUALITY IN THE UNITED STATES* BY J. ROSS ESHLEMAN, BARBARA CASHION, AND LAWRENCE A. BASIRICO

Setting Your Reading Goals

The authors of textbooks attempt to give the broad outlines of differences and interpretations that arise in any field. Your objective in readings organized by comparison/contrast is to get a clear picture of both sides. The title suggests the general issue of concern—inequality. The first paragraph narrows this further by letting the reader know that the authors are mainly concerned here with what kind of inequality? _____

Preview Vocabulary

stratification (8)   the classification or separation into groups based on status

conspicuously (10)   in a manner attracting attention

impoverished (15)   made extremely poor

Annotating As You Read

Look for sections that concentrate on economic and social differences between groups. Write the words "similar" and "different" in the margin, and add some key clarifying phrases, to highlight important differences among groups and between studies. In addition, several key concepts are defined in the text. Identify these and write out full definitions in the margins.

Inequality in the United States

by J. Ross Eshleman, Barbara Cashion, and Lawrence A. Basirico

1   Social inequality in the United States is based on family background, wealth, education, occupation, and a variety of other characteristics. The best way to understand the class system is to look at its various dimensions separately.

The Distribution of Income

2   In 1990, the median income in the United States for people with full-time jobs was $27,866 for men and $19,816 for women (*Current Population Reports,* Series P-60, 1991). The median is the amount at which half of a given population falls above and half falls below. The median household income was $29,943.

3   Another way to look at income distribution is to consider the share of the total U.S. income received by each 20 percent of the U.S. population. Figure 11.1 shows that during the decade of the 1980s, the rich did indeed get richer and the poor got poorer. In 1980, the poorest 20 percent of households received only 4.1 percent of the total available income, but by 1989, that had decreased to 3.8 percent. The richest 20 percent of households received 44.2 percent of the available income in 1980, and that increased to 46.8 percent in 1989.

TABLE 8.2

Percentage of Household Income for each Fifth of U.S. Population, 1980 and 1990

Total Population	Total Available Income 1980	Total Available Income 1990
Highest fifth	44.2	46.6
Second highest fifth	24.8	24.0
Middle fifth	16.8	15.9
Second lowest fifth	10.2	9.6
Lowest fifth	4.1	3.9

Source: U.S. Department of Commerce, Bureau of the Census, *Current Population Reports,* Series P–60, Nos. 167, 168, and 174. U.S. Government Printing Office, Washington, D.C., 1990; from Eshleman, Cashion, and Basirico, *Sociology: An Introduction,* 4th ed., 208.

FIGURE 11.1
Source: Eshelman, Cashion, and Basirico, *Sociology: An Introduction,* 4th ed., 207–213.

4   This income distribution is similar to the distribution of income found in European countries, although in European countries there is a little more equality. Generally, the richest 20 percent earn slightly less than they do in the United States, and the poorest 20 percent earn slightly more. This is before taxes. In European countries, taxes and social programs redistribute earnings much more equally than in the United States.

The Distribution of Wealth

5   Wealth consists of personal property. *Personal property* includes liquid assets (cash in bank accounts), real estate, stock, bonds, and other owned assets. The wealth among the top 20 percent of the population is not evenly distributed. The richest 10 percent of the population holds 67.9 percent of all available wealth in this nation (*Facts on File,* 1986). Even this wealth is not distributed evenly. The top 0.5 percent of households held 26.9 percent of available wealth in 1983, up from 25 percent in 1963, as shown in Figure 11.2. By comparison, the second richest 0.5 percent held only 7.4 percent of the available wealth, and the next 9 percent shared 33.6 percent. The lowest 90 percent of the population shared the remaining 32.1 percent of the wealth, less than their 36 percent share in 1963. Note also in this figure that the average net worth, total assets minus total liabilities, of those in the top 0.5 percent is $8.9 million, compared to an average of $39,000 for 90 percent of the population.

6   Moreover, the very wealthy actually control even more money than they possess. By owning many shares of the major corporations, they influence not just their own fortunes but also those of many others. The Rockefeller family, for example, dominates key banks and corporations and has been known to control assets of more than 15 times their personal wealth.

TABLE 8.3

**Distribution of Wealth and Net Worth,
1963 and 1983**

Sector of Population	Percent of Wealth 1963	1983	Average Net Worth $
Top 0.5%	25.0	26.9	8,900,000
Next 0.5%	6.6	7.4	1,700,000
Next 9%	32.4	33.6	420,000
Lowest 90%	36.0	32.1	39,000

Source: U.S. Facts on File:World News Digest with index 46
(August 1, 1986): 622C2; from Eshleman, Cashion, and Basirico,
Sociology: An Introduction, 4th ed., 208.

FIGURE 11.2

7   As with income, where statistics are available for other countries, they show that the holdings of the wealthy are generally comparable to the holdings of the wealthy in this country. In Britain and in Ireland, the very wealthy have traditionally held an even larger share of their country's wealth than is the case in this country (Brown, 1988). However, in Canada, the largest holders of wealth own a considerably smaller share than is the case in the United States.

Social Status in American Society

8   The earliest studies of stratification in America were based on the concept of status—people's opinions of other people—which can be conferred on others for any reason a person chooses—mystical or religious powers, athletic ability, youth or beauty, good deeds—whatever seems appropriate to the person doing the ranking. It was found that in this country, status was conferred on others on the basis of their wealth. However, wealth used to be more obvious than it is today.

9   A study done in Middletown during the Great Depression found status differences between the business class and the working class. When the study was originally done, the business class lived in larger and better quality housing than did the working class. The very wealthy had elaborate mansions with indoor plumbing and central heating, whereas working-class homes were much smaller and often lacked indoor plumbing; water had to be carried in from an outdoor well. Heating was provided by a wood or coal stove.

10 A more recent study of Middletown (Caplow et al., 1982) found that it had become more difficult to identify classes among the population. The working class now lives in houses that are only slightly smaller than those of the business class, and they contain all of the amenities that modern society provides—not only indoor plumbing and central heating but also self-cleaning ovens, dishwashers, and other laborsaving devices. The wealthy, while living relatively modestly in town, spend more of their money less conspicuously out of town, buying condominiums and yachts in Florida, for example. Today, then, it is more difficult to assign status on the basis of wealth.

Class Consciousness

11 *Class consciousness,* the awareness that different classes exist in society and that people's fates are tied to the fate of their whole class, was studied by Jackman and Jackman (1983), in a national survey. They found respondents throughout the country defined classes in much the same way. When questioned and given a free choice, most respondents assigned themselves to one of five classes, as follows:

1. Poor—7.6 percent considered themselves poor.
2. Working class—36.6 percent considered themselves working class.

3. Middle class—43.3 percent considered themselves middle class, just as the majority of Americans have done for many decades.

4. Upper middle class—8.2 percent put themselves in this category.

5. Upper class—1 percent assigned themselves to this class.

12   Like Weber, respondents in this study used both class and status variables to determine social class. Occupation was a primary consideration, and education was also important, but the amount of money a person had was not given major consideration by this sample. Status issues such as a person's values, beliefs, and style of life were very important in this sample's rankings.

13   Members of the different classes were aware of others in their class and when asked how they felt about people in the different classes, they responded that they felt warmest toward people in their own class. They were also very aware of political issues that affected their class. The poor, for example, would like the government to guarantee good jobs for all, and they would like a higher minimum wage. The upper middle class does not support these programs. The poor would like there to be smaller income differences between occupations, whereas the upper middle class thinks large income differences between occupations are quite proper.

14   Overall, the majority of Americans believe that government should do nothing to create greater equality, even when tax policy changes by government cause greater inequality. People believe our system of inequality is justified and promises to be a productive system for the United States (Dionne, 1990). This is a change from American attitudes in the past. During the depression of the 1930s, for example, Americans thought that the difference in what the wealthy earned from their investments and what the worker earned in wages was unjust, and workers wanted the government to do something to reduce this inequality. During the decade of the 1960s, Americans seemed to forget about the difference between the wealthy and the worker, but they became concerned about poverty and wanted government to increase opportunities for the poor. During the 1980s, Americans appeared to be uninterested in any action by government to reduce inequality. As a result, the rich continued to get richer, and those living in poverty continued to suffer from lack of food, shelter, and other basic necessities.

Poverty

15   Poverty is defined as having fewer resources than necessary to meet the basic necessities of life—food, shelter, and medical care. The U.S. government has developed a measure of poverty that takes into account the size of the family, the number of children, and whether the family lives on a farm. They assume that living on a farm costs less than living in the city. The income level considered impoverished varies with these factors. For a family of four not

living on a farm, the poverty line in 1990 was $12,675. The government reports that in 1990, 13.5 percent of the population, or 33.6 million people were living in poverty. In that same year, 12.2 percent of children lived in poverty.

16   Jobs for poor people would not solve the problems of poverty. Of the adult poor, about 40 percent work at jobs that pay so little that they fall below the poverty line even though they work. The adults who are poor and not working are either retired, ill or disabled, going to school, or keeping house. Approximately one-third of the poor in the United States are children. Only about 5 percent of poor people are adults who could be working but are not, and most of these people do not work because they cannot find work (Eitzen and Zinn, 1989).

17   The level of poverty in the United States is generally higher than in other countries, particularly the proportion of children who are poor. Figure 11.3 gives poverty rates for the United States and other countries. These rates are computed somewhat differently from the way the census computes rates, but they allow comparison with other countries.

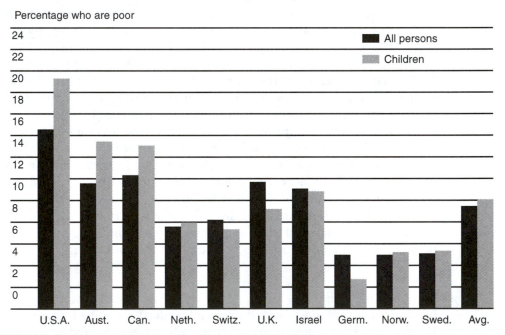

FIGURE 11.3   Comparative poverty rates   *Source*: The 1991 Green Book, Committee on Ways and Means, U.S. House of Representatives, 1991. Based on testimony of Timothy Smeading before the Joint Economic Committee of Congress, May 11, 1959 (Using LIS database). Because of different database, figures differ slightly from official government ones. From Eshleman, Cashion, and Basirico, *Sociology: An Introducion*, 4th ed., 212.

Exercise 11.3

Definitions in the Text

Use your annotations in the margins to provide definitions for these terms.

1. median: _____

2. personal property: _____

3. liquid assets: _____

4. net worth: _____

5. status: _____

6. class consciousness: _____

7. poverty: _____

Mapping Comparison/Contrast

Use information from the text and your annotations to complete the relationship map with these items (two items are used twice).

mansions	much smaller
indoor	carried water
modest in town	only slightly smaller
wood/coal	central

Middletown Class Studies				
	Great Depression Study		**1982 Study**	
	Business Class	Working Class	Business Class	Working Class
Housing				
Plumbing			(same)	
Heating			(same)	

Comprehension Questions

Circle the correct letter choice and fill in the blanks where indicated.

1. According to Figure 11.1, the group that showed the largest decrease in percentage of household income was the

    a. highest fifth.

    b. second highest fifth.

    c. middle fifth.

    d. second lowest fifth.

    e. lowest fifth.

2. According to Figure 11.2, the group whose percentage of wealth decreased the most between 1963 and 1983 was the

    a. top 0.5%.

    b. next 0.5%.

    c. next 9%.

    d. lowest 90%.

3. According to the text, the most important factor in determining status in America has been

    a. wealth.

    b. athletic ability.

    c. good deeds.

    d. religious powers.

4. To determine social class, respondents in the Jackman and Jackman study used used all of the following criteria EXCEPT

    a. occupation.

    b. education.

    c. money.

    d. lifestyle.

5. Americans during the depression of the 1930s felt that

    a. the government should do nothing to create greater equality.

    b. it was natural for tax policy to create inequalities.

    c. having the rich get richer is a productive system.

    d. wages of workers were lower than they should be.

6. In what way did attitudes towards wealth in the 1960s differ from those of the 1980s?

   a. Americans in the 1960s felt the wealthy were justified in what they earned.

   b. Americans in the 1960s felt that government should increase opportunities for the poor.

   c. Americans in the 1960s felt the American system should do more for the worker.

   d. Americans in the 1960s strongly opposed all government attempts to create greater equality.

7. We can infer that the poverty line in 1990 for a family of four living on a farm would be

   a. $12,675.

   b. a figure higher than $12,675.

   c. a figure lower than $12,675.

8. According to the text, which of the following is NOT true?

   a. Jobs for poor people would not solve the problems of poverty.

   b. The pay of about 40 percent of working adults places them below the poverty line.

   c. Poor, nonworking adults are mainly retired, ill or disabled, at school or keeping house.

   d. Only about 5 percent of poor people are adults who are working.

9. In this selection, the authors rely on information from all of these sources EXCEPT

   a. *Facts on File.*

   b. *Current Population Reports.*

   c. the Census Bureau.

   d. *World Almanac.*

10. The authors' attitude toward the topic of the selection, "inequality," is best described as

   a. neutral and objective.

   b. mildly critical of a system that creates inequalities.

   c. strongly critical of a system that creates inequalities.

   d. strongly supportive of the present system in America.

Answer the following based on the data in Figure 11.3:

11. The country closest to the U.S. percentages for both all persons and children in poverty is

    a. Canada.

    b. Australia.

    c. U.K.

    d. Israel.

12. The two countries closest to the average percentages for both categories are

    a. Switzerland and Netherlands.

    b. Sweden and Norway.

    c. U.K. and Australia.

    d. U.K. and Israel.

13. These figures suggest that the continent with the lowest poverty rates would likely be

    a. North America.

    b. Europe.

    c. Australia.

    d. Asia

Write T *for True or* F *for False next to the statement.*

14. _____   The percentage of poor U. S. children is over twice the average of other countries.

15. _____   The figures in Figure 11.3 are exactly the same as official government figures.

■ WORD PARTS 4: COMPARISON AND CONTRAST

Many word parts expressing comparison and contrast are of very high frequency. For example, those expressing the contrast "not"—including *a, dis, un,* and *in* (with variations *il, ir,* and *im*) combine with other words and roots to make thousands of words. Learning this short list, therefore, will more than repay your time.

Word Part	*Meanings*	*Word Examples*	*Your Examples*
a	not	atypical, anonymous	

ambi/amphi	both	ambiguous amphibian
anti	against	antisocial, antidote
contra/counter	against	counteract, contraband
dis	apart, not, opposite, do the opposite of	dissimilar, dissent, disappear, dislike
equi	equal	equinox, equidistant
hetero	other, different	heterodox, heteromorphic
homo	same (also "man")	homonym, homocentric
in/il/ir/im	not	inactive, illogical, immature, irregular
mis	wrong, bad, hatred	misspell, misogamist
non	not	nonconformist, nonsense
oid	resembling	ovoid, spheroid
pseudo	false, fake	pseudonym, pseudoscience
simil	like	similar, assimilate
un	not, do the opposite action	unconcerned, uncover

Exercise 11.4

The words below combine a word part from previous chapters with a word part of comparison or contrast. Use your knowledge of these to answer the questions below without using a dictionary. Circle the correct letter choice.

1. Which of these words means "intense dislike"?

   a. apathy

   b. antipathy

   c. homeopathy

2. Someone who *dissimulates* would be

   a. making others unhappy.

   b. trying to hide or disguise oneself.

   c. equalizing or balancing things.

3. Which of the two words below would we use to refer to a multicultural society?

   a. heterogeneous

   b. homogeneous

4. If you *contradict* your employers, you would

   a. disagree with them.

   b. support them.

   c. try to avoid them.

5. A *nonbelligerent* would be someone who

   a. is very ugly.

   b. is combative.

   c. does not wish to fight.

6. The word *anthropoid* would be used to describe

   a. a lion.

   b. an orangutan.

   c. a lobster.

7. An order that is *unequivocal* is

   a. illegal.

   b. important.

   c. clear.

8. Someone described as an *ambivert* would be

   a. a pervert and moral deviant.

   b. both social and private.

   c. sometimes truthful, sometimes dishonest.

9. A voice that is *inaudible* is

   a. not able to be heard.

b. not pleasant or musical.

c. excessively loud or grating.

10. A person described as a *misanthrope* would be

a. antisocial.

b. a scientist who studies ants.

c. a generous contributor to charity.

REFERENCE FRAMEWORKS: THE ACADEMIC CONNECTION 4

Because it is such a versatile pattern, comparison/contrast appears across the college curriculum in a variety of ways. First, since in any subject we learn new information by relating it to what we know, we are constantly noting similarities and differences in traits, structure, or functions. Also, many survey courses—such as those in history, anthropology, or art—cover wide areas and rely on comparison and contrast in moving from topic to topic. For example, a course in Great American Civilizations that surveys the Inca, Maya, and Aztec civilizations would focus on key similarities and differences in such areas as language, religion, or social organization. In addition, many courses in a variety of fields are built on the idea pattern of comparison/contrast. Below, for example, is a list taken from a representative university course catalog:

Comparative Religions

Historical/Comparative Linguistics

Comparative Animal Physiology

Comparative Vertebrate Anatomy

Comparative Government

Understanding Cultural Differences

Finally, an entire area of study can be built on a comparative foundation. A traditional example has been the field of Comparative Literatures.

You can use your understanding of this pattern to improve your grades on tests and papers. Many test questions, and especially essay questions, ask you to make comparisons and contrasts. You can prepare for these in your classroom note taking and in reading your textbooks by creating pattern maps. Also, think about comparison/contrast when you are planning a report or research paper. If the pattern matches up with what the assignment asks for and with what you wish to say, selecting and organizing your materials becomes a lot easier.

COMPARISON AND CONTRAST: CULTURE AND IDENTITY

Cultural differences provide fuel for an ongoing dialogue on similarities, differences, and values. The following article gives a personal perspective on how cultures can limit or deny choices life offers us—and create serious consequences if certain choices are followed. The narrator here relates events from the personal history of her family. The narrative deals with a specific culture—that of India—but has a much broader application.

PREVIEWING *LALITA MASHI* BY CHITRA BANERJEE DIVAKARUNI

Setting Your Reading Goals

The title is the name of a person. An obvious starting place for determining a main idea would be to ask this question: What is the author/narrator's connection to Lalita Mashi? Read the opening incident in the first few paragraphs and try to figure out what is going on. You'll get a better grasp of the main idea by reading the two concluding paragraphs (42–43). These should give you enough information to complete the following tentative main idea hypothesis:

The author feels connected to her aunt because they both

_____

_____

_____

Preview Vocabulary

stiletto (2)	shaped like a small, slender, tapering dagger
legacies (5)	inheritances; what is passed down from ancestors
mantras (10)	sacred formulas used in prayer and incantation (Hinduism)
astrologer (11)	one who studies heavenly bodies as influencing human history
conches (11)	horns made from shells
bullock (11)	a steer or young bull
dowry (11)	money, property, or goods brought by a wife to her husband at marriage
palanquin (11)	a covered litter carried by poles on the shoulders of four men (East Asia)
jaggery (14)	an unrefined type of sugar

tenuous (17)	not substantial or solidly based
gauge (17)	measure, estimate, evaluate
immaculate (20)	spotless, pure
hookah (20)	a smoking pot with a long tube passing through water (East)
dank (33)	unpleasantly wet and humid
filial (35)	having the relationship of child to parent
wayward (36)	willfully stubborn, disobedient
karma (37)	the totality of a person's existence as it determines fate or destiny (Hinduism and Buddhism)
inexorable (37)	inescapable; unchangeable
translucent (42)	capable of transmitting light

Annotating as You Read

Following the introductory incident, be on the lookout for clues to the author's main point. Pay particular attention to paragraphs 5 and 28, along with the conclusion (42–43). Look for a connection between the title character and the narrator that is more than just a blood relationship. Try to sort out these parallels and differences that involve significant cultural norms and values; you may find it useful to construct your own comparison/contrast pattern map. Also pay attention to time sequence; the details of the story are not given in strict chronological order. Make annotations in the margins where needed to keep these relationships clear.

Lalita Mashi

by Chitra Banerjee Divakaruni

1   The other day I saw Lalita Mashi, my mother's oldest sister. Suddenly, shockingly. But I should have expected it. In recent years she has always come to me this way.

2   I was standing on the platform of the Oakland BART station, my attaché case filled with slides and spreadsheets, on my way to the City, where a committee of heavy-jowled old men were waiting for me to try to persuade them to change the way they do things. Dressed in my power outfit—navy-blue

---

Chitra Banerjee Divakaruni, "Lalita Mashi." (Chitra Banerjee Divakaruni, 1995). Reprinted by permission of the author.

skirt and jacket, deep red silk blouse, pearls, stiletto heels—I felt confident, ready for them. I knew my presentation would go perfectly.

3   Then I saw her. She was sitting by the window of a train going in the other direction, her hair caught back loosely in a knot, her chin propped by her palm. It was a posture I knew so well my breath caught in my throat. And suddenly I was six years old again, back in my grandfather's house in a tiny Bengal village.

4   "Mashi," I called, "Lalita Mashi!" although I knew she couldn't possibly hear me through the double layered glass. I waved frantically, trying to make her look up. But she was intent on something in the sky that only she could see. The warning beeps sounded, the doors closed, the train began to pull away. I dropped my case and started running along the platform, the gleaming electric tracks separating me from her. People stared. Still I ran, stumbling in my high heels, throwing out an arm for balance. Perhaps that desperate movement finally caught her eye, because she looked up. She was too far for me to read the expression on her face—recognition? bewilderment?—but the face itself I knew without a doubt. It was her face, yes, just the way it had been the last time I saw it. Except of, of course, it couldn't be, even if by some unaccountable magic she had remained unchanged by time. Because Lalita Mashi died twenty-four years ago, halfway around the world, in the village of her father, where she had lived (except for one brief year) all her life....

5   Of the many women in my family that I've known and loved, who have shaped my life and thinking, whose legacies of pain and shame and courage I have carried within, why is it I remember Lalita Mashi so clearly? I only knew her for a few years—she died when I was six—and after her death her name was never mentioned in the family. Perhaps it is the mystery that clings to her story, the faint odor of disgrace. Perhaps it is because I, the defiant daughter who left the protection of the family to come to America, who faced their bewilderment and fought their anger, know that she and I are two of a kind.

6   Mashi was born in the early years of the twentieth century in the village of Mashagram in Bengal, the first child of the Mukherjee household. Hers was a respected family; not only was her father—my grandfather—a Brahmin, but he also owned a good amount of fertile paddy land. His was one of the few homes in the village built of brick instead of black mud.

7   A daughter was only born to a family as a loan. Unlike a son, she couldn't carry forth the family name. Nor could she, at the yearly memorial services, offer rice and water to the spirits of departed ancestors. One might as well return her to her true home, her husband's house, as soon as possible. Grandfather knew that a woman's fragile beauty tarnishes soon, her good name even sooner. A grown daughter in the house is more dangerous than a firebrand in a field of ripe grain. Besides, he had two other daughters he needed to find husbands for.

8   This does not mean that my grandfather didn't love Lalita Mashi. She was a girl-child, yes, but his oldest, the first baby he had held in his arms, on whose forehead he had pressed the kiss of blessing. Perhaps he had walked up and down with her on nights when his wife was too tired to do so, whispering to quieten her crying. *Hush, my moonbeam, my little bird.* Even to an Indian father that would count for something.

9   I imagine my grandfather sparing no efforts to find Lalita Mashi a suitable husband, sending matchmakers to all the nearby villages to inquire after young men whose families were of the same standing as his, whose horoscopes matched his daughter's. And when he discovered such a man, he spared no expense for the wedding, inviting people from three villages to admire the style with which a daughter of the Mukherjee house was sent off to her in-laws.

10   I see Mashi being brought into the marriage courtyard, under the silk canopy where the bridegroom is sitting. Red-veiled, wrapped in a red-gold Banarasi silk (the color of married bliss), she keeps her eyes tightly closed, for it would be bad luck to see her husband's face before the priest had recited the proper mantras. Is she frightened at the thought of leaving her familiar world behind? Does she struggle to hold back tears as she walks around the fire with the stranger who is now her master, to whom society has given every right over her body and spirit?

11   The next morning the bride and groom start on their journey home at the exact auspicious moment specified by the family astrologer. Conches sound, women strew their path with flowers and rice and prayers for strong sons, and five bullock carts filled with dowry follow their painted palanquin along the dusty village road.

12   But the old astrologer must have read the signs wrong. For soon my aunt is back again. Only this time she returns weeping, stripped of her jewelry and dressed in the coarse white cloth that widows wear. The servant who brings her back carries a letter from her in-laws. The letter states that they never want to see her face again, for surely it is her bad luck that caused their son to die of typhoid within a year of his marriage....

13   Mashi's story is ordinary enough—the story, I think, of many young widows of the time. She had the misfortune to fall in love. It was a misfortune because though in far off Calcutta changes had begun to take place, in the villages a widow of good family would never be allowed to remarry—if marriage was at all what the man Mashi loved had in his mind.

14   Who it was my mother never knew. Lalita Mashi had whispered a few words to her on Mother's last visit, feverish and hasty, not making total sense. But it was Durga Puja, the busiest time of the year. New clothes had to be stitched for the children and dyed in auspicious colors, sweet coconut-and-jaggery balls to be ground and cooked, the floors decorated with traditional

good-luck designs painted with rice paste. My mother's place was with the other married women, stirring enormous pots of *khichuri,* the thick lentil-rice soup with which all visitors would be fed, frying *brinjals* and yellow squash and fresh-picked sweet potatoes. She wouldn't have had much of an opportunity to be alone with her widow-sister—who was expected to keep to her room—to ask her questions, or even to warn.

15   "But who do you think it might have been?" I ask.

16   She shrugs. The identity of the man is not important. All that matters is the enormity of Mashi's crimes, her betrayal of the family....

17   Lalita Mashi must have known how it would end. All the ancient tales of doomed lovers she—and I—had grown up on would have left no doubts in her mind. Why then did she rush toward destruction, like the rain flies that flung themselves into our kerosene lamps on monsoon nights? Why did she choose to bring shame on the family I know she loved? Why did she risk their hatred, their stern forgetting—not just in this life but even after, into the eternities? I cannot believe it was for the sex, or even for romantic passion. It was, I think, something more complex and deliberate, rising from a deeper, more urgent need. But for proof I can offer, once again, only a brief and tenuous memory:

> Those nights in Grandfather's house, before we went to bed, Lalita Mashi would extinguish the oil lamp by pinching the flaming wick with her fingers.
> "But doesn't it hurt?" I had asked more than once, distressed.
> Mashi had smiled. Only now, years later, I can gauge the sadness of that smile.
> "Sometimes the pain is the only way I know I'm alive, *shona.*"

18   All that month while the family was trying to arrange a match for Susheela, her youngest sister, Lalita Mashi was restless and distracted. She would burst into tears for no reason at all. She burnt the simplest curries, scolded the children for the littlest pranks. Even her mother, busy as she was putting together jewelry and saris for the dowry, noticed the change in her and dosed her with the juice of *tulsi* leaves in case she was coming down with *kalajour,* the black fever. *Jealousy,* whispered the sisters-in-law behind their veils. *Pure jealousy of Susheela.*

19   Was Mashi counting the days with terror until it was well past her time of month, until the nausea and tiredness and aching breasts left no doubts in her mind of her body's betrayal? Was she trying to decide whether to wrench herself away from all that was loved and familiar for an uncertain future from which there was no turning back? Or was the man—tired with waiting or afraid of reprisal—gone already, so that she was contemplating the final choice he had left to her?

20   Sitting face to face with my mother as she braids her hair into tight obe-dience, I remember another day. It is late summer, almost the end of my vaca-tion. Barefoot from play, I run into the dim living room decorated with old-fashioned oil lamps and clouded mirrors in mahogany frames. Heavy shades of *khush-khush* glass, dampened against the heat, cover the windows. Yes, here's grandfather, just as I hoped, reclining in his favorite easy chair, immaculate in his ivory kurta, his hookah in his hand. Maybe I can climb onto his lap and get him to finish the story of the evil magician and the princess of gold mountain.

21   Then I notice the young woman standing in front of him, twisting the edge of her widow's sari.

22   "Please, Father," she pleads, looking down at her hands.

23   "No," says the old man, his voice dispassionate. "I've made my deci-sion already."

24   He closes his eyes and draws on the hookah as though the woman in front of him did not exist. Lalita Mashi makes a small, choking sound and runs from the room, holding her hands to her face. The rush of her white sari stirs the air of the room so that I can smell for a moment the faint, damp fra-grance of the *khush-khush* curtains.

25   What could she have wanted so much? What could have been so forbid-den that her father, usually so loving, would deny her this ruthlessly?

26   "Mashi," I cry, but there is no reply, only the British clock painted with happy shepherds and shepherdesses that ticks and ticks on the wall behind Grandfather's head.

27   It is the last memory I have of Mashi.

28   It is the memory that will finally give me the courage to leave Calcutta, to tear through the suffocating cocoon of family in which we had both always lived, and strike out for the unknown.

29   Three weeks after Mashi disappeared, my mother told me, they found the body in the *dighi*. It had floated up among the *shapla* flowers on the far end, naked and bloated. No one was sure how long it had been in the water.

30   "There was a lot of bad talk," Mother said, "and the marriage the fam-ily had arranged for Susheela fell through." There is no anger in her voice, or blame. Only sorrow.

31   Even now, years later, I dream of Lalita Mashi on that last night. The air is still, as before a storm, and only the cry of a lone jackal, eerily like a woman's, wavers along it. Before she steps over the threshold of the house to which there is no coming back, Mashi stops for a moment outside the new baby's room, listens for a cry. Hesitates, pressing a hand to the growing curve of her belly. Then she is running, her shadow long and trembly behind her, yearning backward to those ocher walls. At the edge of the lake she stops to pick up the stones, choosing the smoothest, roundest ones. The water gleams

faintly in the light of the waning moon. When she steps in, it is not cold like she had feared but warm, warm, a lover's kiss. She pushes off without a sound, as gracefully as though she were a white-plumed waterbird.

32   But what when her arms and legs grow too tired to carry her further, when the stones tied to her sari begin to weigh her down? And the water itself becomes a black hand squeezing her lungs, pulling her under? Does she struggle then, does she cry out her lover's name? Does she try to untie the stones and swim back to shore because the worst life is better than this breathless, choking end?

33   I am not sure. The dream always grows murky at this point, a swirl of rain and wind and dank, black lake mud, the smell of which will persist in my nostrils long after I wake. But her face—I sometimes see it in the last moments of the dream, framed by a bare arm flailing in wet moonlight, its mouth opening in a furious, futile cry. Sometimes it is my face.

34   One time when I wake, weeping, I call my mother in Calcutta.

35   "You killed Mashi, all of you," I cry, liberated from the usual filial courtesies by darkness and fear and pain. "You left her no other course of action."

36   A moment of silence at the other end. Then my mother's voice, calm as always. "She knew the rules, Lalita, the dangers." The edge of warning in her voice is meant for me too—the wayward niece of a wayward aunt.

37   Much as I wish to, I cannot deny her words, the truth in them. What is the truth except that which we have made so by believing in it, generation after generation? And so a new dream is added to my old one. In it the wheel of karma rises, enormous, inexorable, the color of thunder. With a grating roar it rolls forward, gaining on the tiny figure of my aunt, who has set it in motion. She has made no effort to run, to escape it. She believes in it too.

38   But a few weeks later a brief note reaches me. It is in my mother's hand, unsigned—perhaps her attempt at consolation, for a mother must take part in the heartaches of her daughter, even a wayward one.

39   "There were no identifying marks on the body," says the note. "The face was completely eaten by fish. It could have been any young woman."

40   I've seen Lalita Mashi many times since then, in the airport as I rush toward my gate, in a crowded vegetable market, at the other end of a dimly lit restaurant filled with elegant diners. I no longer try to go to her. I know from experience that when I get close enough, she will turn into someone else and give me a polite, inquiring glance.

41   But it doesn't matter. Because I have another picture now inside my head to counter the dream of drowning, the dream of the crushing wheel. In it a young woman is leaving her father's home at night. She stops for a moment outside the new baby's room, listens for a cry. Presses her hand to the growing curve of her belly. Then she steps resolutely over the threshold and begins to walk. She is going to the station at the edge of the bamboo forest where a

night train will stop in an hour's time. She will meet her lover there, and together they will travel to their new life.

42   Or perhaps the woman is alone. There is no man. He left a long time ago, as all men ultimately do. But the woman doesn't care. She knows now that she has always been alone. It is the nature of her condition, of being female, though throughout her life she has tried to hide it—in wish dreams, in gossip, in frenzied activities—like her mother, and her mother, and her mother before her. The realization makes her feel translucent, weightless, as though she could lift off the ground at any moment.

43   The woman's arms swing freely by her side, for she is carrying no baggage. She knows that nothing from her old life will fit into her new one, the one she—and I—cannot quite imagine yet. Not the taboos, not the memories. She will have to create all anew, out of herself, as the mother goddess, Prakriti, does after the end of the world. The bamboo trees rustle like footsteps in the rising wind. She doesn't look back. She walks lightly, this woman, having shed her fears along with her hopes, and, as she makes her way across the moonlit land, I hear her sing.

Exercise 11.5

Circle the correct letter choice.

1. The main idea is partially stated in several places. Which of the following is the most comprehensive statement of the main idea?

   a. Love relationships without social approval are a danger for the participants in all cultures of the world.

   b. Identification with the dilemma of her aunt helped the narrator escape the limitations of traditional family and gender roles imposed on women by society.

   c. The tragic story of her aunt in India, the narrator's battle with her family, finally taking charge of her own life and succeeding in America.

   d. Rather than her betraying her family, it was her family that really betrayed Lalita Mashi.

2. The author states at the end of paragraph 4 that her aunt had died twenty-four years ago. What earlier detail clues us that the narrator is only imagining that she sees her aunt?

   a. "she couldn't possibly hear me through the double-layered glass"

   b. "she was intent on something in the sky that only she could see"

c. "the face itself I knew without a doubt"

d. "It was her face, yes, just the way it had been the last time I saw it."

3. What two reasons given in paragraph 7 motivated Mashi's father to get her married soon?

a. A daughter in the home is a liability, and he had others to marry off.

b. A daughter was only a loan, and Mashi had caused problems already.

c. A daughter's true home is her husband's, and Mashi's beauty was fading fast.

4. What word in paragraph 8 foreshadows her father's later cold rejection of Mashi's last plea (21–24)?

a. perhaps

b. hush

c. even

d. count

5. The prefix *dis* has a number of meanings: "not, without, apart, opposite, do the opposite of." In which of these four words from the article does *dis* mean "do the opposite of"?

a. disappeared

b. distracted

c. dispassionate

d. distressed

6. In the last paragraph the narrator is really describing

a. what Lalita Mashi realized as she was dying.

b. an actual train ride that her aunt took.

c. the narrator's own feelings when she discarded her old life.

d. the futility of trying to escape from the past.

7. The selection deals mainly with the aunt's story, along with a few details of the narrator's life. The author, however, suggests that their situation applies to that of all women. Which paragraph most clearly states that connection?

a. paragraph 5

b. paragraph 28

c. paragraph 36

d. paragraph 42

8. "Lalita Mashi was restless and distracted. She would burst into tears for no reason at all…. *Jealousy,* whispered the sisters-in-law behind their veils. *Pure jealousy of Susheela.*" (18) The sisters-in-law may have committed which logical fallacy here?

   a. false analogy

   b. guilt by association

   c. name-calling

   d. hasty generalization

9. "'There was a lot of bad talk,' Mother said, 'and the marriage the family had arranged for Susheela fell through.'" (30) What logical fallacy may underlie the conclusion this sentence suggests?

   a. false analogy

   b. hasty generalization

   c. faulty causation

   d. guilt by association

Put INF next to any of the following that are inferences strongly suggested by the details of paragraph 2.

10. _____ The narrator feels the committee members are stubborn and close-minded.

11. _____ She is president of the company she is making the presentation to.

12. _____ She believes that clothes are an important factor in combating gender bias.

13. _____ She lacks self-confidence.

Writing Context Sentences

Use the definitions and the general situation clues below to write context sentences of your own. Remember: your goal is to give enough specific clues so that someone unfamiliar with the word could guess its meaning from your sentence.

1. *auspicious:* affording a favorable beginning

   Situation clue: person does well in first test, first games, or first days of work

   Sentence: _____

   _____

   _____

2. *reprisal:* retaliation, revenge

    Situation clue: one person or group injures another

    Sentence: _____

    _____

    _____

3. *ruthlessly:* without pity

    Situation clue: winning something and wouldn't let up on opponent

    Sentence: _____

    _____

    _____

4. *futile:* useless, hopeless

    Situation clue: cramming for a test

    Sentence: _____

    _____

    _____

5. *frenzied:* wildly, uncontrollably excited

    Situation clue: fans at a game or concert

    Sentence: _____

    _____

    _____

Figurative Language

Identify the following sentences from the reading selection as simile, metaphor, *or* analogy.

1. _____ A grown daughter in the house is more dangerous than a firebrand in a field of ripe grain.

2. _____ Why then did she rush toward destruction, like the rain flies that flung themselves into our kerosene lamps on monsoon nights?

3. _____ The water gleams faintly in the light of the waning moon. When she steps in, it is not cold like she had feared but warm, warm, a lover's kiss.

4. _____ *Hush, my moonbeam, my little bird.*

5. _____ It … will finally give me the courage to leave Calcutta, to tear through the suffocating cocoon of family in which we had both always lived.

6. _____ The wheel of karma rises, enormous, inexorable, the color of thunder. With a grating roar it rolls forward, gaining on the tiny figure of my aunt, who has set it in motion.

7. _____ The water itself becomes a black hand squeezing her lungs, pulling her under.

8. _____ She will have to create all anew, out of herself, as the mother goddess, Prakriti, does after the end of the world.

9. _____ The bamboo trees rustle like footsteps in the rising wind.

10. _____ She pushes off without a sound, as gracefully as though she were a white-plumed waterbird.

Mapping Exercises

1. Despite their brief acquaintance, the author clearly feels a close kinship with her aunt: "She and I are two of a kind" (5); "the wayward niece of a wayward aunt." (36) To chart the parallels and contrasts between the author and her aunt, use the details below to complete the pattern map.

   ■ left by train, with or without a man
   ■ decided not to defy family, chose to submit to tradition
   ■ "betrays" family by having an affair and getting pregnant
   ■ be an obedient daughter, stay in family "cocoon"
   ■ drowned herself in despair
   ■ defied tradition and left for America

	Lalita Mashi	Author/Narrator
Trouble began when she		rejected family's protection and role of obedient daughter.
Traditional rule demands she	accept the passive, lonely life of a widow.	
Action each finally took		
Action each might have taken		

2. The author does not stay with strict chronological order in developing her main idea. Below is the order in which various actions were introduced into the text. Rearrange them on the timeline that follows in the order in which they actually would occur:

- The author thinks she sees Lalita Mashi at the BART station. (1–4)
- Mashi was born in the early years of the twentieth century. (6)
- Mashi is married and her husband dies. (7–12)
- The author asks her mother who the man might have been. (15–16)
- Mashi's father refuses her request. (21–24)
- The body is discovered three weeks later. (29)
- Mashi's death is traced in imaginative detail. (31–33)
- Taking control of her life results in new sensations. (42–43)

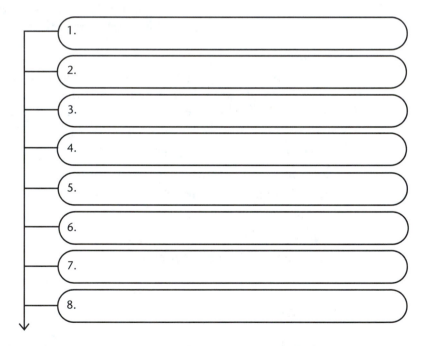

1.

2.

3.

4.

5.

6.

7.

8.

Questions for Writing/Small-Group Discussion

1. "She will have to create all anew, out of herself, as the mother goddess, Prakriti, does after the end of the world." (43) Is it really possible to create an entirely new self? Could you walk away from your family, culture, and current identity and create a new you? Would you wish to?

2. It is much easier to see limitations in other cultures than in our own. Can you give some examples in American culture of the way that gender roles or social mores stifle individuality or unfairly narrow our personal choices?

COMPARISON AND CONTRAST: FALLACIES AND EMOTIONAL APPEALS

A number of misleading reasoning techniques involve comparison and contrast, some of which employ figurative language like simile, metaphor, and analogy. We can identify two logical fallacies among these.

FALSE ANALOGY

Analogies are useful to describe and explain, but danger comes when an analogy is offered as a *proof* rather than an aid to understanding. False analogy occurs in arguments which maintain that because two things share a trait or relationship, they must also share another. Recall the earlier analogy that compared our democratic system to a ship:

> The nation might be compared to a ship, the president to a captain, the government officials to the crew, and the general population to the passengers; an international threat might be likened to a storm.

Suppose at this point, however, that the writer goes on to add this conclusion:

> Therefore, just as with the captain of a ship, in times of peril we must give the president unquestioned authority over the direction of the nation.

The analogy between a ship and the nation may help us *understand* the workings of the government but it does not *prove* anything. The nation is not a ship; the president is not a sea captain. The analogy ignores our Constitution that limits and defines the powers of branches of the government, and it leaves the door wide open by not defining exactly what a "time of peril" is. As an argument, this will not hold water: it is a false analogy.

EITHER/OR THINKING

This fallacy assumes that there are only two—or a limited number—of alternatives. The argument usually attempts to show one is correct simply by ruling out the others. In its crudest form, the fallacy is quite obvious:

> Either you stole the bracelet or your brother did. He was with me at the time, so you must be the one who did it.

Obviously the problem with either/or thinking is that it ignores the possibility of other explanations or choices. In the above illustration, for example, there may be a number of persons with access to the bracelet; or it may have simply been misplaced.

Two appeals to the emotions involving comparison and contrast appear frequently, in political campaigning and in magazine advertisements.

TRANSFER

This technique tries to transfer our feelings about—or the traits of—a person, object, or symbol, to the person or product that is being promoted. In political campaigns, for example, candidates will attempt to be photographed next to national symbols like the flag or at monuments like the Statue of Liberty. Sports teams often select names that contain built-in metaphors of power, speed, or aggressiveness: Raiders, Seahawks, Rams, Bulls. The U.S. Post Office uses the symbol of the eagle, hoping that the suggestion of speed and superiority will transfer to how we view mail handling. Visual advertisements are full of transfer techniques: we are invited to identify with sophisticated models or rugged cowboys smoking cigarettes, or to associate a far-off desert island with a bottle of rum. The text accompanying an advertisement may make an explicit transfer through comparison—"Chevy Blazer: Like a Rock." Sometimes transfers in advertisements imply extended comparisons; in these cases, we can have the suggestion of an analogy rather than a simple simile or metaphor.

TESTIMONIAL

This is a technique that uses a spokesperson to enhance the product or service being sold. It involves transfer when it uses celebrities to speak for—or have their picture associated with—a product. We are invited to transfer our admiration or respect for them to the product they are endorsing. In a slightly different format, testimonial is used for the plain folks appeal—an ordinary citizen who is an arthritis sufferer, for instance, testifying to the effectiveness of a pain product. The problem with testimonial in any form is that, from a rational point of view, endorsement by a nonexpert is not likely to be a valid proof of quality.

Exercise 11.6

Identify the following slogans and advertisements as EO *for either/or;* TRANS *for transfer or* TEST *for testimonial. For transfers that suggest a more extended analogy, write* TA *for transfer/analogy.*

    1. _____ "Now you can be an Olympic hero just by using your Visa Card. Because Visa will make a donation … every time you use your card."

2. _____ "Other distilleries add up to twice as much water to their bourbon as we do. Are they more proud of their water? Or less proud of their bourbon?"

3. _____ "Who better to endorse the all-American, nutrient-rich, wholesome beverage than me?" (Tennis star Pete Sampras promoting milk)

4. _____ "Introducing the unique business class cradle seat. It doesn't simply recline but tilts as a whole, raising your knees and relieving your body of stress and pressure. Lullaby not included." (British Airways ad)

5. _____ "Children are our most important source for tomorrow ... and Amway has more products than you ever imagined, especially for kids."

6. _____ "America: Love it or leave it."

7. _____ "It's no surprise that only the smartest, most aggressive SUVs are able to climb their way to the top of the automotive food chain. What's also a surprise is that's where you'll find Toyota 4Runner."

8. _____ "But that's why now, more than ever, we need the Boys & Girls Club. It's a positive place where thousands of people like Billy Thomas help young people succeed. Does it work? It did for me." (Actor Denzel Washington)

9. _____ "When guns are outlawed, only outlaws will have guns."

10. _____ "Very quiet and serene, the Chevy Blazer has more features than a movie theater. Stretch out and enjoy the view."

CHAPTER REVIEW

Read the following extract, then circle the correct letter choice.

An advantage of a two-party system is that it promotes majoritarian government. Because there are only two parties, one is certain to win a majority of the votes and seats in Congress. There will be no deadlocks caused by several minority parties. The two-party system also enhances government's legitimacy. Winning a majority of the votes means that a party has a clearer mandate to govern.

In contrast, multiparty systems rarely find a single party in control. In Italy, for example, no party is close to having a majority; control passes from different ruling coalitions several times a year. In Israel, neither of the major parties controls a majority and both are forced to bargain with extremely conservative religious parties, which results in tilting national policy in a direction the majority of the voters oppose.

(Welch et al., *American Government*, 4th ed., 153)

1. Which of the following best represents the main idea of the first paragraph?

   a. An advantage of a two-party system is that it promotes majoritarian government.

   b. A two-party system promotes majoritarian government because there will be no deadlocks.

   c. A two-party system promotes majoritarian government and also enhances government's legitimacy.

   d. The two-party system enhances government's legitimacy because one party has the right to do whatever it wants to.

2. Which of the following best states the main idea for the multiparagraph unit?

   a. A two-party system promotes majoritarian government and also enhances government's legitimacy.

   b. A two-party system promotes majoritarian government because there will be no deadlocks, whereas multiparty systems rarely find a single party in control.

   c. A two-party system promotes majoritarian government and also enhances government's legitimacy, whereas multiparty systems rarely find a single party in control.

   d. The two-party system enhances government's legitimacy, whereas in some countries no party is close to having a majority.

3. The *overall* comparison/contrast method of development of the two-paragraph unit is

   a. block.

   b. point by point.

   c. statement of comparison/contrast developed by examples.

   d. none of the above

4. The transition between the two parts of the unit is signaled by which word or phrase?

   a. because

   b. also

   c. in contrast

   d. for example

5. The second paragraph of the contrast unit is developed by a main pattern of
   a. cause/effect.
   b. time sequence.
   c. classification.
   d. description/support.

6. A person described as a "pseudo-intellectual" is
   a. brilliant.
   b. phony.
   c. sophisticated.

Identify the items below with the letter of one of the following:
   A. analogy
   B. transfer
   C. simile
   D. either/or reasoning

7. _____ A teacher often spends less time teaching than acting as a prison warden.

8. _____ You need to decide on a career choice soon. Your mother is a teacher. Your father is a doctor. Which one is it going to be?

9. _____ Walking into a classroom on your first day as a teacher is like leaving your house and walking into a storm. No matter how well prepared you are, you're still not ready for that first blast that may blow all your plans into the air.

10. _____ If you've ever been warmed by the winter's sun, you already know the feeling of Cognac Hennessy.

READING PORTFOLIO   *Comparison and Contrast*

1. *Articles of comparison/contrast are more likely to be found in magazines than in newspapers;* in the latter, you will have more luck in the feature sections rather than the front pages. Articles that compare and contrast are represented in all kinds of interest areas: sports, politics, entertainment, consumer products.

2. *In your summary, try to focus on the main points and judgments being made in the comparison.* Pay particular attention to the patterns in your article: block, point by point, or some other variation. Identifying the pattern combinations and mapping the article accordingly will make your summary easier to write.

3. *You should have a number of options for developing your response section.* If the article is giving a factual, objective comparison of two things, is it accurate? You may use your own experience here to support your view. If an article is evaluative, do you agree with the judgment that one thing is better than the other? If not, support your own views on the topic.

4. *Articles that develop a lengthy analogy are rare and often are very difficult in thought and language.* If you do locate an article that you wish to analyze, check first with your instructor. In evaluating an analogy, you will want to determine how it helps to explain a topic and whether or not it draws any conclusions through false analogy.

5. *Follow the directions as before for length and filing of your article.*

PART III

Persuasion to Action

In Part II, you went beyond the simple gathering of information to questions of proof that require much more active thinking. Persuading a reader to truth, however, is not always the end of an author's intention; a writer may also ask for action to bring about useful changes, create new opportunities, or solve problems. Persuasive writing adds more complexity to our job as readers. We must still look for truth: are the author's facts straight, does the evidence support the analysis? But we must also ask questions of value and action: is the action just and humane, is there a better alternative?

There are two main idea patterns in persuasion. Problem/solution pushes for action mainly on the strength of its proofs and analyses; opinion/reason presents argumentative reasons to the reader, along with appeals to shared values. These two patterns are at the heart of academic dialogue and touch every aspect of our lives. In our personal relationships with friends and family and in our roles within the community, we are constantly identifying and solving problems or giving and receiving advice. Every field of study in college, no matter how informational and factual it may seem at first, will eventually lead you to its own special thorny problems and debatable issues. Finally, throughout all professions, the demand from employers, more and more, is for people who are problem solvers, who can think critically and discuss issues with reason and insight. Learning to recognize, understand, and use these patterns is well worth your time and effort.

In persuasive writing, feelings play a big role and tempers can rise. If we close our minds to protect our self-interests, we can easily lose sight of our commitment to reaching a thoughtful judgment. It is very important that you learn how to recognize the ways in which people manipulate evidence, use faulty arguments, or resort to emotional appeals.

CHAPTER

12

Determining What Needs to Be Done: Problems and Solutions

Crime. Gangs. Drugs. AIDS. Domestic violence, terrorism, hate speech, child abuse, tuition fees, acne, bad breath. Large and small, public and private, real or imagined, such concerns take up a great deal of our time. Newspaper and magazine articles, books, call-in radio programs, and television talk shows provide us with a daily diet of social and personal crises, and offer a wide range of suggestions on how to deal with them. Thus today's media-driven world constantly reminds us of the importance of problem/solution as we struggle in our daily lives.

■ CHAPTER PREVIEW

In this chapter you will

- ■ Review the pattern elements in problem/solution
- ■ Distinguish among truth, value, and action components
- ■ Analyze articles with approaches to a problem area
- ■ Discover how humor and irony can be used effectively in problem/solution
- ■ Meet two logical fallacies common to the pattern
- ■ Analyze an article of problem/solution for your Reading Portfolio

Yerou have already worked at length with the pattern of cause/effect, the core of problem/solution. The difference between these patterns is that pure cause/effect aims only at explaining why something has happened or will happen: why a political election was lost, why a currency has suddenly lost value, why a team will win the Super Bowl. In problem/solution, cause/effect relationships are still central but the focus extends to a situation seen as wrong or bad and in need of fixing. We go beyond why. We want to know why our team lost the Super Bowl, but we may view those causes as a problem that needs to be fixed: fire the coach, replace the general manager, or change team members.

▩ IDENTIFYING PROBLEM/SOLUTION ELEMENTS

The language of problem/solution is a definite help in identifying the pattern and its elements. Often the words *problem* and *solution* or *solve* appear (sometimes in the title) and the other pattern elements require the frequent use of words common to cause/effect (see Chapter 2 for a complete list).

In identifying problem/solution pattern elements, it is helpful to think of an interconnected problem area. What an author might specify as a problem really depends on interest and focus. Problems can be viewed as either causes or effects, and solutions are potential causes, proposed in order to produce an effect: a desirable result. Take, for example, a problem area such as "teenage pregnancy." Under this topic would fall factors which are both causes and effects. A book might touch on many or all of these, but the average article would limit its scope. An author might choose to focus on one of the causes: poor self-esteem might be identified as a central problem, with teenage pregnancy as the effect. The author would then identify causes of poor self-esteem and offer solutions to combat them. Or, working from the other end, another author might choose one of the effects (for example, at-risk children) as the problem. In this case, teenage pregnancy is now the cause, and the solution section may be aimed at doing something about the effects on the child who is at risk: providing parenting classes, compensatory education programs, or foster home placement.

Because different elements can be emphasized, there is a good deal of variety in the pattern of problem/solution. A problem might be seen as so wide-spread and unavoidable (television, for example) that we are concerned only with its effects, since eliminating it is not a realistic option. In this case, the effects/solution sections would dominate. At other times our emphasis may be on a problem and its causes (for example, the dysfunctional family), and our solutions may be short and tentative. Indeed, in cases where a writer has no definite solution, we may be left with only a warning that something must be done and done soon.

Although problem/solution can be the pattern of a single sentence, it is much more likely to be found in larger structures. Whether paragraph or article length, however, the pattern will present some difficulty in formulating the main idea because pattern elements become scattered. In paragraphs and longer passages, one sentence might summarize the problem, another the causes or effects, yet another the solution, but usually no single main idea sentence occurs. Problem/solution is therefore a pattern in which bringing together a divided main idea or creating an implied main idea sentence is more often the rule than the exception.

Using a pattern map often can help you see the relationship of the parts to the whole and help you to determine a comprehensive main idea statement. In the articles in this chapter, pattern maps have been labeled and some paragraph numbers included to help you identify pattern elements. Completing the pattern maps carefully will help you greatly in answering the questions following the readings.

■ COMPONENTS IN PROBLEM/SOLUTION ANALYSIS

Persuasive writing can be very demanding, requiring the reader to be actively, at times emotionally, involved. A reader has three components to deal with in a problem/solution proposal.

TRUTH COMPONENT

This relates to the evidence presented to prove the existence of a problem, its causes and effects, and their connections. Suppose, for example, you read the following problem statement in an article:

> Our rising national debt is being fueled by the skyrocketing costs of health care services.

Your first job is to decide if this problem really exists and whether the analysis of the cause/effect relationship is sound: are the costs of services causing more debt?

- Is debt rising?
- Are health costs escalating?
- Does evidence show a connection?

The proposed solution is, of course, something that has not yet occurred. The author is simply maintaining it will correct or erase the problem. Suppose the author suggests the following:

> We must, unfortunately, cut back severely in the funding of health care programs—such as Medicare—for the elderly.

Just as with analyzing the problem, you must evaluate the evidence to determine whether the solution will work: will it achieve the desired result of reducing the budget deficit?

- Is Medicare funded by budget?
- Can cuts be made?
- Will such action reduce deficit?

At this point, the analysis or the solution must be either rejected as unsound or unsupported by the evidence, or found to be consistent with the evidence at hand.

VALUE COMPONENT

At times you will find a subpattern of opinion/reason used for support, but many times the author simply assumes that the solution is worthwhile and necessary. However, even if you agree with the problem/solution analysis, you still might find yourself uneasy with the proposal because it may conflict with your sense of values. This subjective component may involve a clash between your value system and that of the writer. At this point, you must bring value statements out into the open:

- Are there reasons that will justify it?
- Will it cause more harm than good?
- Is there a better alternative?

ACTION/DECISION COMPONENT

If you initially found the evidence and the cause/effect analysis to be unconvincing, you most likely would have already rejected the entire proposal. If, however, you found these to have merit, your answers to the above values questions will determine whether or not you will undertake and/or support the proposed action:

- I will support it. It is just, fair, the best choice.
- I will not support it. It might work, but it isn't right. There is a better way.

Questions about values provide a good starting point for discussion and written responses. However, discovering implied value judgments requires becoming adept at drawing inferences from the text. Some questions following the articles in this chapter will give you practice in uncovering assumptions and determining value positions.

REFERENCE FRAMEWORKS: PUBLIC ISSUES AND POLITICAL POSITIONS

Many problem/solution issues relate to political questions, and the positions taken by one side or the other side usually rest on shared political assumptions. Knowing a little about political terminology will help you place writers in relation to each other and to mainstream political parties of today.

Political positions are often visualized as creating a political spectrum. Positions to the **left** of center become increasingly **liberal**, whereas those to the **right** of center become increasingly **conservative**. In United States politics, the conservative position is held by the Republican Party—sometimes called the Grand Old Party or GOP for short; its political symbol is the elephant. Conservatives in general favor a more limited role for government; they are often suspicious of new programs promising cure-alls for social ills. They tend to look back to traditional values as the key to keeping the country on the proper path.

Conservatives tend to play down the role of environment in shaping our lives; they are more likely to believe that opportunity for advancement still exists, and they promote the importance of self-help and self-reliance in attaining a fuller life. Traditionally they have been identified as the party of business and the more well-to-do. Most prominent among Republican presidents in the last fifty years have been Dwight D. Eisenhower, Richard Nixon, and Ronald Reagan.

The Democratic Party (the donkey is its symbol) has been the major party on the left—the liberals—in American politics in the twentieth century. Traditionally, their concerns have been more identified with the rights of women, minorities, and the "have nots" of the country. Labor unions have in the past provided major support, but their power has declined in recent years. Democrats tend to emphasize the importance of social conditions in limiting opportunities and maintaining what they believe is an often unfair political and economic status quo. Thus they are more likely to support the role of government in shaping and managing our society through social programs. Presidents Franklin D. Roosevelt, Harry Truman, John F. Kennedy, and Lyndon B. Johnson provided a continuity of liberal ideas through the middle of the century.

PROBLEM/SOLUTION: SUMMARY AND REPORT

The pattern of problem/solution can be used for argument or to summarize objectively and report on actions that were taken. The next two selections illustrate the latter purpose. The first selection below—taken from an American history textbook—presents a historical problem, and its eventual solution, in a neutral and straightforward manner. The second selection summarizes the pros and cons on a problem currently causing a debate on college campuses.

PREVIEWING *THE MARSHALL PLAN* BY ROBERT A. DIVINE, T. H. BREEN, GEORGE M. FREDRICKSON, R. HAL WILLIAMS

Setting Your Reading Goals

Your task in reading a problem/solution summary is to identify clearly the various elements in the pattern. The title alone does not give a clear clue to the central problem. However, by reading the first three sentences of paragraph 1, you should be able to pinpoint what the problem was:

_____

_____

The selection is a part of larger unit on "The Onset of the Cold War." To understand what is happening, pay careful attention to the time period being discussed. Think about the following as you read.

What dates are given in the text?

What big event had concluded only a few years before?

Who are the major countries involved?

What are the main issues being discussed?

Preview Vocabulary

piecemeal (1)	piece by piece; not all at once
obsolete (1)	out of date; no longer in use
demoralized (1)	discouraged, weakened in spirit
infusion (2)	process of putting something into
satellites (3)	smaller nations under a larger nation's control
lobbied (4)	tried to influence
coup (4)	quick rebellion
bonanza (5)	source of great wealth or profits

Annotating As You Read

Circle dates and write notes in the margin to answer the questions above. Write *problem, cause, effect,* or *solution* in the margin next to each element in the pattern as you encounter it. To help locate these, look for and circle any signal words or phrases that state or suggest cause and effect relationships.

The Marshall Plan

by Robert A. Divine, T. H. Breen, George M. Fredrickson, and R. Hal Williams

1   Despite American interest in controlling Soviet expansion into Greece, western Europe was far more vital to U.S. interests than was the eastern Mediterranean. Yet by 1947, many Americans felt that western Europe was open to Soviet penetration. The problem was economic in nature. Despite $9 billion in piecemeal American loans, England, France, Italy, and the other European countries had great difficulty in recovering from World War II. Food was scarce, with millions existing on less than fifteen hundred calories a day; industrial machinery was broken down and obsolete, and workers

Divine et al., *America: Past and Present,* 5th ed., 874–876.

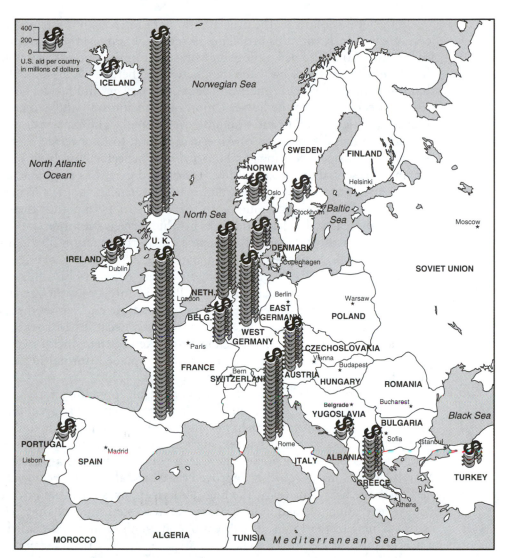

Figure 12.1   Marshall Plan Aid to Europe, 1948–1952   The Marshall Plan, also known as the European Recovery Program, provided aid totaling $13 billion to European countries following World War II. Most went to former allies Great Britain and France but former enemies Italy and West Germany also received substantial aid. To receive the grants, countries pledged to control inflation and lower tariffs.

were demoralized by years of depression and war. The cruel winter of 1947, the worst in fifty years, compounded the problem. Resentment and discontent led to growing communist voting strength, especially in Italy and France. If the United States could not reverse the process, it seemed as though all Europe might drift into the communist orbit.

2   In the weeks following the proclamation of the Truman Doctrine, American officials dealt with this problem. Secretary of State Marshall, returning from a frustrating Council of Foreign Ministers meeting in Moscow, warned that "the patient is sinking while the doctors deliberate." Acheson believed that it was time to extend American "economic power" in Europe, both "to call an effective halt to the Soviet Union's expansionism" and "to create a basis for political stability and economic well-being." The experts drew up a plan for the massive infusion of American capital to finance the economic recovery of Europe. Speaking at a Harvard commencement on June 5, 1947, Marshall presented the broad outline. He offered extensive economic aid to all the nations of Europe if they could reach agreement on ways to achieve "the revival of a working economy in the world so as to permit the emergence of political and social conditions in which free institutions can exist."

3   The fate of the Marshall Plan depended on the reaction of the Soviet Union and the U.S. Congress. Marshall had taken, in the words of one American diplomat, "a hell of a gamble" by including Russia in his offer of aid. At a meeting of the European nations in Paris in July 1947, the Soviet foreign minister ended the suspense by abruptly withdrawing. Neither the Soviet Union nor its satellites would take part, apparently because Moscow saw the Marshall Plan as an American attempt to weaken Soviet control over eastern Europe. The other European countries then made a formal request for $17 billion in assistance over the next four years.

4   Congress responded cautiously to this proposal, appointing a special joint committee to investigate. The administration lobbied vigorously, pointing out that the Marshall Plan would help the United States by stimulating trade with Europe as well as checking Soviet expansion. It was the latter argument, however, that proved decisive. When the Czech coup touched off a war scare in March 1948, Congress quickly approved the Marshall Plan by heavy majorities. Over the next four years, the huge American investment paid rich dividends, generating a broad industrial revival in western Europe that became self-sustaining by the 1950s. The threat of communist domination faded, and a prosperous Europe proved to be a bonanza for the American farmers, miners, and manufacturers.

Exercise 12.1

Mapping Problem Solution
Fill in the map with the appropriate items from the list below.

check Soviet expansion   lack of food

insure free institutions   broken machinery

growing communist influence   stimulate trade
demoralized workers   World War II
winter of 1947   resentment and discontent

PROBLEM:
Economic Breakdown in Europe

1.

2.

3.

CAUSES:

1.

2.

EFFECTS:
Danger of Soviet Expansion

1.

2.

SOLUTION:
The Marshall Plan

1.

2.

3.

Comprehension Question

Mark the following T *for True or* F *for False, according to the selection.*

1. _____ After 1947, the Mediterranean and Greece were the main concerns of the U.S.

2. _____ Prior to the Marshall Plan, Americans had loaned Europe $9 billion for recovery.

3. _____ Communism held no attraction for the workers in post–World War II Europe.

4. _____ Marshall was Secretary of the Council of Foreign Ministers who met in Moscow.

5. _____ Acheson felt it was time to extend American "economic power" into the Soviet Union.

6. _____ The Marshall plan was adopted by Congress on June 5, 1947.

7. _____ The U.S. Congress had no reservations whatsoever about the Marshall Plan.

8. _____ The Soviet Union thought the plan would weaken Soviet control in eastern Europe.

9. _____ Congress was persuaded to back the plan mainly because it would stimulate trade.

10. _____ Despite loans, Western Europe was still very dependent on aid by the end of the 1950s.

Interpreting Graphics

Use the information in Figure 12.1 to answer the questions below.

11. Which of the following would be most useful in figuring out the approximate amount of aid for each country?

   a. a compass

   b. a calculator

   c. a ruler

12. The amount of aid received by Sweden would be approximately

   a. $4,000.

   b. $400,000.

   c. $4,000,000.

   d. $400,000,000.

13. No aid was received by

   a. Portugal.

   b. Bulgaria.

   c. Austria.

   d. Iceland.

14. Aid was given

   a. to European countries who pledged to control inflation.

   b. both to European countries and the Soviet Union.

   c. only to former World War II allies.

   d. all of the above

15. The most aid was received by

   a. France.

   b. The Netherlands and Belgium combined.

   c. Denmark, Norway, and Sweden combined.

   d. United Kingdom.

PREVIEWING *STUDENTS WOOED BY CREDIT CARD PURVEYORS OFTEN OVER-COMMIT THEMSELVES* BY MARY GERAGHTY

Setting Your Reading Goals

The title and the last sentence of paragraph 1 give a clear statement of what the problem is.

Write it here: _____

Your purpose in reading is to assess the severity of the problem and whether or not the solutions seem workable. This may be an issue with which you have had some experience. Think about how much you know about the following:

   What are the going percentage rates for first-time users of credit cards?

   What type of payment requirements are common?

   What sort of penalties are assessed for late payments?

   How much are the annual fees for cards?

Preview Vocabulary

purveyors (title)	one who furnishes or supplies
saturated (1)	totally covered or filled with
pitfalls (2)	danger areas
interdictive (3)	prohibitive
incurring (4)	taking on responsibilities or consequences
frivolous (4)	trivial, not vital or necessary
abyss (5)	a bottomless gulf
"the hard sell" (8)	selling techniques using a great deal of pressure and persuasion
presumably (9)	supposedly, in a way that assumes something to be true
pervasive (11)	occurring throughout or all over
alma mater (12)	literally, "dear mother"; the college from which one graduates

Annotating As You Read

As you did in the previous textbook passage, identify the elements of the problem/solution pattern by highlighting/underlining and writing in the margins. The problem is relatively simple, but there are a number of items in each of the cause, effect, and solution areas. Also you will find some disagreements among the persons cited in the text over whether there really is a problem and, if so, what should be done about it. Mark these various points of view clearly in the margins and in the text.

Students, Wooed by Credit Card Purveyors, Often Over-Commit Themselves

by Mary Geraghty

1   When Visa says it's "everywhere you want to be," college students find that "everywhere" includes their mailboxes, the student newspaper, the student union, the university bookstore, and anywhere else a credit-card application might catch a student's eye. For years, credit-card and phone-card companies, not just Visa, have saturated campuses with promotions aimed at students. The result: Many students go heavily into debt. They struggle to pay their tuition while meeting the minimum monthly payments on several credit-card accounts.

2   Now some college officials are looking for ways to help students avoid the pitfalls of credit-card debt while taking advantage of the opportunity to start building a credit history. Some colleges offer programs during freshman orientation on the wise use of credit. Others—including Northeastern, Tufts, and Widener Universities, and Boston and Rollins Colleges—have prohibited representatives of credit-card companies from soliciting students in person on campus. Some say the bans help to protect students, but others argue that since students are sure to receive credit-card information from other sources, such a policy is ineffective.

Building a Credit History

3   "That doesn't keep their mailboxes from carrying these things," says William E. Stanford, director of financial aid at Lehigh University. "It might be an interdictive thing for at least those particular vendors, but banning their presence on campus doesn't really address the problem." Sean Healy, a spokesman for MasterCard International Inc., says attempts to limit student access to credit are "disappointing" to see. "It's critical for young adults to be able to build a credit history," he says, "and we play a valuable role in that."

Mary Geraghty, "Students Wooed by Credit-Card Purveyors, Often Over-Commit Themselves, Colleges Find" (*The Chronicle of Higher Education,* 1996). Reprinted with permission.

4   Many student-affairs officers say something needs to be done to help students deal with the companies. At a time when students are taking on larger loans to pay for college, credit-card debt can be more dangerous than ever, says Jo-Anne Thomas Vanin, dean of students at the University of Massachusetts at Amherst. Since many universities, including her own, allow tuition to be paid with credit cards, she notes, students may be using the cards to fill the gap between their loan money and the cost of attending college. "We do have a responsibility, because they're incurring this debt more and more to meet the cost of their education." Dr. Vanin says. "There certainly is some degree of what one would call frivolous buying, but I don't think that's the case all the time."

5   Freshman orientation is an obvious place to present information about making wise credit choices, adds Dr. Vanin, who hopes to have a program in place by next fall. Linda Downing, assistant dean and director of student financial planning at Rollins, has seen fewer students with credit trouble since the college began including the subject in orientation sessions for both students and parents. "Part of our focus is to make sure parents are aware that this is something that is going to happen to their children—that they will receive mailings that will give them the opportunity to receive credit cards," she says. Lehigh, too, encourages parents to talk about wise credit choices with students. "We need to give parents the sense that this is an area where students can drop off the cliff and into the abyss," says Mr. Stanford. "That way, parents can help them make better decisions about whether to get a credit card and in what circumstances to use it."

Few Students Show Up

6   The problem with offering seminars on credit has been getting students to show up. Eric S. Godfrey, assistant vice president of student affairs and director of student financial aid at the University of Washington, says the financial-aid office ended its workshops on debt management and proper use of credit cards because "attendance was spotty at best." Now, he says, the information is discussed with individual students when they meet with financial-aid officers. "Our approach has been a little less formal and more on an as-needed, one-on-one basis."

7   At Lehigh, "virtually no one" attended a program about credit decisions during freshman orientation this fall, Mr. Stanford says. "We know that unless we're offering pizza and party favors, we're probably not going to have much luck getting them in the door," he says. In fact, "party favors" of a sort are what often draw students into the world of credit in the first place. Companies show up on campus with T-shirts, note pads, pens, and other freebies for anyone who applies for a card. On many campuses, applications for credit cards are routinely slipped into customers' shopping bags at bookstores. Matthew Schlager, a Northeastern senior, says that students often fill out the applications just for the giveaways, but that once the credit cards arrive, it's tough to throw them out.

Eliminating "The Hard Sell"

8   Janet L. Hookailo, a spokeswoman for Northeastern, says credit-card companies are prohibited from soliciting students on the campus because the university wants at least to "eliminate the hard sell." Vendors, however, simply set up shop right outside the campus, Mr. Schlager says. "They're on a public sidewalk, so they're allowed. It's a prime location, because you need to be on that sidewalk to enter the main gates. You can't avoid them." Mr. Schlager, who did not apply for a credit card until the end of his freshman year, has three cards now, he says, but keeps his debt under control.

9   Ruth Susswein, executive director of Bankcard Holders of America, a non-profit consumer-awareness group, says she applauds universities for making an effort to keep students out of trouble. However, she says, educational programs would have a wider impact if credit-card companies themselves were required to provide them before issuing a card. "The information should be provided before the plastic is," she says. Ms. Susswein suggests that students would show up for the seminars if that was where they had to pick up their cards. "Presumably, the student wants the card. Presumably, the issuer wants to prevent fraud by making sure the card gets to the right person. It's a win-win situation." MasterCard's Mr. Healy calls this "an interesting proposition," but says it has not been considered. The company already provides educational brochures to student applicants, he says.

10   Many universities, including Lehigh, provide credit-counseling services through their financial-aid or student-affairs offices to students who have run into trouble. But it's up to students to seek out the assistance, since universities have no other way of knowing who needs help. "It's a very difficult thing to get into, because before young people have gotten in trouble with credit, they think they're too intelligent to be threatened," says Lehigh's Mr. Stanford. "The ones who really do get in trouble get sufficiently embarrassed by it that they don't come forward to get help."

11   At some universities, however, officials say they are not convinced that enough students are experiencing credit problems to make major changes in educational programs necessary. "We have no evidence to suggest that misuse of credit is a pervasive problem for our students," says the University of Washington's Mr. Godfrey. "But then, we acknowledge readily that information about misuse on a wide scale is difficult, if not impossible, to find."

12   A college has a vested interest in heading off students' credit problems, Mr. Stanford says, because such financial pressure would very likely affect their academic performance. "Equally important to us," he adds, "when they graduate, they're going to be less able to make their annual contribution back to their alma mater."

Mapping Exercise

Use your own notes to create your own problem/solution map. You should be able to include at least three causes, three effects, and four to five solutions.

Comprehension Questions

Circle the correct letter choice.

1. Paragraph 2 is mainly concerned with

   a. causes.

   b. solutions.

   c. effects.

   d. problems.

2. Prohibiting representatives of credit card companies from soliciting students on campus is supported as a solution by

   a. William Sanford.

   b. Matthew Schlager.

   c. Sean Healy.

   d. Janet Hookailo.

3. One argument used to defend student access to credit cards is that

   a. students can pay tuition with it.

   b. students need to build a credit history.

   c. frivolous spending is never a real problem for college students.

   d. students need to learn how to pay off several debts at a time.

4. According to Dr. Vanin, the major danger creating student debt from credit cards is

   a. student gambling.

   b. paying college costs with credit cards.

   c. frivolous buying.

   d. paying off automobile loans.

5. Formal freshman orientation sessions on credit are seen as effective by all EXCEPT

   a. Dr. Vanin.

   b. Eric Godfrey.

    c. Linda Downing.

    d. Mr. Stanford.

6. A problem with helping students deal with credit card debt is that they

    a. often won't show up at seminars on credit.

    b. think they're too intelligent to be threatened.

    c. get too embarrassed to seek help.

    d. all of the above

7. According to Eric Godfrey, an effective way to help students is

    a. orientation sessions.

    b. discussion with parents.

    c. workshops on debt management.

    d. one-on-one discussions with financial-aid officers.

8. According to the article, vendors remain effective because

    a. they can't be prohibited from setting up shop on campus.

    b. most vendors are actually university students.

    c. they're allowed to operate on nearby public sidewalks.

    d. they own prime locations near the main gates.

9. Ruth Susswein

    a. thinks students should not have to attend fraud seminars.

    b. is the executive director of a credit card company, Bankcard Holders of America.

    c. believes that simply offering educational programs would solve the problem.

    d. thinks card companies should give educational programs before issuing a card.

10. The author's position regarding banning credit card representatives on campus is

    a. strongly for the policy.

    b. mildly for the policy.

    c. mildly against the policy.

    d. noncommittal and neutral on the policy.

Questions For Discussion

Work in small discussion groups.

1. What experiences have you had with credit cards or credit card debt? Have you ever signed up for a credit card on or near your campus?

2. Are there other solutions in addition to those suggested in the article? Which do you think would be most effective?

■ PROBLEM/SOLUTION: OPINION AND PERSUASION

Newspapers contain special opinion or editorial sections devoted to columns that comment on, rather than simply report, the news. Both magazines and newspapers utilize writers who are known as columnists—newspeople who write opinion pieces regularly and whose purpose is to persuade the reader to accept the truth of their arguments or viewpoints by supporting these with valid evidence and reasons. In the article below, the author, a syndicated columnist, uses the problem/solution pattern as a vehicle for commenting on a situation in definite need of a remedy.

PREVIEWING *FAT CITY: CORRELATION TIGHTENS BETWEEN OBESITY AND SPRAWL* BY NEIL PEIRCE

Setting Your Reading Goals

Your goal is to understand the author's analysis of the problem and solution and decide: (a) Does a real problem exist? (b) Has the author analyzed the causes correctly? and (c) Is the proposed solution both workable and morally acceptable?

Preread by reading the title and the first paragraph. This should allow you to identify two key elements of the problem/solution pattern:

Problem: _____

Cause:_____

Preview Vocabulary

icon (1)	something regarded as embodying the characteristics of a group, style, or era
circumstantial (3)	indirect, as in evidence that must be inferred
prevalent (16)	widely existing
tenements (16)	houses or apartments, usually in low-income areas
aesthetic (18)	relating to beauty or the quality of living

Annotating As You Read

Again, look for words or phrases that signal cause and effect relationships. Write *problem, cause, effect,* or *solution* in the margin as you encounter these elements in your reading and make any additional notes that might be helpful. Be prepared to use your annotations to complete a pattern map in the exercises that follow.

A common feature of many newspapers and magazine columns is many sub-divided paragraphs, a result of the narrow column format. As you read, think about how you would group these into larger paragraph units; use brackets in the margins to indicate which paragraphs might most logically be merged together.

Since opinion articles deal with controversial subjects, they can create a lively dialogue and invite a response from the reader. Make personal comment notes in the margin wherever you agree or disagree with the author, and wherever you may have any personal observations or experiences to add.

Fat City: Correlation Tightens Between Obesity and Sprawl

by Neil Peirce

1   An obesity epidemic has seized America. And the suspected villain is none other than America's prized development icon—suburbia.

2   So far there's no smoking gun, no irrefutable scientific evidence to prove that our spread-out, overwhelmingly auto-dependent way of living is expanding our paunches and imperiling our health.

3   "It's like global warming," says Robert Yaro, executive director of the New York Regional Plan Association. "There's no conclusive proof. But there's enough strong circumstantial evidence that we better take it seriously."

4   What's indisputable is that we're getting heavier—rapidly. Thirty percent to 50% of Americans, depending on how severe the measure, are now over-weight. Obesity—defined as roughly 30 pounds or more overweight—swelled 60% in the past decade, and now affects 22% of us.

5   One clear reason: almost a third of Americans are basically sedentary, with little or no exercise. Almost three-quarters of adults aren't active enough physically, according to the federal government's Centers for Disease Control and Prevention.

6   And now kids are falling into the same trap. A quarter of American children aged 6 to 17 are overweight, 11% seriously so, says the CDC. Not only have school sports and gym programs declined, but in today's spread-out sub-urbia of roaring freeways and highways, tiny percentages walk to school.

Neil Peirce, "Fat City: Correlation Tightens Between Obesity and Sprawl" (The Washington Post Writers Group, 2001). Reprinted with permission.

7   The implications are serious. Six of every 10 overweight children aged 5 to 10 already have one associated biochemical or clinical cardiovascular risk factor. Almost 80% of obese adults have diabetes, high cholesterol, high blood pressure or coronary heart disease.

8   So why the soaring American Fat Factor? Some people blame couch potato TV-viewing, which is surely a factor. Others finger Big Macs and diet in general.

9   But none of those, say the experts, explain the magnitude of increased obesity in America. Something more pervasive—and damaging—is at work.

10   I like the simple explanation of Thomas Schmid, director of the CDC's Active Community Environments working group: "We sit in cars. We don't walk to the store on the corner. We ride the lawnmower instead of pushing it. We've engineered almost any kind of work out of our lives. That's why we're growing bigger."

11   Look behind most of those reasons and you find lurking an even more persistent, effective culprit—suburban development styles. America's post-World War II streets and community layouts weren't designed for people: They were designed for automobiles.

12   So what did we get? Residences on curvy, dead-end streets (often cul-de-sacs) that feed into high-volume highways leading to segregated uses—shopping malls, office parks, government centers.

13   Traditional street grids encouraged walking and biking by facilitating shortest-possible travels between two points. Contemporary suburban development does just the opposite. Sidewalks are often missing. Roadways are designed for vehicular "throughput" and make foot or bike traffic downright dangerous.

14   William Dietz, the CDC's director of nutrition and physical activity, uses his own suburban workplace as an example: "Some of our staff is in a building 200 yards away. To get there, I have to cross five lanes of traffic, plus hopping a guardrail and walking across an azalea patch. That's how our environment is designed. It's not designed to promote walking." Small wonder government studies show that just between 1977 and 1995, trips that Americans made by walking decreased from 25% to 10%, while trips by auto rose from 84% to 90%.

15   There are disturbing international comparisons. In Italy, 54% of trips are by walking or bicycling; in Sweden (where it's cold and dark much of the year), 49%. In this gloriously hailed Land of the Free and the Brave, we walk or cycle just 10% of the time.

16   Where's the cure? Maybe in reaching back over a century. In the late 1800s and early 1900s, Yaro notes, modern American city planning was pioneered by figures such as Frederick Law Olmsted, who pushed for major parks in our cities on the theory that getting people out into the fresh air and sunshine would combat tuberculosis and rickets then prevalent in the tenements

of industrial workers. The public health and city planning movements developed at the same time.

17   Just maybe, there's a parallel today—that getting more people out of their cars, walking and biking and reengaging an active lifestyle, can cut back on the wave of heart diseases, diabetes and associated diseases now afflicting this nation's people.

18   As long as smoking was an aesthetic issue, notes Yaro, nothing changed. But when it became a public health issue, the public reacted. He predicts the same now: "The correlations are strong, the science will follow shortly. Once the recognition sinks in that our patterns of mobility and development are killing us and imperiling our kids—we're quite capable of forging a new public ethic about these issues."

Exercise 12.3

Vocabulary: Using Word Parts

Use the context, the word part meanings below, and others that you learned previously to match the definitions in the column on the right with the words on the left.

fac = easy   per = through   cor = with, together

1. _____ correlation (title)   a. helping

2. _____ epidemic (1)   b. the degree or relation between two things

3. _____ suburbia (1)   c. not direct, as in evidence that must be inferred

4. _____ irrefutable (2)   d. size

5. _____ imperiling (2)   e. rapid, widespread growth amidst a group of people

6. _____ circumstantial (3)   f. separated

7. _____ indisputable (4)   g. residential areas on the outskirts of a city

8. _____ sedentary (5)   h. characteristic of the present time

9. _____ magnitude (9)   i. incapable of being disproved by other evidence

10. _____ pervasive (9)   j. not capable of being argued about

11. _____ segregated (12)   k. causing danger to

12. _____ facilitating (13)   l. spread throughout

13. _____ contemporary (13)   m. inactive, not moving

Mapping Problem/Solution

Use your annotated notes to fill in the map with the appropriate items from the list below.

obesity   suburban living

auto-dependent lifestyles   get out of cars

cardiovascular risk   fewer gym programs

adopt active lifestyle   diabetes and assorted disorders

couch potato TV viewing   make obesity a public health issue

lack of work in lives

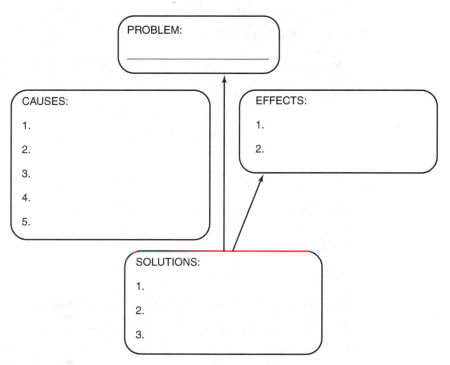

PROBLEM:

_____

CAUSES:

1.

2.

3.

4.

5.

EFFECTS:

1.

2.

SOLUTIONS:

1.

2.

3.

Comprehension Questions

Circle the correct letter choice.

1. By using the word *correlation,* the author avoids the accusation of committing the fallacy of

   a. hasty generalization.

   b. faulty causation.

   c. begging the question.

   d. false analogy.

2. According to the article

   a. 60% of Americans are obese.

   b. 22% of Americans are basically sedentary.

   c. 6 of 10 overweight children aged 5–10 have at least one risk factor.

   d. 25% of American children aged 11–17 are seriously overweight.

3. Obesity is defined as

   a. getting heavier faster.

   b. being overweight.

   c. swelling to 60% of your normal size.

   d. being about 30 pounds overweight.

4. Which of the following is an *effect* of the other three?

   a. "We're growing bigger."

   b. "We don't walk to the store on the corner."

   c. "We ride the lawnmower instead of pushing it."

   d. "We sit in cars."

5. Which of the following could be a *cause* of the other three?

   a. dependence on the automobile

   b. expanding paunches

   c. high cholesterol

   d. coronary heart disease

6. Which of the following is not characteristic of community layouts in America?

   a. They were designed mainly for automobiles.

   b. Highways lead to segregated uses.

   c. Residences are located on dead-end streets.

   d. Street grids encourage walking and biking.

7. Which of the following does Pierce consider to be the main cause of the problem?

   a. couch potato TV viewing

   b. suburban development styles

   c. diet

   d. lack of physical work in our lives

8. Which of the following signals the beginning of the solution section?

   a. "One clear reason ..."

   b. "So what did we get?"

   c. "Look behind most of these reasons ..."

   d. "Where's the cure?"

9. The author presents evidence from all of the following EXCEPT

   a. his own personal experience.

   b. testimony from experts.

   c. governmental studies.

   d. statistics from the CDC.

10. "In this gloriously hailed Land of the Free and the Brave, we walk or cycle just 10% of the time." The tone of this sentence is

   a. solemn and frank.

   b. impartial and neutral.

   c. ironic and sarcastic.

   d. resigned and apathetic.

Subdivided Paragraphs

Group the 18 paragraphs of the article into five units that would create full paragraph structures. Each unit should contain at least three—but no more than four—subdivided paragraphs.

   Unit 1: paragraphs _____.

   Unit 2: paragraphs _____.

   Unit 3: paragraphs _____.

   Unit 4: paragraphs _____.

   Unit 5: paragraphs _____.

PROBLEM/SOLUTION: HUMOR AND IRONY

Humor (especially in the forms of satire and irony) has a long tradition as a very effective literary weapon in arguments over social and moral issues. One of the world's greatest satirists was Jonathan Swift (1667–1745), whose famous essay, "A Modest Proposal," is probably the greatest example of sustained irony in the language. In that essay, Swift dealt with a very serious problem of his time: the poverty and starvation of the Irish people under the domination of the English.

On the literal level, Swift's solution (to butcher and sell the children of Ireland as food) is ghastly, but the informed reader knows that Swift is using irony at a very complex level to propose something quite different. Earlier in this text, you saw examples of verbal irony (saying one thing and meaning the opposite). Irony at a deeper level shows us a contrast between appearance and reality, and thus has traditionally been an effective weapon to reveal vices like hypocrisy, ambition, or blind pride (the last, for example, in the story of King Oedipus). Swift's technique was to create a character or "mask." His ironic narrator does not always just "say one thing but mean another." Rather, the narrator's attitude and assumptions represent a kind of awful extension of his audience's own underlying desires and practices. In rejecting the narrator, then, Swift's readers would be forced eventually to face up to their own hypocrisy and, possibly, to mend their ways.

PREVIEWING *POUNDED BY GRAVITY? LIGHTEN UP* BY DAVE BARRY

Setting Your Reading Goals

The humor of Pulitzer prize-winning columnist Dave Barry is not nearly as grim as Swift's, but he follows in Swift's footsteps in using an ironic narrator to poke fun at some of our attitudes and, occasionally, suggest some serious issues as well. Your goal is to recognize the irony at work and share the humor of the author. Barry uses the pattern elements of problem/solution to provide the organization for his essay. What problem and what solution are suggested by the title?

_____

_____

_____

Preview Vocabulary

compensate (1)	make up for, pay
regimen (1)	a highly structured system, such as for exercise or diet
corollary (5)	a deduction or inference; a proposition that follows naturally from another

Annotating As You Read

The goofy narrator of the essay uses the language of science (he does "calculations" and speaks pseudo-scientific babble) in order to appear objective and factual. Mark examples of this in the text. The chain of cause and effect that is the basis of the narrator's argument would make some sense if the assumption on which it is based were actually true. As you read, identify this definitely false, unscientific premise. Also, the problem/solution structure allows Barry to suggest among the pattern elements a couple of problems that *are* very real and should occupy our attention. Identify and mark these as you read.

Pounded by Gravity? Lighten Up

by Dave Barry

1   I am pleased to report that we finally have a scientific explanation for why everybody in the world is gaining weight. At least I am, and I know it's not my fault. Granted, I do not have the best dietary habits. Sometimes in a restaurant I will order fried, fatty foods ("Give me a plate of fried, fatty foods, and hurry" are my exact words). But I compensate for this by engaging in a strict regimen of vigorously pounding the bottom of the ketchup bottle for as long as necessary. "No pain, no gain," that is my motto regarding ketchup.

2   Nevertheless, I have been gaining weight, and you probably have, too, which is why you're going to be happy to learn that neither of us is responsible. The universe is responsible. We know this thanks to a scientific insight that was had by alert 14-year-old Massachusetts reader Tim Wing.

3   Wing reports that he was browsing through *The Usborne Book of Facts and Lists* when he came across the following fact: Every single day, including federal holidays, 25 TONS of space dust lands on the Earth. This means that every day, the Earth weighs 25 tons more, which means that it contains a larger quantity of gravity, which as you know is the force made up of invisible rays that cause all physical objects in the universe to become more attracted to bathroom scales.

4   What this means, Tim Wing points out, is that "without gaining an ounce, people all over the world are getting heavier."

5   And there is more bad news: At the same time that gravity is increasing, the entire universe is expanding, except for pants. Pants are staying the same size, which means that—and this has been confirmed by extensive scientific tests conducted in my closet—a so-called "33-inch waist" pant will barely fit into a volume that formerly easily fit into a 31-inch waist pant. Albert Einstein accurately predicted this phenomenon in 1923 when he formulated his Theory of Pants Relativity, which also states, as a corollary, that as the universe grows older, "It will get harder and harder to find anything good on the radio."

6   But our big problem is this gravity build-up, which has already started to pose a grave threat to public safety. I refer here to an incident that occurred recently in Fort Lauderdale, Fla., where, according to a Sept. 16 *Miami Herald*

Dave Barry, "Pounded by Gravity? Lighten Up" (Tribune Media Services, 1995).

story that I am not making up, "A loggerhead turtle fell from the sky and hit a man in his white Chevy Nova."

(Scene: The hospital emergency room.)
DOCTOR: Where was the victim hit?
NURSE: In his Chevy Nova.
DOCTOR: OK, let's do a CAT scan, and I want his oil changed immediately.

7   Seriously, the man was unhurt, and so was the turtle, which, according to the *Herald* story, apparently was dropped by a sea gull. But that is exactly my point: Since when do sea gulls—one of the most sure-handed species of bird—drop turtles? The obvious answer is: SINCE TURTLES STARTED GETTING HEAVIER, along with everything else.

8   And as the space dust continues to land on Earth, the situation will only worsen, with chilling results. According to my calculations, at the current rate of gravity build-up, by the year 2038 an ordinary golf ball will weigh the equivalent, in today's pounds, of Rush Limbaugh. Even a professional golfer, using graphite clubs, would need dozens of strokes to make such a ball move a single foot. An average round of golf would take four months—nearly TWICE as long as today.

9   Is that the kind of world we want our children to grow up and develop gum disease in? I think not. This is why we must call upon the scientific community to stop puttering around with global warming and immediately develop a solution to the gravity problem.

(30-second pause)

10   Well, we see that the scientific community has once again let the human race down, leaving it up to us civilians to deal with the situation. Fortunately, I have come up with a practical answer in the form of a:

GRAVITY REDUCTION PLAN

11   Follow my reasoning: The problem is that 25 tons of stuff is landing on the Earth every day, right? So the obvious solution is to put 25 tons of stuff into a rocket every day and blast it into space. It couldn't be simpler.

12   Perhaps you're saying: "But, Dave, how are we going to find 25 tons worth of stuff every single day that is so totally useless that we can just send it into space with total confidence that it could never possibly in any way benefit humanity?"

13   I can answer that question in three simple words: "Fourth Class Mail." Every day AT LEAST 25 tons of material is painstakingly mailed all over the United States and thrown away immediately upon receipt. Solid-waste experts estimate that 78 percent of our nation's landfill capacity is currently occupied by sincere unopened letters from Ed McMahon informing people

that they have almost definitely won $14 million. Why not just load this material directly into rockets? And consider this: If we send up MORE than 25 tons a day, the Earth would actually LOSE gravity. I calculate that every human being on the planet would instantly be six ounces lighter if we also sent Ed up there, not that I am necessarily proposing this.

14   So I say let's fire up the rockets and get this program going before gravity gets so strong that all we can do is lie on the ground, helpless, while turtles rain down upon us. If you agree write to your senators and congress persons today and let them know where you stand. Stress the urgency of the situation. Stress their responsibility as public officials. Above all, stress that there's room in the rocket with Ed.

Exercise 12.4

Pattern Mapping

Use the details below to fill in the pattern map for the article (relevant paragraph numbers are given), then answer the questions below.

- send junk mail into space via rocket
- Americans becoming increasingly overweight
- amount of gravity on Earth increasing significantly
- 25 tons of space dust landing each day

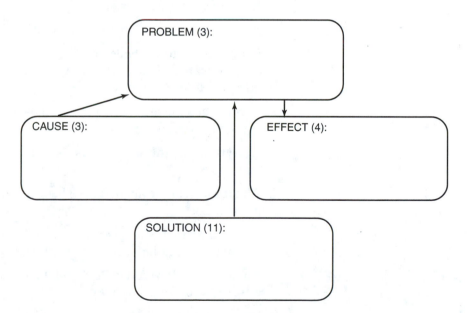

1. Which of the pattern elements on p. 467 is scientifically false?

   _____

2. What two real problems of American life are suggested by the pattern elements?

   _____ and _____

3. Reread paragraphs 5 and 7. What's wrong with the narrator's facts and reasoning?

   _____

   _____

   _____

Fact and Opinion

Barry's humor is not always strictly verbal—saying one thing but meaning another. Much of his humor comes from the way he mixes facts with wildly improbable or flatly untrue statements. In Chapter 6, factual statements were distinguished from opinions in that they can be definitely proven either true or false. For the following claims, write fact *for statements that seem true and for which conclusive evidence could be found. Write* false *for statements that are false or could be proved to be false.*

_____ 1. Tim Wing is a 14-year-old reader from Massachusetts.

_____ 2. Every single day 25 tons of space dust lands on the Earth.

_____ 3. Every day the Earth contains a larger quantity of gravity.

_____ 4. Gravity is the force made up of invisible rays that cause all physical objects in the universe to become more attracted to bathroom scales.

_____ 5. Without gaining an ounce, people all over the world are getting heavier.

_____ 6. Everything in the universe is expanding, except for pants size.

_____ 7. Albert Einstein formulated the Theory of Pants Relativity in 1923.

_____ 8. In Ft. Lauderdale, a loggerhead turtle fell from the sky and hit a man in his white Chevy Nova.

_____ 9. An average golf round in 2038 will be 4 months—twice as long as the average today.

_____ 10. Every day at least 25 tons of Fourth Class mail is mailed and thrown away.

Questions for Writing/Small-Group Discussion

1. Reread paragraphs 11–13. Barry obviously has a low opinion of the value of junk mail. Develop a problem/solution pattern map that would deal with the causes and effects of junk mail and some possible solutions to the problem.

2. Work together in a group to make your own ironic "Modest Proposal." Try to find a problem through which you can make some serious points. Create an ironic narrator who embodies the values and opinions that you think are dead wrong. Make the narrator narrow-minded and short-sighted, praising the wrong things for the wrong reasons, committing reasoning fallacies and missing the obvious truth. You may be able to follow Barry's technique of treating a bogus problem with a ridiculous solution (sending mail into space via rocket) that actually suggests a true problem (junk mail).

PROBLEM/SOLUTION: TWO POTENTIAL FALLACIES

You were introduced to **either/or** thinking in the previous chapter as a fallacy of comparison/contrast, built on the assumption that only two or so alternatives exist. In problem/solution, the fallacy is apt to occur in the solution section where some type of action is proposed. The technique usually involves saying that only two choices exist, and since one is unacceptable, the author's suggestion must be the right one:

> We must imprison every drug addict, or admit we've lost the war and legalize all drugs.

> Defense spending must be drastically reduced now; if not, let's just admit we can no longer afford to support public schools.

> Either we get rid of bilingual education or accept an America with no common language.

A close relative of either/or is what we can call the **slippery slope** fallacy: one small step taken is said to inevitably lead to an uncontrollable sequence with an unfavorable ending. This type of faulty causation usually occurs in two ways in problem/solution. It may be used to create a problem that doesn't really exist, as this example from the previous article shows:

> So I say let's fire up the rockets and get this program going before gravity gets so strong that all we can do is lie on the ground, helpless, while turtles rain down upon us.

Another aim of the fallacy is to reject a solution that may have been proposed:

> Allowing the terminally ill to die may sound humane, but soon thousands of the unwanted elderly and infirm will face mass extermination.

Once schools start promoting contraceptives, an epidemic of immoral and permissive behavior will sweep the country.

Advocates of gun control maintain that they are only after handguns, but rifles, bows, and even knives will quickly become taboo.

To detect these fallacies, apply some of the questions asked at the beginning of this chapter regarding the truth, value, and action components of problem/solution. Has the author offered solid evidence for the existence of a problem? Are there alternatives other than the ones specified? Is the chain of events warned about really likely to occur? Although the examples above may seem very obvious, in actual practice these fallacies may be hidden in fancy language or unstated premises and thus require careful reading and analysis to uncover.

CHAPTER REVIEW

Circle the correct letter choice.

1. In the truth component of problem/solution analysis, your task is to

   a. examine the evidence on whether a problem exists.

   b. determine if the solution offered will work.

   c. determine whether a solution is fair and good.

   d. decide if you will support the action.

   e. all of the above

   f. *a* and *b* above

2. The solution section may

   a. be developed by an opinion/reason subpattern.

   b. give a "how to" of time sequence or advice.

   c. provide a warning.

   d. all of the above

Read the multiparagraph unit below, organized by the pattern of problem/solution, and answer the questions by circling the correct letter choice and filling in the blank where indicated.

The influx of immigrants in recent decades means that many Americans cannot speak English. This concern has prompted calls to make English the official national language. Groups like U.S. English and English First have sounded the alarm: "If this continues, the next American president could well be elected by people who can't read or speak English!"

A constitutional amendment making English the official national language has been introduced in Congress. It is not exactly clear what effect the amendment would have, but election ballots and other government forms now printed in various languages probably would be printed only in English. Bilingual education programs in the schools would be scaled back. The amendment is not intended to restrict private use of foreign languages or their religious or ceremonial use.

Although supporters believe the amendment will solve problems by encouraging immigrants to learn English, opponents believe it will create new problems. The amendment might be a poor way to say "Welcome." If the amendment breeds intolerance and divisiveness rather than unity, it could impede assimilation rather than accelerate it.

(Welch et al., *American Government*, 4th ed., 41–42)

3. Under the provisions of the Constitutional amendment
   a. private use of foreign language would be banned.
   b. religious services would have to be conducted in English.
   c. election ballots would likely be in English only.
   d. ceremonies could not be conducted in a language other than English.

4. Which of the following is a statement of fact?
   a. The next American president could well be elected by people who can't read or speak English.
   b. A constitutional amendment making English the official national language has been introduced in Congress.
   c. The amendment will solve problems by encouraging immigrants to learn English.
   d. The amendment might be a poor way to say "Welcome."

5. All of these are given as reasons for opposing the amendment EXCEPT
   a. it could encourage intolerance.
   b. it would help more immigrants to speak English.
   c. it may slow down assimilation.
   d. it could lead to disunity.

6. "If this continues, the next American president could well be elected by people who can't read or speak English!" This statement illustrates a possible fallacy of
   a. either/or.
   b. false analogy.
   c. slippery slope.
   d. name-calling.

7. "If the amendment breeds intolerance and divisiveness rather than unity, it could impede assimilation rather than accelerate it." From the context, you would guess that *unity* is closest in meaning to

   a. divisiveness.

   b. intolerance.

   c. assimilation.

8. From the context of the quotation in question 7, the opposite of *impede* would be _____.

Match these fallacies to the examples below by writing the corresponding letter in the blank.

A. either/or

B. slippery slope

9. _____ Let us mobilize The National Guard and shut down the borders; the only alternative is to scrap all immigration laws and quotas.

10. _____ If hunting of bears is banned today, tomorrow all forms of hunting will be prohibited.

READING PORTFOLIO   A Problem/Solution Article

1. *Find a magazine or newspaper article that is organized by the problem/solution pattern.* The best choice is one that is a proposal rather than an informational report. In newspapers, you are more likely to find a proposal in the opinion-editorial pages or in a feature section, rather then in the "hard news" sections of a paper.

2. *To be sure you have a good example, find more than one article.* Then work together in small groups (in class or out) to determine which of your article selections is best and how you might approach your summary and response.

3. *For your summary, develop your own problem/solution map.* In your own words, write down causes, effects, problem, and solution in the appropriate section. Then, you can use the map as the basis for developing your summary. This might be a good time to review the section on summarizing in Chapter 5.

4. *In your response, you have a number of options.* Consider the following questions from the truth/value/action components of analysis: Do you agree with the author on the severity and/or causes of the problem? Do you have some objections to the values and/or assumptions of the author—that is, do you think the solution is practical, fair, relevant? Do you have an alternative solution that might work equally well or even better, perhaps based on personal experiences of your own?

5. *Follow previous directions for length and filing of your analysis.*

13

Arguing Over Issues: Opinions and Reasons

What makes a movie so good that you would recommend it to your friends? Why should we support one candidate over another or vote for the latest school bond issue or decide to build a public swimming pool? Why should you choose one college, or one brand of soap, or one person to share your life with, over another? It's an easy thing simply to state our choices, preferences, and value judgments. It is not so easy, however, to come up with sound and relevant support that will convince others to accept our judgments on what is good or bad or what kind of action should be taken.

■ CHAPTER PREVIEW

In this chapter you will

- Examine in depth the pattern elements of opinion/reason
- Find how truth, value, and action components operate in opinion/reason
- Add two more logical fallacies to your list
- Analyze articles on controversial issues
- Discover how editorial cartoons use the pattern of opinion/reason
- Choose from some opinion/reason options for your Reading Portfolio assignment

In opinion/reason, like problem/solution, the reader is invited to accept certain ideas and agree to actions, but there are some significant differences. Problem/solution mainly lets the analysis speak for itself: here is the problem, here is the solution, let's do it. Its concern is more with **how** a solution will work. An opinion/reason article, on the other hand, sees the need to explain **why** an action should be taken. It admits that there is a debate going on, that there is another side, that the audience may be hostile, and that any recommended action must be justified. This difference shows up most clearly in the value/action components of the two patterns. Evaluation and action in problem/solution are mainly left up to readers to decide in their own minds: is the action fair, just, workable, is there a better way? In opinion/reason, questions like these are more out in the open. The writer gives support for statements of fact and opinion that function as reasons justifying the action being called for.

■ PATTERN ELEMENTS IN OPINION/REASON

The main opinion element in this pattern is usually short and simple. Its value component suggests that something is good or bad; its action component recommends that we *should/must/ought to* do something: *vote* for Candidate X, *support* Measure Y, *go see* Movie Z. Like a solution statement, the opinion may be aimed at fixing something, but it may also be praising and supporting something new, positive, and worthy. Sometimes both components of the opinion element are directly stated. In other instances, either is so strongly implied that the reader has no doubt as to what the writer intends. An author urging voters to support a candidate at election time may not feel the need to state the obvious: "Jones is a good choice." Similarly, an article listing the advantages of going to a community college may not directly tell the reader "Go now and enroll."

Most of the opinion/reason pattern is taken up with reasons. These sentences, paragraphs, or multiparagraph units form a structured argument, often with points numbered, that tells why the value judgment and action are right. Their idea patterns come most commonly from description/support, cause/effect, and comparison/contrast. Reasons may be factual but often express opinions. Here is an outline of an opinion/reason argument that would be typical during an election campaign:

Opinion

We should reelect Senator Smith, clearly the best candidate.

or

Senator Smith is the best candidate for Senator. (implied: reelect Smith)

or

We should reelect Senator Smith. (implied: Smith is best candidate)

Reasons why Smith is best and should be reelected:

1. Most yes votes of all Senators on environmental bills (comparison/contrast)
2. Responsible for getting federal funding for educational programs (cause/effect)
3. Spoke consistently in favor of affirmative action (description: behavior)
4. Embodies traditional family values (description: traits)

The reasons, cast in various idea patterns, show a range from fact to opinion: Reason 1 is factual, 4 is clearly opinion, with 2 and 3 allowing for some debate. Be careful not to confuse the pattern of opinion/reason with cause/effect. Both answer the question **why** and both use signal words like *because* and *therefore*. Cause/effect is concerned with **explaining** why things have happened or will happen:

> Marie will return to college to increase her job opportunities and thus her family's security.

> Marie returned to college to increase her job opportunities and thus her family's security.

Opinion/reason, in contrast, offers persuasive reasons in the hope of *creating* certain actions:

> Marie should return to college. A degree will increase her job opportunities and help her family gain security.

These reasons are causes waiting to happen. If Marie is convinced by the argument and does return to college, then those reasons will indeed become causes.

As with problem/solution, opinion/reason may include topical detail (usually near the start of an article) to supply background/framing information. The opinion statement of this pattern is often accepted as the main idea since no single sentence will contain both the opinion statement and the reasons. A more complete main idea statement could be constructed by summarizing the reasons or by adding a listing phrase like "for these/many reasons." Pattern maps for opinion/reason are relatively easy to make (see Figure 13.1).

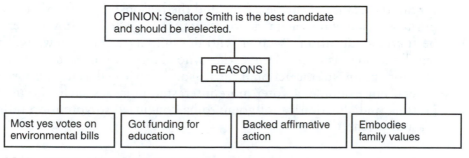

Figure 13.1   Opinion/Reason Pattern Map

■ READING BETWEEN THE LINES

The most important element of an argument, however, may be the part that has been left out. Even though the pattern offers reasons for an opinion, lurking somewhere between those elements are often hidden assumptions that connect the two. Here is where the critical reader may have to make some important inferences. As an example, consider this argument between parents and a teenager. The issue is an all-night graduation party that the student wishes to attend. During the debate, the teenager offers the following reasons to support the proposed action:

1. Other friends are being allowed to go.
2. I've attended school regularly and made good grades.
3. It's a once-in-a-lifetime event.
4. I've never gotten into any serious trouble.

On one level the parents would deal with the truth of these statements, which could be decided from the facts. Between the opinion and these reasons, however, is the unstated issue of whether these are *good* reasons or at least *good enough* to outweigh opposite views. It is the broader assumptions or premises that lie behind each of the above statements that really connect the opinion and reason into a complete argument.

1. If other parents feel an activity is safe, it must be OK.
2. School performance should secure special rewards and override parental fears.
3. Normal rules and regulations should be lifted for special occasions.
4. Trouble won't happen to those determined to avoid it.

Chances are the parents will very quickly shift their counterattack from the truth of the reasons (which they might have to concede) to the question of whether the underlying assumptions are valid.

Something similar could happen in the example of electing Senator Smith. A voter might concede the truth about what Smith has done, and yet not vote for Smith because of the beliefs behind the reasons: that affirmative action is positive, that environmental action is vital, that the federal government should be funding education. A voter who doesn't share these views will not see Smith's actions as good. Even a voter who agrees with these assumptions may still not approve of the action if the reasons are viewed as less important than others. For example, a voter more interested in issues such as crime, immigration, and abortion is not going to be convinced to vote for Smith by the reasons given.

▓ FALLACIES COMMON TO OPINION/REASON

At the beginning of this unit, you were told to look out for abuses in arguments trying to persuade you to action: appealing to emotions, manipulating evidence, committing fallacies in reasoning. Earlier in this text you learned about one technique common in political arguments: name-calling or mudslinging. Two other fallacies that relate to evidence and reasoning in an argument are begging the question and card stacking.

BEGGING THE QUESTION

This is a traditional term for dodging an issue. It occurs when a conclusion has already assumed the point it is supposedly out to make. Look carefully at this statement:

> "No informed voter would support an ill-designed amendment such as this one."

The opinion is clear: the amendment is bad and should be rejected because it is "ill designed." The proof that it is ill designed is that "no informed voter would support it." But why not? The only answer is: because it is ill designed. In other words, the author's proof already assumes the conclusion, and the argument goes in a circle. For another example, we can go back to Dave Barry's article in Chapter 12 where he uses begging the question for comical effect. Barry's loopy narrator is concerned about the big problem of "gravity build-up, which has already started to pose a grave threat to public safety." As proof of gravity build-up, he relates the incident where a turtle fell from the sky and hit a man in a car. The narrator notes that "the turtle … apparently was dropped by a sea gull" and then draws this conclusion:

> "But that is exactly my point: Since when do sea gulls—one of the most sure-handed species of bird—drop turtles? The obvious answer is: SINCE TURTLES STARTED GETTING HEAVIER, along with everything else."

Here the narrator offers "proof" that gravity build-up exists and everything is heavier by citing the example of the turtle. However, to explain why the turtle would fall, he must assume a build-up in gravity. By thus "begging the question" the narrator avoids (as he does throughout the essay) the burden of really proving that gravity is increasing significantly.

CARD STACKING

As its name suggests, this fallacy relates to manipulating evidence, and more often refers to what is left *out* of an argument than what goes in. Honest debate requires acknowledging the opposition argument and facing all the evidence squarely. That doesn't happen in card stacking. What is said may be true, but it may not be the whole truth. The person presenting the argument has carefully selected only those facts that offer support and ignored the rest. For an example, we can return to the previous argument for the election of Senator Smith. A number of reasons for reelection were offered. But suppose these facts had been left out: that Senator Smith had voted against "get tough" crime measures and welfare reform, or that the senator was under indictment for laundering illegal contributions. These facts, if true, would certainly change the picture for most voters. For a reader, the best way of combating card stacking is to maintain a skeptical attitude and to have enough background information from other sources—or to seek it—to know when the whole picture is not being given.

The articles in the rest of this chapter involve issues often discussed on television and radio, as well as in print. As you read, identify the pattern elements and examine the evidence and reasoning carefully for emotional appeals and logical fallacies. Consider also whether there are any unstated assumptions or value judgments that are necessary to complete the argument. The comprehension questions in the exercises will help you focus on premises, assumptions, fallacies, and inferences in this pattern.

■ OPINION/REASON: SUMMARIZING PROS AND CONS

Informational prose summarizes debate rather than participates in it. That is, its goal is to clearly and objectively present the issue and the arguments for and against it, without taking sides. The selection below, taken from a textbook in sociology, is a good example of a clear and comprehensive summary of an issue that generates much heated discussion.

PREVIEWING *POLICY DEBATE: SHOULD STRICTER ENVIRONMENTAL PROTECTION MEASURES BE ENACTED?* BY J. ROSS ESHLEMAN, BARBARA G. CASHION, AND LAURENCE A. BASIRICO

Setting Your Reading Goals

Your purpose in reading is to understand both sides clearly, evaluate the arguments and evidence, and, if you wish, decide on which side of the issue you stand. From the title it is clear that the issue is whether or not _____.

A summary of an argument usually follows a listing of the arguments both pro (supporting) and con (attacking) a stated viewpoint. The first paragraph gives the focus for discussion. Complete it here:

"A variety of environmental protection groups, scientists, and politicians have suggested that _____."

Preview Vocabulary

stringent (1)	strict, harsh
emission (1)	something given off
curtail (3)	shorten or end
speculative (4)	based on opinion, not certain fact
miniscule (6)	very tiny
unwarranted (7)	not called for or justified

Annotating As You Read

Follow the arguments for and against by writing PRO next to every reason given to support environmental regulation and CON next to each reason given to oppose it. To help locate these reasons, pay particular attention to verbs that point to a statement of reason, e.g., "say" and "contend." There are a number of other verbs that perform this function; circle them as you read and mark the statements as directed above.

Policy Debate: Should Stricter Environmental Protection Measures Be Enacted?

by J. Ross Eshleman, Barbara G. Cashion,
and Laurence A. Basirico

1   Measures to protect the environment through the regulation of consumer and industrial behavior have accomplished a great deal over the past few decades, but many feel that a great deal more is needed. A variety of environmental protection groups, scientists, and politicians have suggested that further regulatory steps be taken, such as

- Ban chlorofluorocarbons (CFCs) and other ozone-depleting chemicals.
- Enforce air-quality standards established by the Clean Air Act.
- Insist upon stringent vehicle emission standards, and require auto manufacturers to produce cars that can yield at least 40 miles per gallon of gasoline.
- Reduce the number of miles people drive by requiring carpooling.
- Ban, highly restrict, or reformulate products that are environmentally unsound, such as gasoline-powered lawnmowers, charcoal lighter fluid,

---

Eshleman, Cashion, and Basirico, *Sociology: An Introduction*, 4th ed., 523–524.

some kinds of deodorants, polystyrene foam (Styrofoam™), varnishes, adhesives, and hundreds of other products.

■ Require rapid reductions in sulfur emissions.

2   There are many other regulatory measures like these that many consider to be necessary to prevent further environmental destruction (Melville, 1988). Yet, despite Americans' heightened environmental consciousness, there still is considerable debate as to whether the government should impose stricter environmental regulations on consumer and industrial behavior. Perhaps this is because many of the proposed environmental regulations would significantly affect both consumer and industrial behavior.

3   Opponents of strict environmental regulation believe that the aforementioned types of measures would seriously damage the economy and, thus, lead to a decline in our standard of living. It would be very costly in terms of money, time, and reorganization for industries to meet some of the stricter environmental regulations. Opponents therefore contend that the cost and complexity of complying with stricter environmental regulations would discourage investment, hinder the construction of new plants, cut into profits, create unemployment, lead to a loss of production, and generally curtail economic growth (Currie and Skolnick, 1988).

4   Advocates of strict environmental regulation argue that putting short-term corporate profits ahead of a cleaner environment is dangerously shortsighted. For example, in 1974, scientists warned of the dangers to the ozone layer that result from the chemicals—such as CFCs—used in aerosol sprays and other products. For many years, manufacturers of CFCs dismissed the warnings as speculative and fought proposed government legislation to restrict their usage on the grounds that eliminating them would lead to serious economic losses. In 1985, however, when a hole in the ozone layer was discovered over Antarctica, the public took notice. CFCs began being phased out of production, nearly two decades after scientists' warnings. The result of acting nearly two decades too late, according to advocates of stricter environmental regulations, is that humans are exposed to higher levels of dangerous ultraviolet rays.

5   While most opponents of environmental regulation would probably agree that we would all be better off with a cleaner environment, they contend that a certain amount of pollution and environmental destruction is an unavoidable by-product of industrial society. This is part of the price that must be paid for a high standard of living. Opponents feel that the economic dislocation that would be caused by strict environmental regulation would have negative consequences not just for industry, but for all of society. For example, the taxes that large corporations pay help to support public schools, public hospitals, fire departments, police departments, and many other services. In many communities, most of the tax base to support these services is provided by large corporations. Decreased profits for industry mean that less tax

money would be paid by them and, thus, less money would be available for public services. In order to maintain the same level of service, the tax burden would have to be passed on to the citizens. Opponents of stricter regulation contend that the problem would be even worse for poor people in underdeveloped nations that now can benefit from the economic and technological growth associated with industrialization.

6   Advocates maintain that while environmental regulation may involve short-range costs to the economy, the long-range economic impact actually is positive. A study conducted by the Council on Environmental Quality found that environmental controls would lower industrial productivity by only a minuscule amount and would entail one-time expenses (Currie and Skolnick, 1988). While the cost of stricter environmental regulation could be significant, advocates say that there is no evidence that there would be substantial negative effects on investment. On the contrary, they suggest that environmental regulations carry the potential for increased economic growth. For example, an EPA study projected that unemployment would decrease slightly as a result of newly created jobs in antipollution-equipment industries and services. Another study, conducted by the Conservation Foundation, found no evidence that environmental regulations had caused industries to avoid locating in states with stricter regulations. As Currie and Skolnick note, "California, for example, which has very stringent environmental regulations, also had the largest gain in manufacturing jobs of any state during the 1970s."

7   Finally, some opponents of stricter environmental regulation feel that this type of control is an unwarranted intrusion of the government into our lives and contradicts our free-market economy. They feel that government should not control individual behavior or private producers unless it is absolutely necessary. Advocates of environmental regulation, however, say that it is absolutely necessary for the government to step in because it is unrealistic to trust the free market and consumers to make prudent decisions about environmental effects.

Exercise 13.1

Recognizing Reasons in Arguments

Below are 12 reasons listed in the article to support the two sides. Use your annotated text to write PRO *for the six reason* supporting *increased regulation and* CON *for the six reasons* opposing *it.*

_____   Regulations did not cause industries to avoid locating in states with stricter regulations.

_____   Regulation would seriously damage the economy and standard of living.

_____ A certain amount of pollution and environmental destruction must be tolerated.

_____ There is no evidence of major negative effects on investment.

_____ Unemployment will go down with new jobs in antipollution industries and services.

_____ Cost/complexity of compliance would generally curtail economic growth.

_____ More regulation is an unjustified intrusion into our lives.

_____ Putting short-term profits ahead of a cleaner environment is a dangerous policy.

_____ Corporations would pay fewer taxes, and citizens more, with more regulations.

_____ Regulation may cause short-range costs but has long-range positive economic impact.

_____ Government must regulate wisely because free market and consumers won't.

_____ Short-term costs of regulation are offset by a positive long-range impact.

_____ People in undeveloped nations who benefit from industrialization will be worse off.

Comprehension Questions

Circle the correct letter choice and fill in the blanks where indicated.

1. Which of the following is NOT a step favored by environmental protection advocates?

    a. Require auto manufacturers to produce cars getting 40 miles per gallon of gasoline.

    b. Reduce the number of people involved in carpooling.

    c. Ban or restrict products that are environmentally unsound.

    d. Require rapid reductions in sulfur emissions.

2. All of the following words are used to introduce argumentative reasons EXCEPT

    a. "feel." (1)

    b. "believe." (3)

c. "argue that." (4)

d. "benefit." (5)

e. "maintain." (6)

3. Opponents believe that complying with stricter environmental regulations would

   a. discourage investment.

   b. hinder the construction of new plants.

   c. lead to a loss of production.

   d. all of the above

4. Write the main idea of paragraph 4: _____

   _____

   _____

   What signal phrase provides a clue to your choice? _____

5. All of the following words and phrases are used to signal differences between pro and con positions EXCEPT

   a. for example.

   b. yet.

   c. on the contrary.

   d. however.

6. CFCs

   a. were phased out of production in 1974.

   b. were eliminated because they caused serious economic losses.

   c. were discovered over Antarctica in 1985.

   d. contributed to exposing humans to higher levels of ultraviolet rays.

7. One point that both proponents and opponents of stricter regulation would probably agree on is that

   a. we would all be better off with a cleaner environment.

   b. a certain amount of pollution and environmental destruction is unavoidable.

   c. we must pay a high price for a high standard of living.

   d. none of the above

8. The reason presented in the first part of paragraph 5 is developed by the pattern of

   a. classification.

   b. cause/effect.

   c. whole/part.

   d. time sequence.

9. The contention by those favoring regulation that its long-range economic impact is positive is supported by

   a. a study conducted by the Council on Environmental Quality.

   b. an EPA study on unemployment.

   c. a study conducted by the Conservation Foundation.

   d. all of the above.

10. The authors of this textbook selection

   a. feel that regulation is an unwarranted intrusion into our lives.

   b. feel that government should not control individual behavior.

   c. maintain that it is necessary for the government to regulate the environment.

   d. do not reveal their own positions on the issue of regulation.

ISSUE AREA: CONTROLLING TECHNOLOGY

One form of argument is the "running debate"—that is, articles and/or letters to the editor written as responses to others previously published, which may be followed by even more counterargumentative responses. The two articles below are a part of a such a running debate over a highly charged issue—the control of new technology in the future. The authors involved have highly impressive credentials. Alvin and Heidi Toffler have a long history of writing popular accounts on the promise and dangers of technology, including their best seller, *Future Shock*. Bill Joy is a respected figure in technology; he is the chief scientist of Sun Microsystems and chairman of a presidential commission on the future of internet technology research.

To judge the arguments involved in debate, the reader needs some background information regarding technical terms. Here, the authors refer often to three technologies of growing importance in the future, known collectively by the acronym GNR:

Genetic engineering designates a branch of biology dealing with splicing and recombining genes to create new species or biochemicals.

<u>N</u>ano-science or nanotechnology relates to a more theoretical and speculative subject: hypothetical methods of creating microminiature equipment by manipulating small units of matter (atoms and molecules) as if they were part of a machine.

<u>R</u>obotics refers to the design and use of increasingly sophisticated robots.

PREVIEWING *MORE TECHNOLOGY, NOT LESS* BY ALVIN AND HEIDI TOFFLER

Setting Your Reading Goals

The Tofflers are responding to an article written by Bill Joy in *Wired* magazine. Their strategy is to counter his arguments with their own to support a position essentially the opposite. The Tofflers present an argument that mixes the pattern of opinion/reason with problem/solution—that is, their opinions are a solution to a perceived problem, and they must back up their analysis with valid and supportable reasons if a reader is to accept their position. Your goals are to (1) identify and understand the reasons given for their position, (2) determine whether or not their analysis of the problem and solution is accurate, and (3) decide whether the argument they present is well-supported and persuasive. A good place to start is the title, which states in brief form their opinion. What stand (opinion) are they taking on the issue?: _____

_____

_____

Preview Vocabulary

relinquish (2)	giving up something desired or wanted
self-replication (2)	the act of reproducing one's self
scenarios (6)	outlines for possible events, real or imagined
static (6)	unchanging, fixed
proliferation (8)	extremely rapid increase
Hiroshima (9)	city in Japan where first atom bomb was dropped, ending World War II
ethos (10)	the characteristic attitudes and beliefs of a group
apparatchik (12)	a member, especially an official, of a Communist party; a bureaucrat
Rousseauian (14)	characterized by the philosophy of Jean Jacques Rousseau (1712–78), which championed a high degree of individual freedom, feeling, and expression
nihilists (14)	those whose destructive actions show rejection of customary beliefs and values

Annotating As You Read

One important strategy in a running debate is to summarize the position of an opponent in previous writings so that it can be attacked. Annotate your text (particularly in the first half of the article) regarding key points that the Tofflers attribute to Bill Joy, and note their reasons for rejecting his positions. Identify key elements in the pattern of opinion/reason and problem/solution, and be prepared to map these patterns, using your annotated notes, in the exercises that follow.

More Technology, Not Less

by Alvin and Heidi Toffler

1   One of America's leading technologists has caused a great stir by provocatively admitting that he sees "some merit" in the Luddite reasoning of Theodore Kaczynski, the Unabomber, who once terrorized scientists whose inventions he thought were enslaving the human race.

2   Bill Joy, chief scientist at Sun Microsystems and the chairman of the presidential commission on the future of Internet technology research, has gone so far as to call on the scientific community to "relinquish" research that might lead to the domination of the human species by the "destructive self-replication" of technologies made possible by genetics, nano-science and robotics.

3   According to Joy's essay in the April issue of *Wired* magazine titled "Why the Future Doesn't Need Us," the alarm bell went off when it recently became clear, thanks to new advances in molecular electronics, that computer processing speeds would match the capacity of the human brain by the year 2030. Theoretically that might make possible robots as smart as humans—and as processing capacities develop further, smarter; indeed, smart enough to reproduce themselves.

4   Joy is not a Luddite; he is a serious man raising a responsible warning, and certainly knows a lot about computers. He has spent 25 years on computer networking where, as he himself writes, "the sending and receiving of messages creates the opportunity for out-of-control replication." All of us are now familiar with the damage that computer viruses can wreak.

5   But he too easily accepts the Unabomber's argument that the human race "might easily permit itself to drift into a position of such dependence on machines that it would have no practical choice but to accept all of the machines' decisions." Or else, that the need for control of such processes would lead to a takeover of society by an elite that "domesticates" the masses like animals.

Alvin and Heidi Toffler, "More Technology, Not Less," (NPQ, Blackwell Publishers, Summer 2000).

6   This reasoning is far too either–or. These are not the only alternatives. The scenarios that both Kaczynski and Joy present are essentially mechanistic and mono-causal. They ignore the rich complexity of the physical and social environment, which is filled with thousands, if not millions of negative feedback loops that, in fact, damp down most runaway processes before they reach their ultimate limits. In fact, they assume that computer capacity grows, while the human brain remains static.

7   But must it? The very technologies they regard as most dangerous— robotics, genetics and nanotech—may very well help us expand the human brain's capabilities and make it possible for us to use those technologies in completely new ways. Recent advances in stem cell research, for example, challenge the assumption that the brain's capacity is fixed. Like Kaczynski, Joy underestimates the ability of humans to mess things up, to rebel, to create, whether by chance or not, counter-technologies, and to step back from the brink of disaster.

8   Speaking of runaway processes, one of the most amazing facts about the 20th century is not the invention of the atomic bomb, but the fact that after one demonstration of its power, the human race managed for more than half a century never to use one again. That does not mean we won't, and the dangers of proliferation are real. Nonetheless, the record so far has been remarkable. We managed to chain the chain reaction.

9   We, too, worry about some of the effects of technology, whether self-replicating or not, and raised warning flags long ago. In *Future Shock* (1970), we forecast cloning of mammals and, eventually, humans; we warned about the misuse of genetic engineering (even the possibility of race-selective genetic weapons); we discussed the danger of eugenic manipulation and a "biological Hiroshima." In *War and Anti-War* (1994), we wrote about replication in the form of "self-reproducing war machines."

10   Unfortunately, Joy's proposed remedy is potentially more frightening than the disease. He recommends that we not only "relinquish" certain technologies (stuffing genies back into bottles, as it were), but that we limit the search for certain kinds of knowledge. Of course, the search for knowledge is always limited—by funds, by cultural blind spots, by political and other forces. Yet within this reality, the ethos of science has always included a belief in free, unhindered curiosity and research. Joy's proposal strikes at the heart of that ethos, which has, for the last three centuries, deepened our knowledge of the universe we live in and made possible not merely atomic bombs and industrial pollution, but longer life spans, a reduction of pain and hunger, and the blessings of what limited democracy we have.

11   If, in fact, we set out to limit the range of scientific curiosity, the obvious question is: Who decides? The Ayatollah Ali Khamenei? The Chinese Communist Party (which regards even run-of-the-mill farm statistics as state

secrets)? Saddam Hussein? The limitations will be imposed by those in power, and they may do exactly the reverse of what Joy proposes.

12   More fundamentally, trying to restrain the search for knowledge to stem the "destructive self-replication of technology" is an attempt to limit the self-replication of knowledge itself. That is no more possible for an American computer scientist than for a Chinese apparatchik. Fortunately, you just can't turn off 6 billion brains. If you could, you would send the entire human race time-traveling back into the 12th century.

13   The solution? There isn't an easy one. But the answer is probably more technology, not less. We will need new technologies that shut down systems on their way out of control. We have such technologies now in everything from jet planes to home space heaters. Pharmaceutical companies are on their way to finding precisely how to use proteins in our DNA for these purposes.

14   Joy's fear of "destructive self-replication" is warranted. His clarion call for responsible discussion of this issue is well taken. But his extreme pessimism is not. Cancer is an example of a runaway, self-replicating process. But do any of us anymore believe there is no cure for cancer? Along with worrying about self-replication, it is worth thinking about the following lines from *Future Shock*:

> "The incipient worldwide movement for control of technology, however, must not be permitted to fall into the hands of irresponsible technophobes, nihilists and Rousseauian romantics. Reckless attempts to halt technology will produce results quite as destructive as reckless attempts to advance it."

Kaczynski would never agree with that. But we'll bet Bill Joy does.

Exercise 13.2

Mapping Opinion/Reason

From the list of statements below, fill in the map with the one *statement of opinion and the* five *accurate reasons that the author offers to support the opinion.*

- "Dangerous" technologies can actually expand the human brain's capabilities.
- Safeguards to control runaway process simply do not exist.
- Self-replicating robots will soon be a definite threat to take over the world.
- The scenarios of opponents are mechanistic, mono-causal, and too pessimistic.
- Humans can create counter-technologies that shut down runaway processes.
- We must not needlessly restrict advancement of technologies.
- GNR technologies lend themselves solely to dangerous purposes.

- Limiting the search for knowledge goes against the ethos of science.
- The power to control technology may end up in the hands of evil leaders.
- Restraining the search for knowledge will actually promote it.

OPINION:

1.

2.

3.

4.

5.

1. The Tofflers agree with Joy that

    a. there is a very real danger that humans will become controlled by machines.
    b. reckless attempts to advance technology will produce destructive results.
    c. computer capacity grows, while the human brain remains static.
    d. humans lack the ability to create effective counter-technologies.

2. The authors believe that Joy is

    a. too optimistic about the future of technology.
    b. as delusional as the Unabomber.
    c. a serious, experienced man raising a responsible warning.
    d. fundamentally a Luddite.

3. Which of the following examples or phrases used by the authors is strictly neutral, with no emotional connotations or value judgment overtones?

    a. a Luddite
    b. Internet technology research
    c. "domesticates the masses like animals"
    d. Saddam Hussein

4. "Kaczynski and Joy … ignore the rich complexity of the physical and social environment, which is filled with thousands, if not millions of negative feedback loops…. In fact, they assume that computer capacity grows, while the human brain remains static." (6) This passage illustrates which method of development?

    a. simple restatement

    b. positive/negative restatement

    c. clarification

    d. order of importance

5. To challenge the assumption that the brain's capacity is fixed, the authors point to all of the following EXCEPT

    a. the tendency of humans to become machine dependent.

    b. stem cell research.

    c. human ability to create counter-technologies.

    d. human handling of the atomic bomb for more than half a century.

6. The authors admit to a degree of technological concern over

    a. the cloning of mammals and humans.

    b. race-selective genetic weapons.

    c. eugenic manipulation.

    d. all of the above

7. The authors' strategy in comparing Joy's solution to "stuffing genies back into bottles" is to accomplish all of the following EXCEPT to

    a. make his "remedy" seem somewhat ridiculous.

    b. show that Joy is serious, well-informed, and not a Luddite.

    c. suggest that his solution is actually impossible.

    d. discredit his argument for limits on technology.

8. One beneficial result associated by the article with free scientific research is

    a. atomic bombs.

    b. industrial pollution.

    c. longer life spans.

    d. increasingly limited democracy.

9. The authors believe that enacting the limitations proposed by Joy on "the range of scientific curiosity" would result in

    a. the control of America by Saddam Hussein.

b. increasing the ability of dangerous men in power to misuse technology.

c. stopping the "destructive self-replication of technology."

d. sending the entire human race back into the 16th century.

10. The quotation from *Future Shock* (14) mentions "irresponsible techno-phobes." Another term for "technophobe," used in the first part of the article, is _____.

PREVIEWING *ACT NOW TO KEEP NEW TECHNOLOGIES OUT OF DESTRUCTIVE HANDS* BY BILL JOY

Setting Your Reading Goals

The Tofflers article was a response to Bill Joy's article in *Wired*. Here Joy responds—though not by name—to a number of articles, including that by the Tofflers, attacking his views. His purpose is to defend further his original position and, like the Tofflers, he does so through an argument combining opinion/reason with problem/solution. Your goals are to (1) identify his reasons for his position, (2) determine whether or not his analysis of the problem and solution respond convincingly to the points raised by the Tofflers, and (3) compare the two opposing sides to decide which argument is best supported and most persuasive.

   The title states in brief form an opinion clearly opposite to that of the Tofflers. What is Joy's opinion regarding the issue?: _____

_____

_____

Preview Vocabulary

grinding (1)	hard, heavy to the point of wearing one down
delusional (3)	characterized by a false, continuing belief despite clear evidence to the contrary
contagious (4)	capable of being spread by direct or indirect means
quantitative (4)	capable of being objectively measured
pestilences (5)	serious or fatal infectious diseases, especially of large proportions
devastated (5)	laid waste to, destroyed completely
augmented (6)	increased, enhanced by
substrate (7)	a substance acted upon
repugnant (10)	distasteful, offensive
catastrophic (11)	disastrous

Annotating As You Read

As with the previous article, you need to identify, mark, and make notes on key elements in the pattern of opinion/reason and problem/solution. You will be asked to map these patterns, using your annotated notes, in the exercises that follow.

Act Now to Keep New Technologies Out of Destructive Hands

by Bill Joy

1   In the 20th century, nuclear, biological and chemical weapons of mass destruction (WMDs) were developed by the military, having little or no commercial value. WMD development and manufacture required large-scale activities and often-rare raw materials. The knowledge of how to create these WMDs was not made widely available. Three new 21st century technologies—genetic engineering, nanotechnology and robotics (GNR)—are being aggressively pursued by the commercial sector because of their promise to create almost unimaginable wealth. Using them we will be able to cure many diseases and extend our lives, eliminate material poverty and grinding physical labor, and heal the Earth.

2   But, these new technologies may also pose an even greater danger to humankind than weapons of mass destruction. It is critical to notice that the scale of the activities needed to practice the GNR technologies is rapidly declining, and that these do not need rare raw materials. More and more, the knowledge needed to design with these technologies is freely available on the Internet. The advancing power of computing will allow this design to be done on a personal computer, and manufacture of these designs is becoming inexpensive, using widely available equipment, for good or evil purposes.

3   Writing in the *Seattle Times,* William Calvin, a neurobiologist at the University of Washington, wrote: "There is a class of people with 'delusional disorders' who can remain employed and pretty functional for decades. Even if they are only one percent of the population, that's 20,000 mostly untreated delusional people in the Puget Sound area. Even if only one percent of these has the intelligence or education to intentionally create sustained or widespread harm, it's still a pool of 200 high-performing sociopathic or delusional techies just in the Puget Sound area alone." The malevolent actions of such individuals and small groups using the GNR technologies pose a large and even mortal danger to our civilization.

4   This threat will manifest itself, for example, as genetic engineering techniques provide the ability, perhaps in about 20 years, to use software

Bill Joy, "Act Now to Keep New Technologies Out of Destructive Hands", *News Perspectives Quarterly,* V. 17 (Center for the Study of Democratic Institutions, 2000), 12–14.

to create new, highly contagious and deadly "designer pathogens." Nano-technologists have similarly recognized that out of control nanobots could destroy the biosphere; a first quantitative study of this possibility of "Global Ecophagy" by Robert Freitas was recently published in response to the article I wrote on this subject in *Wired* in April. His study is quite troubling, showing the clear dangers we face from unrestricted nanotechnology and the extreme difficulty and enormous scale required of any "defense."

5   Such pestilences are beyond our direct experience. The Black Death killed a third of the population of 14th century Europe and smallpox devastated the native population in the Americas in the 16th century, but these are distant historical events. Even the influenza pandemic of 1918 is largely out of living memory. Antibiotics and improved sanitation have given us grace from such disasters, at least for a time. But to believe such things cannot recur is untrue and our failing memory of them is quite dangerous.

6   Since technologies are creating these new dangers some have hoped for the answers to be technological too, some sort of defense. But a strong defense against genetically engineered pathogens would seem to require a nearly perfectly augmented immune system, which seems quite unlikely in the time-frame of interest; this may even prove to be impossible without large-scale reengineering of the germline of our species. A "doomsday nanoshield" appears to be so outlandishly dangerous that I can't imagine we would attempt to deploy it. As with nuclear technology, the destructive offensive uses here have a seemingly deeply sustainable advantage over defensive efforts.

7   Robotics poses a different threat—the creation of a new life form that may escape our control. Some have romantically imagined that we would achieve near-immortality by becoming robots. But replacing our bodies with silicon while retaining our humanity will not eliminate the risk I am discussing here, unless we can somehow simultaneously eliminate human evil. I think it is also clear that we are not the natural life form in this imagined new computational substrate, where there would be little need for sex, no need for relearning, and perhaps no strong notion of individuality. It's not clear—Hollywood notwith-standing—that there is any practical way to protect our continued existence in the presence of a more powerful robotic species.

8   An alternative to defense might be escape to the stars, as Carl Sagan dreamed. But there seems insufficient time and most people couldn't go, so we have to look for answers closer to home.

9   We live in an economic and political system that puts its faith strongly in the individual. Freedom was born in Greece roughly 2500 years ago when we agreed to limit our actions, thus giving birth to modern civilization. This idea of putting faith in the individual is the basis not only of Greek democracy, but also underlies the Enlightenment ideal, modern democracy, and capitalism. But we must now realize that we are creating such incredible power that we cannot sanely give this power to all individuals, some of whom are

clearly not sane. Our civilization, a society of laws, is grounded in the benefits we receive by limiting our actions; this social contract is clearly threatened by illimitable individual power.

10   The risk of our extinction as we pass through this time of danger has been estimated to be anywhere from 30% to 50%. I believe that such high risks are far beyond completely unacceptable and that we must therefore take some strong action to reduce this risk. Though we can't eliminate the risk through technology, we should still build some partial defenses to reduce the risk, and also need to look for sensible non-technical steps. Historically, the doctrine of Mutually Assured Destruction (MAD), which seems to have helped to contain the nuclear threat in the past half-century, is such a non-technical approach; going forward let us hope we can find less morally repugnant mechanisms.

11   We can do some simple and obvious things to reduce the risk: have scientists and technologists take a Hippocratic oath, do assessment of the risks of new technologies in an open public process, force enterprises which wish to use dangerous technologies to take insurance against the catastrophic risk so that less risky paths are favored, limit the access to dangerous technologies by practicing them in secure international laboratories even though the work being done in these laboratories is on behalf of commercial enterprises, and finally relinquish development of the most dangerous forms of the new technologies such as unrestricted nanotechnology. We should engage a wide discussion of these and other sensible steps.

12   If we do not retain, as a civilization, control over these new technologies, and allow individuals to release self-replicating GNR technologies into the world, then we will cede control over our future to extreme individuals and accidents. A half century ago, Einstein warned us that the nuclear age had come and changed everything but our way of thinking, and that we were thus drifting toward unparalleled catastrophe, bequeathing the power of widespread destruction to the nation states. Now, with the confluence of powerful, widely available information technology with these new self-replicating GNR technologies, we are drifting toward a further, even larger potential catastrophe, on course to put our collective fate in the hands of the extreme individuals that undeniably exist in the world.

13   We must act collectively to reduce this grave threat, while getting most of the benefits of the new technologies. We can do this only if we fully face the new dangers, act decisively, and soon.

Exercise 13.3

Mapping Opinion/Reason

From the list of the following statements, fill in the map with the one statement of opinion and the four accurate reasons that the author offers to support the opinion.

- The knowledge and equipment to design dangerous technologies is available and cheap.
- Our social contract clearly requires that we place no limits on individual power.
- Delusional people using GNR technologies pose a large danger to our civilization.
- The risk of extinction can be eliminated through technology.
- Though we derive benefits from new technologies, we must limit them to reduce the grave threats they can pose.
- Without limitations, extreme individuals and accidents will control our future.
- GNR technologies can provide no benefits other than to the wealthy commercial sector.
- Destructive uses of pathogens and robots can easily be countered by defensive efforts.
- Genetic engineering could lead to deadly pathogens or biosphere-destroying nanobots.

OPINION:

1.

2.

3.

4.

Comprehension Questions

Circle the correct letter choice.

1. Bill Joy's strategy in beginning his article with weapons of mass destruction (WMDs) is to

   a. criticize the military for committing to something having little or no commercial value.

   b. show how development of WMDs depleted our sources of rare raw materials.

     c. emphasize the even greater dangers that GNR technologies pose.

     d. draw a parallel between the desirable benefits of WMDs and GNRs.

2. Which of the following is NOT advanced as a reason why GNRs are a danger?

     a. The practice of GNR technologies is rapidly declining.

     b. GNR technologies do not need rare raw materials.

     c. The knowledge needed to design with these technologies is freely available.

     d. Manufacture of these designs is becoming inexpensive.

3. According to Joy, which of the following is true?

     a. People are classified as having "delusional disorders" if they cannot remain employed and pretty functional for at least a decade.

     b. There are an estimated 20,000 mostly untreated delusional people in the United States.

     c. About ten percent of delusional people have the intelligence to create sustained or widespread harm.

     d. As many 200 high-performing delusional techies could exist in just the Puget Sound area alone.

4. The author identifies two new major threats as

     a. the study of genetics and the creation of new software.

     b. designer pathogens and nanotechnologists.

     c. nanobots and the biosphere.

     d. out of control nanobots and designer pathogens.

5. All of the pestilences below were actual historical occurrences EXCEPT

     a. global ecophagy.

     b. the Black Death.

     c. smallpox in the Americas.

     d. the flu epidemic of 1918.

6. The author feels a practical and effective defense against creations of new and dangerous technologies would be

     a. an augmented immune system.

     b. large-scale reengineering of the germline of our species.

     c. replacement of our bodies with silicon while retaining our humanity.

     d. none of the above

7. According to Joy, which of the following is NOT true of our democratic system?

   a. Our system puts its faith strongly in the individual.

   b. Democracy in Greece gave birth to modern civilization.

   c. Democracy demands equality of power for all individuals.

   d. Faith in the individual underlies modern democracy and capitalism.

8. Joy believes the risk of our extinction

   a. has been greatly over-exaggerated.

   b. is at an unacceptably high level.

   c. requires us to eliminate the risk through technology.

   d. means we must accept a morally objectionable doctrine such as MAD.

9. The author believes the risk from dangerous technologies can be reduced by

   a. having scientists and technologists take a hypocritical oath.

   b. discussing and debating openly the risks of new technologies.

   c. forcing citizens to purchase catastrophic risk insurance.

   d. banning the development of dangerous technologies in international laboratories.

10. The author feels our only choice is to

   a. keep control over these new technologies.

   b. allow individuals to release self-replicating GNR technologies into the world.

   c. cede control over our future to extreme individuals and accidents.

   d. all of the above

Use the articles by the Tofflers and Joy to complete the exercise below.

Exercise 13.4

Vocabulary: Using Word Parts
Use the word part meanings below and others you learned previously to match the definitions in the column on the right with the words (taken from the previous two articles) on the left.

voc = call	*eu* = good, well
patho = disease	*phage* = one that eats or destroys something
demos = the people	*re* = again
if = without, not	*con* = with

pro = forth   *pan* = all
fluence = flowing   *eco* = environment or habitat

1. _____ provocatively   a. causing improvement in the hereditary qualities

2. _____ mono-causal   b. coming or merging together

3. _____ eugenic   c. happen again

4. _____ malevolent   d. in a manner that arouses to action or feeling

5. _____ pathogens   e. spread throughout the population of a region

6. _____ ecophagy   f. showing ill will; wishing harm to others

7. _____ pandemic   g. without limits

8. _____ recur   h. microorganisms that cause disease

9. _____ illimitable   i. destruction of an environment

10. _____ confluence   j. having only one cause

Logical Fallacies and Emotional Appeals

1. The Tofflers attack Joy's "extreme pessimism" over the dangers of uncontrolled replication, defending their call for more technology with this statement: "Cancer is an example of a runaway, self-replicating process. But do any of us anymore believe there is no cure for cancer?" Supporters of Joy might argue that this line of reasoning commits the fallacy of

   a. begging the question.

   b. faulty causation.

   c. false analogy.

   d. guilt by association.

2. The Toffler argue that both Kaczynski and Joy present scenarios where humans move rapidly from dependence on machines to total loss of control. They feel there are "other alternatives" and that "this reasoning is far too either–or." Those who agree with the Tofflers might find Joy guilty of committing what emotional appeal similar to "either/or"?

   a. hasty generalization

   b. slippery slope

c. guilt by association

d. circular reasoning

3. In several places in their article, the Tofflers attempt to link Bill Joy to the positions of the Unabomber. Supporters of Joy might accuse the Tofflers of which faulty line of reasoning in doing this?

a. hasty generalization

b. faulty causation

c. false analogy

d. guilt by association

Determining Tone

Below are terms designating tone that may or may not fit the authors of the two readings. On the basis of your reading, fill in the blank that best describes the degree to which a tone dominates an article.

Write J in a blank to describe a tone that fits Joy's article.

Write T in a blank to describe a tone that fits the Tofflers.

If a tone fits both articles to the same degree, write B.

Leave blanks empty if a tone fits neither article.

Degree to Which Article Reflects This Tone

Tone	Strongly	In a few places
somber		
flippant		
sincere		
forthright		
frustrated		
earnest		
concerned		
vacillating		
intense		
neutral		
worried		

| nonchalant | _____ | _____ |
| impassioned | _____ | _____ |

Mapping Problem/Solution

Both articles build their arguments by merging the pattern of opinion/reason with a problem/solution analysis. Below is a list that mixes together elements from the problem/solution pattern from both articles. Fill in the two maps that follow with the appropriate items from the list below. The number of blanks in each map indicates how many items from each category need to placed in the map.

<u>Problem:</u>
- Ill-advised attempts to limit range of scientific curiosity in new technologies
- Future of mankind threatened by unrestrained technologies

<u>Causes:</u>
- Ignoring negative feedback loops that control runaway processes
- Believing in faulty mechanistic and mono-causal scenarios
- Advances in genetics, nano-science, and robotics
- Widely available information and cheap materials to create technology
- Underestimating human ability to create counter-technologies
- New, unrestricted self-replicating GNR technologies

<u>Effects:</u>
- Deadly "designer pathogens"
- Undesirable limitations imposed by dangerous rulers
- Attempt to limit the self-replication of knowledge itself
- Destruction of biosphere by robots
- Free, unhindered curiosity and research threatened
- Domination of our species by robots

<u>Solutions:</u>
- Relinquish development of dangerous technologies
- Hippocratic oath for scientists and technologists
- New technologies that shut down out of control systems

- Continue research guided by ethos of science
- Assess and control risks of new technologies

TOFFLERS

PROBLEM:

CAUSES:

1.

2.

3.

EFFECTS:

1.

2.

3.

SOLUTIONS:

1.

2.

JOY

PROBLEM:

CAUSES:

1.

2.

3.

EFFECTS:

1.

2.

3.

SOLUTIONS:

1.

2.

3.

Group Discussion and Debate

For this exercise, form groups of six. Divide up—three on each side—with one side taking the anti-limitation position of the Tofflers and the other the pro-limitation position of Bill Joy.

1. Discuss how any recent events or scientific innovations would support your position for or against placing limits on technology.

2. Using the issue of cloning, develop arguments and cite examples that would give support to your position for or against placing limits on experimentation.

■ OPINION/REASON IN EDITORIAL CARTOONS

Over the last century, the editorial cartoon has been a potent weapon for driving home critical opinions on highly charged political, social, and moral issues. These cartoons can convey their points through all types of idea patterns. A cartoon, for example, may attribute good or bad characteristics to leaders, compare and contrast candidates, assign responsibility for actions to individuals or institutions, or identify problems and suggest solutions. Editorial cartoons are, however, most closely associated with the opinion/reason pattern. Despite the fact that cartoons are mainly pictorial, a clever cartoonist can convey both an opinion and the reasons for it (more often implied than directly stated).

Cartoons often use humor, but their messages are usually quite serious, and making sense of editorial cartoons can be difficult for a number of reasons. First, they require background knowledge on issues and some frames of reference on history and political terminology. Various parts of the cartoon may be labeled— NAFTA, CIA—or well-known political and social leaders may be drawn in caricatures that the reader is expected to recognize. Another difficulty is the use of certain symbols as a kind of common shorthand in cartoons. For example, the donkey represents the Democrats, the elephant and the initials GOP (Grand Old Party) stand for the Republicans, the figure of Uncle Sam represents the United States, and so on. A third difficulty lies in understanding how the parts interrelate in a cartoon to express the message. Cartoonists often use comparisons or analogies to express their ideas. For example, suppose a political party has promoted a funding bill for schools that the cartoonist thinks is inadequate. The cartoonist might convey his opposition by portraying a roofer (with a donkey or elephant face) futilely attempting to fix a huge hole in the roof of a school building with inadequate tools or materials.

To interpret an editorial cartoon correctly, the reader must analyze closely. As an example, look carefully at the cartoon in Figure 13.2 which expresses a very strong opinion about how the news media handle certain events.

Figure 13.2   (*Source*: BIZARRO © 1987 by Dan Piraro. Reprinted with permission of Universal Press Syndicate. All rights reserved.)

To make sense of the cartoon, we must first identify the participants and the context. From what the speaker is doing (holding a mike, addressing a camera) we would assume that he is a TV news reporter; the presence of a TV camera and photographers indicates coverage of a perhaps sensational story. The comments of the reporter support these inferences and help clarify the situation. However, to understand the cartoonist's *attitude* towards what's going on, we have to look carefully at the word choice and the way in which the reporter is portrayed. The negative words "badger and harass" clearly indicate the issue (coverage of events by the media) and the cartoonist's opinion (the media should not act in such a manner). The actions in the cartoon combined with the text and the way the reporter is drawn (prim, unfeeling) allow the reader to recognize several reasons for the opinion:

- Such coverage is an invasion of one's right to privacy in the home.
- Media actions amount to harassment.
- The motivation is purely for money ("for the sake of a few rating points").
- Exploiting the grief of others is disgraceful and inhuman.

One note of caution: don't confuse editorial cartoons with the comics. Comic strips or single-panel comic cartoons, it is true, may deal with social themes or serious ideas through humor. Occasionally a comic strip with strong political content might be placed in the editorial section—*Doonesbury* is an example of this. For the most part, however, editorial cartoons do not have continuing characters. They deal with a single, specific issue. They stand alone, or occasionally accompany an opinion essay or editorial, and can be found in the editorial pages or clearly marked as "opinion" in some other location.

Exercise 13.5

Analyze the cartoon in Figure 13.3 by determining the elements, interpreting their relationships, and identifying the issue, position, opinion, and reasons. Then answer the questions.

1. The issue in the cartoon is indicated by the things that the teacher is carrying. What group heading would you give to these? _____

_____

2. In developing its point of view, this cartoon relies on the reader's being able to make inferences regarding description/support ideas. Based on the way

Figure 13.3   (*Source*: Signe Wilkinson, Cartoonists & Writers Syndicate. Reprinted by permission.)

they are pictured, what words would you use to describe the characteristics and behaviors of

a. the teacher: _____

b. the parent: _____

c. the child: _____

3. From these descriptions and the statement of the teacher in the cartoon, circle the correct letter choice for the author's opinion on the issue.

a. Teachers should be trained better to meet all the needs of students.

b. Parents need to take back responsibilities that the schools have had to assume.

c. Parents should remove children from public schools and place them in private ones.

4. From the combination of elements in the cartoon, we can infer several reasons that would support the cartoonist's opinion. Put an X next to three reasons below that are most strongly implied:

a. _____ Parents are immature and irresponsible.

b. _____ Teachers are complaining too much.

c. _____ Children are out of control.

d. _____ School facilities are inadequate.

e. _____ Teachers are overburdened.

CHAPTER REVIEW

Write T for true or F for false next to the statements.

1. _____ The value component in an opinion/reason pattern is always directly stated.

2. _____ The action component in an opinion/reason pattern is always directly stated.

Circle the correct letter choice.

3. Which statement below is opinion/reason?

a. Minnie should quit her job as a waitress because it will lead to nothing in the future.

b. Minnie quit her job as a waitress because she felt it was a dead end.

4. Which of the following is an example of begging the question?

   a. Principal Wilson's policies are idiotic and foolish.

   b. Education is the key to the future.

   c. Any responsible parent will agree that school uniforms benefit students.

   d. Either we have school uniforms or gangs will overrun the schools.

5. Card stacking is a technique that

   a. involves manipulating evidence.

   b. may rely on ignoring points favorable to the opposition.

   c. can best be combated by a skeptical attitude and background knowledge.

   d. involves all of the above.

Read the following passage and answer the questions by circling the correct letter choice.

> To diminish malnutrition, should government simply give the poor more financial aid and let them spend it as they see fit? Or should the poor be given aid that can be used only to buy food, such as food stamps?
>
> On the one hand, the poor should not be treated like children. Adults in poor families should be allowed to decide how they spend their family income and not be made more dependent on government than they already are. Some may not spend it "wisely" as the larger public might define it, but neither do all other Americans. Then, too, the coupons themselves are a sort of stigma. Some people, particularly the needy elderly in rural communities, are too proud to use the stamps.
>
> On the other hand, giving the poor food stamps ensures that money will be used for food. Extra money cannot be demanded by a landlord for rent, spent on other needed items, or wasted. Some, but not all, who argue in favor of food stamps rather than increased cash aid think the stigma of food stamps is good. It might deter some people from asking for aid when they do not really need it.
>
> (Welch et al., *American Government*, 4th ed., 511)

6. The issue discussed in the passage is

   a. whether food stamps will be abused.

   b. in what form assistance should be given.

   c. whether assistance to the poor should be given or not.

   d. how the media portrays those on welfare.

7. Those favoring cash assistance offer all of the following reasons EXCEPT that

   a. the poor need to make decisions.

   b. cash makes the poor less dependent.

    c. the poor spend more wisely than the larger public.

    d. some are too proud to use food stamps.

8. Reasons given in support of aid through food stamps include all the following EXCEPT that

    a. aid will be used for food.

    b. recipients will not have to pay rent.

    c. extra money won't be wasted.

    d. the stigma of food stamps can discourage the unneedy.

9. The same reason—seen as "good" by one side and "bad" by the other—may be used on both sides of an argument. Which of the following is an example of that in this passage?

    a. Aid may not be spent wisely.

    b. The poor need to make decisions.

    c. Landlords might abuse the system.

    d. Food stamps carry a stigma.

10. The main pattern of organization in the passage is a combination of opinion/reason with

    a. comparison/contrast.

    b. cause/effect.

    c. classification.

    d. time sequence.

READING PORTFOLIO   *Opinion/Reason Article*

    1. *For examples of opinion/reason in newspapers, look first and foremost in the opinion-editorial ("op-ed") section of the paper.* Opinion/reason also appears in the work of regular columnists in other specialty sections, or, occasionally, as a featured front-page article clearly designated as commentary and with the author identified. In magazines, op-ed essays often appear in feature columns of well-known commentators or guest writers.

    2. *There are a number of options you can select from.*

Option A: Opinion Article

The articles you read in this chapter are all examples of this most common type. Look for an article that takes a stand on an issue and justifies it. Get a grasp of the main argument by identifying the *issue* and the author's *position* (pro or con), making a complete *opinion statement,* and listing the *reasons.* From these you should have no difficulty constructing your summary. Your response section is a good place to evaluate the evidence for the author's reasons and "read between the lines." Does the evidence support the reasons? Are the reasons "good" ones? Are there other major hidden assumptions? Has evidence been distorted or left out (card stacking)? You may also give a quick counterargument with your own reasons. Another approach to the response section would be to discuss any *personal* application the issue may have for you.

Option B: Editorial Cartoon

Be sure to select a cartoon that implies one or more reasons as well as an opinion. Also find one on an issue that you have some background on. Identify the various elements and any analogies in the cartoon and explain how they work together to express the issue, position, opinion, and reasons. In your response, you can address concerns similar to those in Option A.

Option C: Review of a Review

This assignment requires you to find an article that summarizes and evaluates a movie, TV show, or live performance. This requires that you must also see the show. Your main purpose is not *writing* a review, but *reviewing* one and responding to it. Summarize the reviewer's discussion of plot and character, the opinion given about the production, and the reasons for the judgment. Then, give your own assessment. Is the reviewer correct or partially correct? Or has the review totally missed the boat? Give your own reasons for your judgment.

3. *Again, you'll find it helpful to work together with a group to evaluate selections and rough drafts and make needed revisions before submitting a final draft.* Follow previous directions for length and filing of your article.

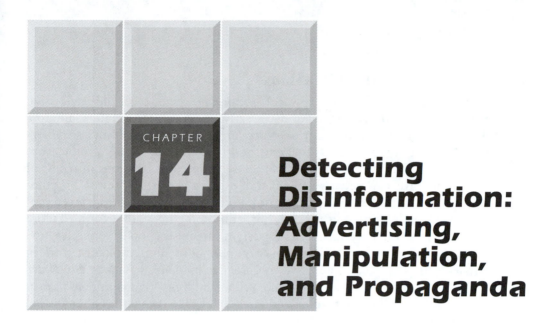

CHAPTER

14

Detecting Disinformation: Advertising, Manipulation, and Propaganda

During the past few decades, in the wake of Watergate, Iran–Contra, and other scandals, the American public began to hear the word *disinformation* used to refer to communication that is intentionally misleading. Whether it be slick advertising or national propaganda, deceptive communications share a common strategy: to confuse people as to the real purpose behind a presentation by making them believe they are getting "the facts" when they are really being misinformed and manipulated. As you will see, persuasive techniques can range from the generally tolerable methods of soft-sell advertising to the dangerously deceptive practices of con men and propagandists.

■ CHAPTER PREVIEW

In this chapter you will

- Get advice on how to analyze an advertisement
- Analyze a typical advertisement
- Evaluate one aspect of the issue of advertising aimed at young people
- Learn to spot techniques of manipulation in personal and public relationships
- Uncover the real assumptions that propaganda works on
- Find and analyze an advertisement or an example of deceptive communication for your Reading Portfolio

◼ MANIPULATION IN ADVERTISING

Caveat emptor—"let the buyer beware"—expresses the code of the advertising world. Of course, advertising is not necessarily an evil. It has a tradition dating back to the ancient world, and it does provide a service in making consumers aware of the variety of products that exist to fill their needs. Many products are of high quality, and the advertisements themselves are the creations of teams of clever people. Ads can be very artistic and, especially in the form of TV commercials, quite humorous. Still, the bottom line for advertisements is to sell, not to inform. The competition in selling is fierce and sometimes ads are aimed more at creating a need for a product than in satisfying an existing one. No matter how mild a technique may seem, some form of emotional manipulation is at work in advertisements. This section will give you practice in analyzing ads and includes an article on one key issue—advertising to schoolchildren—that continues to provoke debate. The following reading will introduce you to the basics of analyzing an advertisement.

PREVIEWING *HOW TO ANALYZE AN AD* BY PHIL SUDO

Setting Your Reading Goals

The first two words in the title of the article clue you that you will be working in a familiar pattern.

That pattern is _____.

When published in *Scholastic Update,* the article carried this subhead: "Advertisers use all kinds of strategies to get your attention and your dollars. By asking some basic questions, you can learn to cut through the hype." These two sentences should give you enough information to determine a main idea hypothesis for the article:

_____

_____

_____

Preview Vocabulary

maximize (4)	make as great as possible
tailored (4)	designed specifically for
ritzy (6)	expensive, exclusive
fostering (8)	encouraging, promoting
critique (9)	analyze critically

Annotating As You Read

Note here how the author has written his subheadings in the form of questions. As you read, make notes in the margin for information on classification (kinds of ads), the target, the sales pitch, and the subtext.

How to Analyze an Ad

by Phil Sudo

1   No one likes to be a sucker. If you don't pay attention, though, ads can make you one. You can protect yourself by learning how to analyze ads. Once you understand the strategies and techniques advertisers use—the buttons they're trying to push—you can spot attempts at manipulation and make better, more critical decisions about what's being advertised. You can even heighten your appreciation of ads—which ones you think are good and which ones you think are bad.

2   So the next time you notice an ad, ask yourself some of these questions:

What Kind of Ad Is It?

3   The majority of ads are called *product ads*—those intended to promote the millions of different goods and services for sale, from baking soda to banking. Other kinds of ads include: *corporate ads,* which promote a company's image or philosophy rather than a product; *political ads,* which aim to generate votes for a candidate or against an opponent; and *public-service ads,* which offer help, promote a cause, or seek donations.

What's the Target?

4   One reason we ignore so many ads is because they're not aimed at us. Advertisers seek to maximize an ad's effectiveness by identifying a *target market*—the audience they want most to reach. To do so, they divide the market into categories: by age, sex, income level, education, geographic region, ethnic background, political leaning, life-style—the list goes on and on. A maker of hockey sticks, for example, is going to target young males who live in cold-weather areas and take part in sports. Thus, its hockey-stick ads would be tailored to appeal to the likes and desires of that market alone.

5   A company with a wide target audience, like McDonald's, will develop several different ads, each aimed at a specific segment of the market—one for

---

Phil Sudo, "How to Analyze an Ad", *Scholastic Update,* May 7, 1993 (Scholastic Inc., 1993).

teenagers, one in Spanish, one for black families. It may cost more than having a single ad designed for everybody, but it is a more calculated, direct method of selling.

Where Is the Ad Found?

6   It makes no sense for the seller of arthritis medication to run an ad on MTV, or for a skateboard maker to advertise on Oprah. Advertisers seek to place their ads in media viewed by their target audience. A public-safety department, for example, might put a billboard about seat belts near a site where accidents are high. Similarly, a ritzy mail-order house might send its catalogues only to ZIP codes like 90210 and other high-income areas.

What's the Sales Pitch?

7   The foundation of an ad is the sales pitch. To make the pitch, ads play on our needs and desires—those basic, often instinctive forces that motivate us to do something. Says one corporate marketing director, "Fear, envy, vanity, health, utility, profit, pride, love, and entertainment. If you ever spend money, it will be for one of those reasons." Here is where your guard should go up. If you can identify the buttons an ad is trying to push, you can avoid manipulation.

What Is the Subtext?

8   All ads have a subtext—that is, a meaning beneath the surface. The subtext of an ad is often what causes the most controversy, usually for fostering sexism or racial and ethnic stereotypes. Ads for laundry detergent, for example, are sometimes criticized for portraying women only as housewives.

9   By looking at the deeper level of ads, you can critique not only the attitudes of the advertiser, but our culture at large—what we value, how we see ourselves. With that knowledge, you can buy into those values or not. At least you'll know you're not getting suckered.

Exercise 14.1

Comprehension Questions

Circle the correct letter choice and fill in the blanks where indicated.

1. This article is an example of which type of "how to"?

    a. process (time sequence)

    b. advice

2. List the four types of ads distinguished in the article.

_____   _____

_____   _____

3. "It makes no sense for the seller of arthritis medication to run an ad on MTV." (6) Why?

_____

_____

_____

4. "Fear, envy, vanity, health, utility, profit, pride, love, and entertainment." In the context of the idea pattern of paragraph 7, these are

a. causes.

b. effects.

5. Explain the difference between the *sales pitch* and the *subtext*.

_____

_____

_____

Exercise 14.2

Figure 14.1 is an example of what is considered a legitimate commercial advertisement. The questions that follow relate back to those posed in "How to Analyze an Ad." In discussing the sales pitch aspect of an ad, you will need to apply some of the terms you met earlier in this text on emotional appeals. The most important of these are repeated here.

name-calling: "mudslinging," the use of value words to hide a lack of real evidence by attaching an unfavorable label or a name to a person or an idea.

glittering generalities: statements that seem to say something but are really giving only a vague positive value judgment.

bandwagon: a technique that appeals to our urge to join with the majority or the in-group associated with being modern and sophisticated.

plain folks: an appeal to our belief in the wisdom of the common man and our suspicion of the rich or highly educated.

It suggests both Fortune 500 and Indianapolis 500.

Calfnap-grained leather-trimmed seats. Cavernous space thanks to its innovative cab-forward design.

A premium 120-watt Chrysler/Infinity Spatial Imaging™ Sound System with no fewer than 11 speakers. And, of course, driver and front passenger air bags. Why, with all that, you'd think we made this car exclusively for the corporate elite. Enter a 214 horsepower, 24-valve, 3.5 liter V6 engine. Road-touring suspension and low-speed traction control. Plus a wide track for superior handling. And you'd be apt to think racing elite. Chrysler LHS. Whatever circles you drive in, you'll be comfortable in both. For more information, call 1-800-4-A-CHRYSLER.

Chrysler LHS
form follows function

Figure 14.1   Advertisement for Chrysler LHS

(The Chrysler LHS ad is used with permission from Chrysler Corporation.)

transfer: the direct or implied use of comparisons for associating the traits of a person, object, or symbol to a product that is being promoted. One common subtype of transfer in advertising is **identification:** we want to be the glamorous or exciting person pictured in the ad.

testimonial: a transfer technique that uses celebrities to speak for and/or have their picture associated with a product.

1. This ad best fits into which of these categories?

   a. product ads

   b. corporate ads

   c. political ads

   d. public-service ads

2. Associations of the product with Fortune 500 and Indianapolis 500 are examples of

   a. bandwagon.

   b. plain folks.

   c. testimonial.

   d. glittering generalities.

   e. transfer.

3. Reference to Fortune 500 most emphasizes the vehicle's

   a. power.

   b. economy.

   c. safety.

   d. luxury features.

4. Reference to Indianapolis 500 most emphasizes the vehicle's

   a. power.

   b. economy.

   c. safety.

   d. luxury features.

5. The feature LEAST emphasized in this ad would be

   a. power.

   b. safety.

   c. economy.

   d. comfort.

Questions for Writing/Small-Group Discussion

"By looking at the deeper level of ads, you can critique not only the attitudes of the advertiser but our culture at large—what we value, how we see ourselves." (9) What values are revealed by the ad above? Do you share them? Why or why not?

FAIRNESS IN ADVERTISING

We may grant that advertising is necessary, but its techniques and its targets can create a good deal of controversy. The following article deals with a very sensitive issue: commercialization of our schools. The author is a professor of education and the director of the Center for the Analysis of Commercialism in Education, University of Wisconsin.

PREVIEWING *HOW ADS IN SCHOOLS COMPROMISE OUR KIDS: IT'S THE REAL THING* BY ALEX MOLNAR

Setting Your Reading Goals

The overall pattern of the article mixes problem/solution (though a solution is only implied), along with some reasons the author gives to support his attack on what he considers to be the problem. From reading the first and last two paragraphs, you should be able to identify the specific problem about which the author is concerned: _____

Preview Vocabulary

osteoporosis (13)	bone disorder involving loss of bone density and brittleness of bone
subsidize (17)	buy aid or support through a grant of money (sometimes considered a bribe)
pervasiveness (19)	condition of being spread throughout

Annotating As You Read

Look for and mark the problem, the causes, and the effects; in the last two paragraphs, try to formulate some solutions the author seems to be implying. Mark and make brief notes on any reasons the author states for his opposition to certain practices in the schools. Also mark EX in the margin for any key examples introduced to clarify points.

How Ads in Schools Compromise Our Kids: It's the Real Thing

by Alex Molnar

1   Over the past 20 years, educators have increasingly turned to corporations to raise money by participating in a variety of activities. Some of the projects are laudable, but many are not. One of our most disturbing trends is schools attempting to raise money by engaging in activities that undermine their curricular message and, in some instances, promote unhealthy student lifestyles.

2   Shortly after the 1998 school year began, a district administrator in Colorado Springs, Colorado, sent a memo to all principals in the district. The subject was how to encourage students to drink more Coca-Cola. If that sounds like an unusual priority, consider that the administrator was responsible for the district's signing an exclusive contract with Coca-Cola.

3   The administrator's memo, which attracted the attention of the *Denver Post, Harper's Magazine, The Washington Post,* and *The New York Times,* pointed out that under the terms of the contract, in which the district agreed to allow only the sale of Coca-Cola products in its schools, students would need to consume 70,000 cases of those products for the district to receive the full benefit of the agreement.

4   The memo urged principals to "allow students to purchase and consume vended products throughout the day," and to "locate machines where they are accessible to the students all day." The administrator even offered to provide schools with additional electrical outlets if necessary. Enclosed with the memo was a list of Coca-Cola products and a calendar of events intended to help promote them.

5   The exclusive contract with Coca-Cola is representative of one of the fastest growing areas of schoolhouse commercialism. According to the Center for Commercial-Free Public Education, in April 1998 there were 46 exclusive agreements between school districts and soft-drink bottlers in 16 states. By July 1999, a little over a year later, there were 150 such agreements with school districts in 29 states—and the numbers continue to rise.

6   These contracts can produce situations like that which occurred two years ago at Greenbrier High School in Evans, Georgia, when Principal Gloria Hamilton made international headlines by suspending senior Mike Cameron. He was with a group of 1,200 classmates who lined up in the

---

Alex Molnar, condensed from "How Ads in Schools Compromise Our Kids: It's the Real Thing", *Principal* (National Association of Elementary School Principals, 80, Nov. 2000), 18–21.

school parking lot to spell out the word "Coke." This was to be the highlight of Greenbrier's "Coke in Education Day," during which about 20 Coca-Cola executives were on hand to lecture on economics, assist home economics students in baking a "Coke cake," and help chemistry students analyze the sugar content of Coca-Cola. Photographers using a crane were prepared to capture the defining moment on film—when Cameron exposed a shirt that boldly spelled out "Pepsi."

Disrespect?

7   According to Cameron, he not only received a dressing down from the principal in her office, but was told that he was being suspended for disrespect—and for possibly costing the school $10,000 in prize money offered by Coke to the winning high school in a national marketing campaign. Newspaper reports of the incident were hardly flattering. Under the headline, "Student's Act of Cola Defiance Was Refreshing," the Norfolk, Virginia, *Virginian-Pilot* editorialized, "Enlightened, responsible corporate investment of time and money can be of significant help to hard-strapped schools everywhere; but to make the boosting of a business a part of the day's curriculum is counterproductive."

8   Close kin to exclusive marketing deals are marketing incentive programs that enlist schools to steer students and their families to certain brands. These have long been a staple of corporate marketing efforts in schools. For example, Campbell Soup's Labels for Education program, launched in 1973, now reaches 50 million school children, while Pizza Hut's Book it! reading incentive program, launched in 1984, is in 53,000 schools. The popularity of these and other incentive programs, such as General Mills' Box Tops for Education, Giant Foods' Apples for the Students, and AT&T's Learning Points has led to a number of variations.

Check the Acronym

9   In 1996, Blockbuster video stores launched a program in Hawaii called Viewing Can Reward, where districts received videocassette recorders when their students or family members turned in punch cards showing that a combined total of 5,000 movies or video games had been rented. Also in 1996, Pepsi-Cola initiated a School Caps program in 110 schools. Students were asked to collect blue bottle caps from select Pepsi products and turn them in to their school, which received a nickel per cap.

10   While schools may receive some money from such programs, marketers reap the lion's share of the financial rewards. In 1997 the *Boston Globe* reported that General Mills had "managed to switch thousands of Special K eaters over to marshmallow-laced Lucky Charms by giving cash to students."

Students at one elementary school had collected 27,000 General Mills box tops (117 per student) in a General Mills promotion paying the school 15 cents per box top.

11   Incentive programs are at best considered by some a type of "cause-related" marketing; by purchasing a product or service, customers can promote a worthy cause. Pizza Hut's Book it! program rewards school children who meet reading goals with Pizza Hut products. This associates the pizza with the social goal of literacy—and at the same time promotes its consumption.

12   Incentive programs have a social and economic downside, as General Mills found out when the Catholic Diocese of Gary, Indiana, ordered Box Tops for Education out of its schools because the General Mills Foundation had awarded a grant to Planned Parenthood of Minnesota. (In response, the foundation "phased out" the grant.) Exclusive agreements also carry a heavy price. Health experts are concerned about the rising amounts of soft drinks young people consume, and the consequent harm to their health. In slightly less than 30 years, the annual consumption per capita of soda more than doubled, from 22.4 gallons in 1970 to 56.1 in 1998.

13   The Center for Science in the Public Interest found that a quarter of the teenage boys who drink soda consume more than two 12-ounce cans daily and that 5% drink more than 5 cans. Girls, although they drink about a third less soda, face potentially more serious health consequences. With soda pushing milk out of their diets, an increasing number of girls may be early candidates for osteoporosis.

14   Richard Troiano, a National Cancer Institute senior scientist, says data on soda consumption suggests a link with childhood obesity: Overweight children tend to take in more calories from soda than those who are not overweight. With childhood obesity rates virtually doubling in 20 years, William Dietz, director of the nutrition division at the U.S. Centers for Disease Control and Prevention, suggests, "If the schools must have vending machines, they should concentrate on healthy choices, like bottled water."

15   Rather than promoting healthy choices, though, it appears that exclusive agreements put pressure on school districts to increase the number of vending machines in schools in order to increase sales of soft drinks. Colorado Springs is just one example. Last year, Daniel Michaud, business administrator for the Edison, New Jersey, public schools, told *The Washington Post* that, prior to signing an exclusive contract with Coca-Cola, few of the district's schools had vending machines. After signing the contract, most district high schools had four machines, middle schools had three, and elementary schools had one. As a student at a Rhode Island high school with an exclusive contract commented, "There's really nothing else to drink."

High-Stakes Game

16   It is unlikely that the trend toward exclusive agreements with soft-drink bottlers will abate in the near future. G. David Van Houten, Jr., Coca-Cola senior vice president, says schools "are important to everyone, and it has recently become a high-stakes game for that very reason. How much is that [school] business worth? I doubt we'll ever be able to answer that question fully. But we're going to continue to be very aggressive and proactive in getting our share of the school business."

17   Other ways to get that business are described by the Center for the Analysis of Commercialism in Education, which identifies seven sometimes-overlapping kinds of commercial activity in schools:

1. **Sponsorship of programs and activities.** Corporations pay for, or subsidize, school events and/or one-time activities in return for the right to associate their names with these activities.

2. **Exclusive agreements.** Schools agree to give corporations exclusive rights to sell and promote their goods and/or services in a school or district. The school or district gets a percentage of the profits from the arrangement. Such agreements may entail granting a corporation the right to be a sole supplier of a product or service.

3. **Incentive programs.** These corporate programs provide money, goods, or services to a school or district when students, parents, or staff do a specified activity, such as collecting product labels or cash register receipts.

4. **Appropriation of space.** Corporations pay to place corporate logos and/or advertising messages on school scoreboards, rooftops, bulletin boards, walls, and book covers.

5. **Sponsored educational materials.** Instructional materials are supplied to schools by corporations and/or trade associations.

6. **Electronic marketing.** Corporations provide electronic programming and/or equipment for the right to advertise online to students, families, or community members.

7. **Privatization.** The management of schools or school programs by private, for-profit corporations or other nonpublic organizations.

18   The American people are poorly served when our public schools become educational flea markets open to anyone with the money to set up a table. But that is what the relentless assault on funding for public education and repeated calls for "cooperation" with the business community are pushing schools to do.

A Trend to Watch

19   The effort to integrate the schoolhouse into corporate marketing plans by securing control of school-based advertising media may well be the trend to watch over the next decade. If so, we can expect schools to serve as launch pads for marketing campaigns with multiple tie-ins for a variety of products and services aimed at children and their families. Yet, despite the pervasiveness and rapid growth of schoolhouse commercialism, educators and the education press have been largely silent about—or, worse, cheerleaders for—this fundraising approach. The failure of the education community to critically assess the impact of commercial activities on the character and quality of schools reveals an ethical blindness not worthy of a profession that seeks to serve the best interests of children.

Exercise 14.3

Vocabulary

Use the context to match the words on the left with the meanings on the right.

1. _____ laudable (1)

    a. a taking over of something for one's own use

2. _____ priority (2)

    b. lessen, diminish

3. _____ counterproductive (7)

    c. involve, require

4. _____ abate (16)

    d. something given importance to

5. _____ entail (17)

    e. worthy of praise

6. _____ appropriation (17)

    f. producing an effect opposite to what was intended

Mapping

Use your annotations of the text to fill in the problem/solution map. The solution is implied.

- promotes unhealthy life-styles: osteoporosis/obesity
- educators must evaluate programs to separate good from bad
- assault on funding for public education
- pressure to "cooperate" with business community
- silence or "cheerleading" by educators/education press
- curricular message of schools is undermined

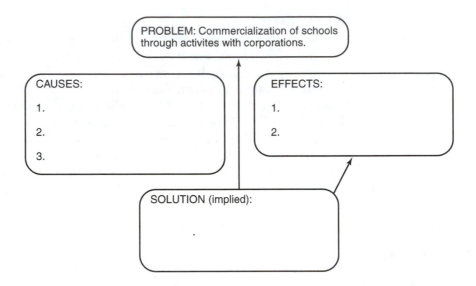

Comprehension Questions

Circle the correct letter choice and fill in the blanks where indicated.

1. Which of the following is NOT a reason the author puts forward for opposing commercial programs in the schools?

    a. Most of the money goes to marketers, not the schools.

    b. They have a social and economic downside.

    c. They can carry a heavy price in harmful consequences to health.

    d. They can sometimes provide a way to promote a worthy cause.

2. Mike Cameron was criticized for his prank with his "Pepsi" shirt by

    a. a *Virginian-Pilot* editorial.

    b. the author of this article.

    c. his principal.

    d. all of the above

3. "In 1997 the *Boston Globe* reported that General Mills had 'managed to switch thousands of Special K eaters over to marshmallow-laced Lucky Charms by giving cash to students.'" (10) Which one of the following can we infer from this statement?

    a. Students switched because they preferred the taste of Lucky Charms.

    b. Lucky Charms is a product of General Mills, but Special K isn't.

    c. The *Globe* thinks Lucky Charms is a healthier product than Special K.

    d. Giving money is not an effective way to gain product support.

4. "Pizza Hut's Book It! program rewards school children who meet reading goals with Pizza Hut products. This associates the pizza with the social goal of literacy—and at the same time promotes its consumption." (11) This statement criticizes Pizza Hut for using which emotional appeal technique?

    a. transfer

    b. glittering generality

    c. bandwagon

    d. name-calling

5. We can infer from the example involving General Mills, the Catholic Diocese of Gary, Indiana, and Planned Parenthood of Minnesota that

    a. General Mills had long been opposed to the aims and goals of Planned Parenthood.

    b. General Mills discontinued its grant to Planned Parenthood because of economic considerations.

    c. The response of General Mills showed its refusal to compromise its principles.

    d. General Mills would soon phase out its Box Tops for Education program.

6. The author lists seven types of commercial activity in schools:

    a. Sponsorship of programs and activities

    b. Exclusive agreements

    c. Incentive programs

    d. Appropriation of space

    e. Sponsored educational materials

    f. Electronic marketing

    g. Privatization

    Write the *two* that the article mainly focuses on:

    _____   _____

7. The author's attitude regarding the educational community is that

    a. economic conditions leave it no other choice than to cooperate with marketers.

    b. even if educators spoke out, they would have little effect on the situation.

    c. they share a large part of the blame for shameless commercialization in schools.

    d. a strong anti-commercialism effort by the schools will be the new trend.

8. The author draws evidence for his position from all of the following EXCEPT

    a. incidents reported in the press.

    b. studies from various centers and institutes.

    c. quotations from experts and others in the field.

    d. the author's personal experience as a school administrator.

9. Which of the following best describes the author's purpose in the article?

    a. expose a problem badly in need of a solution

    b. objectively lay out the facts on both sides so debate can occur

    c. promote a switch from incentive programs to exclusive agreements

    d. get rid of all projects involving corporations and schools

10. The author's tone in the article is best described as

    a. subtle and humorous.

    b. blunt and unsparing.

    c. vindictive and sarcastic.

    d. playful and ironic.

Question For Discussion

1. Sometimes in courses or in casual discussions, you may find yourself "playing the devil's advocate"—that is, defending a position you don't really believe in just for the sake of argument. This can, however, force all participants to make a more careful examination of their own assumptions. Form discussion groups wherein one side, whatever its true beliefs, defends commercial activities in schools, and the other side opposes the activities.

■ BEHIND THE MASK: DECEIT IN RELATIONSHIPS

We may fear being used by impersonal, well-funded forces beyond our control, but we can be manipulated equally on a personal level and on a smaller scale in issues that can affect family, community, and work. In the following article, the author, a teacher in the public schools, criticizes the techniques by which power can be abused in parent-child and management-employee relationships.

PREVIEWING *STOP THE MANIPULATIVE TRICKERY* BY FAITH NITSCHKE
Setting Your Reading Goal

Your first task is to analyze and understand the authors viewpoint, before you can respond to it. Preview by reading the title and the first paragraph. From this you can make an hypothesis on:

The issue: _____

The opinion: _____

Preview Vocabulary

preclude (1)	prevent
negate (5)	deny, nullify
placates (6)	satisfies by yielding to, appeases
sans (8)	without
facilitator (10)	one who makes things easier; leader, moderator
substantiated (11)	supported with proof, verified

Annotating As You Read

In this opinion/reason pattern, the author argues against a negative action. Therefore, be on the lookout for a recommendation offering some positive counteractions. In the margin, note reasons and recommendations as you encounter them.

Stop the Manipulative Trickery

by Faith Nitschke

1   I've come to the conclusion that "people management/communication" courses ought to be banned, and this is coming from a person who is against

---

Faith Nitschke, "Stop the Manipulative Trickery," from *The Fresno Bee*, 11/2/92. Reprinted by permission of The Fresno Bee.

censorship. The reason I distrust such courses is they preclude honest relationships and depend upon manipulation. Manipulation is dishonest. It's a way of using people, a belief in "the end justifies the means."

2   One of the easiest places to manipulate people is in the parent-child relationship. Any adult is superior to a child intellectually (for a while, at least) and can easily use manipulation to control behavior.

3   Let's say you are struggling with your 2-year-old who continues to play with the television remote control. My son's preschool teacher advised that when your child is doing something you don't like, distract him away. So I was to bring out a toy or something else he'd have. I hated that. I felt the problem with this distraction technique is that it didn't address the real problem—that the child was playing with something that he shouldn't have been playing with. Sure, I can outsmart a 2-year-old (most of the time, anyway), but what have I taught him?

4   The half-knowledge some graduates of these courses operate with is quite disturbing. I had a college student who once wrote, "I am a good listener. I look directly at the speaker, I lean into them a bit, and I nod my head occasionally while they're speaking."

Smoothing over Your Concerns

5   Another thing I really hate about these "management" courses is that they negate authentic response. I swear, if one more person says, "I'm so happy you brought that up. We really need to hear your concerns," I'm going to challenge him to a duel.

6   Schools do it all the time. "It's so nice to have concerned parents," we say. Barf. My advice to you is stay on the line until you get an answer to your question, not a piece of sweet talk that temporarily placates you.

7   I am also coming to distrust the line, "If I'm hearing you correctly, this is what you seem to be saying." Then the person shapes your words ever so slightly differently, and all of a sudden, the discussion is going in a direction that seems to have little connection with your previous comments.

8   Here's another way it works: Get a group of people together who aren't behaving as you wish them to. (You already know how you want the problem solved.) Explain the problem to them (sans solutions, of course). Then ask for their input. We call this grassroots or site-based management.

9   Listen for any reference to your solution—have a list of key words memorized. Then when someone stumbles onto anything that resembles your key word, you pop in and say, "If I am hearing you correctly, you seem to be talking about a need for _____." Bingo, they've arrived at just the

10   spot you wanted them to be at and now they can adopt your own precon- ceived solution as if it were their own.

It's like when you're at a meeting to solve some problem and you go through the entire brainstorming process only to find that before the meeting is over, the facilitator hands out already printed material on the very solution your group has "independently" arrived at. Amazing.

11   This assumes a pessimistic view of humanity, that people are only capable of mediocrity, not brilliance. Let's put the problem at "A" on a continuum and the solution at "Z." We are at "A" trying to solve the problem. The hinted, preprinted material gets us to "C." The facilitator is happy—a bunch of people have just substantiated his worth. The people at the meeting are happy—the stupid meeting is over and they can get back to real work.

12   Supposedly, however, the beauty of the human condition is that we learn from our past mistakes, which this approach denies: "C" is as far as we can get, and we should be happy with "C."

13   But why not give us "C" at the beginning of the meeting and build on it? Perhaps we can get to "G." And next week, perhaps another group can get further.

Trying to Isolate You

14   The line I hate the worst, though, is, "You're the first person who has ever complained about this." If someone says this to you, beware! What you should immediately do is start talking to other people. Your question poses a threat to those in power. The one thing they don't want you to know is that there are others who feel the same way as you do. You know, the power in numbers thing. So they make you feel as if you are some isolated nut.

15   Another way to combat this approach is simply not to care if you are the only one who feels this way. This is how I handle the "you are really some weirdo" implication. Who knows, I may be the only one with enough courage to say what everybody else is thinking. Besides, I read Emerson in my formative years.

16   I think it's possible for us to have open, authentic communication with each other, workers to workers and workers to management, when we are sincere in our intent to do so. It will mean that we are open, that we put all our cards on the table at the beginning of the negotiations, that we speak honestly and directly, and that we throw out that lousy book on people management/communication techniques.

Exercise 14.5

Pattern Mapping

Complete the map below. Relevant paragraph numbers are given in parentheses.

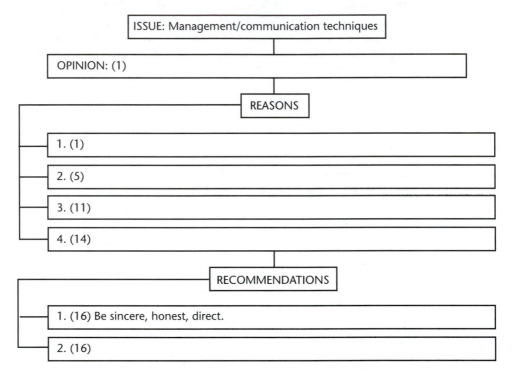

ISSUE: Management/communication techniques

OPINION: (1)

REASONS

1. (1)

2. (5)

3. (11)

4. (14)

RECOMMENDATIONS

1. (16) Be sincere, honest, direct.

2. (16)

Comprehension Questions

Circle the correct letter choice.

1. Paragraph 3 relates to paragraph 2 by

   a. providing a contrast.

   b. suggesting a solution.

   c. giving an illustration.

   d. showing the effect of a cause.

2. The author objects (3) to the distraction technique for all of the following reasons EXCEPT that

   a. it's manipulative.

   b. it didn't make the child stop.

   c. it didn't deal with the real problem.

   d. the child didn't learn anything.

3. In paragraph 4 the example shows that management courses create students who

   a. exhibit mastery of good study techniques.

   b. value appearance over reality.

   c. know the importance of student-teacher relationships.

   d. have a clear notion of what a truly good listener does.

4. The author implies that people who say things like "I'm so happy you brought that up. We really need to hear your concerns" (5) are

   a. phony.

   b. good problem solvers.

   c. confused.

   d. open-minded.

5. A person who says "If I'm hearing you correctly, this is what you seem to be saying" (7) is

   a. unintentionally misunderstanding you.

   b. not actually hearing you correctly.

   c. attempting to paraphrase your ideas accurately.

   d. hearing correctly but twisting your meaning.

6. The example given in paragraphs 8–9 suggests that manipulation

   a. is carefully calculated in advance.

   b. is more concerned with control than truth.

   c. requires a certain amount of acting.

   d. all of the above

7. In paragraph 10, the word *amazing* is used to show

   a. genuine wonder.

   b. appreciation of the discussion process.

   c. disgust with the technique.

   d. approval of the facilitator's actions.

8. By using the example with alphabet letters (11–13), the author hopes to show that

   a. most people are capable only of mediocrity.

   b. everybody is happier if we don't push our thinking too far.

   c. most workers need to be rigidly directed to get anywhere at all.

   d. people are better problem solvers when they're not manipulated.

9. Which of the following is the best statement of the implied idea of multi-paragraph unit 14–15?

   a. You can solve the problem of being isolated by talking to others or refusing to care.

   b. Talking to people is better than pretending not to care.

   c. Employees who talk to others pose a threat to those in power.

   d. You should resist isolation for two reasons.

10. The author believes authentic communication can occur if workers and managers

   a. are sincere.

   b. avoid deceptive negotiation.

   c. avoid manipulative techniques.

   d. all of the above

Questions for Writing/Small-Group Discussion

1. Find some information on Ralph Waldo Emerson. Who was he? Why is he mentioned here?

2. Have you ever had the experience of being manipulated—or being the manipulator—in a similar situation? How did you feel at the time? Later?

3. The author offers some advice on handling situations where communication is dishonest. Add one or two suggestions to her list.

▦ PROPAGANDA: A CAPACITY FOR SHEER EVIL

Propaganda—the systematic spreading of material favorable to one's interest—is often looked on rather tolerantly as a necessary irritant of international relations: our enemies use it, our allies use it, and we use it, in war and in peace. The history of the last century, however, has shown that propaganda can be a ruthless tool with a tremendous capacity for evil when used by unscrupulous, amoral people. It rejects the values of rational discussion by resorting to emotional appeals and logical fallacies. At its core, for example, propaganda is nothing more than a large-scale game of card stacking: ignoring anything counter to one's position. Another common technique of propaganda is *stereotyping*, the creation of a rigid, inaccurate portrayal of individuals and groups. Stereotyping also usually leads to another underhanded practice, *scapegoating*, by which individuals or groups are unfairly made a focus of blame and persecution. At the center of both of these techniques rests a vicious emotional appeal that you have analyzed and identified previously in this text: name-calling.

The potential destructiveness of propaganda is nowhere more evident than in its use in the wars and political conflicts of the twentieth century. It played a major role, for example, in the war machine of Nazi Germany in World War II, a conflict responsible for the deaths of well over 40 million citizens and soldiers, including the calculated genocide of 6 million European Jews. In the last selection in this text, you will read an explanation (and what amounts to a shameless defense) of propaganda by a man whom history has justly labeled one of the true monsters of all time.

PREVIEWING *WAR PROPAGANDA* BY ADOLF HITLER

Setting Your Reading Goals

The name most often associated with the Nazi horror is Adolf Hitler. In the mid-1920s, between the two world wars and while in prison after leading an unsuccessful uprising, Hitler wrote *Mein Kampf* (My Struggle). In it he stated his political and racial views and gave a blueprint of the ruthless methods which he was to install in Germany in the years of his dictatorship (1933–1945). The selection here is from Vol. I, Chapter VI.

Preview Vocabulary

loftiest (6)	highest, most noble
aesthetics (8)	philosophical study concerned with the theory of beauty and the fine arts
intelligentsia (13)	the intellectual elite

Annotating As You Read

In this selection Hitler is out to show how the use of propaganda is essential to ensure the war aims of an aggressor—and how Germany failed to use it properly in World War I. As you read, try to formulate an answer to this question: On what grounds does Hitler justify the deliberate distortion of truth and the manipulation of the masses? Use the margins to ask questions and make any counterarguments where appropriate.

War Propaganda

by Adolf Hitler

1   But it was not until the War [World War I, 1914–18] that it became evident what immense results could be obtained by a correct application of propaganda....

Excerpts from *Mein Kampf* by Adolf Hitler, translated by Ralph Manheim (Houghton Mifflin Company, 1943, renewed 1971).

2   Did we have anything you could call propaganda?

3   I regret that I must answer in the negative. Everything that actually was done in this field was so inadequate and wrong from the very start that it certainly did no good and sometimes did actual harm.

4   The form was inadequate, the substance was psychologically wrong: a careful examination of German war propaganda can lead to no other diagnosis.

5   There seems to have been no clarity on the very first question: Is propaganda a means or an end?

> Read—and reread—the next few paragraphs very carefully. Make sure you clearly understand the meaning of the first three sentences of paragraph **6** before you move on.

6   It is a means and must therefore be judged with regard to its end. It must constantly take a form calculated to support the aim which it serves. It is also obvious that its aim can vary in importance from the standpoint of general need, and that the inner value of the propaganda will vary accordingly. The aim for which we were fighting the War was the loftiest, the most overpowering, that man can conceive: It was the freedom and independence of our nation, the security of our future food supply, and—our national honor....

7   The German nation was engaged in a struggle for a human existence, and the purpose of war propaganda should have been to support this struggle; its aim to help bring about victory.

8   When nations on this planet fight for existence—when the question of destiny, "to be or not to be," cries out for a solution—then all considerations of humanitarianism or aesthetics crumble into nothingness....

9   And since these criteria of humanitarianism and beauty must be eliminated from the struggle, they are also inapplicable to propaganda.

10   Propaganda in the War was a means to an end, and the end was the struggle for the existence of the German people; consequently, propaganda could only be considered in accordance with the principles that were valid for this struggle. In this case the most cruel weapons were humane if they brought about a quicker victory; and only those methods were beautiful which helped the nation to safeguard the dignity of its freedom.

11   This was the only possible attitude toward war propaganda in a life-and-death struggle like ours.

12   If the so-called responsible authorities had been clear on this point, they would have never fallen into such uncertainty over the form and application of this weapon: for even propaganda is no more than a weapon, though a frightful one in the hand of an expert.

13   The second really decisive question was this: To whom should propaganda be addressed? To the scientifically trained intelligentsia or to the less educated masses?

14   It must be addressed always and exclusively to the masses.

15   What the intelligentsia—or those who today unfortunately often go by that name—what they need is not propaganda but scientific instruction. The content of propaganda is not science any more than the object represented in a poster is art. The art of the poster lies in the designer's ability to attract the attention of the crowd by form and color....

16   A similar situation prevails with what we today call propaganda.

17   The function of propaganda does not lie in the scientific training of the individual, but in calling the masses' attention to certain facts, processes, necessities, etc., whose significance is thus for the first time placed within their field of vision.

18   The whole art consists in doing this so skillfully that everyone will be convinced that the fact is real, the process necessary, the necessity correct, etc. But since propaganda is not and cannot be the necessity in itself, since its function, like the poster, consists in attracting the attention of the crowd and not in educating those who are already educated or who are striving after education and knowledge, its effect for the most part must be aimed at the emotions and only to a very limited degree at the so-called intellect.

19   All propaganda must be popular and its intellectual level must be adjusted to the most limited intelligence among those it is addressed to. Consequently, the greater the mass it is intended to reach, the lower its purely intellectual level will have to be. But if, as in propaganda for sticking out a war, the aim is to influence a whole people, we must avoid excessive intellectual demands on our public, and too much caution cannot be exerted in this direction....

20   The art of propaganda lies in understanding the emotional ideas of the great masses and finding, through a psychologically correct form, the way to the attention and thence to the heart of the broad masses. The fact that our bright boys do not understand this merely shows how mentally lazy and conceited they are.

21   Once we understand how necessary it is for propaganda to be adjusted to the broad mass, the following rule results: It is a mistake to make propaganda many-sided, like scientific instruction, for instance.

22   The receptivity of the great masses is very limited, their intelligence is small, but their power of forgetting is enormous. In consequence of these facts, all effective propaganda must be limited to a very few points and must harp on these in slogans until the last member of the public understands what you want him to understand by your slogan. As soon as you sacrifice this slogan and try to be many-sided, the effect will piddle away, for the crowd can neither digest nor retain the material offered. In this way the result is weakened and in the end entirely canceled out....

23   What our authorities least of all understood was the very first axiom of all propagandist activity: to wit, the basically subjective and one-sided attitude it must take toward every question it deals with. In this connection, from

the very beginning of the War and from top to bottom, such sins were committed that we were entitled to doubt whether so much absurdity could really be attributed to pure stupidity alone.

24   What, for example, would we say about a poster that was supposed to advertise a new soap and that described other soaps as "good"?

25   We would only shake our heads.

26   Exactly the same applies to political advertising.

27   The function of propaganda is, for example, not to weigh and ponder the rights of different people, but exclusively to emphasize the one right which it has set out to argue for. Its task is not to make an objective study of the truth, in so far as it favors the enemy, and then set it before the masses with academic fairness; its task is to serve our own right, always and unflinchingly.

28   It was absolutely wrong to discuss war-guilt from the standpoint that Germany alone could not be held responsible for the outbreak of the catastrophe; it would have been correct to load every bit of the blame on the shoulders of the enemy, even if this had not really corresponded to the true facts, as it actually did.

Exercise 14.6

Comprehension Questions

Circle the correct letter choice.

1. This passage as a whole combines the pattern of opinion/reason mainly with

   a. comparison/contrast.

   b. whole/part.

   c. how to: time sequence.

   d. how to: advice.

2. What does Hitler mean by saying that propaganda "is a means and must therefore be judged with regard to its end"? (6)

   a. A rational means will always lead to a justified end.

   b. You can justify any method whatsoever if you're convinced the end is good.

   c. Both methods and aims must be equally morally justifiable.

   d. The end of propaganda is to provide a rational choice between two views.

3. In paragraphs 8–10, Hitler provides a rationale for saying that war can be "humane" and "beautiful" if it

   a. ensures national survival as quickly as possible.

   b. follows humanitarian rules for the conduct of war.

   c. provides safeguards for artists and thinkers during war.

   d. is justified in the eyes of a majority of the world's nations.

4. Hitler seems to imply in paragraphs 6–11 that relationships between nations must necessarily be

   a. rational.

   b. antagonistic.

   c. cooperative.

   d. built on mutual respect.

5. According to paragraphs 18 and 19, propaganda should

   a. build on a foundation of rational discourse.

   b. be aimed at the lazy and conceited "bright boys."

   c. emphasize emotion to the exclusion of reason.

   d. all of the above

6. We can infer from Hitler's comments (19–22) that he believes the average man is

   a. highly capable of self-government.

   b. a potential thinker and problem solver.

   c. a slow-witted sheep to be led.

   d. born with natural rights to liberty and free speech.

7. It might be argued that the points Hitler makes regarding the relation of propaganda to posters and advertising (15–18, 24–26) are based on what logical fallacy?

   a. faulty causation

   b. hasty generalization

   c. guilt by association

   d. false analogy

8. According to Hitler (22), what is the function of slogans?

   a. to brainwash the listener

   b. to adapt propaganda to the audience's limited intelligence

   c. to prevent memory loss

   d. all of the above

9. Given Hitler's views, the possessive pronoun *our* in the phrase "serve our own right, always and unflinchingly" (27) would likely refer specifically to which group?

   a. all citizens of any nation

   b. his elite group of strong-arm leaders

   c. all residents of Germany

   d. all citizens of democracies

10. Hitler's assertion that "it would have been correct to load every bit of the blame on the shoulders of the enemy, even if this had not really corresponded to the true facts, as it actually did" (28) is all of the following EXCEPT

   a. fact.

   b. propaganda.

   c. false.

   d. unsupported by evidence.

Questions for Writing/Small-Group Discussion

1. In paragraph 26, Hitler refers to propaganda as "political advertising." Do the aims and methods of regular product advertising and propaganda differ? If so, how?

2. "When nations on this planet fight for existence–when the question of destiny, 'to be or not to be,' cries out for a solution–then all considerations of humanitarianism or aesthetics crumble into nothingness." (8) In debating this issue, what counterarguments would you use?

3. Are you aware of, or have you experienced, instances where agencies of our government have engaged in propaganda? Is propaganda justifiable in wartime? During "cold" wars? Now?

4. Do the ends ever justify extreme or inhumane actions (means)? Can you give examples where they would?

CHAPTER REVIEW

Circle the correct letter choice.

1. An advertisement listing a hotline number for AIDS victims most likely would be a

    a. product ad.

    b. corporate ad.

    c. political ad.

    d. public-service ad.

2. An ad detailing a chemical corporation's commitment to an environmental cleanup project would be an example of a

    a. product ad.

    b. corporate ad.

    c. political ad.

    d. public-service ad.

3. An ad for blue jeans would be an example of a

    a. product ad.

    b. corporate ad.

    c. political ad.

    d. public-service ad.

4. An insurance ad showing an elderly couple sunning on a tropical island beach would be built around the technique of

    a. transfer.

    b. bandwagon.

    c. testimonial.

    d. glittering generality.

5. Ads for milk featuring pictures of celebrities with milk mustaches would be a variation on the technique of

    a. glittering generality.

    b. bandwagon.

    c. testimonial.

    d. plain folks.

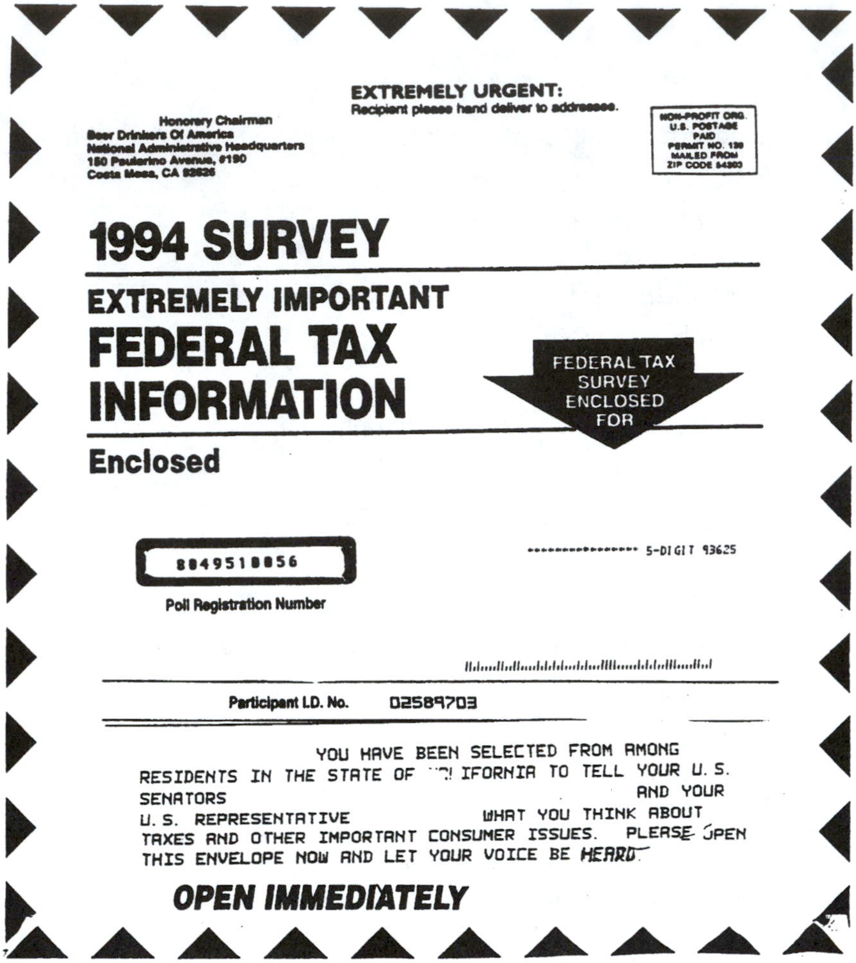

Figure 14.2

Analyze the communication in Figure 14.2, then answer the questions that follow.

6. The sponsors want this "survey" to appear to be sent by whom?

_____

_____

7. Why did the sponsors want to suggest that particular identity as sender?

_____

_____

8. What purposes do you think the "Poll Registration Number" and "Participant ID No." are there to serve?

_____

_____

9. "EXTREMELY URGENT: Recipient please hand deliver to addressee." What does this really mean? Why is it included?

_____

_____

10. The actual source of this "survey" is what group?

_____

_____

READING PORTFOLIO   *Analyzing Disinformation*

This assignment gives you a chance to analyze any communication that you believe has a strong element of disinformation. You may find it easier in this assignment to mix summary and response, evaluating various elements as you go along. If you feel this approach is best, discuss it first with your instructor.

Option A

Analyze an ad of your own choosing. To do well on this assignment, you need to pick your ad very carefully. Most ads in newspapers are straightforward products ads. They may include a picture or a drawing, but there are few subtle appeals. The best source for ads is a magazine printed on high-quality ("slick") paper. Look for an ad that has some complexity; the more elements working in the ad, the more you will have to write about. Use these guidelines to write a summary and response.

Summary

1. Give a brief, objective description of the main details in the ad. Unless you submit the original ad, you may need to add descriptions for the reader of such things as the intensity of colors being used or other details that might not be clear in a black-and-white copy.

2. Identify any of the following emotional appeals in the ad and explain how, in the context of the ad, they deliver the sales pitch:

bandwagon	glittering generalities
plain folks	transfer
testimonial	

<u>Response</u>

1. Comment on the values or images the ad promotes, and whether or not there is a subtle and possibly objectionable subtext.

2. Discuss the effectiveness of the ad. Would it tend to make its target audience buy the product? Would you be likely to buy it?

Option B

Look for an advertisement that has a definite element of deceit. Words like *amazing, scientific,* or *unbelievable* are usually signals of an ad that is a rip-off.

<u>Summary</u>

1. Give a brief, objective description of the contents and identify the product/service being pitched in the ad.

2. Describe any other details not clear in a black-and-white copy.

3. Examine the evidence closely for false or unsubstantiated aims.

4. Analyze closely the terms of any supposed guarantees.

<u>Response</u>

1. Explain your reasoning in concluding that the ad is bogus.

2. Discuss the effectiveness of the ad.

3. Would it tend to make its target audience buy the product?

Option C

Look for deceptive advertising or junk mailings regarding political campaign ballot proposals or candidates.

<u>Summary</u>

1. Identify the issue, proposition, or candidates.

2. Give some framing information to help the reader put the communication in context.

<u>Response</u>

1. Analyze for faulty evidence and for the fallacies.

2. Try to identify who the real people might be behind a front—e.g., trial lawyers posing as a consumer group on an insurance measure.

Glossary of Terms

Analogy: an extended comparison between two generally very different things that share one or two significant relationships or characteristics. Analogies use the more familiar to explain the unfamiliar.

Bandwagon: an emotional appeal that urges us to base our actions on our desire to be with the majority or with a special "in" group.

Beliefs: concepts we hold to with little or no factual evidence.

Clarification: a restatement of an idea in a simpler and easier to understand form.

Connotation: the feelings, emotions, or value judgments that a word may carry.

Context clues: signals that lead a reader to make an educated guess (inference) as to the meaning of a word

Cross-classification: an error in reasoning that occurs when we use sorting factors that overlap—e.g., sorting apples into red, green, and small.

Deductive reasoning: a formal reasoning process wherein conclusions are drawn from other statements (premises).

Denotation: the factual, literal reference of a word.

Directional shifts: movement from one idea to another (often an opposite), usually signaled by contrast words like *but, however,* etc.

Divided main idea: a controlling idea that is directly stated but not contained in a single topic sentence. Common in idea patterns with many elements.

Either/or thinking: an error in reasoning based on the assumption that there are only two—or a specified, limited number—of alternatives or factors, ignoring the possibility of other explanations or choices.

Emotional appeals: a variety of unfair persuasive techniques using emotionally charged words (see name-calling, glittering generalities, bandwagon).

Evidence field: an area of experience we accept as a sanctioning authority.

Factual statements: statements we agree can be proved to be either true or false.

False analogy: an error in reasoning that assumes that because two things share a number of traits or internal relationships, they must also share another. Confuses the use of an analogy as an aid to understanding with what constitutes valid proof.

Faulty causation: errors in reasoning involving cause and effect, usually the result of assuming that because one thing follows another, it has necessarily caused it. Often identified by the Latin phrase *post hoc ergo propter hoc*—"after this, therefore caused by this."

Frames of reference: connected guidelines of facts, concepts, and definitions in various fields that help you to understand new information by relating it to a larger context.

Generalizations: broad statements based on more than one observation or action, or conclusions drawn about a group or class of things.

Glittering generalities: empty statements that sound great but on closer examination aren't really giving anything but vague opinions; they are particularly common in politics and advertising.

Guilt by association: an error in reasoning used to attack or discredit by suggesting that because an object shares one trait with another, it must share others.

Hasty generalization: the fallacy of trying to cover too much ground with too little evidence. Also called *sweeping generalization.*

Idea: any statement (complete sentence) made about a topic.

Idea patterns: common patterns by which a variety of questions are answered. Include description/support, comparison/contrast, time sequence, cause/effect, classification, whole/part, problem/solution, opinion/reason.

Implied main idea: a controlling idea of a paragraph or larger unit that is suggested rather than directly stated.

Inductive reasoning: process of inferring general statements from particular facts and events.

Inference: a reasonable guess based on partial evidence.

Listing phrases: combinations of number words and pattern element words (e.g., "there are several types of ...") used to express main ideas with multiple or compound elements.

Logical fallacies: unintentional or deliberate errors in reasoning and inference.

Main idea: (also called *controlling idea, thesis,* or in the case of paragraphs, *topic sentence*). A central connecting idea for a unit of communication that, by focusing on one dominant question about a topic, limits, controls, and unifies what is included.

Metaphor: a comparison linking the characteristics of two unlike things.

Multiparagraph units: groups of paragraphs that function together in developing part of the overall main idea.

Name-calling: using value words to unfairly attach an unfavorable label or a name to a person or an idea. Also called "mudslinging," "poisoning the well," *argument ad hominem* (argument against the man).

Opinions: reasoned judgments that may be changed or even given up after further debate and evaluation of evidence.

Order of importance: a method of development in which an author uses key signal words—e.g., "most important"—to emphasize the key point that the reader should remember.

Paraphrase: a rephrasing of an author's ideas in one's own words.

Plagiarism: the theft of someone's ideas or language by passing them off as one's own.

Plain folks: a favorite technique of advertisers and politicians who try to appeal to the population at large by capitalizing on our belief in the wisdom of the common man and our suspicion of elitists or "eggheads."

Negative/positive restatement: a form of restatement in which essentially the same idea is stated in both a positive and a negative form.

Purpose: author's intention or goal in writing: to inform, to prove, to persuade to action.

Restatement: a sentence, following an initial statement of an idea, that states the same idea in slightly different and frequently more specific words.

Rhetorical question: a question that really is a statement that answers itself; used for emphasis or effect.

Sarcasm: a form of verbal irony that ridicules by suggesting the opposite of its literal meaning or surface tone.

Simile: comparisons between unlike things using *like* or *as.*

Specific details: support for main ideas in the form of *major* detail (major pattern elements) or *minor* detail (additional support and development).

Subdivided paragraph unit: a unit of writing, usually found in newspaper columns, in which what normally would be one complete paragraph has, for visual effect, been broken into a number of smaller paragraphs.

Subpattern: a pattern of organization used to develop the main pattern.

Summary: a shortened, rephrased version of a piece of writing that still provides the key elements.

Supporting material: material used to develop ideas, including statistics, studies, examples, testimony of experts.

Testimonial: a technique that uses a spokesperson to enhance the product or service being sold. It involves transfer when it uses celebrities to speak for—or have their picture associated with—a product.

Tone: the writer's attitude toward his subject and his reader as revealed in the text.

Topic: means the same as a "subject." Topics are stated in fragments. Topical organization gives us a wide range of information on various aspects of a topic by answering a series of questions like *who, what, when, where, why, how.*

Transfer: an emotional appeal often built on figurative comparisons that attempt to take our feelings about, or the traits of, a person, object, or symbol and transfer them to the person or product that is being promoted.

Word parts: meaningful word segments of one or more syllables including roots (base parts of a word), prefixes (word parts added before roots), and suffixes (word parts that follow roots and usually change the part of speech of a word.)

Credits

Capron, H.L., *Computers: Tools for an Information Age*, 6th ed. Copyright © Reprinted by permission of Pearson Education, Inc.

Carlson, Neil. R. and William Buskist, *Psychology: The Science of Behavior*, 5th ed. Copyright © 1997 by Allyn & Bacon. Reprinted/adapted by permission.

Coon, D., *Introduction to Psychology: Exploration and Application*, 7th ed. Copyright © 1995. Reprinted with permission of Wadsworth, an imprint of the Wadsworth Group, a division of Thomson Learning. Fax 800 730-2215.

Divine, Robert A., T.H. Breen, George M. Fredrickson, and R. Hal Williams, *America Past and Present*, 5th ed. Copyright © 1999 by Addison-Wesley Educational Publishers Inc. Reprinted by permission of Pearson Education, Inc.

Eitzen, D. Stanley and Maxine Baca Zinn, *In Conflict and Order: Understanding Society*, 7th ed. Copyright © 1995 by Allyn & Bacon. Reprinted/adapted by permission.

Eshleman, J. Ross et al., *Sociology: An Introduction*. Copyright © 1993 by Allyn & Bacon. Reprinted/adapted by permission.

Henslin, James M., *Sociology: A Down-to-Earth Approach*, 3rd ed. Copyright © 1997 by Allyn & Bacon. Reprinted/adapted by permission.

Kagan, *Western Heritage* 5th ed. Copyright © Reprinted by permission of Pearson Education Inc., Upper Saddle River, NJ.

Kaler, James B., *Astronomy! A Brief Edition*. Copyright © 1997 by Addison-Wesley Educational Publishers Inc. Reprinted by permission of Pearson Education, Inc.

Lefton, Lester A. *Psychology*, 5th ed. Copyright © 1994 by Allyn & Bacon. Reprinted/adapted by permission.

O'Connor, Karen and Larry J. Sabato, *American Government: Continuity and Change*. Copyright © 1997 Allyn & Bacon.

Powers, Scott K. and Stephen L. Dodd, *Total Fitness*, 2nd ed. Copyright © 1999, 1996 by Allyn & Bacon. Reprinted by permission of Pearson Education, Inc.

Starr, C., *Biology: Concepts and Applications*, 2nd ed. Copyright © 1994 Wadsworth, Inc.

Wallace, Robert J. and Robert J. Ferl, *Biology: The Realm of Life*, 3rd ed. Copyright © 1996 by HarperCollins College Publishers. Reprinted by permission of Pearson Education, Inc.

Welch, S., et al., *American Government*, 4th ed. Copyright © 1992 West Publishing Company. Reprinted by permission of West Educational Publishing.

Index